This book is a must-read for anyone who values the integrity of the judicial system and the effective delivery of justice. Court administration has evolved far beyond its historical focus on preserving the king's peace and purse or accommodating the chief judge. The authors clearly trace this evolution and explain the increasingly complex demands of modern court management. They thoughtfully examine the purposes and responsibilities of courts and the wide array of legitimate stakeholders they serve – far more diverse and nuanced than those of private-sector organizations driven primarily by shareholder interests. Beginning with leadership, the book demonstrates how essential skills and practices can be aligned to engage stakeholders and foster a court culture that delivers justice effectively and consistently. *Fundamentals of Modern Court Administration* is both a practical guide and a compelling argument for reform. I strongly recommend it to judges and court administrators alike, particularly those seeking a more collaborative, sustainable model of court governance.

Hon. Pamela Dembe, *President Judge, Court of Common Pleas of Philadelphia County, First Judicial District of Pennsylvania (Ret.)*

Fundamentals of Modern Court Administration is a rare and timely contribution to a field that is central to the rule of law yet too often underserved by comprehensive scholarship. Blending theory with real-world practice, the authors illuminate, among other important fundamentals, the essential roles of leadership, culture, caseflow, technology, and community engagement in delivering justice effectively. This book is an indispensable resource for judges, court administrators, scholars, and students committed to strengthening courts in an increasingly complex world.

Pamela Harris, *Maryland State Court Administrator (Ret.) and President International Association for Court Administration*

Fundamentals of Modern Court Administration stands as a seminal contribution to the global literature on judicial systems. Unique in its scope and intellectual ambition, this volume offers an incisive, elegantly structured framework that speaks to the operational demands of contemporary courts, and to the deeper institutional values that sustain the rule of law and uphold legal certainty across jurisdictions. From an international vantage point, the work is nothing short of indispensable. The authors succeed admirably in weaving together theory, practice, and comparative insight, providing a consistent paradigm for understanding the complex ecology of the administration of justice. Their analysis of leadership, culture, caseflow, technology, and community engagement demonstrates scholarly rigor and a profound understanding of how courts must evolve to deliver justice that is timely, accessible, and worthy of public trust. This book is, in every respect, a masterwork achievement – authoritative, illuminating, and richly deserving of the widest readership.

Luis Maria Palma, *Professor of Court Administration and Judicial Studies, Argentina and International Universities, and Past President, International Association for Court Administration*

Students and practitioners of court administration have long sought guidance in learning and refining their craft. *Fundamentals of Modern Court Administration* is a rare and invaluable contribution that delivers. Drawing on decades of experience, scholarship, and practice, the authors bridge the longstanding gap between theory and the real-world demands of leading courts. This book thoughtfully examines not only how courts function, but why they exist, grounding modern administrative practice in enduring judicial purpose. Its treatment of leadership, culture, caseflow management, operations, technology, human resources, strategy, stakeholder collaboration, funding, and community engagement reflects a deep understanding of the complexity of courts as institutions and human organizations. Equally important, the authors emphasize sustainability – developing systems, leaders, and practices that endure beyond individual tenures. Students of court administration, emerging leaders, and seasoned executives will find this book indispensable. It belongs on the desk of anyone committed to strengthening the judiciary's capacity to deliver justice fairly, effectively, and with public trust.

David W. Slayton, *Court Executive Officer, Superior Court of Los Angeles County and Past President National Association for Court Management*

Fundamentals of Modern Court Administration

Fundamentals of Modern Court Administration offers a comprehensive and practice-grounded framework for understanding and leading modern courts as complex public institutions. Drawing on foundational theories from public administration, organizational behavior, and judicial governance, the authors integrate decades of court management literature together with their professional experience to bridge the gap between theory and practice.

At the core of the book is a unifying Fundamental Areas of Court Administration model, which organizes court governance and management responsibilities into interconnected operational and aspirational domains. The text systematically examines strategic planning, leadership, court culture, caseflow management, budgeting, operations, human resources, technology, community engagement, and stakeholder collaboration – anchored in the purposes and responsibilities of courts.

Methodologically, the book emphasizes applied analysis, long-range strategic thinking, and experiential learning. In practice, it provides concrete approaches, examples, and cautionary insights drawn from real court environments. Designed for students, judges, administrators, and policy leaders alike, this work serves as both an instructional guide and a professional reference for advancing effective, ethical, and resilient court administration.

Giuseppe M. Fazari is a professor of criminal justice at Monmouth University and a former chief administrator and court executive for the New Jersey Judiciary.

Marcus W. Reinkensmeyer is Dean for the Institute for Court Management Fellows Program, National Center for State Courts.

Alexander B. Aikman is a former executive of the National Center for State Courts and served as a management consultant to scores of trial and appellate courts nationwide.

Fundamentals of Modern Court Administration

Giuseppe M. Fazari,
Marcus W. Reinkensmeyer, and
Alexander B. Aikman

Routledge
Taylor & Francis Group
NEW YORK AND LONDON

Designed cover image: Getty Images

First published 2027
by Routledge
605 Third Avenue, New York, NY 10158

and by Routledge
4 Park Square, Milton Park, Abingdon, Oxon, OX14 4RN

Routledge is an imprint of the Taylor & Francis Group, an informa business

Library of Congress Cataloging-in-Publication Data
Names: Fazari, Giuseppe (Giuseppe M.) author | Reinkensmeyer, Marcus Wm. author | Aikman, Alexander B. author
Title: Fundamentals of modern court administration / Giuseppe M. Fazari, Marcus W. Reinkensmeyer, Alexander B. Aikman. Description: 1. | New York : Routledge, 2026. | Includes bibliographical references and index.
Identifiers: LCCN 2026022736 (print) | LCCN 2026022737 (ebook) | ISBN 9781041168744 paperback | ISBN 9781041168751 hardback | ISBN 9781003686804 ebook
Subjects: LCSH: Court administration—United States | Courts—United States—Management | Justice, Administration of—United States
Classification: LCC KF8732 .F39 2026 (print) | LCC KF8732 (ebook)
LC record available at https://lccn.loc.gov/2026022736
LC ebook record available at https://lccn.loc.gov/2026022737

ISBN: 978-1-041-16875-1 (hbk)
ISBN: 978-1-041-16874-4 (pbk)
ISBN: 978-1-003-68680-4 (ebk)

DOI: 10.4324/9781003686804

Typeset in Univers
by codeMantra

For Michael Anthony and Vincent Philip, the bassists of the band playing in my head. With great expectation that the courage, sacrifice, and wisdom of the extraordinary women and men who preceded us always inspires and informs so that the spirit to progress remains unbroken. Delivering your right uppercut such as the one I dreamt here is then only a matter of time and effort.

Giuseppe M. Fazari

To my loving wife, Anita, and our cherished children, Katie, Christina, and David, whose steadfast support and enduring love have shaped every step of our journey.

Marcus W. Reinkensmeyer

My wife Ruth, a wise and committed supporter, whose encouragement has enriched my life and career. To my mentors, Larry Sipes and Ed McConnell, my colleagues at the courts, and my co-workers at the National Center for State Courts whose guidance, dedication, and example inspired my path in public service.

Alexander B. Aikman

Contents

About the Authors

Giuseppe M. Fazari is a professor of criminal justice at Monmouth University and a former chief administrator and court executive for the New Jersey Judiciary. His Management Musings column appears quarterly in the NACM Court Manager, and he is the author of *Courthouse Confidential: Unveiling Lessons Learned in Leading and Managing Trial Court Organizations.* He serves as Regional Vice President of the IACA. He holds an MPA and a PhD in higher education administration from Seton Hall University and is a Fellow of the Institute for Court Management.

Marcus W. Reinkensmeyer is Dean for the Institute for Court Management Fellows Program, National Center for State Courts. He has served as an administrator at the state and local court levels in Arizona and Illinois, a presenter, consultant, and Past NACM President. He presently serves on the IACA North American Regional Board. He holds a BFA from Michigan State University, an MPA from Northern Illinois University, and is a Fellow of the Institute for Court Management.

Alexander B. Aikman is a former executive of the National Center for State Courts and served as a management consultant to scores of trial and appellate courts nationwide. He was the Deputy State Court Administrator of Oregon and a court administrator of El Dorado County Superior Court, California. He has taught numerous courses on court administration and is the author of *The Art and Practice of Court Administration.* He holds a JD and LLM from The University of Chicago.

Acknowledgments

The authors gratefully acknowledge the many individuals who have contributed to this work, either directly or indirectly. This book has been shaped by their leadership, scholarship, and dedication to the field of court administration over the past several decades, as well as by the lessons we have learned throughout our own professional experiences. We are deeply grateful for their influence and generous contributions to the profession.

We are honored to begin the book with an insightful Foreword authored by Mary Campell McQueen, President Emerita of the National Center for State Courts (NCSC). Mary's exhortations regarding the field of court administration resonate profoundly today, given her substantial achievements in court reform and access to justice. We extend our heartfelt gratitude to Mary for her exemplary leadership, enduring contributions to the field, and ongoing support of judicial administration throughout the years.

We express gratitude to the initial reviewers of our book proposal for their invaluable insight regarding the content, scope, and value of this publication: Pamela Harris, President of the International Association for Court Administration (IACA) and former Maryland State Court Administrator, and Norman Meyer, former Clerk of Court for the United States District Court, New Mexico. Our deep appreciation is also extended to the reviewers of the final draft particularly, The Honorable Pamela Dembe, former President Judge, Court of Common Pleas of Philadelphia County, First Judicial District of Pennsylvania, Luis Maria Palma, Past President of IACA and Professor of Court Administration and Judicial Studies at Argentine and International Universities, and David Slayton, Court Executive Officer of the Los Angeles Superior Court, for their generous allocation of time and supportive feedback.

While we may inadvertently overlook some noteworthy individuals, we are thankful and acknowledge our gratitude to the distinguished leaders and pioneers of the field. Among other roles, they served as trusted mentors who courageously spearheaded the initial efforts and wide range of initiatives in the professionalization of court management: Chief Justice Warren E. Burger, Carl Baar, Samual D. Conti, Edward C. Gallas, Geoff Gallas, Ernest Friesen, Gordon M. Griller, Collins E. Ijoma, Harry Lawson, Dale Lefever,

Barry Mahoney, Edward B. McConnell, Larry L. Sipes, Harvey Solomon, Maureen Solomon, Daniel Straub, and Arthur T. Vanderbilt.

We appreciate the continuous efforts and ongoing work of numerous court improvement organizations and their dedicated staff. Collectively, these entities advance the study and practice of court management through interdisciplinary research, educational programs, leadership networking, and comprehensive publications on court administration. Among other consortiums that include regional associations, the prominent organizations include the American Bar Association, American Judges Association, American Judicature Society, Bureau of Justice Assistance, Bureau of Justice Statistics, Conference of Chief Justices, Conference of State Court Administrators, Federal Judicial Center, Institute for the Advancement of the American Legal System, Institute for Court Management (ICM), International Association for Court Administration, Justice Management Institute, National Association for Court Management, National Association of Judicial Educators, National Association of Presiding Judges and Court Executive Officers, National Center for State Courts, National Judicial College, and State Justice Institute. We thank the editorial team at Routledge Taylor & Francis Group, especially Senior Editor Ellen S. Boyne, Editorial Assistant Maia Berliner, Production Editor Helen Birchall, and Copyeditor Tom Bedford. In addition, we are grateful to the support extended by the organizations where we are presently employed, including Monmouth University and the NCSC.

Finally, and most importantly, we are profoundly grateful and indebted to our families for their encouragement and the solitude they afforded us throughout the development of this book. While space does not permit individual recognition of each family member, this acknowledgment is meant to express our sincere appreciation to all of them. We are especially thankful to our spouses – Maria Lagonigro Fazari, Anita M. Reinkensmeyer, and Ruth Grace Aikman – for their unwavering support and thoughtful counsel.

Foreword

> The expediency of carrying justice to every man's door is obvious – but how to do it is far from apparent.
>
> – Chief Justice John Jay

When John Jay was appointed as the first Chief Justice of the Supreme Court of the United States in 1789, he recognized that justice in our new nation varied in almost every state and was primarily provided through its courts. As Jay observed, the "expediency," the wisdom and necessity, of providing "justice for all" was evident, but how to build a justice system of tribunals and selecting leaders to ensure an independent judiciary was far from apparent.

As Alexander Hamilton argued in *Federalist No. 17*, the administration of justice "contributes more than any other circumstance, to impressing upon the minds of the people affection, esteem, and reverence towards government." Russell Wheeler writing in his essay observing the U.S. constitutional bicentennial quoted Hamilton in noting that the "ordinary administration of justice" is the most powerful source of the public's trust and confidence in its government. Wheeler traced the early evolution of court administration to the Progressive Era's reform efforts when government accountability and efficiency became central to public service. He describes that purpose as enabling courts to resolve disputes fairly, expeditiously, and economically – a definition that continues to guide the work of court leaders today. As Harry Lawson once observed, the "innovation" or "new-fangled notion" called court administration has matured into an indispensable leadership model supporting the administration of justice. From Chief Justice John Jay to Chief Justice Warren Burger, the role of court administrators has developed into a recognized profession of visionary and dynamic leaders dedicated to upholding the Rule of Law. Since the Friesen and Gallas' publication *Managing the Courts* in 1971, a rich body of research, scholarship, and practical guidance has shaped the field.

In *Fundamentals of Modern Court Administration*, Fazari, Reinkensmeyer, and Aikman carry this tradition forward. They have skillfully merged decades of literature, empirical research, and personal experience into a comprehensive, modern guide for court leaders. Their emphasis on collaborative leadership, problem solving, and solutions based upon best practices provides readers with an essential framework for negotiating the complex realities of judicial administration in the 21st century. By offering both a practical roadmap and an inspiring vision, *Fundamentals of Modern Court Administration* equips today's court leaders to sustain and advance the public's trust and confidence in the courts and answers the question of how to create a system of trusted, fair, and impartial courts as envisioned by Chief Justice Jay in 1789.

Mary Campbell McQueen
President Emerita
National Center for State Courts

1 Introduction and Fundamental Areas of Modern Court Administration

The Rationale for This Book

Tocqueville (1875) remarked how all issues of import in American society eventually end up in the forum of the courts (Schleifer, 1980).[1] This adjudicative responsibility suggested by Tocqueville and to the courts is, in fact, no small matter. Arguably, in many respects, the organizational and management side of the judiciary is equally as critical to the delivery of justice. Structurally and administratively, courts have many characteristics similar to those of the most complex organizations in the public and private sectors. In fact, when it comes to managing these institutions, many have argued that the judiciary can be more confounding because of its shared management authority between judges and administrators, coupled with the clashing cultures of key independent professionals the court interacts with during case adjudication. These professionals include prosecutors, criminal defense attorneys (both public and private), civil attorneys, law enforcement officers (who provide security and serve as witnesses), social service agencies assisting defendants and litigants in family law matters, and probation and parole agents employed by executive-branch agencies. This distinct feature, among others, makes the court a difficult organization to oversee and lead. Moreover, it is particularly relevant for non-judicial administrators and senior managers who often serve at the pleasure of their judicial employers.

The responsibilities consigned to court administrators are almost always consequential, as even the most perfunctory of tasks may impact freedoms and justice. These issues and the relative uniqueness and complexity involved in managing courts are explored in our Fundamental Areas of Court Administration model presented in Figure 1.1.

DOI: 10.4324/9781003686804-1

Figure 1.1 Fundamental Areas of Court Administration

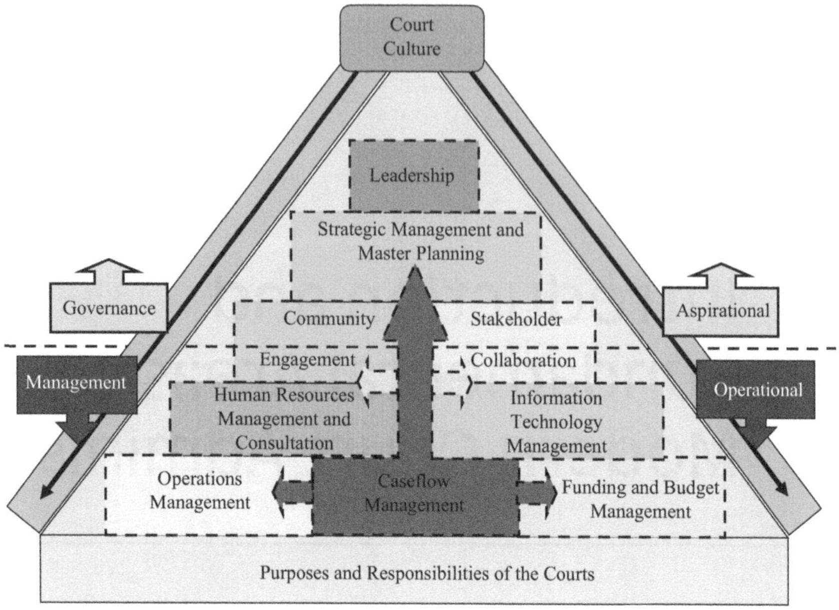

Fundamentals of Modern Court Administration

A fuller understanding of the roles and responsibilities that define court administration is gained over time, after much commitment, and through a variety of work experiences. In his book *Outliers*, Gladwell (2008) posited that it takes an estimated 10,000 hours of practice to become an expert at something (approximately 6 years at 8 hours per day for 210 days a year). He derived that number by studying some of the most "successful" people in the world. For court administrators, 10,000 hours may underestimate what is needed to become a true subject matter expert, given the many human and institutional complexities that influence success. Nonetheless, Gladwell's point is a salient one: practice is time-consuming and not easy, but it leads to expertise. We hope this book will help readers shorten and illuminate the practice part of that journey, at least somewhat.

The roles and responsibilities of court administration depicted in Figure 1.1 illustrate the integrated elements that comprise the fundamental areas of court administration from our perspective. This paradigm was developed and modified over several years of working in and with trial courts. The use of a triangle in this context to visualize these dynamic elements represents the stability of the judicial branch and a fully functioning court, which should be independent of political whim and influence. Its foundation, which collectively embodies the tradition and formal procedure of the judicial branch, rests and is guided by the purposes and responsibilities of the courts. The judiciary's stability and predictability provide vital support for the Rule of Law, thus enabling economic development, the government's sustained legitimacy, and support of democratic institutions. The dotted lines in the figure around each functional area represent the permeability of work areas, as well as related skill sets required within most court systems; they show an idealized distribution of work among these functions, also recognizing the fluidity of associated tasks and the dynamic organization in which many courts operate.

The purpose of this depiction is to provide an overview and context for the key functional areas that encompass the work of a court administrator. For those unfamiliar with the court administration field, the roles and responsibilities of court professionals are often unrecognized or largely obscure. Outsiders may have limited knowledge of the courts based on their perceptions of judges and attorneys, or they may be unaware of the existence of such a profession. Even organizations and individuals that interact with the courts often lack understanding of how the organization is managed and the complexities involved in judicial administration. In fact, administrators may encounter significant disconnects in support for management, even among entities that are loosely coupled and work directly with the court organization (e.g., sheriffs, prosecutors, defense counsel, community advocates, host funding bodies, legislators, etc.). We briefly explain each component of Figure 1.1 below, prior to delving into detailed discussion in the balance of the book.

Three components define as well as limit courts as institutions: purposes and responsibilities (without which there are no courts), shown in Figure 1.1 as the foundation of the model; local court culture, depicted as encompassing all operations; and leadership, required for the court to move forward with innovations and system improvements best serving the public. In this paradigm, the court's strategic plan sets out a long-range preferred vision, mission, and guiding principles. The strategic plan also facilitates the alignment of court operations, resource allocation, and organizational development efforts with the mission of the court. Two other dimensions of the model, governance and management, are the subject of extensive discussion in the pages that follow.

Purposes and Responsibilities of the Courts

The purposes and responsibilities of courts are the foundation for everything that courts do. They determine and inform not only what judges do in their adjudicative roles, but also how judges in their administrative roles, along with managers and staff, perform and make administrative decisions. Professor Ernest Friesen, the first Director of the Institute for Court Management (ICM) and a renowned, seminal leader in court administration, identified the following purposes of courts that have been widely accepted (NACM, 2004):

1) Assure individual justice in individual cases
2) Assure the appearance of individual justice in individual cases
3) Provide a forum for the resolution of legal disputes

4) Protect individuals from the arbitrary use of governmental power
5) Create a formal record of legal status
6) Deter criminal behavior
7) Rehabilitate persons convicted of crime
8) Separate some convicted people from society

More recently, the National Association for Court Management (NACM) in its 2016 CORE Curriculum for court leaders broadened this list by adding the following two purposes:

1) Protect vulnerable populations from the abuse of power in any form
2) Promote coordination with justice, public health, social services, and other agencies to address common problems underlying the court's criminal and civil caseload, including substance use and mental health

Arguably, the first of these newly identified purposes might be encompassed by Friesen's first purpose – to do individual justice in individual cases – but it also is broader in scope and thus can be distinguished. The second reflects a refinement of court purposes drawn from the growth in the last 25-plus years of "therapeutic" and "problem-solving" courts that address issues of substance abuse, mental health, and other personal and family dysfunctions (e.g., anger management issues that threaten others) that are seminal in some criminal, civil, juvenile, and family cases, among other case types. It deserves inclusion in the list for today's courts because judges increasingly are seeking new ways for coordination of multiple agencies to holistically address litigant issues that have brought them to court, rather than adjudicating one issue or incident in isolation. Another purpose of courts that is seldom mentioned but should be noted: Support and preservation of American democracy under law. This, too, might be thought to be subsumed in the other ten purposes, but like the purpose of protecting vulnerable populations and constraining the arbitrary use of government power, it has other components that justify highlighting it specifically.

With some exceptions such as stand-alone probate courts or administrative courts, these articulated purposes of courts are generally universal to the judicial branch of government and to each court, regardless of size, location, or jurisdiction. They separate courts from almost all other public institutions, including law enforcement and other agencies that comprise the justice system, some of which are responsible for several, but not all, of these charges. The purposes are the foundation – the guiding principles – that provide court leaders with the all-important *meaning* of their work. The purposes serve as the framework and focus for courts, aligning their priorities with the institution's mission and vision. In the face of ever-challenging and changing demands, often with limited resources, the purposes guide courts in establishing their priorities.

Moreover, the purposes form the basis for aligning a court's performance, organization, practices, and governing policies. By doing so, courts ensure that accountability and transparency to the public are carried out diligently, upholding justice and the public's perception of it.

Court Culture

The concept of "local legal culture" was first introduced into court administration by Church and associates (1978) and defined there as "the practices and expectations of judges and attorneys in a community about the acceptable pace of litigation." This definition was developed in the context of a study of how 21 urban courts managed civil and criminal cases, how long those cases took to resolve, and what seemed to work well in courts with expedited case disposition times while not compromising justice in the process. Time has shown that the local legal culture concept applies equally to all case types, not just civil and criminal cases. This definition has been used and accepted within the judiciary for many years and still works when applied to case management.

Ostrom et al. (2007) have examined and redirected the definition to apply to courts as institutions. This is an important addition to the field, but administrators should be careful to distinguish institutional culture from the local legal culture related to the pace of litigation in a court. The model developed by the latest study has two dimensions of organizational culture: Sociability and Solidarity. Within their construct, there are four court cultures: Hierarchal, Networked, Autonomous, and Communal. These cultural typologies are associated with and defined by four styles: rule-oriented (Hierarchical Culture), judicial consensus (Networked Culture), self-managing (Autonomous Culture), and flexibility (Communal Culture).

Institutional court culture plays a crucial role as an overarching reality for five key dimensions of the organization: dominant case management style, judicial and court staff relations, change management, courthouse leadership, and internal organization. While there are no universally accepted or ideal court cultures, experience has demonstrated that leadership judges and administrators often favor a specific type of court culture when leading the court. Moreover, court cultures tend to evolve over time.

In *Organizational Culture and Leadership*, Schein (2004) defined organizational culture similar to the definition used in *Justice Delayed* as related to case management:

> A pattern of shared basic assumptions that was learned by a group as it solved its problems of external adaptation and internal integration, that has worked well enough to be considered valid and, therefore, to be taught to new members as the correct way to perceive, think, and feel in relation to those problems.

Culture, akin to character, shapes an organization's destiny only after being preceded by thoughts, actions, and habits. The court's culture encompasses its values, attitudes, beliefs, and customs, which influence its "normative" practices and the way its members approach problem-solving and fulfill their roles. As depicted in Figure 1.1, organizational culture permeates all administrative elements of the court due to its profound influence on management and operation. It even shapes leadership types and styles that effectively accomplish existing and new tasks. Indeed, there are few forces or conditions more impactful to an organization than its culture. Courts are no exception.

Leadership

Being an effective leader is fundamental to the role and responsibility of a court administrator. Leadership types and styles can and do vary, but the consummate court administrator is at the same time the personification of a leader. The literature on leadership is extensive, but it generally falls into one of two genres – the "how-to" and types of leaders and the principles or fundamentals of leadership. Henslin (2019) cited two types of leaders. The instrumental leader (or task-oriented leader) is focused on keeping the group moving toward its goals. The expressive leader (or socio-emotional leader), in contrast, builds personal bonds, attempts to reduce friction in the group, and is usually more popular than the instrumental leader. He also identified three basic leadership styles: authoritarian (gives orders), democratic (tries to reach consensus), and laissez-faire (highly permissive).

A key difference between leadership in the courts and the private sector is the necessary involvement of the presiding judge, ideally working closely with the court administrator in a two-person executive leadership team. The administrator must have the judge's endorsement, approval, and support to be the leader of a particular initiative, especially if judges are affected or believe they are affected. Even with the leadership team working together and the presiding judge agreeing to the change, a single judge or small cadre of judges not regularly involved with court administration can potentially reject or undermine those changes despite being supported by a majority of judges and staff. In smaller courts, a single judge can potentially stop a change because others may be unwilling to challenge the dissenting judge.

Judges have constitutionally protected decision-making independence in case-related rulings. As professionals, their commitment to impartiality begins during their careers as attorneys. Additionally, their defined impartial role instills in them a strong sense of service. This sense of service is further emphasized by the fact that judges generally do not owe their appointment or election to anyone on or within the court. This distinguishes them from many other groups of professionals and most managers in private-sector, non-profit, or educational institutions and executive-branch agency (except for department or agency leaders who are independently elected).[2] The leadership styles and governance models relevant for courts are now well defined, but this extra layer of complexity may place added stress on the ability of even the best appointed leaders to manage, improve, or change operations.

Caseflow Management

Caseflow management is at the center of the functions performed by a court because ultimately the courts exist to bring cases to a just resolution as quickly as the circumstances of each case warrant. Caseflow management is about facilitating this core business process as effectively and efficiently as possible for every case. The types of cases vary, and the nuances of each type can vary, but the principles of effective case management are generally well understood and universal. Whatever specific procedures are developed for different case types and for individual cases, the process of case management touches every aspect of court operations. Accordingly, caseflow management informs and drives all other operational roles and responsibilities of modern court administration. Thus, caseflow management is portrayed in Figure 1.1 as a central function, right above the purposes and responsibilities and with arrows connecting to all other court functions. Collectively and individually, all other administrative areas exist to support this core court function.

Funding and Budget Management

Court funding and budget management involve planning, preparing, presenting, justifying, monitoring, and adjusting the budget as needed, along with identifying budget priorities. Budget management also includes the court's responsibilities to ensure the collection of imposed fines, fees, and penalties, as well as the collection of bail for criminal defendants who fail to appear in court. Like case management, budget management impacts and touches every other aspect of court administration's cost-center components. Budget management is linked and driven by both strategic and long-range master planning. As with all other government agencies, courts do not set their own budgets but must adhere to the parameters allocated by the funding authority. Budget management generally involves decision making that accounts for the environment, process, and individual strategies such that policies and programs are not simply supported by aspirational hopes but also have the financial backing to realistically achieve desired ends (Rubin & Babbie, 1997).

Operations Management

Operations management is a catchment area of court administration that covers a wide spectrum of both general and specialized court services. Each is an important function or responsibility of a court, supporting the functions identified in Figure 1.1. Key components of "operations" are jury management, interpreting services, mailroom services, reporting and transcription services, telecommunications and video conferencing, fleet management, facilities and grounds, safety and security (including probation in some courts), emergency management and continuity of operations (COOP), and records management.

Human Resources Management and Consultation

Courts are fundamentally a people business and not just from the perspective of the public served, but also because of the large cadre of judges and staff who are responsible for doing the work of the court. Recruiting and managing the human capital of the court involves a specific set of knowledge, skills, and abilities (KSA). The skill set includes recruiting, hiring, labor/management relations, training, position control, evaluation and feedback, policies and procedures, progressive discipline, surveying staff needs and opinions, incident reporting, compensation study and analysis, and workforce forecasting.The presiding judge is generally responsible for communicating with other judges on administrative matters. While the lead judge may be the one to principally correspond with line judges on administrative issues, this does not suggest that the lead judge is "managing" other judges in the traditional sense of the word. And the most effective court administrators communicate in the same way; that is, they can effectively convey program information and context to prompt action while remaining deferential to the bench. When it comes to judicial "management," an administrator will generally fill what we regard to be a consultative role for the presiding judge on organizational fit or a specific management issue involving a judge.

Information Technology Management

Technology is an inescapable as well as increasingly indispensable element of modern court administration and the ability to fulfill its purpose and responsibilities. Current and emerging technologies hold the promise of expanded court access, advancements in procedural fairness and efficiencies in daily court operations. Almost universally, increasingly sophisticated information systems are used for case and financial management, as well as public facing e-court services. Increasingly, technology is improving court communication with jurors, litigants, attorneys, many outside stakeholders, and the public. Chapter 9 addresses the rapidly expanding use of artificial intelligence (AI) in the legal system, both from the standpoint of court operations and the changing practice of law. Our discussion considers the practical application of such technologies in tandem with the whole new set of emerging philosophical and ethical issues related to machine learning applications.

Many courts are turning to social media, but still predominantly rely on their websites to provide information about cases, court services, and procedures to enable the digital filing of documents and evidence by litigants. Websites also are the vehicle for the sharing of press releases and for sharing data and budget information about court operations. Technology is also used to obtain actionable performance metrics and data analytics to guide court system improvements. Transparency and accountability are improved as the use of court technology expands.

The availability of these improvements is not uniform across the nation. Most of these advanced developments exist or are in the planning process in many courts, but not for all courts. Broad use of technology beyond basic case management information systems, particularly in rural and less-affluent communities, remains a still-unrealized goal. In courts with significant or substantial use of technology, an administrator's challenge is to sustain what exists, upgrade existing technology on a regular basis, and continue to expand the use of technology. Courts with less technology and resource constraints can work with the community and state-level judicial branch officials to overcome limitations.

Community Engagement

Community engagement supports and improves the accessibility and transparency of a court. It also puts a "human" face on the courthouse that can improve public support for needed and desired improvements, particularly if these require budget increases. Yet, community engagement is an area that often is overlooked when court leadership is managing multiple internal and external demands. Because the judiciary often must be its own public advocate, with some support from the public and private Bar, staying abreast of community concerns is critically important. The challenge is ever present because of ethical constraints on judges and staff that foreclose some communication strategies applicable to other public officials and agencies. Much community engagement today involves judges taking the lead in reaching out to community service groups, schools, and the Bar. The administrator and, possibly, one or more staff should supplement these efforts by continually looking for opportunities to hear from the community and to share information about court services. There is a medley of programs and approaches that modern courts have leveraged to create a comprehensive community relations strategy. These are discussed in Chapter 10. Media relations and volunteer coordination also fall within the scope of community engagement, as does seeking feedback from those using the court and, more broadly, from the community. These efforts are indispensable to address the need for courts to be *perceived* as doing justice. And just as importantly, it also helps to advance recognition among the public that the court is fair and accessible.

Stakeholder Collaboration

Stakeholder collaboration is an inherent part of managing a court because the court depends on many external agencies and individuals to function. A representative list includes the local prosecutor's office, the public defender's office, private criminal attorneys, private civil attorneys, legal aid attorneys, public and private social service agencies serving and supporting people involved in court cases, schools, local and state correctional institutions, local and state law enforcement – and, sometimes, federal agencies (normally many independent agencies), local probation offices that are not part of the judicial branch, state motor vehicle agencies, and local political bodies and officials. Consequently, regular and frequent collaboration with the numerous stakeholders that affect the work of the court is a necessity. It involves the politicking (with a lower case "p") that the administrator must do to ensure that the working relationship and communication with justice system stakeholders is ongoing and effective. Examples of formal, local collaborations include a speedy trial committee, case management committee, criminal justice coordinating committee, domestic violence coordinating committee, drug court forum, bar association meetings, minority concerns council, and security and facilities committee. Each of these convenings involve multiple stakeholders coming together on a regular basis to address shared issues and to consider systemic improvements. Informal, one-on-one meetings also can facilitate and, if necessary, improve collaboration and understanding.

There is one other somewhat-loosely connected and closely tied organization that needs to be acknowledged here: the independently appointed or elected clerk of court. This position exists in many state court systems, most often at the general jurisdiction court level. In most of those states, the clerk is responsible for the creation and preservation of the court. In a few states the clerk has other responsibilities involving executive branch functions, too, while also responsible for serving the court and the public regarding the record of proceedings.

The clerk's office is both tied to the court through its function and may be "loosely coupled" (McQueen, 2013) because the court does not typically select, evaluate, discipline, or dismiss the clerk. Most clerks take their responsibility to the court and the public very seriously and continually work to satisfy court recordkeeping requirements. Some clerks put greater emphasis on the independent role of the clerk's office, separate from the court. To that end, they may see their role as a neutral and independent guardian of the record to assure that no judge or attorney contaminates or inappropriately changes the official court record. In some courts, a case management information system is "owned" and controlled by the clerk and a second system is "owned" and controlled by the court (judges). The two systems may not necessarily communicate with each other, and the system controlled by the clerk may lack information judges believe is necessary to aid their work. The latter factor normally is the basis for the court having its own, separate system. A court administrator hired by and responsible to the judges must collaborate with the clerk almost daily. The court administrator must engage leadership skills to keep the two entities working together toward the same ends or to mediate different perspectives of what either the clerk or the judges need to do their jobs. In the end, collaboration with the clerk is an essential element of the administrator's responsibilities.[3]

Strategic Management and Master Planning

Organizations, including courts, should evaluate the current state of affairs (retrospective), as well as strategizing what the court should achieve administratively or organizationally in the next 3, 5, 10, and 20 years (prospective). Akin to the function of human resources, these areas require specific KSAs. In *Leaders Make the Future*, Johansen (2012) discusses foresight (the ability to look over the horizon and see the big picture), insight (the ability to be discerning and determine what is most important), and action (the ability to make decisions on the best path forward). This long-range perspective is particularly important in master planning for new courthouses, renovation of existing facilities and flexible infrastructure planning to support remote and hybrid hearings in the post-pandemic era. Modern court administration facilitates a comprehensive approach to master space planning while encompassing environmental factors and capital funding strategies. All of these skills are critical to strategic management. Court administrators are tasked to forecast, develop, implement, and evaluate to assist the court in establishing realistic strategic goals. Once plans are finalized, court administrators and staff are typically tasked to achieve them.

* * * *

No single diagram or classification of duties, functions, and tasks encompasses all that is involved in court administration or expected of an administrator. The balance of this book explores in detail the fundamental components of court administration and, when appropriate, the limits of relying solely on this "static" model in the universe of real-time, real-world court administration. And as Leonardo da Vinci urged centuries ago, we endeavored to offer both theoretical insights – research and consensus opinions on best practices – and practical examples based on our own experiences, observations, and the experiences of others within the profession.

In 1969, the Chief Justice of the United States, Warren E. Burger (1990), asserted:

> The courts of this country need management, which busy and overworked judges, with drastically increased caseloads, cannot give. We need a corps of trained administrators or managers to manage and direct the machinery so that judges can

> concentrate on their primary duty of judging. Such managers do not now exist, except for a handful who are almost entirely confined to state court systems. We must literally create a corps of court administrators or managers and do it at once.

More than 50 years have passed since Chief Justice Burger remarked on this urgent need. Today, court administrators are employed at all levels (local, state, and federal) and in all types of court systems (limited, general, and specialized jurisdictions). In the years since Chief Justice Burger's plea, the court administration profession has expanded and become more complex, paralleling the changing and growing demands of society, some of which are expressed as laws. Consequently, the need for this professional administrative arm of the courts is, if anything, more clearly recognized today than it was more than five decades ago. In some respects, courts are analogous to hospitals and universities. Just as doctors and professors rely on administrators to manage hospitals and universities, so, too, judges depend on the competence of management professionals to effectively and efficiently lead and administer court operations. This book illuminates these crucial judicial branch leadership and management functions.

How do administrators incorporate court management literature and applicable general management findings into their short- and long-term vision for the organization? What does this practical implementation look like? How are the overarching judicial administration responsibilities, such as "core competencies," "best practices," and "performance standards," effectively executed? Our goal is to provide instructive insights into the core aspects of the court administration profession. For instance, when the profession emphasizes the development of "strategic planning" as a core responsibility of administrators, what does this entail in the court setting? While administrators understand the concept of strategic planning, how is it strategically planned, developed, implemented, and evaluated within the court environment? Are there specific deliverables, and if so, what are they? Clearly, strategic management in courts resembles planning in other public sector departments, but it possesses unique characteristics. Therefore, how is strategy optimally developed, managed, and executed in the court setting? These and similar questions are crucial for both aspiring managers, including students and those new to the profession, and seasoned court administrators in organizing their thoughts and focusing their efforts.

Relative to other management disciplines, court administration is still in its infancy. Since the appointment of Ed Gallas, who is recognized as the country's first trial court administrator (Friesen et al., 1971), there have been scores of books and articles written about the court administration profession – most of which were of a very specific nature dealing with a particular subject matter. There have been notably fewer publications of comprehensive textbooks in the last 40 years, however, offering an overarching overview which bridges the gap between the concepts and principles of the field with the practical application of those tenets drawn from actual court environments (Aikman, 2007). This particular text is guided by two questions that led to the design of the Fundamental Areas of Court Administration model. First, what can be determined from the relevant literature that incorporates the ten fundamentals of the paradigm? Second, how have these fundamentals been applied (made relevant) in practice in the courts?

The disparity between theory and practice in court management varies significantly across the nation and beyond, influenced by various factors, primarily the organization and culture of a specific institution and its leadership. This book presents a proposed paradigm for court administration, outlining the ten fundamental areas that administrators must address in managing a court. It delves into the opportunities and limitations of applying and managing within these principles within a court setting. For instance, it explores how the literature defines "operations management" in organizations and identifies the best practices and key tasks associated with effective "operations management." Additionally, it examines how practical challenges in practice align with the literature's insights. This book aims to provide approaches – not necessarily solutions – that have been successfully "operationalized" in certain courts and address common issues that administrators encounter and will continue to face.

Theory and Application

Leonardo da Vinci, perhaps one of the earliest historical figures to blend theory and practice, left behind remarkable insights. Imagine da Vinci savoring an apple, fully experiencing its taste and texture. He would document his observations, comparing them to those of others and other fruits. da Vinci's approach to learning was experiential, questioning the accepted thinking and practices of his time. He considered himself a man without letters but a disciple of experience, valuing keen observation. This approach involved observing in a way that captured and engaged with the experience itself.

Knowledge, da Vinci contended, comes from a myriad of sources which can be drawn upon to develop a deeper understanding and, through this process, determine a course of action. He was impressed "with the urgency of doing" and stated, "knowing is not enough; we must apply." He did not hold to this one-sided perspective either, remarking, "He who loves practice without theory is like the sailor who boards [a] ship without a rudder and compass and never knows where he may cast" (da Vinci, 1519/1970). In short, he understood the need for both, from whichever point one starts. This dual perspective guides the development of this book, particularly as it relates to judicial branch leadership.

The extent to which experience informs us should not be easily dismissed. Theoretical knowledge teaches the why and is built upon prior factual knowledge. A theoretical framework is important because it illustrates why a court program, project, process, or procedure can or *should* work. It also provides an overview to inform action taken, substantiates why a particular action should be pursued, and helps formulate strategy. A theoretical framework allows individuals to learn from their experiences to approach problem-solving in a systematic manner, instead of having to rely solely on random trial and error. For instance, a report on differentiated case management (DCM) informs administrators of the principles and essential functions of this approach in caseflow management. However, a theory that could fully explain every aspect of the caseflow management process would contain so many details and contingencies that it would be unwieldy and ultimately obstructive. Implementing and evaluating theoretical frameworks are thus crucial steps in the process. DCM is where practice informs and fleshes out the theory as it pertains to that particular court.

Practical knowledge facilitates the administrator acquiring expertise that crystallizes the relevant issues. Whereas the theory defines the forest, practical knowledge provides a local narrative of the trees, vegetation, and landscape. This up-close-and-personal day-to-day work can support or reject aspects of what the theory suggests as *the* "best practice," taking into account dynamics of the local court environment. The best practice may be appropriate under given circumstances that only application can verify. And practical knowledge can only be gained by immersing oneself in the actual work of courts. Through this tedious process one can fill the theoretical gaps because experience accounts for the intangible and the subtlety of issues that are almost always present in those real-world environments. Perhaps best practice that ostensibly produces desired outcomes should be customized to reflect the court's vision, resources, personnel, and local court culture – factors that only its leadership would know and be in the best position to consider *because* of their experience. It is all the same a challenge; applying practical knowledge in the court milieu requires both art and skill. Court administrators and judicial branch leadership teams must be receptive to new ideas and innovation, willing to build consensus, and then, most importantly, to act. As da Vinci observed, "people of accomplishment rarely sat back and let things happen to them. They went out and happened to things" (da Vinci, 1519/1970).

These two ostensibly opposite perspectives are not mutually exclusive. Rather, because both theory and practice are vitally important, they can and should come together to generate expected system improvement outcomes. Practice is useful in solving a specific problem. Theory provides a principle-based starting point and high-level roadmap for doing so.

Theories and practices often exist in separate thought silos, hindering effective collaboration. Retreating to these silos leads to less effective and unproductive efforts as informed perspectives are not utilized for mutual benefit. To engage and benefit from diverse perspectives, it's crucial to review the literature and quantify the extent and influence of identified variables. This book aims to bridge these silos and foster understanding among court organizations. Our intended audience is inclusive, encompassing faculty and students of public administration studying courts as organizations, seasoned leadership judges and court administrators, newcomers to the field, mid-careerists, and experts in specialized areas of court management.

Explanations Applicable to This Book

Those who write about courts use two terms for the administrative side of courts: judicial administration and court administration. The former normally is used by judges, the latter by administrators. Researchers, by and large, use both. In this book, we will use court administration because our focus is on administrators and court staff. This publication strongly advocates the collaborative judge/administrator leadership model and explores the challenges facing court administrators, senior managers, and staff.

Except for the title "judge," there are no agreed-upon titles across all states for court administrators or for the judge's assigned administrative responsibilities. Accordingly, any designation used in this book might appear to overlook judges or administrators in some states. That is certainly not our intent.

The judge with the legal or titular final administrative authority of a trial court varies state to state and, sometimes, depending on the jurisdiction of a court. The dominant titles are "presiding judge" or "chief judge" and more esoteric titles include "assignment judge." For the balance of this book, we will refer to the judge with primary administrative responsibility as the "presiding judge" to identify this judge, as "chief judge" may imply a status and authority that few presiding judges possess.

Chief administrative officers in courts have many formal titles across the nation: court administrator, trial court administrator, chief executive officer, court executive, and chief administrative officer. The person who manages the staff and senior managers and ultimately is responsible for non-judicial operations is referred to here as the "court administrator." In this book, we will specifically use the term "court administrator" to identify the person with final administrative authority in the court administration arm of the court. Our use of these terms – "presiding judge" and "administrator" – is generic and not intended to exclude those in any federal, state or local court assigned a different job title.

Nothing said in this book – positive or negative – is intended or should be interpreted to suggest that it applies to all judges in the nation or in individual courts. The vast majority of judges across the nation have good-to-great administrative/management understanding and knowledge and are supporters of court administrators and staff. Judges universally are committed to the purposes and values of courts, so case studies and deviations noted in this book are never intended as a criticism of judges as a whole. They are noted to illustrate challenges and to serve as caveats for those studying or working in the courts.[4]

Most judges seek to improve the administrative process and decisions by improving management's decision-making process. They constantly seek improvement and, even if they might have preferred that a particular decision be different, they adhere to the adopted procedure and follow all rules and statutes. They minimize or ignore any potential individual difficulties or differences for the greater good of the court. Even so, as discussed further in the Leadership chapter, we note that the role of judges differs from that of policymakers in almost all other organizations and even from those of other elected or appointed public officials. Judges are what sociologists refer to as "loosely coupled independent professionals" and courts are akin to the term used to describe higher education milieus – "loosely coupled silos," which in practical terms led a former presiding judge of a general-jurisdiction court in the Midwest to suggest that judges are independent professionals forced to share office space (Aikman, 2011). The commitment of many judges to the court as an institution and to following common rules or procedures that define administrative practices may be placed behind their commitment to their professional perspective and the adjudicative independence guaranteed by every state constitution. Adjudicative independence is essential and must be protected at all costs. But for some judges, some administrative processes designed to assure internal or external uniformity and public access may be perceived as unduly restraining their adjudicative independence. The line between essential adjudicative independence and institutional administrative imperatives may be seen by these judges as dashed or advisory in nature.

The chapters which follow address essential components of court administration practice, the inherent tension between policy and practice, and executive decision making in the realm of modern court governance. Given the increasingly rapid pace of societal change, our discussion also encompasses preferred future visions of the court as a public institution, bearing in mind the fundamental purposes and responsibilities of courts and the Rule of Law. It is our collective belief that the transformative work required for the "next generation" can be most effectively advanced by court leadership executive teams, including presiding judges, court administrators, and other relevant individuals. For effective leadership, these teams must cultivate a strong sense of genuine collaboration within the court and with judicial branch stakeholders. Fortunately, for the field, our rich history of court administration provides a wealth of organizational models, best practices, and other resources to guide court leadership teams in the important decisions which lie ahead. The synthesis and practical application of such guidance in the practice of court administration are the central focus of our proposed court leadership strategies.

Notes

1 Tocqueville also argued that "scarcely any question arises in the United States which does not become sooner or later, a subject of judicial debate; hence all parties are obliged to borrow the ideas, and even the language, usual in judicial proceedings in their daily controversies."

2 Judge Kevin Burke, a former presiding judge of the Hennepin County District Court (Minneapolis) generally describes judges as "independent professionals forced to share office space."

3 In the federal court system, the appointed Clerk of the Court serves as the court executive overseeing both clerk and court administration functions. In the Superior Court of California and many other limited jurisdiction courts across the country, an appointed court executive or court administrator oversees both court administration and clerk functions.

4 Normally, the authors prefer to and will cite and rely on more universal data. Anecdotes are used throughout the book, however, when our experience indicates that the anecdote is not isolated, but representative of many courts or judges.

References

Aikman, A. B. (2007). *The art and practice of court administration.* Taylor & Francis Group.

Aikman, A. (2011, June). Why not... add court administration to new judges' orientation? *Thinking Out Loud*, 2.

Burger, W. E. (1990). Court administrators: Where would we find them? In B. Anderson (Ed.), *Delivery of justice: Proposals for changes to improve the administration of justice* (pp. 32–35). College of William and Mary Press; West Publishing Company. (Original speech delivered August 12, 1969).

Church, T. W., Jr., Carlson, A., Lee, J.-L., & Tan, T. (1978). *Justice delayed: The pace of litigation in urban trial courts* (Report). National Center for State Courts.

da Vinci, L. (1970). *The notebooks of Leonardo da Vinci.* Dover Publications. (Original work published 1519)

Friesen, E. C., Gallas, E. C., & Gallas, N. M. (1971). *Managing the courts.* MICHIE.

Gladwell, M. (2008). *Outliers: The story of success.* Little, Brown and Company.

Henslin, J. M. (2019). *Sociology: A down-to-earth approach* (14th ed.). Pearson.

Johansen, B. (2012). *Leaders make the future: Ten new leadership skills for an uncertain world* (2nd ed.). Berrett-Koehler Publishers.

McQueen, M. C. (2013). *Governance: The final frontier.* National Center for State Courts. www.hks.harvard.edu/sites/default/files/centers/wiener/programs/pcj/files/ES-StateCourts-GovernanceFinalFrontier.pdf.

National Association for Court Management (NACM). (2004). *Core competency curriculum guidelines: What court leaders need to know and be able to do.*

National Association for Court Management (NACM). (2016). *NACM core competencies, Purposes and responsibilities.* https://nacmnet.org/nacm-core/.

Ostrom, B. J., Ostrom, C. W., Hanson, R. A., & Kleiman, M. (2007). *Trial courts as organizations.* Temple University Press.

Rubin, A., & Babbie, E. (1997). *Practice-oriented study guide for research methods for social work* (3rd ed.). Brooks/Cole.

Schein, E. H. (2004). *Organizational culture and leadership* (3rd ed.). Jossey-Bass.

Schleifer, J. T. (1980). *The making of Tocqueville's democracy in America.* University of North Carolina Press.

Tocqueville, A. de (1875). *Democracy in America* (H. Reeve, Trans., Vol. 1, pp. 283–284). N.P.

2 Purposes and Responsibilities of Courts

Starting in the 1960s, Professor Ernie Friesen, a noted pioneer and leader in modern court administration, would ask judges and lawyers their thoughts on the purposes of courts. After several years of obtaining their input through facilitated meeting discussions, he synthesized their answers in the 1970s into the eight purposes noted in the Introduction. This list has been presented to judicial-branch conferences and training sessions across the nation for decades and included in numerous documents of the field, one being the National Association for Court Management's (NACM) (2004) *Core Responsibilities*. Friesen's list has clearly stood the test of time.

The list has served as the foundation for discussions about the purposes of courts, including the *CORE* collaboration, for the past half-century. It has been recently referred to as the "traditional" statement of the purposes of courts. That is not to say that in other workshops and meetings over the years individuals did not suggest that something was missing or that one of the items should be edited, but in the end, Friesen's enumeration has been the touchstone for most discussions on the topic. Only recently have other ideas begun to gain traction, particularly in Institute for Court Management (ICM) workshops devoted to purposes and responsibilities (Batty, 2016). Thus, in its core curriculum for court leaders, the NACM (2016a) adds two new purposes that reflect the growth and broad acceptance of "problem-solving" and "therapeutic" courts as new ways for courts to address social issues which are mostly apparent in criminal, juvenile, and family-related cases but also include homelessness, mental health, and addiction matters.

In response to NACM's endorsement of Friesen's list and the addition of the two new purposes, Batty (2016) suggested that the entire list should be re-examined and rephrased. He proposed the following six reformulations of the courts' purposes based on

DOI: 10.4324/9781003686804-2

his synthesis of discussions in the ICM courses he led on purposes and responsibilities that takes into account the pioneering work of Friesen:

- To preserve order in society
- To reconcile relationships
- To protect those who cannot protect themselves
- To protect individuals and society from the abusive use of power
- To provide appropriate services to aid "at-risk" children and their families while safeguarding the community
- To demonstrate accountability for the effective, efficient use of public resources

Following Batty, V. Eugene Flango, a recognized researcher and author on court administration issues, responded with reformulated purposes of his own. Both Batty and Flango urged a re-evaluation of the current articulation of courts' purposes by a broad group of people familiar with courts (representing both the government and the public) rather than having individuals continue to propose their own lists.

Regardless of whether any new statement gains the broad acceptance accorded by Friesen's statement, the ongoing responsibility of court leaders is to ensure that judges and court staff understand the purposes of courts. These purposes transcend the leadership and culture of the court. While the tenure of leaders eventually ends and the current court culture can change, these fundamental purposes and responsibilities of the courts endure. This is easier said than done in practice because sometimes the important succumbs to the urgent (Covey, 1989). Court leaders, however, who can retain a focus on the purposes of courts can avoid this pitfall.

Within the paradigm, the fundamental Purposes and Responsibilities of Courts addresses a question that all members of an organization should be able to answer: What foundational principles guide the organization's service and mission? Accordingly, this central element from which we begin this text concerns the "why" aspect of court administration. The other ten fundamentals represent the "how" features of the profession. Mission, vision, goals, and strategies for accomplishing objectives are generally reviewed briefly by human resource personnel (courts included) during new employee orientation.

The footing is the most important part of any physical structure. There is simply no substitute from which an arrangement rests, as Ralph Waldo Emerson (1870) remarked: "The beautiful rests on the foundations of the necessary." A well-established base, therefore, provides stability to the organization upon which the weight of its operations can function and be made practical. Everything in the present form, as well as what can come to be expected in the future, is supported and draws meaning from this foundational base.

Court leaders have discovered that inquiring about the purposes of the courts with internal stakeholders yields a diverse range of intriguing responses. These responses encompass a variety of answers, some of which may cause even the most dedicated and focused administrator to cringe. Some responses will be spot on and recite one or more of Friesen's eight purposes. Other reactions are straightforward with many responses including the word "justice." Ask what justice *means*, however, and the responses get more varied, devolving often into the specifics of the respondents' technical expertise, job subject matter, or physical work area (what we do when we occupy this space).

The same seems to hold true in the classroom. For instance, students completing a task force exercise for implementing a differentiated case management (DCM) system often reference "justice" in their project statements, but seldom do they provide reasons for the change and justify it based on the court's purposes and responsibilities. In other words, why should the court and other stakeholders invest resources and time into keeping the calendar "current"? What are some of the tangible consequences of delay and its impact on both internal and external stakeholders and their organizations? What changes and problems have occurred that would warrant the procedural changes that are being suggested? Where are the pitfalls in how cases are currently being managed and how can the process be corrected with the DCM plan that is being outlined? Each of these points can be tied to one or more purposes of the courts. The purposes and responsibilities should be regularly communicated by court administrators so that the mission of the courts is clear to those the institution must rely on to actually achieve it.

Dale Lefever, a faculty leader for workshops on creating and managing change presented by the ICM of the National Center for State Courts (NCSC), would remind participants, "If they don't know why, the price is too high." Although he was referring specifically to change management, his cautionary advice was equally applicable to staff knowing and understanding the purposes and responsibilities of courts. In short, court leaders are responsible for assuring that court staff comprehend and take seriously this foundational information. The NACM (2015) states:

> The most fundamental aspect of court leadership is an understanding of the purposes and responsibilities of the court and providing the leadership to ensure that these continuously guide court operations, policies, and procedures.

It adds:

> These fundamental purposes and responsibilities of courts apply regardless of the specific jurisdiction in which a court functions and provide both the philosophical and legal framework for the daily work of all court leaders. They also delineate the essential differences between the role court leaders [fill] and [the roles of]... professionals who work in other public sector entities.

With respect to "responsibilities," *The CORE* states:

> [T]he primary responsibility of the judicial branch is to provide an impartial forum for the resolution of disputes. This ensures the rule of law and protection of individual rights. Over time, this fundamental responsibility of the judicial branch has been expanded to encompass other areas of importance, including but not limited to the following:
>
> - Ensuring access to the court process for all who seek it.
> - Managing the business of the court in a manner that promotes efficiency, transparency and the opportunity for fair and timely disposition of the cases filed.
> - Exercising leadership among other justice-related agencies to develop strategies that join the interests of all three branches of government.

The purposes and responsibilities of the courts provide the overarching values by which the organization is steered. This perspective impacts everything from basic day-to-day public service functions to the long-term issues affecting the court's ability to meet and exceed benchmarks, such that it strains efforts to recruit, retain, and promote the court's most valuable (and costly) commodity – its employees. In some instances, problems become so pervasive and the court so dysfunctional that external "experts" and consultants are brought in to assess the circumstances and provide a series of recommendations. Ultimately, the administrator will find that there was no recondite knowledge shared in the final analysis, but rather or more simply, a void in the process or "way of thinking and doing things" that invariably comes into play when human beings are brought together to work. Consider the following excerpt from an internal coach's report evaluating what was regarded as an underperforming team:

> The accounts receivables office employing 16 employees in the Potenza Municipal Court[1] has been undergoing a period of deep turmoil among its staff and leadership for several years. The interpersonal conflict and the failed interventions have left the local administrator and the employees discouraged, apprehensive, and at times, paranoid. Some of the observations I noted during my visits included making excuses, a lack of communication between team members, and contentious interpersonal communication patterns leading to a stressful work environment. The support of the presiding judge, court administrator, and liaisons at the general jurisdiction level have been instrumental in helping the employees gain perspective and move toward greater cooperation. The following are my preliminary recommendations for your consideration:
>
> - Related trainings that have been discussed should cover the following topics: Establishing Direction, Promoting Change, Stability, and Order, Motivating Employees,

Personality Spectrum, Effective Communication, Emotional Intelligence, and Case Management.

- Staff and supervision require tools for personal development, workshops, and self-assessment instruments as appropriate to those trainings.
- The court's leadership needs continued support and feedback. They will require an evaluation of reorganization efforts over the course of the next 6 to 12 months.
- The team should continue to implement new tools and documents to support the workflow.

As noted by Lipsky (1980), these recommendations address issues among street-level bureaucrats that reflect a broader organizational problem: a lack of alignment with the organization's objectives. This lack of alignment is caused by inadequate communication and intervention from the court's leadership and a human resources orientation that is grossly deficient. In this example, the coach takes the role of the consultant who tells you what time it is with your own watch. The problem, in other words, is relatively obvious, but the changes that are sought require validation from someone outside the group before the recommendations are taken seriously and instituted. When the court's leadership teaches and demonstrates purpose, its employees are aggrandized through their shared understanding in the overarching importance of their work.

The court's purposes transcend all of its leaders, notwithstanding their knowledge, skills, and abilities. Gallas (2007) believed that there must be three basic presumptions at the heart of court administration. First, courts do not exist for administrators to manage them. Second, justice is the overarching goal of the court, and therefore if ever a conflict exists between justice and management, the ultimate goal must always take precedence. Previously, Friesen (2002) argued that "administrative processes are subordinate to the judicial processes that apply the rules to particular cases." These first two assumptions and the implications directed at management are buffered by the third conjecture, wherein Gallas (2007) stated that justice is immeasurably more the result of management than case law, statutes, or constitution. Plato (n.d., Book VI) noted in *Laws*:

> It is obvious to anyone that legislation is a tremendous task and that when you have a well constructed state with a well framed legal code, to put incompetent officials in charge is a waste of good laws, and the whole business degenerates into farce. And not only that, the state will find its laws are doing damage and injury on a gigantic scale.

Administrators manage the courts, but they must always do so to advance the purposes of courts and deliver upon the responsibilities of their courts rather than acting for some other interest or influence bearing down on the organization's leadership. Using purposes as the touchstone of decision making largely makes the difference between a court that merely exists and one that meets its intended mission. As Zorza (2002) asserted, the importance of that mission should never be understated:

> Without the protection of courts, the core of our society dies. Without courts that are practically and effectively accessible, our society still dies, but more slowly and less obviously. The shell remains, but the essence is gone.

The court's "product" – justice – is in some ways abstract. The purposes and responsibilities drive the action at all levels of the organization that produce this end product, intangible as it may be. This foundation – well-established – should be what motivates staff to come to work and do what they do. Finally, the purposes of the court can support leaders seeking operational changes by showing gaps between what is being done and what should be done to move the court closer to achieving its purposes and responsibilities.

Arguably, courts have an inherent advantage over almost all other institutions in this regard given that most staff choose to work for courts because the institution is special, because they help individuals, businesses, and society achieve justice and because they understand they are contributing to the delivery of justice. Court leaders have to call on and build on staff's predispositions by assuring that all of the purposes are known, and that staff see the connection between what they are doing and those purposes.

Individual Justice in Individual Cases

Every case filed in a court has a story behind it that affects people – even those filed by or involving corporations and government entities – be it a traffic ticket, a misdemeanor or felony crime, a divorce or annulment, a dispute over money or property, the care and protection of at-risk individuals, or any of the countless other matters individuals, businesses, and governments bring to courts for resolution. Less well recognized is that every case is driven by its own facts; law that may appear to apply to all may or may not apply based on the individualized facts. Sometimes, equity issues can affect outcomes. The specifics of a case can materially impact how a case is decided. Like a fingerprint, all cases have distinctions that come to characterize the individual stories. Thus, doing individual justice in individual cases (each and every case) is the essence of what courts are to do on all matters. Even when some courtroom processes appear rote, such as some high-volume traffic or parking calendars, the obligation to do *individual* justice remains. The obligation extends to everyone working for and in a court.

Cases represent individuals requiring care because each file holds the narrative of what is likely the most challenging and volatile period of a person's life. Think of the eight-year-old girl – a witness in her own case where a supposed family friend is accused of having sexually assaulted her from the time she was five. The 15-year-old who has lived with three different foster families since having been put up for adoption when he was an infant and now stands before the court charged, among other things, with possession of stolen property. The patient who fell victim to malpractice. The single father arguing for child custody. A property owner seeking relief. And the list goes on ad infinitum; many cases are similar, and yet they are each unique in that all cases have distinctions that come to characterize the individual's story. However, managing a case with the consideration it warrants is burdensome. It requires a great deal of thought in the labyrinth of decisions that can be made by the host of stakeholders on the direction of the file (person) and the time that it is allotted.

Given the high volume of cases coming to courts, the quantitative and statistically driven paradigm of cranking out files – if x, then y – may seem appealing. There is a certainty to it – an arbitrary line distinguishes the good and bad. The exposure and discomfort associated with resolving even non-straightforward matters are clearly delineated. Such a system provides for a more sterile environment and certainly takes considerably less time from our judicial system, but at what cost? Individual rights and liberties are sacrificed for the sake of expediency. However, the very purpose of a court is to not restrict that which is unrestricted – the fullness of an individual's experiences, all of which contribute to their current social position. When the court's attention is diverted from individual cases, there is no need for it. Instead, we are left with a human supply chain where fact patterns are quantified, and "decisions" are delivered. Individual justice is at the heart of the court's responsibilities. Unlike any other institution, it recognizes that while life continues at a normal pace for everyone else, the litigant's life slows, becomes arduous, and in some cases, is forever altered.

The universe is found in the details of things, places, and people – and the relative importance of these variables can sometimes be underappreciated. The truth is similarly found by scrutinizing a given set of conditions – and not in a superficial kind of way that is consumed in a 30-second sound bite of information afforded by a myriad of media outlets. This is critically important to the idea of individual justice. The specifics of a case should dictate how it is managed by the court. The courts, therefore, have an obligation to make the best decision they can, based on the unique circumstances presented before it. Obviously, the strength and certainty of precedents are subject to change with the passage of time, emergence of new information, and evolution of public sentiment. For instance, in *Schenck v. Pro-Choice Network* (1997), the United States Supreme Court (USSC) upheld the constitutionality of prohibiting protestors under the Freedom of Access to Clinic Entrances Act from breaching a 15-foot "buffer zone" around abortion clinics and from giving unsolicited counsel to individuals entering the clinic. In *Scheidler v. National Organization for Women* (2006) the USSC reversed course that anti-abortion protestors could be prosecuted under racketeering statutes.

How do we know if individual justice is being accomplished? Consider a group of criminal division trial courts in a large, urban district. Each criminal division judge is responsible for an individual calendar, which is coordinated with an assigned group of assistant prosecutors (APs) and assistant public defenders (APDs). Judges are generally accountable for three primary functions: 1) calendar/caseflow management; 2) report preparation, which comprises interviews, investigations, assessments, report writing and reviewing, and secretarial support; and 3) records management. The local court backlog standard for active pending cases in this particular district provides judges with flexibility to individually consider and exercise discretion on which cases should be disposed within a standard 60-day (filing to indictment) and 120-day (indictment to resolution) timeframe.

Backlog is monitored closely at both the local district level, as well as the state level. At the district level, numerous reports detailing case management performance are reviewed on a regular basis with individual courts compared against one another. Table 2.1 exemplifies one such report. Judges are ranked in descending order based on backlog sizes.

Table 2.1 Backlog Reduction Goals by Judge

Judge	*Backlog Reduction to Reach 10%*	*Total Backlogged Defendants*	*Total Defendant Caseload*	*Backlog Percentage*
A	0	3	125	2
B	2	19	175	10
C	2	18	158	11
D	5	20	155	13
E	4	16	121	13
F	6	19	128	15
G	12	26	143	18
H	15	32	170	19
I	17	28	113	25
J	28	41	134	31
K	58	77	190	41
L	78	98	204	48
M	47	59	121	49
N	82	102	205	50
O	49	61	119	51
Division Total	393	619	2,261	27

Clearly, some judges are performing better than others vis-à-vis speedy trial outcomes. Does this mean that Judge A, ranked first among his peers with a 2 percent backlog, is delivering the most individual justice in the district? Not necessarily. In fact, this particular judge was not unlike many other judges and was extraordinarily competitive with respect to these performance metrics, which incidentally were promulgated to the entire division on a monthly basis. He prided himself at being at the top of the list, but the speed at which he insisted on the cases being resolved by counsel had a deleterious effect on some of the cases' outcomes. Some decisions went so far as being reversed by the appellate court for issues stemming from lack of due process. Even more concerning is that some underperforming judges use adverse conditions, such as overly expedited case management, to undermine the legitimacy of performance measurement.

Individual justice requires thoughtful decision making that also takes into account overarching goals and performance standards. At the same time, all cases (as evidenced by DCM) are not created equally, and some may legitimately require more time. A balance, therefore, which the prudent judge and administrator recognize, must be struck.[2] As central as benchmarks are to the system, they should not be used to disregard aspects of a case that can cause it to fall outside of time standards. Eventually, discounting such peculiarities does not go unnoticed, as one ADP remarked (Fazari, 2008):

> Whatever happened to caring about how well cases were handled by the parties compared to how quickly the cases are "processed"? Using terms such as "standard" and the dreaded "backlog" mean terms so that justice and fairness are de-emphasized for the greater goal of efficiency. Judges are under greater pressure to move cases. That pressure is transferred to prosecutors and defense lawyers. Ultimately, victims and defendants bear the stresses placed upon the system. They become the real losers in any case management system.

An AP commented in a similar vein (Fazari, 2008):

> Disposing of backlogged cases pre- and post-indictment is important. However, judges and the central office need to understand criminal cases are the most important. Leeway must be given even on old cases because the eye to resolving cases should be justice, NOT the age of the case.

In practice, the individual justice equilibrium will demonstrate that there is such a thing as a "healthy backlog," meaning that although performance standards will apply to the lion's share of the docket, there will be instances wherein cases (for good reason) fall outside general parameters. Whether they are ignored or not fully understood, speedy trial standards are quintessential of courts. For the courts, while case outcome is a critical factor in evaluating if justice was accomplished, the case management *process* is equally important because it determines whether justice *can* be achieved. Gallas (personal communication, February 4, 2008) remarked that ultimately, case management is about engendering the "same or better justice in a shorter period of time." Central to this process is time, which is measured in part by the "dreaded backlog." Taken wholly, the court will find that its failure to meet performance standards ordinarily equates to its failure to deliver justice and its promise as a system. Having said that, the court must concomitantly ensure that each case receives the time and resources it requires, recognizing that what serves justice in an individual case may not always advance aggregate performance goals.

Appearance of Individual Justice in Individual Cases

The appearance of individual justice is distinct from providing individual justice and thus it is distinguished as a separate purpose of the court. This purpose relates to the level of predictability and consistency by which the court applies the laws governing similar cases. The perception and understanding by the public that the court can be relied upon to apply the law equally is a keystone to maintaining a civilized society. Court rulings are meaningful to the constituency and order follows in society when the majority perceives the consistent and equitable application of law. Accordingly, it cuts to the questions of accessibility and fairness.

We acknowledge that the concept of "justice" is not universally applicable. It varies among individuals, regions within a country, "tribes" (in the broadest sense), and from country to country. Consequently, what a judge may perceive as upholding "justice" in a particular case might not be viewed similarly by the involved parties. In fact, many judges believe that regardless of the outcome, at least one party will leave the courtroom dissatisfied and convinced that justice was not served. As a result, they may feel that while it remains an admirable aspiration, it remains unattainable. However, research does not support this notion. Regardless of one's philosophical or political stance on "justice" in an individual case, courts must ensure that all litigants and those observing the court's proceedings believe that the judge(s) and the institution strive throughout the process to uphold justice. Therefore, the appearance of doing individual justice in individual cases is as crucial a purpose as actually doing justice. This implies that there is a level of predictability and consistency in how the court applies the laws governing similar cases. Moreover, these actions align with the majority of society's perception and understanding that the court can be relied upon to apply the law impartially.

Research shows that if courts provide "procedural justice," both parties to cases and those observing courts will see that a court is doing justice, including those against whom a judge or jury may rule (Center for Court Innovation, 2011). Parties who do not prevail in their case still believe they received justice if they believe they received procedural justice. Procedural justice refers to how litigants believe they – and their families, friends, witnesses, and attorneys – were treated in the courtroom and throughout the courthouse. The components of procedural justice include courts being understandable, accessible, respectful, and trustworthy in the eyes of the people who use them. Were all involved in the process treated equally? Were litigants for whom English is not their first language given interpreter services? Did the judge seek to assure that all parties understood what was being said, including reference to legal terms that are second nature to lawyers and judges but not to lay people? The appearance of doing justice is not solely the responsibility of judges; staff and management also contribute to procedural justice.

Procedural justice also includes accessibility and fairness. Was the court accessible to the litigant regardless of age, gender, religion, disability, dominant language, sexual orientation, or socioeconomic status? Were parties given a fair chance to present their positions? Were forms and court documents, including orders, understandable and usable by self-represented litigants? Were court records readily accessible? Did the court treat the individual with respect and dignity, including the judge listening respectfully and the party (or their attorney) having an opportunity to voice their version of events in the courtroom and in filed documents? Was the litigant provided with the same level of treatment as anyone else, regardless of their social status or lack of legal representation? Additionally, other aspects of accessibility contribute to procedural justice, such as well-maintained courthouses (clean, with functional furniture and equipment, proper heating and air conditioning, and signage to aid visitors), and staff who provide excellent service with a positive attitude.

The pre-trial intervention (PTI) program is one example demonstrating how the court fulfills this purpose. PTI is a diversionary program that provides defendants, generally first-time offenders, with an opportunity to avoid criminal prosecution that would typically occur because of the crime the defendant is alleged to have committed. It is open to anyone qualifying under a specific set of rules. The goal of the community-based program is to deter future criminal behavior by applying rehabilitative constructs. Eligibility is ordinarily limited to first-time adult offenders, who reside within the state and whose crime is considered a minor violation. Defendants who have a prior record of conviction, are on parole or probation, or have been previously diverted are generally excluded from the program. For those who have had some prior involvement, the court can be compelled to consider "individual" circumstances to allow entry into the program.

The appearance of individual justice is applied by assessing the totality of circumstances that brought this particular defendant into court. With respect to criminal offenses, questions relating to frequency, severity, criminal history, and the likelihood of reoccurrence all factor into how the matter is resolved and ultimately the perception of how the case was resolved. Accordingly, some of the generally relevant questions that should be considered by judges and administrators in ensuring an equitable delivery of justice in all cases are listed by Solomon and Somerlot (1987) and organized in Table 2.2.

Table 2.2 Outline of Case Management Information for Judges and Managers

Individual Trial Judge and Case Management Supervisor or Leader	***Presiding Judge and Court Administrator***
Case-related questions: • What has happened in this case? • How old is it? • What is the status? • What should happen next and by when?	Overall status of division caseload: • How many cases are nearing one year? • What is the backlog?

Calendar-related questions:
• What is the overall status of my calendar?
    • What are the total number cases?
    • What is the age and status of pending cases?
• What are the old cases?
    • Why are they old?
    • What is required to dispose them?
	Problem areas:
	• Case types, procedural issues, particular judges, staff, external agencies, etc.?

The notion of perceived justice is a bifurcated concept. The first part of it addresses how the court administers justice with respect to the litigants that come before it. The second aspect focuses on how the system is perceived in handling matters wherein political and administrative "insiders" are implicated. This is where a canon of ethics and standards by which administrators and staff should be trained on and thereafter abide are particularly important. The NACM Model Code of Conduct for Court Professionals (2018) serves as an appropriate reference for these points. Among other points, members should not use or attempt to use their official positions to secure unwarranted privileges or exemptions for themselves or other people. A probation officer who, in an effort to avoid receiving a ticket after being pulled over for a moving violation, shows the police officer his badge would be in violation of this standard. Another scenario where a court employee who is in a relationship with a private attorney provides her with information on confidential juvenile records would contravene the canon which precludes members from disclosing confidential information to any unauthorized person.

Consider a scenario where a small claims motion is being presented in court. A data entry clerk walking in and out of the court is fluent in Spanish and perceives interpreting inaccuracies by the court's interpreter, who is a relatively new employee. This is no small matter because taking one action over another can have an adverse impact on perception, can lead to a mistrial, etc. In this instance, bilingual staff should understand that stepping outside of their role to comment on the court's interpreting services could jeopardize the perceived integrity of the judicial system. Interrupting the proceeding, notwithstanding having the best of intentions, can prove detrimental to the perceived legitimacy of the court. This may seem obvious, but the level of comfort a "judge's team" (including the sheriff's officer assigned to the court) have with one another (which can naturally develop over time) sometimes leads to complacency in procedure.

The court administrator, senior managers, and staff play crucial roles in ensuring procedural fairness. Their actions significantly impact how court users perceive their experience, and whether they were treated fairly. If a poll were conducted among court users, how would litigants respond regarding their treatment and overall experience in court? Moreover, how would the court rate itself without knowing the public findings? Judges and court administrators, like other working professionals, often tend to view their performance more positively than others perceive it. An Arizona judge cited by Peak (2004) expressed this notion succinctly:

> Judges and court administrators are not likely to view themselves in a negative light. As part of an organization that creates a certain amount of respect and awe for itself, it is not surprising that the [judge] and the court administrator may believe that they are better than they actually are. As a result, their top members frequently believe that the awe displayed toward them is intrinsic to their person, and not to the office.

Humility, as T.S. Eliot (1951) opined, is "the most difficult of all virtues to achieve; nothing dies harder than the desire to think well of oneself." Perceptions should be juxtaposed against empirical data drawn from both internal and external stakeholders so that practices are objectively assessed, and policies and procedures are developed and implemented with these findings in mind. Appearances are mutable, but critically important all the same. Court leaders need to assure stakeholders that achieving this purpose is high on their priority list. An excellent way to provide that assurance is to collect and evaluate data which will substantiate (or refute) the exceptional job they believe the court is doing.

Access and fairness focus on the public's perception of their experience in the courts. Understanding how actions can be perceived by the public is the basis for this purpose. The court benefits by incorporating committees and working groups that evaluate access and fairness issues, so that the importance of this purpose is firmly embedded into the culture of the court system. This evaluation demonstrates the realization that the organizational decisions and operations of every service counter, data entry point, and courtroom impact the ability to earn the public's confidence in the courts.

A Forum for Dispute Resolution

The cornerstone of an orderly and civilized society lies in the court's capacity to resolve matters conclusively. Failure to achieve this objective poses a risk to individuals who resort to self-resolution of their grievances, and in cases of crimes, an accused may commit additional offenses. Unnecessary delays in case resolution lead to simmering family disputes, potentially causing adverse effects not only for the parties involved but also for other family members.

The court as a "forum for dispute resolution" has three elements: timely dispositions, finality, and access. Timely dispositions mean each case takes no more time to be disposed than the facts and circumstances of the case require, consistent with the court assuring due process. A fuller discussion of caseflow management and how it achieves these goals is provided in Chapter 5. Finality means people can learn the outcome of their cases and get on with their lives. A right to appeal is part of the finality process to enable correction of any possible legal errors by a trial judge (or an intermediate appellate court), but once that final appeals process ends, the dispute/case ends. Parties are expected to accept the court's decision and implement its provisions, if any. The parties and society at large benefit from knowing that this matter is formally resolved and will not be relitigated. The public should believe they are coming to court to resolve a conflict, and not simply because they have no alternative for dispute resolution.

Within the construct of resolving disputes, the judge listens, staying attentive to all the cues (both verbal and non-verbal), deliberates over the evidence, considers all sides of the arguments, and structures their own legally based conclusions of what occurred on the basis of the information provided, and most importantly, their interpretation of those facts. Ultimately, it is the truth that the court seeks. The judge's interpretation of course is grounded by their own knowledge and experience. Imperfect as the process is, it seems to be the best way, yet devisable, to arrive at the truth and to apply the law.[3]

Serving as a forum where disputes are decided is not an unambiguous process because it necessarily requires the public's trust and confidence. In his address to the American Bar Association (ABA), *The Causes of Popular Dissatisfaction with the Administration of Justice,* Roscoe Pound (1906) articulated the complexity of this process. More than 100 years later, it resonates now as it did then. He explained the causes of dissatisfaction with *any* legal system in four points. The first involved the necessary mechanical operation of rules. The uniformity that the law attempts to create does not appeal to a community that does not think uniformly. Courts face challenges because not all controversies are identical. While attempting to cater to the needs of most people, judges are often perceived as falling short due to the need to strike a compromise between administrative extremes, such as judicial discretion and legislative bureaucracy. Ultimately, the negotiation does not necessarily result in this *idea* of justice because the community is diverse and its notions of justice are likewise varied. Second, there is an inevitable difference in the acceptable rate of progress between law and public opinion. The period between legislating the law and administrating it is not fixed to public opinion. As Pound (1906) observed, the change in law must be prompted by the change in "moral or intellectual or economic" thought. It is during this interim, critical period that the court leaves a lasting impression in the public's mind. Third, there is a general and popular assumption that the administration of justice is an easy task which anyone can competently manage. While he conceded this to be a greater issue for some states than others, the public generally does not realize the stakes involved in "maintaining the highest scientific standard in the administration of justice." Fourth, impatience of restraint is prevalent. When individuals are forced to reconcile their activities for the interests of the group, it makes them (to varying extents) unyielding to such restraint. The perceived sacrifice (nota bene) that is brought to bear by these imposed limitations can intensify one's proclivity to resist, which manifests itself in a variety of ways depending on how much "sacrifice" is meted out.

The causes of dissatisfaction lying in the peculiarities of the Anglo-American legal system are inherent in the individualist spirit of the common law practice. Common law impedes what the courts can realistically do and the remedies that it can offer to the public. Considering the adversarial nature of the judicial system, the community frequently misinterprets "the purpose and end of the law" as a sort of game with winners and losers. Individuals restrained covet the authority of those wielding such power because the matters being controlled involve strong, emotional ties to their well-being. Moreover, given that courts are left to interpret the law, whatever shortcomings it has are perceived to be due to interpretation as opposed to applicable legislation. The interpretation by virtue of what it is (or attempts to do) is problematic. It is as Derrida (2014) observed in stating that when something occurs, it vanishes – only the cinders remain. The cinders are not in their present form as they were when the event took place; one can never reassemble what actually occurred.

A proverbial picture is being painted in the courtroom, but how will it be interpreted? The "legal game" alluded to by Pound (1906) refers to the adversarial courtroom process, in which attorneys' resourcefulness in researching, arguing, and applying precedent provides a clear advantage that does not go unnoticed by spectators. Reconstructing the past takes the form of testimony in court (reassembling the cinders if you will) but, testimony once taken, narrows the number of possible interpretations and is "then left to pass away." The testimony provides a degree of truth to what occurred, but at the same time, the court delimits the infinite versions of the story which were previously possible. The testimony is (Derrida, 2014):

> An interpretation, one among others. At each syllable, even at each silence, a decision is imposed: it was not always deliberate, nor sometimes even the same from one repetition to the other. And what it signs is neither the law nor the truth. Other interpretations remain possible and doubtless necessary.

These difficulties, among others, that the court confronts cannot be forestalled entirely, according to Pound (1906). Knowing that these realities are inevitable, what is the court to do? Licht (1993) explained the most appropriate course of action:

> The Court's power lies... in its legitimacy, a product of substance and perception that shows itself in the people's acceptance of the Judiciary as fit to determine what the Nation's law means and to declare what it demands... The Court must take care to speak and act in ways that allow people to accept its decisions on the terms the Court claims for them, as grounded truly in principle, not as compromises with social and political pressures... Thus the Court's legitimacy depends on making legally principled decisions under circumstances in which their principled character is sufficiently plausible to be accepted by the Nation.

Court administrators acknowledge the truths that these scholars and philosophers addressed about the restrictions that testimony presents, the implications that it poses to the purposes of the courts and its effect on public satisfaction. Having said that, administrators do not accept public dissatisfaction as a fait accompli by virtue of "the system" and the bureaucracy in which it attempts to function. The thoughtful administrator monitors, evaluates, and implements change to improve processes, notwithstanding these realities. Administrators who are well grounded in the purposes and responsibilities of the courts accept them not as realities, but as challenges (not insurmountable, but onerous); to do otherwise would be to deny, or at the very least shortchange the public on, the administrator's role in this important capacity. Part of "making legally principled decisions" is derived from a fair, consistent, and efficient administrative process – and that responsibility rests squarely with the administrator.

Preserving the idea of the court as a "forum for dispute resolution" requires an ongoing evaluative process that continually assesses emerging issues, changes in law or procedure, and directives that potentially affect service to the public. "Business Process Re-Engineering" as it known to be is not so much a goal for court leaders, as it is an organizational value. It rejects the notion of being the object of political stalemates, staffing models, technological improvements, legislative and policy changes, and administrative and structural modifications. Conversely, it impels focus and seeks to build success around the purposes and responsibilities of the court despite the challenges that the system confronts – like inevitable public dissatisfaction. Business process re-engineering requires committed leadership that communicates the organizational vision and expectations to meet those objectives. It is on this very foundation of judicial and executive commitment, which must be well established, that administrators can effectively manage system intricacies to ensure that the judicial process is, if nothing else, fair so that everyone is provided the same opportunities in accordance with law, rule, and policy.

Protection of Individuals from the Arbitrary Use of Governmental Power

The Rule of Law and government of limited powers are impossible without an independent judiciary. The nation's framers believed this independent branch of government would safeguard citizens from the legislative and executive branches' overreach in protecting individual rights, liberty, and property rights. Moreover, the independence of the judiciary reduces the likelihood of the majority suppressing the rights of the minority. The judiciary's role in a free society seeks to ultimately strike a balance on the appropriate use of government power.

For instance, in *Miranda v. Arizona* (1966), the USSC ruled that defendants have a right to remain silent and be represented by counsel when being questioned by police. Balancing this protection, the court allowed exceptions for convictions obtained, even after the Miranda warning was not provided such as those circumstances when there is an urgent need to obtain information in the interest of "public safety" or when the defendant is not explicit in their desire to want an attorney and to remain silent. In *United States v. Eichman* (1990), the court protected a minority view by ruling that the Flag Protection Act of 1989, which criminalized the burning and certain other forms of destruction of the United States flag, violated an individual's rights guaranteed under the First Amendment. In *Brown v. Board of Education* (1954), the court sought to safeguard minority rights by nullifying the "separate but equal" doctrine as it pertained to racial segregation in public schools.

The grand jury system is another good example of how the court ensures that policing agencies do not abuse their executive authority by assuring that the probable cause threshold is met as a part of the indictment process. The following excerpt from an orientation script drafted for a presiding judge to use in addressing newly summoned grand jurors reveals the importance of the function:

> The function of the grand jury is to determine whether there is sufficient evidence to establish that a crime has been

> committed and that the accused committed it. The grand jury serves as a screening mechanism to ensure that before persons are required to stand trial on a criminal charge there be an adequate basis for it, and also serves to prevent citizens from being exposed to the rigors of a criminal trial when the charge is baseless. The grand jury as a part of the criminal justice system is an institution of ancient origin which has existed for many centuries. Its continued existence is guaranteed by our state constitution and this constitutional guarantee is a recognition that the grand jury protects the rights of every person and breathes the spirit of the community into the enforcement of the law. As prospective grand jurors, you have been randomly selected from throughout the county to represent your fellow citizens in carrying out this vital function. If selected, you will bring to the grand jury the attitudes and experience of the citizenry. In a very real sense, you will function as the conscience of the community.

One facet of the courts' responsibility which could be better administered, and for that matter communicated to the public, is the issue of bail. Judges are the decision-makers with respect to setting a reasonable bail of an arrested person. Consider the case where a defendant charged with aggravated sexual assault on a minor was out on bail when he committed a homicide a few months later. Unsurprisingly, the high-profile nature of the homicide case coupled with the defendant's criminal history placed the court under intense scrutiny and public criticism. A comprehensive review of procedures in setting the bail showed that the court, however, proceeded appropriately. The denigration of the court in setting the defendant's bail in this case demonstrates how profoundly flawed the public's understanding is with respect to the right of bail. The primary purpose of bail is to provide the court with some level of assurance that the accused will appear for the next scheduled court event. It is a constitutional right, which cannot be denied and used as a punitive measure before the defendant is convicted of any crime. To do so would ignore the presumption of innocence which is afforded to all persons charged with a crime. The court considers a variety of risk factors and certainly has discretion when setting bail, but the presumption of innocence remains. Some defendants, perhaps many, are ultimately found to be guilty as charged. However, because there is no way of knowing this beforehand, all defendants must be treated as though innocent until proven otherwise.

Many members of the public seem to believe that if a person is arrested, they are probably guilty. Such critics do not recognize that by protecting the rights of those accused of crime – including some who almost everyone would agree represent the worst in humanity and often are dangerous to others – courts also are simultaneously protecting everyone's constitutional rights. One cannot exist without the other. A democratic society relies on this principle. In *The Search for Justice*, Shapiro (Shapiro & Warren, 1996) responded to inquiries about his ability to sleep following what was one of the most divided trials in American history. As part of the defense team that resulted in O.J. Simpson's acquittal for a double murder, when at least half of America believed him to be guilty, Shapiro (Shapiro & Warren, 1996) explained how he is capable of getting a good night's rest without any trouble:

> It's convenient, when confronted with the virulence of modern crime, to forget history, both ancient and recent, which is full of object lessons illustrating what happens when the rules that govern a people's conscience are, for whatever "expedient" reason, set aside... until that moment in many people's lives when they or someone near and dear to them is arrested for something as simple as drunk driving or as complicated as insider trading. And then the first question asked is "Where are my rights?" Until and unless that moment happens, crime isn't committed by "us"; therefore, those accused of crimes aren't "us," and "they" are not entitled to the same constitutional protections that "we" are entitled to. Or, as one defense attorney once put it, "Everybody in town hates my guts – until two o'clock in the morning, when their kid gets arrested."

The Keeper of the Record

One of the primary purposes of courts is to make a formal record of legal status. In a world in which movies, television, news outlets, and other sources of information focus almost exclusively on the commission, solving, and prosecution of crimes, this purpose is largely lost in the public's consciousness. Yet, it consumes a large portion of judge and staff time. Making and preserving the official court record is thus a fundamental function of court administration, apart from representing a large cost center. Friesen observed that the resources associated with making and preserving the official record may constitute up to 65 percent of a court's budget (United States Bureau of Justice Assistance, 2014).

Virtually every action taken by a court establishes or confirms an individual's "legal status." Accused individuals are either found guilty or not guilty. This status is established in a court, but the court must also maintain and disseminate it to other components of the criminal justice system. Additionally, it must make this record accessible to everyone as a public record of the court's actions and the accused's legal status. If the record is inaccurate or incomplete, it can compromise people's freedom, access to government benefits, the right to vote, employment opportunities, and, in some cases, housing. Similarly, if the court fails to adequately protect the integrity and long-term viability of the record, whether in physical or digital format, or in any future format, similar risks may arise.

Likewise, this holds true in the myriad of civil matters with which courts deal. Without court sanction, no one can enforce a contract and establish the legally proper remedy under that contract, establish a right to damages for injury to their person and/or property, establish ownership of personal or real property, confirm the proper distribution of a deceased's property when it is contested, formally and legally end a marriage (thus creating the right to remarry, if desired) and establish custody and support rights and obligations, gain emancipation, adopt a child, or establish that someone needs the protection of a guardian or conservator. In each individual case, a judge determines responsibility for one party or absolves one or more parties of responsibility, thereby establishing rights and responsibilities and legally concluding the dispute.[4] Equally critical, the court maintains an official record of its actions to ensure clarity and avoid any questions from the parties. Moreover, this record serves as a valuable resource for the community at large and other government entities, providing them with information about each party's status, rights, and responsibilities. If a court does not make a full and accurate record and assure that the record of its actions is available to all,[5] facets of the social contract under which we all operate would not be possible and social order would be threatened by individuals or businesses helping only themselves.

In the courtroom drama film, *...And Justice for All*, defense attorney Arthur Kirkland, played by Al Pacino, entertained audiences in this pivotal scene (Jewison, 1979):

> That man is guilty! That man there, that man. That man is a slime! He is a slime! If he's allowed to go free, something really wrong is going on here! You're out of order! You're out of order! The whole trial is out of order! They're out of order! That man, that sick, crazy depraved man raped and beat that woman there, and he'd like to do it again! He told me so! It's just a show! It's a show! It's "Let's make a deal!" "Let's make a deal!"

Similar film and television dramas portray (and sometimes perpetuate) the myth of the court as this theatrical showcase of events and actors. In these Hollywood milieus, justice is always done notwithstanding the virtues and shortcomings of its characters. Although there are some instances in a court administrator's career where one can identify with a set of circumstances that "were made for TV," the day-to-day management of the courts does not reflect what is conveyed in popular culture.

Albeit not the most compelling of fundamental court functions, one of the principal reasons for the court's existence is to make a formal record of legal status. Court recordkeeping may seem lackluster, filled with legalese, and can sometimes take up volumes of storage space (both physical and technological) in maintaining it. Moreover, in interpreting the law to make the record, some citizens may come to regard it as defying common sense, not understanding that judicial determinations are derived from established legal principles and standards rather than intuitive or colloquial reasoning.

Cases proceeding into the appellate division of the judiciary enter a sort of think tank wherein the court, at least in part, relies on the official court record to formulate an opinion and render a judgment. Appellate court hearings are filled almost entirely by judicial insiders – judges, staff, and law clerks – and attorneys. The record includes copies of the trial court proceeding's documents filed by parties, a transcript, and may include an audio or video of hearings and appearances – all of which are reviewed in determining whether the law was correctly applied. The trial courts are therefore compelled to get the record "right."

Making the formal record accounts for almost two-thirds of the court's activity and, consequently, the lion's share of its resources. Moreover, this recordkeeping activity is rarely challenged. For instance, trust and estate matters are not typically disputed, but the accuracy of these records is crucial for maintaining the continuation of relations and property distribution among the affected parties. Courts also execute adoption orders, probate wills, and grant default judgments on uncontested matters or when the litigant fails to perform a legal duty, fulfill an obligation, or observe a promise. These actions serve to record the legal status of the parties involved. Additionally, collection cases are often filed to enable the court to issue a judgment that can be enforced.

Nationally, only 2 percent of civil cases are resolved by trial, and more than 90 percent of all criminal filings are disposed of by plea bargain. As dull as it may seem to the unaffected outsider, keeping the record is paramount to the court's purposes and has extraordinary importance. The court's failure to properly document, store, and protect the record can be equally as injurious as failing to render an appropriate judgment. The timeliness by which the record is created is also instrumental to whether the court is fulfilling its purpose. The extent of time elapsing between when the court events occurred and the official record is made may have a correspondingly deleterious effect on the court's purpose. The welfare of individuals is frequently held in abeyance until such point when the court finalizes the legal status of the matter by documenting and making the record available. Until such formal record is made, the closure sought in business dealings and personal relationships remains indeterminate. The record of the legal proceeding legitimizes it by documenting the steps and process the court undertook in the case. To that end, the record manifests transparency in and accountability of the justice system; it is not just some ordinary textual process because if the record is not accurate or accessible, it has an indelible effect on the public's perception of the courts (Carver & Mahoney, 2002).

Much like the affect it can have on the appearance of individual justice, complacency can also inherently set in when it comes to managing the record, oftentimes because of the burdensome process and high volume by which it is created. In an effort to impress upon its court clerks the value and implications of their day-to-day work (most of which concerns handling the record), consider the "golden rules" in Table 2.3 that a district court used as a part of its training curriculum.

Table 2.3 Court Clerk Golden Rules

1. General documentation	Court clerks must be attentive during all court proceedings and accurately record court events.
2. Calendar	Court clerks must review the calendar upon completion to ensure its accuracy and that entries correspond with the case management system. Judges, attorneys and court staff rely on the calendar court clerks create for court.
3. Court file	Court Clerks must accurately and legibly document the pertinent identifiers on the court file so that it may be easily referenced.
4. Photocopies	Court clerks must ensure that copies of any materials made by the court and included in the case file are legible.
5. "Original" copies	Court clerks must ensure that original copies are stamped "original" and included in the file as a part of the formal record of the case.
6. Bench warrants	Court clerks must always bear in mind that bail must be set within 48 hours.
7. Custody status	Court clerks must always check the custody status of a defendant *before* writing up a bench warrant.
8. Master schedule and backlog list	Court clerks must monitor and modify the schedules and other data associated with these lists so that it reflects the most updated information.
9. Discussion	Court clerks must not speak about any case, or anything related to a case outside of the courtroom.
10. Always act and dress appropriately, especially in the courtroom	Court clerks must adhere to the protocols in the Code of Conduct for Judiciary employees and "Work Attire" policy.

Deterring Criminal Behavior

When individuals are convicted of a crime, the courts serve as the forum where the public can bear witness to the punishment and associated sanctions. To that end, one of the byproducts of this purpose and responsibility is necessarily to deter crime. That deterrence, however, is based on public perception, which is affected by the efficiencies and outcomes of the court's processes.

The philosopher and founder of the classical school of criminology, Cesare Beccaria, posited that the inherent hedonism of human beings can proliferate crime. He argued that swift, certain, and relatively severe punishment helps to ensure an orderly society and deter criminal activity (Siegel, 2023). In short, law exists to safeguard the rights of both society and the individual and its principal purpose is to discourage criminal behavior. The emphasis of this school is on situational forces. Crime is viewed as a function of free will, rationality, and personal choice. Punishment is a deterrent to crime because rational actors weigh the costs and benefits of committing the act. Fear of punishment, in short, is what principally keeps people in check.

Deterrence is based on the notion that humans are driven by hedonism, seeking pleasure and avoiding pain. They are also rational decision-makers who carefully consider the costs and benefits of each action. Deterrence has two main aspects: general and specific. General deterrence aims to influence the behavior of potential criminals by serving as an example of the consequences faced by convicted individuals. The fear of experiencing the same punishment as a current defendant can deter potential criminals from committing crimes. Specific deterrence focuses on reducing the likelihood of recidivism among convicted offenders. The goal is to deter individuals from committing future crimes by emphasizing the potential for more severe penalties if they do so.

Counterbalancing punishment against the criminal act was critical, because excessive punishment was thought to compromise the integrity of the state. Jeremy Bentham (1789/1948), the founder of utilitarianism and inventor of the panopticon, believed that the processes of the criminal justice system should be predictable, with laws known by the public. He also argued that punishment was itself evil and should only be used to divert a greater wrong; therefore, penalties should be proportionate to the crime and only insofar as deterring would-be offenders.

Theorists of this school underscored three elements of deterrence: 1) celerity, 2) certainty, and 3) severity. Celerity refers to the speed by which punishment is administered relative to when an alleged crime is committed. It has been long held that the likelihood of general deterrence increases the closer the punishment is instituted to the commission of the crime. This nexus is a key perspective behind the rapid-response approach used in many of the problem-solving and therapeutic courts, as discussed below. Certainty refers to ensuring that persons are held accountable for their crimes. Severity aims to match the punishment relative to the seriousness of the offense. Severity is regarded as the least important criterion of the three because deterrence is most likely to occur when celerity and certainty are prioritized and ultimately achieved. Research shows that individuals respond favorably and have greater levels of compliance when there is consistency in expected behavior which is equally and swiftly enforced (Grasmick & Bryjak, 1980; Hawken &

Kleiman, 2009; Paternoster, 1989, 2010; Paternoster et al., 1997). Recidivism rates for those who are imprisoned challenge the view that severity which includes long-term incarceration is an effective deterrent.[6] Accordingly, the more severe, certain, and swift the sanction in relation to the crime, the greater the system's ability to control criminal behavior.

The courts' role in achieving these three components of deterrence, however, is somewhat limited. Courts can manage and largely control the pace of litigation – subject to assuring due process, which we discuss further in Chapter 5. The link between the commission of a crime and the imposition of a sentence is a key factor in both specific and general deterrence, but it is only one of many. Scores of other factors influence the certainty of a guilty finding that leads to some form of punishment: whether law enforcement apprehends an offender and develops credible evidence;[7] the policies, decisions, and procedures in the prosecutor's office; defense counsel's decisions and strategies (and, often, their budgets); and then the fact that each judge operates independently from each other judge in making legal and – when there is a bench trial – factual decisions; plus, finally, because the outcome is rarely assured in jury trials. The court-based factors are the result of constitutional or statutory policy decisions that are entirely beyond the control of court administration and almost entirely in the control of judges. The severity of punishment is based on decisions by the legislature in almost all states when it classifies the relative seriousness of crimes and dictates specific incarceration periods or a range of incarceration terms for some crimes.

Unnecessary delay obviates this purpose of the courts such that the public is less likely to bear witness to the punishment and the correlation between offense and penalty. As a result, punishment no longer serves as powerful a deterrent to those who would otherwise contemplate similar conduct. Moreover, delay weakens the constituency's confidence and acceptance in the court's legitimacy to competently address crimes against the people.

There is validity in the deterrent effect that punishment has on rational individuals. Research demonstrates that the celerity and certainty of punishment are particularly relevant in deterring future unwanted behaviors of probationers. Scholars posited that probationers are deterred when violations are accompanied by a sanction. This action-consequence principle-procedure jettisons any preconceived notion by the probationer that particular violations are enforced and prioritized or that some probationers are more accountable for their actions than others. These studies substantiate that individuals respond favorably and have greater levels of compliance when there is consistency in expected behavior which is equally and swiftly enforced (Grasmick & Bryjak, 1980; Hawken & Kleiman, 2009; Paternoster, 1989, 2010; Paternoster et al., 1997). Delaying (or worse, failing) to execute an appropriate sanction is less likely to resonate with a probationer as more time passes, particularly one with unchecked addiction issues. As a result, the failure of an untimely caseflow process lessens the likelihood of deterring unlawful behavior. Furthermore, it conveys an impression to other probationers that the process is arbitrary and can prompt them to test the limits of what they perceive to be an inconsistent system.

A comprehensive enforcement program (CEP) for jurors who failed to respond (FTR) or failed to appear (FTA) for their scheduled date of service offers another example in the power of deterrence. In accordance with Boatright's (1998) suggestion that courts enforce juror summonses, the court sought to increase the overall juror yield and expressed an interest in uncovering whether these measures would impact the response rate of future pools. The study showed the viability of using the CEP as a management policy and procedure to compel prospective jurors to comply with the jury summons. The preparation and follow-up required to process delinquent jurors placed an extraordinary burden on the court's staff and resources, but the results of enforcing the summonses substantiated the need.

The findings demonstrated that given the resources that Order to Show Cause (OTSC) hearings require to process the jurors, they should only be conducted semiannually. Table 2.4 shows that only six percent of the selected prospective juror pools were unaccounted for following the OTSC hearing. The volume of prospective jurors that are summoned was simply too large to hold all of them accountable, but longitudinal data of the CEP showed that if the pools were regularly and randomly selected and the information on outcomes was promulgated to the community, it increased the overall response rate. This one relatively straightforward program is a microcosm of the larger, more complex policies, such as sentencing guidelines, that are served with respect to this purpose of the courts. Because the CEP demonstrates that enforcement and transparency strengthen compliance, ignoring its lessons would undermine the court's legitimacy and accessibility, producing consequences far more significant than the program's operational costs.

Table 2.4 Failed to Respond Distribution for the Selected Jury Pools

Status Period	***FTR Distribution***	
	N	***% of Pool***
2 weeks following Summons	807	67
Following 1st Reminder	458	38
Following 2nd Reminder	236	20
On Service Date	183	15
Post OTSC Hearing	77	6

Note: A total of 1,200 prospective jurors were summoned for the two service dates.

Rehabilitation of Persons Convicted of Crime

Ralph Waldo Emerson (1860) stated, "Treat a man as he is, and he will remain as he is. Treat a man as he could be, and he will become what he should be." Emerson captures the essence of rehabilitation as a goal of punishment although correction systems by and large have fallen short in transforming offenders into becoming what they "should be." The challenge for courts is to differentiate those who can and should be rehabilitated (through a period of probation or term of incarceration).

Reconciling this particular purpose with the courts presents a unique problem because rehabilitation is generally assigned to corrections, an executive branch function. The best a judge can do is to guess whether someone should be given a chance at rehabilitation while on probation or be incarcerated with the hope that the institution has a program that will help. Even if a judge tries to order correctional authorities to provide a specific program or approach for a prisoner, legally it is only a suggestion that need not be followed – and often it is not.

Rehabilitation recognizes that outcomes (circumstances which brought the defendant to the court) are affected by more than rational choice. Criminal behavior exists on a continuum with relatively minor and benign unlawful acts at one end and the most heinous and malicious of crimes at the other. Theories abound centering on a variety of causes, incorporating a plethora of possible solutions. A myriad of programs operating at all levels of government and private enterprise, supported by millions of dollars, offer explanation. Despite the research dollars and societal resources that are afforded, there remain as many questions as there are answers. To discuss those reasons at length, however, is the subject of a different book and we bring it up here only to give this discussion context.

Theory provides a good framework for possible causes. Practice shows that seldom is the source a singular one. Crime is partly (at the very least) influenced by an individual's social location and psychological development. In fact, individuals reared in the same corporal community go on to live very different lives from one another because behavior is shaped by a confluence of factors. This does not suggest that the community ("environment") has no impact, but it does imply that there are other variables at play beyond those centered simply on community. The court has a responsibility to use its authority and discretion to rule with the intention of bringing about change in the individual – to return them to society as a law-abiding person.

This *specific* responsibility rests squarely with the court, in part, because the totality of circumstances is evidentiary and can be considered in this forum. Thus, the court is in the unique position to discern the extent to which a variety of criminogenic risk factors such as poor or non-existent familial care and supervision, childhood abuses, exposure to a peer network of criminals, the internalization (differential association) of antisocial values and normative behavior, or an unsuitable educational system impacted the individual. When the right program is offered at the right time, the court can facilitate the path that can help ameliorate some of these impactful issues so that the person can become a more productive member of society.

Drug courts have a track record of rehabilitating and reintegrating defendants into the community. Studies have shown a drug court approach that involves intensive supervision and random drug testing generates greater cost savings compared to traditional incarceration methods. Moreover, drug court graduates have lower recidivism rates than defendants who are processed through traditional means of adjudication. Part of the reason is because treatment programs, which generally last between three and five years, are individually structured and are closely monitored by an assigned drug court judge and team. The results, as remarked by one drug court graduate, show the impact of this alternative program:

> If ever there has been something that changed my life, it was drug court. I want to thank Judge Jones[8] who never gave up on me. He knew before I did that, I needed this program. And thanks to this program, I'm proud to finally be the father that my kids can count on. I also want to thank the whole drug court team for seeing me through this. I know this is just the beginning, but at least I have the tools now to give myself a future. I couldn't have done it without you.

The former heavyweight boxing champion, Mike Tyson, who delivered the keynote address at a drug court graduation, understands intimately the repercussions of addiction and the importance that these kinds of court programs can have on defendants (Terruso, 2013):

> I'm really proud of these graduates right here because now this is the first time in all your life you can start fresh. To overcome this adversity, we all came out looking like wounded warriors, but we won. It's all about living and wanting to. Most of us we don't feel comfortable in our skin that's why we do this. You stop drugs by stopping pain.

The rehabilitative responsibility of the court also involves contrasting the derived benefits and potential risks and costs of these programs, wherein the primary focus is rehabilitative with other alternatives including a term of incarceration. Court administrators understand that they are important partners in the criminal justice system and so must astutely manage those programs within the court's purview to ensure that expectations are empirically justified by the ends. Consider the analytical model that is being studied at Lehigh University for the Pennsylvania Department of Corrections. The assessment framework integrated systems utilized in other industries, combining mathematical modeling, optimization, process control, and logistics to determine how to meet the varied needs of inmates, including education, healthcare, addiction treatment, mental health services, and anger management (Terlaky, 2016). The courts are pivotal to these system integrations. Perhaps more importantly, the court is central to these kinds of public policy directions because the justice system relies on its knowledge and expertise, to springboard the change it seeks in that targeted population to ultimately reduce recidivism and deliver on its purpose and responsibility to the public.

Therapeutic and problem-solving courts (e.g., drug, mental health, veterans, and homeless courts), the first of which was created in the late 1980s, strongly argue against this view of courts' limited role in offender rehabilitation. These courts share four common features: addressing a person's condition(s) and/or circumstances rather than treating his/her conduct as a crime;[9] providing rapid attention and response to each person's failure to comply with conditions set by a judge and regular monitoring of progress; easing of conditions and limitations as progress is made addressing the issues that led to participation in the special court; and the court marshaling and overseeing coordination among the needed social, addiction, mental health, and, sometimes, education resources. Clearly and explicitly, rehabilitation is a central, widely accepted purpose of these special courts.

There are three factors that challenge the view and confirm rehabilitation as a purpose of courts. The first relates to the origin of these courts. The first drug court was started by a Florida court and a single judge who was exasperated with repeat cases involving drug offenders and who looked for a new way to deal with the challenges of these cases when the only available options were incarceration or probation. Every judge handling these cases knew that neither option was appropriately dealing with the underlying addiction issues that resulted in a perpetual docket of repeat offenders. At that time and for the next several years, neither this court nor any of the similar courts established were authorized by statute; all were envisioned, designed, and implemented solely within the judicial branch. In the years that followed, a number of states have created legislation which defines and authorizes specific problem-solving and therapeutic courts. The states that have created these laws implicitly have articulated and expanded rehabilitation as a purpose of courts, at least through these specialized courts. Absent these laws, the idea of rehabilitation as a purpose of courts is less clear.

The second factor is the judge's role in each of these courts. The court's ability to marshal resources to apply to the social and mental-health concerns addressed in these specialized forums is unique to judges, their convening role in the criminal justice system, and their ability to interact with the broader body politic. Judges have demonstrated remarkable success in both areas.

Further, judges are successful in leading these courts because they are much more "hands-on" in administering them; they apply the proven elements of deterrence (quick response and negative consequences for failing to follow program conditions), and the judges assigned to these calendars normally have personalities well-suited to the purposes and operations of these courts. Each of these factors enhances the chances of rehabilitation, as proven by numerous follow-up studies.

The third factor is the relatively small number of cases and defendants handled in these specialized courts. The cases and their results are important to the courts and, especially, to those who are admitted to a program, but their impact on the total criminal caseload is limited. There are several reasons for this, but two are most critical. The first relates to the restrictions normally placed on who can be admitted to these programs. Admission policies are normally negotiated with the prosecutor's office. Many prosecutors and judges are sensitive to possible public reaction if a client of the program were to commit another crime while enrolled and undergoing treatment. Oftentimes, there is an interest and increased scrutiny in establishing and determining "likelihood of success" metrics for those admitted to the program. Expectations and standards consequently delimit the type of instant charges (and criminal history and defendant as a result) that are acceptable; in most instances cases are limited to misdemeanors where the facts did not involve any violence. Defendants' criminal case history can also exclude them from the program; generally, only those with no prior convictions or a small number of convictions for the same type of offenses(s) and no convictions for violent crimes are permitted to participate. Thus, in many of these specialized courts, the deck is stacked at the outset toward low-risk, first-time offenders and likely program success. Given the clientele of many of these specialized courts, it is reasonable to ask if they truly further the rehabilitative purpose of courts. The second constraint relates to the court's ability to support rehabilitation: it depends on whether non-judicial entities – such as probation departments and community service providers – have the capacity to deliver the intensive services required by court-ordered programs. Because courts cannot control the resources of these partner agencies, they must tailor their programs to what is feasible given existing capacity.

It should also be noted that probation services are not always a part of the judicial branch. In a number of states, probation is an executive branch function reporting to a state agency or a local funding body, e.g., county management. In jurisdictions where probation is operated under the executive branch, the court may have little to no input on models of probation supervision, program services, and governing policies.

This situation does not discount the impact that individual program work and effort can have on case outcomes, but it also recognizes the equivalent effects of other factors such as access, social class, wealth, inter alia, that courts must bring to bear in steering individuals toward a more productive, law-abiding existence. The community cannot guarantee a good family to every child, but it can assure a purposeful and responsible justice system that acknowledges realities and seeks to dutifully administer, when appropriate, rehabilitative, diversionary programming. Does the symbiotic relationship amongst all these factors mean that court purposes include rehabilitation or does it bolster the argument that rehabilitation is not a judicial function, and therefore not a purpose of courts? We leave the resolution of this debate to others, but note that the issue, considering the interplay of social, institutional, and individual variables, is far less clear than has long been accepted.

Separation (When Necessary) of Some Convicted People from Society

The meaning of "when necessary" has been a focus of debate for decades vis-à-vis whether separation of some convicted persons is a function of courts. It has been renewed at the federal level and in some states in recent years. It primarily focuses on mandatory minimum and fixed range sentences, designed to curtail, if not eliminate, a judge's discretion. The number and nature of crimes for which legislatures have decreed some level of mandatory sentencing varies from state to state.

Even when there are numerous crimes on the "mandatory sentencing" list – always involving some predetermined time in prison – they always apply to felonies. This leaves the decision to judges about separation from society (if only for a few days) for the majority of convicted defendants concerning misdemeanors, because those types of cases dominate criminal dockets. If there is legislatively mandated incarceration for a fixed period or range of years, judges still must impose the sentence following conviction. In all other cases, however small of a fraction it may represent, the responsibility for decisions about separating a convicted defendant from society belongs to judges.

This purpose of separating some convicted people from society compels the court to take "last resort" action either because the defendant's record chronicles a history of failed efforts to reintegrate them or that the criminal act constitutes abject cruelty or pathological wickedness in defiance of basic human decency. Athens (1992) described it as *virulency* – the last of four stages in the "violentization" process:

> He now firmly resolves to attack people physically with the serious intention of gravely harming or even killing them for the slightest or no provocation whatsoever... He has suddenly been emboldened and made venomous at the same time.

Courts are responsible for separating convicted people to safeguard other members of society. This purpose is ostensibly ever-present.

Consider Durkheim's (1895/1982) position which stated that society will never rid itself of crime because, apart from it being present "in all societies of all types," we will always be confronted by "men who have behaved in such a way as to draw upon themselves penal repression." He contended that crime is natural to the social order and, in fact, serves a *functional* purpose toward its stability and operation. Courts are responsible for ensuring that unnecessary delays in incarceration do not perpetuate other opportunities for "dyed-in-the-wool" offenders to commit additional crimes while awaiting disposition.

Research has shown that the court's failure to meet time to disposition standards can unduly delay and obfuscate cases, which when initially filed were relatively simple to resolve. In some of those instances involving bailed defendants, the longer it takes the case to reach disposition, the more likely the defendant will be arrested with other defendants on other charges. Consequently, a poorly managed court and the backlog that it perpetuates can become a vicious cycle that feeds off itself.

When a determination has been made for incarceration, it should be grounded on creating symmetry; that is, the sentence is in proportion to the crime committed. Proportionality, hence, links the length and kind of incarceration (jail versus prison) to the severity of the violation. An individual's criminogenic nature and criminal history should be assessed by incorporating both risks and needs to maximize the individual's ability to learn from intervention strategies, while also safeguarding the community in the interim or, to the extent the law allows, to permanently incarcerate the offender.

Evidence-based practices and associated training for personnel are essential so that the court can tailor sanctions (not exclusive to detention) to balance individual and community needs. Some general measures are cited by the Pew Center (Warren, 2009), but a potentially important tool for these purposes is the presentence report (PSI), which is completed by either a probation officer or other appointed personnel. In order for the PSI to be of practical use to the court, however, it should include the defendant's demographic information, criminal and court history, medical health status, substance abuse history, psychological health status and treatment history, employment background, financial status, family history, military service background, education, home and neighborhood environment, plea agreement, offense circumstances and special factors related to the offense, case analysis including circumstances, if any, contributing to the present offense and assessment of the defendant's personality, problems, and potential for non-incarceration diversionary alternatives noting available community assistance and resources.

Studies have shown that evidence-based sentencing and corrections practices are far more effective than traditional approaches in reducing recidivism and correctional system costs. The public safety policy brief by the Pew Center encapsulates the leading research into the following ten cost-effective evidence-based practices that courts should use in collaborating with the other branches of government and relevant agencies (Warren, 2009).

1) Establish Recidivism Reduction as an Explicit Sentencing Goal
2) Provide Sufficient Flexibility to Consider Recidivism Reduction Options
3) Base Sentencing Decisions on Risk/Needs Assessment
4) Require Community Corrections Programs to be Evidence-Based
5) Integrate Services and Sanctions
6) Ensure Courts Know About Available Sentencing Options
7) Train Court Officers on Evidence-Based Practice
8) Encourage Swift and Certain Responses to Violations of Probation
9) Use Court Hearings and Incentives to Motivate Offender Behavior Change
10) Promote Effective Collaboration Among Criminal Justice Agencies

NACM's Two Additions to Friesen's Purposes

Addressing these new, separate purposes, the NACM (2015) states: "Over time, these fundamental purposes of the courts expanded to include other areas of emphasis." Batty (2016) stated something similar in support of his proposed purposes, but with a little more specificity: "[A]fter 40 years in this field, I have seen firsthand the broadening public expectations of courts, as well as the upsurge of certain societal trends or emphases that bring to the fore new possibilities for purposes."

One can debate whether the first addition is a new purpose or an implicit part of Friesen's, "to protect individuals against the arbitrary use of governmental power." In recent years more attention has been given within court administration and the public at large to issues affecting foster children, abandoned and neglected children, adults and, specifically, seniors who are dependent on others for care, and elders whose financial resources need to be protected and preserved under court supervision. Frankly, none of these issues are new. Regardless, NACM's articulation of a need to protect "vulnerable populations" appears to reflect a heightened level of consciousness. Another reason expressed for this new observation is a growing recognition that corporations and others with substantial financial resources have used their wealth to tilt litigation results in their favor.

The *CORE's* second new purpose appears to be a clear response to the relatively recent and widespread embrace of problem-solving and therapeutic courts. Until the advent and growth of these courts, no one known to us formally suggested this level and kind of coordination was a purpose for which courts were created. The coordination and cooperation supported by this purpose always have been part of leadership's administrative responsibilities, but never an independent "purpose."

NACM's two *CORE* additions to Friesen's list, coupled with the proposals from Batty, suggest that any broad effort to re-examine the purposes of courts should start with a common understanding of the words: "purpose" versus "responsibilities" versus "effective and needed management." Otherwise, continuing debates and uncertainty about questions such as whether coordination is a "purpose" are inevitable.

Responsibilities

We again quote *The CORE* on its statement of courts' responsibilities (NACM, 2015):

> [T]he primary responsibility of the judicial branch is to provide an impartial forum for the resolution of disputes. This ensures the rule of law and protection of individual rights. Over time, this fundamental responsibility of the judicial branch has been expanded to encompass other areas of importance, including but not limited to the following:
>
> - Ensuring access to the court process for all who seek it.
> - Managing the business of the court in a manner that promotes efficiency, transparency and the opportunity for fair and timely disposition of the cases filed.
> - Exercising leadership among other justice-related agencies to develop strategies that join the interests of all three branches of government.

The principal thing to note is that *The CORE* states the first "responsibility" of courts is the third "purpose" in Friesen's list. Further, it is notable that in the discussion of a key competency called "purposes and responsibilities," NACM's guidance on "responsibilities" is limited to the above statements. The later document, *Court Administration: A Guide to the Profession*, does not address this area of guidance (NACM, 2016b). There appear to be two reasons why the "responsibilities" discussion has been so truncated. The first is the very long list that might be created to define a court and an administrator's responsibilities. Second, trying to define a court's responsibilities may lead to the type of discussion suggested above, about the definition of purpose. When leadership organizations in court administration formally revisit courts' purposes, it may be advantageous to address "responsibilities" at the same time as "purposes."

If the past is a prologue, then court administrators need not look beyond the prior decade of trends in judiciaries to understand the implications that the purposes and responsibilities will have for generations to come. We anticipate a sustained "new normal" reliant on a limited number of judges and court staff providing higher levels of service to meet growing public demands. Coupled to these expectations, there will be an ever-increasing requirement of performance accountability to demonstrate taxpayer returns on dwindling coffers. At the same time, we expect that the judiciary's role in society will increase and become even more complex, given emerging technologies, alterations in traditional family compositions, continued delineation of the offender population with diversionary approaches, and the increasing reliance on specialized courts and therapeutic programs. The tea leaves suggest that court leaders can best navigate these changes through a firm grasp on the fundamental purposes of courts, the very foundation from which they draw meaning.

Notes

1 Pseudonym.

2 We regard such balance in accordance with the teaching and training adage that while justice delayed is justice denied, justice rushed is justice crushed.

3 In Plato's *Phaedrus*, Socrates discusses the pros and cons of the written word with Phaedrus, saying, "I cannot help feeling, Phaedrus, that writing is unfortunately like painting; for the creations of the painter have the attitude of life, and yet if you ask them a question they preserve a solemn silence... when they [words] have been once written down they are tumbled about anywhere among those who may or may not understand them, and know not to whom they should reply; to whom not; and if they are maltreated or abused, they have no parent to protect them; and they cannot protect or defend themselves."

4 We are talking here of proceedings in a trial court. Each party retains a right to appeal an adverse ruling to a higher jurisdiction review trial court or to an appellate court, depending on the matter involved and state law.

5 Subject to certain limitations on access established by statute. There also are retention schedules for records that are established by the legislature and/or statewide court rules that may result in records of some matters being destroyed after a period of time. Other statutes or rules may require indefinite retention of some records, which create unique challenges for both paper and digital records.

6 Long-term incarceration may be justified for other reasons, but the relationship between deterrence and long-term incarceration is debatable.

7 Even before capture, criminal acts must be known by law enforcement. Victimization studies conducted for decades by the BJA, U.S. Department of Justice, show a significant gap between being victimized and reporting the victimization to law enforcement.

8 Pseudonym.

[9] Normally, these courts require one of two options: The defendant must plead guilty, but the plea is vacated and charges are dismissed upon successful completion of the program; or criminal charges are suspended during participation, but reinstated if the defendant fails to complete the program successfully.

References

Athens, L. H. (1992). *The creation of dangerous violent criminals.* University of Illinois Press.

Batty, K. (2016). It's time to expand the traditional purposes of courts. *Court Manager, 31*(4), 6–9.

Bentham, J. (1948). *An introduction to the principles of morals and legislation.* Kegan Paul. (Original work published 1789)

Boatright, R. G. (1998). *Improving citizen response to jury summonses: A report with recommendations.* American Judicature Society.

Brown v. Board of Education, 347 U.S. 483 (1954).

Carver, J. A., & Mahoney, B. (2002, June). *How to conduct an assessment of your court's record-making operations: Executive summary.* The Justice Management Institute for the National Court Reporters Association.

Center for Court Innovation. (2011). *Procedural fairness in California: Initiatives, challenges, and recommendations.* Judicial Council of California.

Covey, S. R. (1989). *The 7 habits of highly effective people: Powerful lessons in personal change.* Free Press.

Derrida, J. (2014). *Cinders* (N. Lukacher, Trans.). University of Minnesota Press.

Durkheim, É. (1982). *The rules of sociological method* (W. D. Halls, Trans.). Free Press. (Original work published 1895)

Eliot, T. S. (1951). *Selected essays.* Faber.

Emerson, R. W. (1860). *The conduct of life.* James Munroe and Company.

Emerson, R. W. (1870). *Society and solitude* (Vol. 7). In *The works of Ralph Waldo Emerson* (Fireside ed., p. 52). Houghton Mifflin.

Fazari, G. M. (2008). *An assessment of criminal case management in the Superior Court of New Jersey, Essex Vicinage.* Institute for Court Management, National Center for State Courts.

Friesen, E. C. (2002). Court leaders: Survivors or agents of change? In G. M. Griller, E. K. Stott Jr., & J. Fallahay (Eds.), *The improvement of the administration of justice* (7th ed., pp. 31–47). American Bar Association, Judicial Division.

Gallas, G. (2007, June). *The justice discipline* [Lecture]. Phase II, Leadership and Management in the Courts and Justice Environment, Court Executive Development Program, Institute for Court Management, Williamsburg, VA.

Grasmick, H. G., & Bryjak, G. J. (1980). The deterrent effect of perceived severity of punishment. *Social Forces, 59*(2), 471–491.

Hawken, A., & Kleiman, M. (2009). *Managing drug-involved probationers with swift and certain sanctions: Evaluating Hawaii's HOPE* (NCJ No. 229023). National Institute of Justice. www.ncjrs.gov/pdffiles1/nij/grants/229023.pdf.

Jewison, N. (Director). (1979). *...And justice for all* [Film]. Columbia Pictures.

Licht, R. A. (1993). *Is the Supreme Court the guardian of the Constitution?* The AEI Press.

Lipsky, M. (1980). *Street-level bureaucracy: Dilemmas of the individual in public services.* Russell Sage Foundation.

Miranda v. Arizona, 384 U.S. 436 (1966).

National Association for Court Management (NACM). (2004). *Core competency curriculum guidelines: What court leaders need to know and be able to do.*

National Association for Court Management (NACM). (2015). *The core.* https://nacmnet.org/nacm-core/.

National Association for Court Management (NACM). (2016a). *NACM core competencies: Purposes and responsibilities.* https://nacmnet.org/nacm-core/.

National Association for Court Management (NACM). (2016b). *The court administrator, Court administration: A guide to the profession.*

National Association for Court Management (NACM). (2018). *NACM model code of conduct for court professionals* (with commentary). https://nacmnet.org/wp-content/uploads/Model-Code-of-Conduct-for-Professionals-with-commentary.pdf.

Paternoster, R. (1989). Decisions to participate in and desist from four types of common delinquency: Deterrence and the rational choice perspective. *Law & Society Review, 23*(1), 7–40.

Paternoster, R. (2010). How much do we really know about criminal deterrence? *Journal of Criminal Law & Criminology, 100*(3), 765–823.

Paternoster, R., Brame, R., Bachman, R., & Sherman, L. W. (1997). Do fair procedures matter? The effect of procedural justice on spouse assault. *Law & Society Review, 31*(1), 163–204.

Peak, K. J. (2004). *Justice administration: Police, courts, and corrections management.* Pearson Education.

Plato. (n.d.). *Laws* (B. Jowett, Trans.). Massachusetts Institute of Technology. https://classics.mit.edu/Plato/laws.html.

Pound, R. (1906). *The causes of popular dissatisfaction with the administration of justice* [Speech]. Speech delivered at the American Bar Association. https://law.unl.edu/RoscoePound.pdf.

Scheidler v. National Organization for Women, 547 U.S. 9 (2006).

Schenck v. Pro-Choice Network, 519 U.S. 357 (1997).

Shapiro, R. L., & Warren, L. (1996). *The search for justice: A defense attorney's brief on the O.J. Simpson case.* Warner Books.

Siegel, L. J. (2023). *Criminology* (8th ed.). Cengage.

Solomon, M., & Somerlot, D. K. (1987). *Caseflow management in the trial court: Now and for the future.* American Bar Association.

Terlaky, T. (2016). *The optimal prison stay, mathematically modeled. Resolve: A Focus on Lehigh Engineering 1.* P.C. Rossin College of Engineering & Applied Science, Lehigh University. https://engineering.lehigh.edu/research/resolve/volume-1-2016.

Terruso, J. (2013, July 16). Mike Tyson speaks at Newark drug court graduation. *NJ.com.* www.nj.com/essex/index.ssf/2013/07/mike_tyson_speaks_at_newark_drug_court_graduation.html

United States Bureau of Justice Assistance. (2014, March 31). *Video of Professor Ernest Friesen speaking about the purposes of courts* [Video]. YouTube. www.youtube.com/watch?v=saHb06PNadQ.

United States v. Eichman, 496 U.S. 310 (1990).

Warren, R. K. (2009, May). *Arming the courts with research: 10 evidence-based sentencing initiatives to control crime and reduce costs* (Public Safety Policy Brief No. 8). Pew Center on the States, Public Safety Performance Project. https://cdpsdocs.state.co.us/ccjj/Resources/Ref/2009-05_PEW_Arming-TheCourtWithResearch.pdf.

Zorza, R. (2002). *The self-help friendly court: Designed from the ground up to work for people without lawyers.* National Center for State Courts.

3 Court Culture

Defining Court Culture

Court culture comprises an institutional set of values, assumptions, attitudes, beliefs, and customs that are shared by the judges of a court and court staff. The court culture strongly affects the daily practices of the institution through language, including symbols and gestures which influence the behaviors of its members. The court culture is developed by groups within that organization to cope with external influences and internal change. The values and beliefs held by a court and its employees contribute to that court's unique environment; that being, no two courts are alike, notwithstanding the universal purposes and responsibilities which guide all judiciaries. The culture of a specific court predates the appointment of any judge or administrator, albeit these officials are responsible for further shaping the culture so that it remains aligned with the purposes and responsibilities of the court.

Common meanings of court culture include observed behavioral regularities that evolve in teams or departmental units, dominant values espoused by the court, formal and informal rules of the work environment for forging and maintaining relationships within the organization's social system, and the general "feeling" created by the way employees are managed and interact. Court culture, and more generally, organizational culture (because courts are not an exception when compared to other institutions in this regard), can also be described as the set of values underlying Quinn's (1988) statement, "This is how we do things around here." Those values direct all aspects of how the court's employees collectively effectuate "normative" practices, confront challenges, and resolve issues because of an indoctrinated mindset that extends beyond any one person (including its leadership judges and administrators). This dynamic does not suggest that the court's leadership is devoid of duty or that those obligations are otherwise abridged in shaping the court culture, but rather it demonstrates the enormous and often painstaking undertaking it requires.

The process of socialization serves to imbue the court's patterns of basic values and assumptions into its new and existing members.

DOI: 10.4324/9781003686804-3

Occupational socialization is the continuous process by which an employee acquires the values and assumptions of the court's occupational social system. This perpetual socialization process includes both intentional influences, such as formal training and new employee orientation programs, as well as unintentional influences, such as break room and individual work unit cultures. Moreover, values and behaviors formed and prompted through the court's occupational socialization can be appropriate or inappropriate; that being, the difference between a constructive and harmful court culture. Behaviors within court organizational structures will persist as long as aggregate attitudes and expectations of members remain unchanged.

Part of the challenge for court administrators, particularly for those who were hired externally from another court or public or private entity, is to fully grasp the essence of the local court culture because it is not readily apparent. Moreover, it takes considerable time for those factors that influence behaviors and processes and are embedded in the institution to become obvious, even for the most astute of court managers. In some instances, practices observed by the court administrator may simply be the "norm" of one employee or small group of non-conformists that are mistaken for what is the prevalent, widespread normative organizational culture. For instance, the manner in which an employee assigned to a civil reception desk interacts with litigants may be indicative of *only* that one employee or work unit and not that of the entire court organization. At the same time, the fact that inconsistent practices between management units are *permitted* to exist at all may be a part of the cultural subtext. Divergences in management practices may indicate negligence or an unsuccessful effort to align the court's mission and values across disparate groups and departments. In other instances, indicators of what appear to be a bona fide part of the court culture may be fleeting and not long-term fixtures of the environment. A new manager, for example, may find that as they become more acquainted with individual staff and processes, the work ethic reverts to its customary form which was present prior to their arrival. In this instance, the brief period of transitional change may have been done in a purposeful manner to get in the "good graces" of the new manager.

In *Jacobellis v. Ohio* (1964), United States Supreme Court Justice Potter Stewart remarked, "I know it when I see it," in describing the threshold test to decide whether material at issue was obscene and unprotected speech. Culture, likewise, has an amorphous *feel* to it that is exceedingly difficult to clearly quantify and index. Instead, individuals get a sense of an organization's culture through interactions and observations. And, just as a "good" organizational culture is beneficial to employees, which in turn transmutes into better public service, a "bad" culture can be equally as influential in a highly detrimental way (Craig, 2014). Indeed, cultural attributes that guide the court's daily practices are specific to its traditions, norms, and values of what is considered the "cornerstone" of democracy, and thus are quite different from the traditions, norms, and values one would find in any private enterprise or other public institution. Apart from those overarching ideals of an independent judiciary, culture within individual courts is further delineated by the historical practice and leadership of that particular court. The institutionalization of culture can at times be difficult to define, but, similar to what Justice Stewart pointed out in describing perceptions of obscene material – individuals come to know the court culture when they see it.

Although court culture is a nebulous concept, Schein (2004) provides a clear and comprehensive definition of organizational culture that the court manager can reference, describing it as an:

> Empirically-based abstraction... a pattern of shared basic assumptions that was learned by a group as it solved its problems of external adaptation and internal integration, that has worked well enough to be considered valid and, therefore, to be taught to new members as the correct way to perceive, think, and feel in relation to those problems.

Accordingly, court culture is the *individuality* of the organization which guides employee behaviors and approaches in both their day-to-day, routine work, as well as long-term feelings about the job they do for the court. Court culture reflects how well attuned staff are with the purposes and responsibilities of the courts and in what ways they integrate their tasks and projects into those fundamental constructs.

As depicted in Figure 1.1, court culture is situated at the peak and is superimposed over the model because it envelops each core function and responsibility from which the court operates. The court's culture, therefore, is one of the most prominent of responsibilities for court leadership to address, given its extensive influence on the court's governance, management, aspirations, and operations. The court's culture is defined by its internal value system, which supports quality assurance and continuous learning and operationalizes the court's mission and vision through strategic initiatives, managerial practices, workplace relationships, and the customary daily practices of court operations. Each aspect by itself can have an enormous impact on the court. For instance, variations in standard operating procedures for managing court work can produce substantial differences between two otherwise similar local courts. This is because organizational culture guides those ordinary processes vis-à-vis how administrative decisions are made (at different levels, by whom and when), the level of responsibility assigned to various staff members, and the degree to which internal stakeholders are tractable to protocol and adept in responding to unforeseen problems. Apart from the wide-scale effect it has on the formation of the court, culture also impacts who "comes, stays, and goes." Recruiting and retaining adroit court staff rely, in large part, on the impressions external prospective job candidates have of the court organization and the relationships and opportunities from which internal stakeholders benefit – all of which are captured in the organization's culture.

A chef salad metaphor is one example used in our trainings to understand the full extent by which culture profoundly affects an organization. By way of example, the ham, turkey, cheese, boiled eggs, tomatoes, cucumbers, and of course lettuce signify the different divisions or units of the court. The salad dressing constitutes the organization's culture. While the various areas of specialty such as case management, information technology, finance, operations, human resources, etc., are each distinctive in their composition, expertise, and core objectives (tomato, ham, cheese), it is the organizational culture (balsamic vinegar) which pervades and otherwise *colors* the court's "way of doing business," irrespective of that division of labor and subject-matter expertise. Shifting of focus or attempts to shape the court's organizational culture so that it aligns with the core values and mission of the judiciary is a time consuming and sometimes fruitless endeavor because of the challenge in ridding the organization of its lingering past. Similarly, consider the difficulty in rinsing a salad of its dressing as it coats the ingredients. It would require the court manager (chef) to rinse it thoroughly and yet stuck between the nooks and crannies of the lettuce and absorbed in parts of the meats and vegetables, you will likely still find remnants of that old vinaigrette, despite the manager's repeated and best efforts to replace it with a different overlay.

Importance of the Court's Culture

Presiding judges and court administrators who can skillfully guide, shape, and shift the organizational culture are *genuine*, effective judicial branch leaders. We submit this, acknowledging the important "X" factor that culture has on court organizations. As the Fundamental Areas of Court Administration model demonstrates, case management is at the heart of the profession because all institutional activity centers around this principal charge. However, the court culture will dictate the overall effectiveness in how case management and court functions are operationalized ("how we do things around here"). True cultural change is borne from the court leadership team, which hones the culture in spite of the pitfalls and time-consuming nature this work almost always entails. The decision not to engage the cultural issues of the court (however the administrator finds it to be) and simply acclimate, work and manage within the existent culture is always an easier path in the short term. Conversely, the administrator's bold decision to develop strategy and facilitate change around the court culture is to cross that wide chasm that separates the transformational leader from the mere transactional one.

It is critically important for court leaders to be attentive to organizational culture because it will often determine whether the court is successful in achieving its mission and objectives. Research suggests that planned organizational change oftentimes fails because the institutional leadership disregarded the overarching import of the institution's culture (Kotter, 1995; Spencer & Watkins, 2019). Transactional leaders, therefore, can only accomplish whatever is presently being achieved because goals that seek to elevate the court from the status quo require that the culture be addressed to mitigate the risk of failure. Administrators who are focused only on transactional dimensions of the organization typically accept the prevailing value system of the court and are ensconced in its customary practices, irrespective of productivity levels or lack thereof. They manage by simply "keeping the lights on" in contrast to transformational leaders, who take on the risks of achieving more venerable goals, sometimes doing so even at their own professional peril.

A compelling court culture attracts the best and brightest individuals who are considering a career in the judiciary, both for bench and court staff positions. Individuals responsible for recruiting prospective court personnel exude confidence about the difference and contributions that are made with a career in the courts. Competent and trusted court leadership builds an enriching culture; it can retain and promote the next generation of leaders. Employees who are inspired by the mission of the court are committed and highly dedicated, thus ensuring the positive legacy and credibility of that court. These staff can also serve as institutional advocates for persons external to the organization on the relative importance that an independent judiciary has in a free, democratic society.

The most successful courts recognize the cascading effect that their culture has on the institution and its employees and thus define, execute, and align the cultures to ensure that the entire judicial branch is "dressed" in the intended value system. Culture is a pervasive influence within the organization, which affects interaction, decision making, teamwork, and incentives (formal and informal rewards and punishments for conforming to expected norms and values). Accordingly, organizational culture establishes the direction in how the court seeks to accomplish its ends. A strong and well-intentioned court culture manifests engaged staff, who are likely to support and contribute to organizational initiatives, rather than immediately resisting and disrupting system improvement changes.

Culture is the unique way that the court delivers on its purpose and responsibilities to the public. The court culture can create alignment among the different units and divisions of the judicial branch. An effectively administered organizational culture in the court ensures that teams of managers and staff are ultimately working toward one common mission and vision, however distinct the individual tasks and operations. Organizational alignment is also pertinent to *all* stakeholders (internal and external to the court) – attorneys, litigants, witnesses, community advocates, media representatives, political figures, law enforcement, jurors, corrections personnel, current and prospective employees who think about the court from various perspectives. Most importantly, the court culture provides institutional leadership with direction and crystallizes how resources should be allocated and prioritized.

A disaffected court culture will be encumbered by disengaged teams of people who are often working for self-interested ends. Along this vein, organizational culture is a critical factor, and in many ways a key differentiator, in court performance. Courts that have a virtuous basis from which they operate will ultimately improve benchmark outcomes because they *value* continual improvement, incorporating new ideas and best practices in accomplishing organizational goals. In light of the difficulty in defining the court culture, the challenge for administrators is, in part, tying this relatively abstract concept to performance metrics. However culture is defined, findings across an array of industries demonstrate strong positive correlations between workplace culture and employee performance. As we denote in the last section of this chapter, court administrators should aim to define the culture so that it can be empirically assessed. Baseline data should be collected along specified parameters, such as absenteeism, employee turnover rate, disciplinary infractions, performance advisory ratings, among other personnel variables, so that the net positive or negative affect on workplace culture can be linked to organizational changes. Other areas with relevant data points include case management, budget utilization, user satisfaction (National Center for State Courts [NCSC], 2005), and program efficacy.

Differences in organizational norms and practices among domestic courts become even more pronounced when contrasted with international entities. The willingness to understand organizational culture hence involves the *purposeful* intent on the part of leadership to engage and form connections. Consider some of the cultural differences that were experienced in a large, urban court which routinely collaborated with and hosted delegations from an array of countries. Jurists and administrators from Italy, for instance, are always quite formal and in meeting someone for the first time, first names are seldom used. Instead, university graduates who have titles are expected to be introduced – *dottore* for liberal arts, *avvocato* for law, *ingegnere* for technical fields, and *professore* for both professors and medical doctors. In Nigeria, prior appointments are generally considered important, particularly as it relates to government officials. Making prior appointments and arrangements were likewise important when it came to delegations from New Zealand; also, as a matter of course, they were customarily early for appointments. Japanese delegates greeted judges and staff very formally with a long and low bow and would often expect to exchange business cards. Delegates who were close colleagues with one another would address each other by their first name, but otherwise or in formal settings they would always address each other by last name followed by the word *san*. Korean delegates would often express their gratitude for the time spent in the court by giving hosts gifts (candy bowl, wallet, decorative wall fan, etc.). Japanese delegates would often do the same and it was later learned that gift giving was considered a necessity rather than simply a courteous gesture. Giving a thoughtful and proper gift to the host was perceived as a true expression of friendship, gratitude, and respect. The form of gift giving is also very specific – the timing (at the end of the visit), the wrapping (never in white paper because of its association with death), and ensuring that you receive the gift with both hands to demonstrate humility and respect. Nigerians would sometimes provide gifts as well – the most notable of which would be if the visitor purchased the host a pair of shoes. Notwithstanding the origin country where the visitor arrived from, in all instances, the guests visiting the court would most often gravitate toward judges and staff who had taken the time to learn about or had some prior knowledge about their home country's culture and way of life. Culture, hence, is important if for no other reason than because it enables the manager to connect to others – the same people from whom they must gain trust and respect to shape the court and shift it forward.

Court Culture Framework

The way in which an institution adopts its cultural identity occurs over a long period of time, as the organization's employees respond and adapt to change and overcome challenges that are prompted by a host of internal and external factors. Courts are not an exception to this ongoing process and so the existent culture is not a speculative reality that materializes from any single event or given day. Instead, it is a manifestation of the ongoing experiences that the court's judges and employees come to understand while learning to develop responses specific to their organization. As newly hired judges and employees are assimilated into the court, they become increasingly familiar with the local court culture (likely different to varying degrees from that of their prior employment) while learning to adapt. The faster they become accustomed to the business processes and relationship-based structures of the new court, the sooner they become comfortable with change in organizational environments which they are experiencing. To that end, most new employees will make an earnest effort to quickly acclimate themselves to curtail the stress that logically follows when anyone begins work in a new environment.

There are many organizational frameworks from which culture can be described. Suffice to say we do not delve into all of them, but instead review one particular model noted by Brian J. Ostrom and associates (2007), with which we have experience studying and applying to actual court environments. We preface the application of the model with the characteristics we believe come to define organizations and are relatable, irrespective of industry. Edgar Schein (2004) believed that there are three levels in an organization's culture: artifacts (first level), values (second level), and assumed values (third level). The first level, artifacts, is connected to those aspects of the organization that are readily viewed, heard, and felt by individuals. For instance, work attire policy, court facilities, mission and vision statement, quality of customer service, level and extent of community engagement, etc., constitute artifacts and are considerably important regarding their influence on the workplace culture. Consider the example in Table 3.1, demonstrating how artifacts can differentiate workplace cultures in specific courts.

Table 3.1 Workplace Culture Artifacts by Selected Court

Northeast County Court	***Southeast County Court***
• A work attire policy is instituted and is generally followed by managers and staff.	• No formal workplace attire protocol exists, and staff report to work however they feel is appropriate.
• The court conducts a formal two-day orientation that is separate and apart from the statewide program during which new employees are acquainted with, among other things, the purposes and responsibilities of the courts.	• Apart from the statewide orientation program, staff do not undergo any uniform training and are immediately assigned to their unit and respective supervisor.
• The court has regularly scheduled monthly meetings of top-level managers in which an agenda, minutes, and action lists are reviewed and discussed.	• Meetings are arbitrarily scheduled and in most instances are focused on short-term, task-driven assignments that have become emergent issues.

The case study in Table 3.1 shows the implications of three artifacts (work attire, new employee orientation, and meeting regimen) and the significant differences it can pose on court culture. Managers and staff of Northeast County Court wear professional attire so that they are more easily distinguishable from the public they are serving and strictly follow the work attire policy of the organization. They are more fully acquainted with the mission and vision of the court immediately upon their hiring and are shown how their daily work fits into the larger scheme of administering justice. Meetings are formal sessions and include detailed expectations and performance measures. Conversely, in the other court, the few artifacts characterize an entirely different work culture. Employees in Southeast County Court have an indifferent attitude toward their appearance to the public and abdicate most of the responsibility to engage new employees and the importance of the court's work to the state's central office. The structure of Southeast meetings conveys the court as being short-sighted because they handle only those issues which have devolved into urgent status. The fact that the information is not documented in any consistent manner leads one to believe that these same issues will be addressed in the future as though they are occurring for the first time; thus, the court is not one which builds upon its knowledge and training through its experience of addressing and resolving problems. On strictly this basis, Northeast can be seen as being aligned with a more formal and professional culture, whereas Southeast follows a laissez-faire work culture where employees are not as well trained and guided toward continued learning and improvement.

The second level comprises the values of the employees. The values of managers and staff working in the court play a critical role in determining the institution's culture. The thoughts, attitudes, and beliefs of employees about the organization impact the way work gets done, problems are resolved, and relationships are maintained. Overall mindset and perceptions in how employees view the work of the courts, together with their short- and long-term contributions regarding those ends, greatly influence the court culture. By valuing crucial skills, court managers can improve the quality of their leadership and inspire engaged employees who are passionate about the mission and vision of the court. Assessments of values can be captured in instruments such as CourTool 9 which provide a snapshot of employees' perceptions (NCSC, 2005). Findings can be used by managers to both gauge and shift the organizational culture by pinpointing areas that may require focused training.

Assumed values constitute the third level of organizational culture. While assumed values are not quantifiable, they impact the culture of the organization all the same. More importantly, this level of organizational culture is the most difficult for managers to address and change because assumed values tend to be the most ingrained in the institution. These values include obscure standards that affect the organization's practices, despite never being discussed. Assumed values are "understood" principles and are an important component in determining the culture of the court. Notwithstanding the adverse impact that these assumed values may have on employee morale and the overall tenor of the court, these principles may also suggest that judges need not adhere to the same standard of conduct given their position in the organization.

Despite the external environment in which the court finds itself, the norms and expectations for most courts remain unchanged. Not unlike other complex bureaucracies, this is what makes culture unique to each court and consequently difficult to change. Even in those instances when an "outsider" brings the concerns regarding culture to the attention of the court leadership, it often goes unheeded if the reality is contrary to an assumed value. Consider the remarks of one juror on a satisfaction survey who was in the process of voir dire and complained about the judge smoking a cigar in his chambers during a recess period:

> My overall experience was okay, but I think it is objectionable that the sheriff's officers stand in the same court where a judge picking a jury is allowed to smoke, but are threatening to fine people if they are smoking too close to the building outside. It's a double standard by a place that is supposedly about equal justice for all.

Interestingly, when this survey response was highlighted and shared with the presiding judge of the division, his response was "we have to see if the county can replace Judge Jones'[1] chambers' windows so he can get more ventilation." The assumed value was never questioned, rather it was an unspoken truth that this particular juror simply did not understand "how we do things around here." These unspoken rules and norms form the third level of the court culture.

Church (1982) studied aspects of culture in government work and was the first to coin the term, "local legal culture." This concept described the collective views of judges, court staff, and attorneys regarding the pace of case disposition. Research by Ostrom and associates (2005) focuses on culture as well, but is largely focused on the internal workings of local courts. The framework is useful in that it operationalizes court culture along measurable constructs, which can be practically applied to key work areas of the court, and linked to performance outcomes. The framework provides administrators with specific information in determining the extent to which change is warranted. Along the same vein, the benefit of using a model (and this one in particular) is that it also allows court administrators (over the course of managing different courts) to clarify issues that are relevant to that specific court in contrast to those of other courts that they have observed and managed. For instance, the model helps to identify what differentiates the work culture in one court from another. Why does case disposition time differ (sometimes significantly) between two courts that are virtually identical and have similar caseloads, and how can these differences be explained? What specific strategies should a court employ in changing its culture to meet its objectives?

Table 3.2 depicts the organizational framework set forth by Ostrom and associates (2007) along the fourfold typology of culture: (1) Communal – judges and administrators emphasize the importance of getting along and acting collectively; (2) Networked – judges and administrators emphasize inclusion, creativity, innovation, and coordination to establish a collaborative work environment and effective court-wide communication; (3) Autonomous – judges and administrators emphasize the importance of allowing each judge wide discretion in conducting business; and

(4) Hierarchy – judges and administrators emphasize the importance of established rules and procedures to meet clearly stated court-wide objectives. Together, these typologies form four quadrants, each representing a set of organizational and discrete factors. Among other considerations, each typology identifies the criteria of effectiveness that are currently followed by organizations, the leadership and managerial competencies that are most effective, and the underlying culture of the institution. Along the same criteria, the framework identifies those factors that *should* be pursued by the court's leadership, irrespective of whether it matches current operations.

Table 3.2 Court Culture Classification Typology

Typology	*Summary Description*
Communal	❖ Judges and administrators emphasize getting along and acting collectively • High sociability, low solidarity • Emphasize importance of acting collectively • Mutually agreed upon norms • Flexibility key to management • Willing to discuss alternative approaches • Rather than established rules and firm lines of authority, mutually agreed upon norms • Go forward if everyone agrees
Networked	❖ Judges and administrators emphasize collaborative work environments and effective communication • High sociability, high solidarity • Policies developed through consensus of bench/ staff • Seek collaboration to make decisions without full agreement • Sharing of power to achieve desired outcome • See role of justice system partners
Autonomous	❖ Judges and administrators emphasize allowing judges wide discretion to conduct court business • Low sociability, low solidarity • Emphasis on giving each judge wide discretion to conduct business • Limited discussion and agreement on court-wide performance goals • Difficult to implement a court-wide policy
Hierarchical	❖ Judges and administrators emphasize established rules and procedures to meet court-wide objectives • Low sociability, high solidarity • Emphasize importance of clear rules and procedures • Achieve advantages of order and efficiency • Effective leaders are good coordinators and organizers • See value of standard operating procedures and chain of command

The culture-types are distinct from one another – each of which represents a particular set of assumptions – and courts will generally emphasize one of the four. Comparatively, the typologies also highlight competing sets of values. For instance, whereas the autonomous court emphasizes decision making residing within the individual judge and manager (internal control mechanics), the networked culture is centered on mutually agreed-upon practices to guide short- and long-term processes (external control mechanics). The differences among the four typologies are important because leadership competencies are sought and judged, and strategic plans are developed and instituted in the context of the organization's culture. The desired outcomes of the organization are consistent with its values, which drive ongoing development and determine the tools that are employed in achieving those objectives. For instance, teamwork, collaboration, and interpersonal relationships are indicative of the techniques in a networked culture. Other methods such as benchmarking, competitiveness, and controlled processes are indicative of hierarchical structures.

The framework also incorporates two dimensions of court culture: 1) solidarity: the degree to which a court has clearly understood shared goals, mutual interests, and common tasks; and 2) sociability: the degree to which people work together and cooperate in a cordial fashion. For instance, a professional sports team is characteristic of an organization with a high level of solidarity because of the clear set of goals, duties, and responsibilities. Conversely, a soccer team of children would exemplify an organization with low solidarity. An organization with high sociability would be one where co-workers go out to lunch together and perhaps, in some courts, have drinks together after work or see each other on weekends, schedule vacations as a group, etc. Low sociability among employees is when very little to no interaction occurs outside the organization's work hours and its defined objectives. Table 3.3 outlines the solidarity and sociability dimensions in accordance with court culture typology.

Table 3.3 Court Culture Dimensions

Dimension	***High/Low***	***Corresponding Typology***
Solidarity	High	• Networked • Hierarchical
Sociability	High	• Communal • Networked
Solidarity	Low	• Communal • Autonomous
Sociability	Low	• Autonomous • Hierarchical

The central value of the instrument is that it can juxtapose individual perceptions with aggregate findings. Meaningful training can then be developed so that it targets disconnects between various groups (by specific occupation or unit within the court) and their perceptions of the existent and preferred culture. Moreover, results can be used by the court's leadership so that cultural shifts run parallel to the vision and mission of the organization and are aligned with the court's strategic plan in achieving those ends (Ostrom et al., 2007). For instance, assessments may show the need to increase the allocation of resources to areas of need (i.e., better management of interpreters, pro se litigants, jurors, etc.), as well as attention to new or revised procedures (i.e., PSI assignment and distribution, staff rotation, etc.).

The model has been useful for organizing and understanding a wide variety of organizational concepts, including theories related to organizational effectiveness, leadership roles, and competencies. For example, some court organizations and respective leaders are viewed as effective if they are transformational in nature. Other courts and managers, conversely, are viewed as effective if they are consistent in administering court operations. This framework accounts for those unique differences, while at the same time demonstrating to what extent shifts in the culture are desired. Institute for Court Management training in caseflow management includes a Court Culture Assessment Instrument that is used to assess five key dimensions of court culture, including dominant case management style, judicial and court staff relations, change management, courthouse leadership, and internal organization (Ostrom, 2008). For the purposes of elaborating on the court culture framework in this chapter, the dominant case management style dimension is used to exemplify findings from a case study court that compared responses from both judges and administrators, as well as a wide-ranging sample of administrators who completed the assessment. In completing the questionnaire, participants were asked first to assess their respective court vis-à-vis how it currently operates with respect to its dominant case management style, and second how they would prefer the court to operate as noted in Table 3.4.

Individual assessments of judges and administrators are averaged and plotted onto the diagram in depicting a pictorial of the current and preferred court culture regarding its dominant case management style. This sample demonstration can be further delineated in determining several aspects of the court culture, including the "type" of case management culture that dominates each division of the court (civil, criminal, family, etc.), the relative strength of that culture within that division or court, variations internal and external to the court, and the extent of disparity between current and preferred states.

The following discussion shows the empirical application of the organizational culture framework to actual court environments by contrasting the differences between the perceptions of judges and administrators in a large, urban court, Northeast District Court.[2]

Table 3.4 Court Culture Assessment Instrument

Dominant Case Management Style		***Current***	***Preferred***
I **Communal**	There is broad consensus regarding performance objectives; however, centralized leadership by judicial and administrative staff is deemphasized, and innovation is actively encouraged. Consequently, multiple acceptable approaches exist for individual judges to interpret and implement court rules, policies, and procedures.		
II **Networked**	Expectations regarding the timing of important procedural events are derived from an operational policy developed through the intentional engagement, planning, and collaboration of the full contingent of judges. Adherence to established objectives is actively promoted and reinforced by the presiding judge.		
III **Autonomous**	Deliberation and consensus regarding the significance of court-wide performance goals and objectives is limited. Individual judges retain considerable discretion to determine the timing for the completion of important procedural events.		
IV **Hierarchy**	Judges demonstrate a strong commitment to the consistent application of caseflow management practices, such as early case control, coordinated scheduling, and firm trial settings, supported by administrative and courtroom personnel. Written court rules and procedures are consistently observed and applied by judges throughout the court.		
Total		100	100

This is followed by a separate review involving the assessments drawn from a sizeable sample of administrators. The assessment showed a significant difference in jurists' perspectives regarding their current and preferred organizational culture. Judges of the noted court perceived the current culture as one of relatively low sociability that is mostly hierarchical and rule-oriented in nature. Judges generally sought a shift in the court so that it relies less on uniform policies and procedures and instead becomes an increasingly more adaptable court where decisions are centered on judicial consensus.

Administrators' assessments in Northeast District Court likewise showed significant differences between their current and preferred culture with respect to the Dominant Case Management Style. Interestingly, however, the current and preferred changes are in stark contrast to judges' perspectives. Administrators' perceptions of the current culture demonstrated a sizable shift in moving the court away from what they believed was a flexible and autonomous court. They sought to shift the organization toward a model that, while building on consensus, is grounded in a more hierarchical structure organized around uniform rules, procedures, performance measures, and accountability.

The observations and experiences drawn from the Northeast case study demonstrate how the preferred culture was significantly different from what *actually* existed. The outcomes, however, are consistent with other research findings, which show that judges have a general desire to manage their caseloads so that decisions are made with the best interests of the public in mind. Judges are also amenable to managing the caseload using different methods, if those decisions are reached by consensus with other colleagues on the bench. While both groups seek to move the court toward a higher level of solidarity, they differ in terms of *how* that change should be instituted. Administrators desired a lower degree of sociability functioning within a hierarchical structure, while judges advocated a networking environment to achieve increased solidarity in the court.

Given similar results in his research, Ostrom (2008) likened administrators to engineers wherein they seek clear rules, a step-by-step approach, and "systems-focused" change/analysis to re-engineer the organization. Conversely, judges could be compared to psychologists, who seek a collaborative, inclusive approach, and a "human-focused" method to institute change. Bearing this in mind, judges and administrators should seek to converge their expectations and establish general themes that they have agreed to work on, including overcoming the notion of "separate fiefdoms," developing an effective presiding judge and court executive team, and setting meaningful performance goals and mechanisms for accountability. In the case of the Northeast District Court, once the differences were made known, a discussion relating to the methods by which to achieve the preferred conditions was spearheaded by the court administrator with the support and urging of the presiding judge. The discourse generated several ideas including clarifying expectations over what should occur at each event hearing;

clarifying expectations for counsels' level of preparedness; implementing firm and reliable schedules; and establishing a firm continuance policy.

The perspective of Northeast District administrators and staff, who sought a court culture characterized by a rule-oriented hierarchical court, which develops policy and procedure around consensus, while still allowing for some flexibility and autonomy is not an anomaly. These findings are consistent with the overall view of a sizable sample of administrators who assessed the culture of their respective courts. The total sample included 698 administrators from a variety of small, mid-size, and large court systems across a wide geographic segment of the United States and its territories. Table 3.5 and Figures 3.1 and 3.2 depict the aggregate mean and median assessment scores of the respondents' current and preferred culture. Table 3.5 enumerates the corresponding assessment scores by the dominant case management style. These findings show results similar to those of the Northeast District case study; that being, administrators sought a considerable shift from a flexible, autonomous court to one which is organized around consensus and standardized measures.

Table 3.5 Administrators' Mean and Median Court Culture Assessment Scores by Dominant Case Management Style

Dominant Case Management Style	***Mean***		***Median***	
	Current	***Preferred***	***Current***	***Preferred***
Communal	23	17	20	15
Networked	22	31	20	30
Autonomous	30	13	30	10
Hierarchical	25	39	20	40

Figure 3.1 Kite Diagram of Administrators' Perceptions of Current and Preferred Court Culture (Mean National Sample)

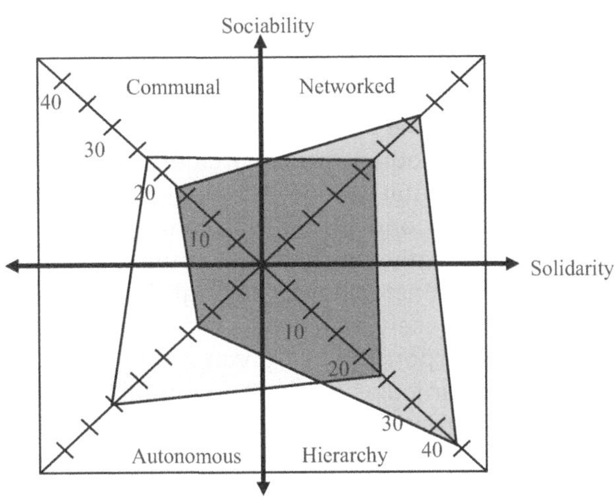

Figure 3.2 Kite Diagram of Administrators' Perceptions of Current and Preferred Court Culture (Median National Sample)

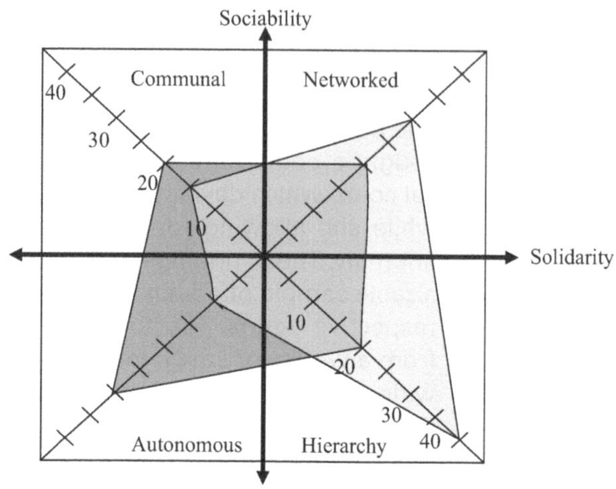

Notwithstanding the traditional roles and functions of courts grounded in purposes and responsibilities, the processes that individual courts employ in achieving those ends are dependent upon their unique organizational cultures. Having said that, our empirical findings show that there are patterns in those courts where changes to the current court culture are sought. Court practitioners generally expressed a desire to diminish the autonomous features of court culture. Notably, administrators perceived the existing culture as highly autonomous and aimed to reduce that autonomy substantially. Both administrators and judges desire greater solidarity in managing the caseload and instituting organizational changes. Administrators and judges are divided, however, in the degree of sociability to achieve solidarity when it comes to managing cases, with judges seeking more of a networked culture.

Although we found general consistencies among cultural preferences of stakeholders, there are no "right" and "wrong" cultures per se for court organizations. Each culture fosters its own form of "doing things," while concurrently minimizing, however purposeful, other ways of managing the same processes. Insofar as some courts are more adaptable and encourage innovative change, others prefer greater stability and lead mainly through incremental change. Accordingly, modern courts do not fit exactly into any one of the four cultural typologies and, perhaps more importantly, we find that court leaders do not universally favor one distinct culture. The "right" culture for a court is the one that most closely matches its strategies to accomplishing its purposes and responsibilities given the specific issues and challenges of *that* particular court. The cultural realities of a court can bolster or restrict its ability to be effective and ultimately successful, depending on whether it provides an integrated, consistent, and shared value system and common approach in its institutional development.

Shifting the Court Culture

Schein (1992) noted that "culture is the most difficult organizational attribute to change, outlasting organizational products, services, founders and leadership and all other physical attributes of the organization." The veracity of this observation is especially true for court organizations, given the nuances that are unlike those of many other institutions. For this reason, we carefully chose our chapter subheading to describe it as "shifting" and not simply "changing." Our experience has found that changing the court's culture occurs by *shifting* it over a long period of time. Akin to efforts to reduce delay, it is court reform all the same and again, as Arthur Vanderbilt stated, "is not a sport for the short winded" (Mahoney & Bakke, 1995). Moreover, our experiences indicated that change in the courts is an incremental one and when executed with a purposeful commitment, may require several years to wholly implement. There are multiple reasons why this is the case, but changing the culture is particularly burdensome because it often relies on moving people in and out of leadership roles (this includes judges), (re)training, and an acclimation period. In the meantime, all of this must occur without any abject failure in order to assure those within the organization that the direction the court is taking is the right one and sustainable as well. However positive or toxic the work culture may be, the court's leadership is at the foundation of sustaining and improving upon a constructive culture or shifting a harmful and unproductive one. This remains true regardless of whether the leadership team "inherited" the culture; to not address it for reasons of not wanting to "rock the boat" means a purposeful dereliction of duty and not *actually* leading the team. While it certainly requires a core set of management skills to "keep the lights on," the judicial branch leader is defined not by maintaining the day-to-day operations of the court, but rather by elevating them to the next, higher plane; this work necessarily requires a deliberate shifting of the culture so that the court is effectively aligned with its responsibility to address contemporary issues.

The organizational impact of leadership on the court culture cannot be overstated, given its capacity to affect and institute change. Proactive court leaders will seek out (as opposed to assume) how well aligned their perceptions are to those of their employees. Among other data points that are collected, survey instruments include questions such as: Do court employees work in a manner that goes beyond what is minimally expected? Do employees go beyond what is specified in their job description for the sake of the greater purpose of the job? Do employees feel that their manager is fair, ethical, knowledgeable, and competent? Do employees believe that the court's leadership provides appropriate direction (the mission and strategy to accomplish objectives) that is also clear? One large-scale study found, unsurprisingly, that employees who rated their leaders' skills highly also had a better working relationship with them (May et al., 2004).

Managers generally view themselves more positively than how their staff view them. In one large, urban court where we conducted a training assessment, managers were asked to rate their leadership skills on a five-point Likert scale. More than 85 percent of the managers rated themselves as "good" or "excellent" in overall leadership. In the follow-up question that asked them why they gave themselves a particular rating, one manager remarked, "Because I have always been a natural born leader and am generally exceptional in everything I do." Almost 90 percent of the managers who took part in the assessment rated themselves higher in at least one of the five areas of leadership that were measured (decision making, communication, problem solving, strategy, and influence) in comparison to the survey responses from staff.

Management literature refers to these manager perspectives of self-worth as "blind spots." In the foregoing survey, more than 50 percent of the managers had three or more blind spots. The most common blind spot was their ability to be "influential" followed by "decision making." When misalignments between perceived and actual skill levels endure, it limits the manager's effectiveness and ability to personally develop within the leadership role, at best, and at worst, it can be an enormous detriment by adversely impacting the court on a wider and more influential scale.

Shifting the court culture requires an administrator who is adept at leading and managing their employees. Research conducted by the National Association for Court Management (NACM, 2004, 2015, 2016) consistently supports our experience that administrators who successfully shift court culture possess the following five skills:

1. Decision-making (ability to evaluate the available alternatives and make timely decisions)
2. Communication (ability to articulate the court's mission, vision, and strategies using a variety of mediums)
3. Problem Solving (ability to apply their background and experience to assess ongoing challenges and direct continual improvement in processes, procedures, and general operations)
4. Strategic (ability to set priorities, establish timelines, and align resources)
5. Influential (ability to build trust and strengthen relationships within the court)

For those administrators who are new to the court and unfamiliar with the unique culture of that environment, apart from the forgoing skill set, we found that there are five essential lessons learned that are important for administrators to recognize. These lessons can be very helpful for the administrator's work in assessing and shifting the organizational culture to maximize the likelihood of being successful. First, and this is above all: to thine own self be true (Shakespeare, 1603/2009, 1.3) or more simply, know thyself. Effective leaders start off by assiduously nurturing self-awareness and endeavor to engage in ongoing self-assessment, whereby they attempt to objectively identify how to build upon their strengths while mitigating their weaknesses. What are one's motivations in wanting to be a court administrator? Whatever they may be, to what extent are these motivations sustainable? A salary increase, for instance, may be a motivating factor, but it can quickly dissipate given the significant (and evolving) responsibility the position brings to bear. Discounting pecuniary motivations, Gladwell (2008) mentioned that autonomy, complexity and a connection between effort and reward are what "most people agree, the three qualities that work must have if it is to be satisfying. It is not how much money we make that ultimately makes us happy between nine and five. It's whether our work fulfills us." Accordingly, the desire and ability to lead efforts and play a central role in implementing change to improve the system of justice would have a longer shelf life. It is desire (what does one *want* to do and not what one *can* do) that will sustain a court administrator over the long haul – and as alluded to earlier, serving in the courts to enhance and maintain our quality of justice reminds one more of a marathon than the 100-meter dash.

Second, know thy presiding judge. The court administrator title is, in its truest sense, oxymoronic – a more appropriate designation would be "servant leader" (Greenleaf, 1970). While the court administrator is putatively the administrative leader, the position exists principally to serve the public good and concomitantly support the presiding judge in their vision for the organization. In this latter regard, the administrator must have a keen awareness of their place in the organization – the leader, whose authority is parameterized by the fact that they are not the principal driver of the court. Working together as a leadership team, the presiding judge and court administrator navigate the organization's journey (strategic planning, consultation, etc.) to a desired destination: attainment of the court's mission and vision.

In effecting cultural change in the court, the administrator must demonstrate adaptability – which is different than being a sycophant – to work with the presiding judge's management approach, once the administrator has developed a clear understanding of the judge's character, leadership and communication style, expectations, and institutional goals. The administrator bears responsibility for adjusting to the judge's leadership framework, while simultaneously sustaining an open and constructive dialogue in which ideas and concerns may be exchanged freely. The foundation of this relationship must rest on the most essential element of the executive-component – trust. As confidence in the relationship is being established, the administrator must allow for the perspective of the court's unique culture to settle in, while strategically and incrementally instituting organizational changes in collaboration with the presiding judge. Incidentally, the mirrored roles of the court administrator and presiding judge help to develop the essential component of trust that the relationship requires and from which the court culture is enhanced.

Third, know thy managers. Assessing the quality and mindset of personnel is a responsibility common to all managers and supervisors. However, the court administrator must, for the most part, perform these assessments as they pertain to upper and middle management. This process requires a comprehensive understanding of the daily responsibilities, intellectual orientations, and attitudinal dispositions of the court's leadership and support structure. Effecting cultural change demands substantial insight into managers' strengths, weaknesses, leadership styles, and – most critically – their underlying motivations. A manager's ambitions, including the reasons and incentives for seeking or maintaining employment within the court system, are central to understanding individual behavior. Although personality traits are often readily observable, they should not be conflated with character, which typically emerges only over time. Over the course of our experience, we have found that a properly motivated manager is likely to pursue professional development to address recognized deficiencies, whereas a disengaged manager may allow existing strengths to erode. Consequently, a court administrator cannot fully understand managerial capacity without first identifying what motivates each manager. The strategic task, then, is to align these motivational drivers with targeted areas of organizational change. For instance, if the administrator seeks to shift the court so that it begins to focus more on performance-based metrics, the administrator may assign one of the court's highly analytical managers to a pilot program to assess various measures.

In understanding the court's leadership, an awareness of the social style where these role players fall is important in forging and then shaping relationships in pursuit of the court's mission. Ideally, although one cannot change a manager's preferred style, an administrator should be able to influence their approach, considering different circumstances and people, particularly judges. The administrator's and judge's knowledge of, and ability to identify, these leadership styles enables a more informed understanding of the court's management support network. Like an astute teacher, a good manager is discerning of the psychologies of individual staff to effectively motivate and lead them.

In an interesting analogy, Highet (1950) noted a reference where students were described as "salt, sugar, flour, and chalk" – substances that appear the same, but differ significantly in terms of their features and uses. The court manager must, likewise, be able to recognize, appreciate, and draw on the strength of differences as they exist among their judges and staff. Moreover, while differences exist, the court manager must seek to create a "court identity," that is, what it means to work and professionally grow in that particular court, which in turn can be shared by judges and staff so that it is eventually embedded into the culture. Court administrators must be willing to set aside staff differences and resolve conflicts for the purpose of building alliances with the staff who do the *actual* work and judges who wield considerable power. Table 3.6 depicts the four styles in accordance with the common characteristics, misconceptions, and motivations associated with each of them (Merrill & Reid, 1981).

Table 3.6 Common Characteristics, Misconceptions, and Motivations of the Four Social Styles

Analytical	***Driver***
• Characteristics: plans, researches, collects data, analyzes, exact, detail-oriented, perfectionist, cautious, skeptical, prepared, and thorough • Misconception: They do not have feelings and do not know how to have fun • Motivation: Desires respect	• Characteristics: direct, dutiful, practical, decisive, fast-paced, lead not follow, results, on time, and on task • Misconception: They are impersonal and pushy • Motivation: Desires results
Amiable	***Expressive***
• Characteristics: wants to get along, people-oriented, dislikes conflict, supportive, helpful, builds relationships, giving, honest, and picks up on subtleties • Misconception: They place too much emphasis on relationships and move too slowly on decisions • Motivation: Desires approval	• Characteristics: energetic, inspiring, fast, flamboyant, playful, creative, rapid reactor, flexible, non-linear, and tests limits • Misconception: They are flighty, joke around too much, and are not task-oriented • Motivation: Desires recognition

Fourth, patience is paramount. The success of the courts – like that of any other organization, public or private – relies on their adaptability. Changing approaches as circumstances dictate is pivotal to organizational progress. This requires time, and generally considerable portions of it are demanded irrespective of whether the administrator is willing to supply it. The difference between success and failure will sometimes rest on supplying (and sacrificing) the time, knowing full well the precious nature of this commodity. This principle is true for both the organization at large, as well as the individual administrator. Soon enough, all administrators find that the court is not a perfect working environment. There are processes that even the tyro administrator will come to understand as not being optimal and the need for change will be apparent. As with leaders of any organization, but particularly those working within the public sector, the court administrator functions within a professional "fishbowl," subject to heightened visibility and scrutiny (Fazari, 2015). The position carries significant accountability and potential liability; accordingly, all administrative decisions, including those that may initially appear routine or inconsequential, must be approached with deliberate consideration. At the same time, effective leadership requires maintaining a balance between excessive deliberation and undue impulsiveness, so that there is sufficient decisional fluidity to support the organization's daily operational needs. Patience is important, but it should not be used as a prop to delay decisions.

The administrator will occasionally be confronted and confounded by circumstances that they did not create and scarcely control. Nonetheless, the court administrator is charged with resolving the situation as it exists in its present form. The history of dysfunction stemming from the court culture, if you will, matters less than addressing it in its current state, irrespective of how it got to be that way. Ultimately, a shift in culture is needed and skilled leadership teams can succeed, but even in the best of circumstances it will not occur without challenge. This requires one to take the necessary time to learn the dynamics of the organization, how work gets completed, the stakeholders who are principally responsible for the output, and how to use the abilities of reliable staff who are candid in their feedback to achieve desired ends.

Court administrators will encounter setbacks, some of which arise from the unintended consequences inherent in professional bureaucracies. This reality is inevitable. Budgetary constraints, antiquated processes, and personnel decisions that reinforce the status quo are among the persistent obstacles that can impede innovation and diminish the resolve of even the most capable and well-intentioned administrators. The most effective response to such bureaucratic inertia is a combination of patience, perseverance, and a strategic management orientation. Achieving a desired and improved organizational state requires sustained effort over a considerable period of time. These views regarding the incremental and often marginal pace of change in organizations such as courts are also clearly articulated in the scholarly literature (Lindblom, 1959). The court's vision, and the ability of its leadership to articulate it in compelling and influential ways, is therefore essential because it shapes the organization's strategic direction.

Resistance to change may manifest in different ways across an organization. In some instances, opposition arises immediately in response to proposed initiatives; in others, the most substantial resistance emerges only once changes begin to gain "traction." The strongest reactions typically occur when longstanding practices – often described as "the way we have always done it" – are materially altered and the change becomes operational rather than merely conceptual. In court organizations, such resistance is frequently framed as an appeal to tradition, reflecting the inherently traditional nature of judicial institutions. While traditions serve an important role and merit thoughtful consideration, they should not be invoked to obstruct innovation, suppress new ideas, or foreclose alternative approaches to accomplishing work. Accordingly, although the retention of institutional knowledge is essential, the administrator must exercise discernment in determining which practices remain valuable and which warrant revision or replacement.

The pursuit of excellence, rather than adherence to tradition alone, should function as a central source of organizational motivation. Some court leaders with long tenure may reference the "other time in the 1990s" when such a change was suggested, but it did not always work; the implicit suggestion of course being that the court ought not to try and change it again in 2026 and beyond. Such reactions should be anticipated, as they are characteristic of the human responses that typically accompany change. The critical issue is not the change itself, but the transition it requires, since all changes eventually become established practice. The transition, thus, is what needs to be managed well – crossing the great chasm that is perceived to be wide, dreadful, and difficult to navigate.

A novice administrator can benefit from understanding and valuing the inherent resistance to change. The following questions illustrate common concerns individuals may raise when faced with change in general, and more specifically, with shifts in established ways of working. The answers – or absence of answers – to these questions, together with individuals' perceptions, help explain why resistance to change is to be expected and can offer leaders insight into the issues that must be addressed to mitigate its effects (Fazari, 2022):

1) What will the change look like?
2) How will I transition from current practices to new ones?
3) What if I am not competent in the new approach?
4) Whose decisions will affect me?
5) What will happen to my co-workers?
6) Who initiated this change?

The final lesson learned is to seek counsel from a trusted mentor. For a variety of reasons, some individuals will be vocal and active in their attempts to undermine the leader as the transition deepens and the strategic direction broadens, even when the presiding judge supports the change. Others will "silently root" for the leader's failure. Leaders across industries and organizational contexts encounter similar dynamics, and court administration is no exception. Some resistance stems from the personal impact of change and the perceived threat to individual self-interests. For others, cultural shifts that increase accountability and responsibility disrupt established comfort zones, making resistance an expected response. Additional resistance may arise from basic emotional reactions, such as the perception that the administrator lacks sufficient qualifications or experience, or that political considerations (as opposed to demonstrated leadership ability) played a role in the appointment (Fazari, 2015). These experiences can be instructive if the administrator is receptive to them. We submit that there is considerable merit to the argument that administrators can sometimes learn more from adversaries than from allies.

The new administrator should be able to draw enormous value in regular discussions with a trusted mentor, who can add unbiased perspective and guidance to management dilemmas.[3] While the court administrator position requires constant interaction, it is concurrently a lonely one. With the exception of the presiding judge, with whom the "executive component" is formed and hopefully well grounded, there are few individuals with whom the court administrator is likely to confide. A trusted mentor, who has endured the trials and tribulations of being a court administrator (or served in some leadership capacity), will be that voice of authenticity that however scarce prior to appointment as a court administrator will be in even shorter supply afterwards.

Others' perceptions of the court administrator position often overshadow a newcomer's intended approach to the role. A court administrator may observe that individuals interact and behave differently at meetings or events depending on whether the presiding judge or the administrator is present. By virtue of the title alone, individuals may alter their behavior toward the court administrator in ways that can unintentionally filter or sanitize critically important information before it reaches them. As a result, the administrator may not receive all the facts necessary to make the most informed decisions (Fazari, 2022). Accordingly, administrators should not hesitate to actively seek input and feedback from credible sources and subject-matter experts, and to consult with mentors who can assist in evaluating and contextualizing that information when making important decisions.

Having discussed the most critical skills and lessons learned in shifting the culture, how does the court leadership team go about *actually* shifting it? More specifically, how does the team transcend what can appear to be an entrenched value system and approach toward work that is equally matched with ardent resistance whenever any change is introduced? In the same way one would eat an elephant – one bite at a time; that is, changes should be instituted incrementally so that they are planned and managed systematically. Except for small-sized courts with relatively low caseload volumes, attempts to shift the culture by centralizing changes are seldom successful because, among other reasons, judges have wider latitude regarding individual practices of their court. Silo mentality, thus, is a critical barrier toward efforts to shift the court culture.

Competent leaders recognize that court culture is not imposed, but rather strategically developed through their influence and engagement with staff. Court leadership teams who have a keen understanding and acceptance of this reality will find that their changes have a long-lasting effect because they will not be viewed as any one person's "pet project," but rather as a collaborative work in which ownership is mutually shared. This is the underpinning separating procedural change from substantive, sustainable organizational change. Shifting the culture will certainly require changes in procedure, but substantive change occurs when aggregate attitudes and expectations of employees come into alignment with the desired change.

Knoster et al. (2000) offer a framework for understanding systems of change. While this model has been applied to a variety of organizations other than the judiciary, it can be made to correspond just as easily to the context of the courts. Accordingly, complex change occurs when court leaders effectively bring together the composite of vision, skills, incentives, resources, and an action plan. Each represents a key element because the absence of any one of these dynamics will confound leadership efforts and manifest outcomes other than what was intended. A plan to shift the culture, therefore, must be able to address each of one these elements as a part of its short- *and* long-term process. To that end, the court's leadership must be able to operationalize the following questions as it pertains to each of the process's critical elements:

1. Vision – what is the guiding statement and is it clear and compelling to inspire action from those stakeholders who can significantly impact the process?
2. Skills – are the role players sufficiently prepared and competent enough to undertake the work needed to make the desired changes in shifting the culture?
3. Incentives – what are those things and performance measurements that the court leadership can utilize to help keep role players incentivized in achieving the desired ends?
4. Resources – what types and kinds of resources does the court realistically have and require to make the desired changes?
5. Action Plan – has the court's leadership equipped the organization with a comprehensive and clear blueprint to navigate the process of accomplishing the desired ends in the specified period?

Leaders can shape and manage court culture, but they must first identify and measure it correctly. The culture of "high-performing" courts (Ostrom & Hanson, 2010) is one which operationalizes the conceptual framework discussed in this chapter. These courts incorporate the desire to shift the culture into their strategic planning; that is, leadership is adept at accurately perceiving the current "status quo," considers alternative approaches to processing the inputs and outputs of case management, develops a vision to guide the court's direction toward its mission, and formulates and executes strategic initiatives by establishing priorities, milestones, and performance metrics. Courts that are effectively managed also communicate accomplishments regularly, advocating and linking institutional interests with those of external stakeholders, including the executive and legislative branches, justice system partners, and the public.

Court Culture Operationalization

Court organizations are enterprises driven and operated largely on human capital. While the associated pecuniary costs are discussed in the Funding and Budget chapter and the recruiting, training, and progressive discipline are addressed in the Human Resources Management chapter, we introduce here the summary core competencies of court managers as they relate to the Fundamental Areas of Court Administration given the remarkable impact of these competencies on the current and preferred culture. This is not to say that court administrators who inherit managers who lack these respective competencies are doomed to fail at developing a more effective culture. Understandably, administrators are rarely in a position upon appointment to "clean house" and, for a variety of reasons, this should *not* be an immediate objective. Instead, Table 3.7 enumerates the competencies that should be institutionalized by current managers and advanced as new hires are made. We preface this human resources related matter here, because the greatest court commodity is its people and a necessary first (and ongoing) step to shifting the culture is to ensure that its leaders are skilled at the art and practice of management. These requisite competencies must be continually developed. In accordance with the recommendations on how to achieve a high-performing court (Ostrom & Hanson, 2010), the model operationalizes these competencies by linking them to key principles, emphasizing measurable and sustainable practices, and focusing on a limited set of performance-based outcomes.

Table 3.7 Court Administrator Core Competencies

Fundamental Area	***Competency Summary***	***Operationalization***
Leadership	Demonstrates the characteristics indicative of good leadership, including a commitment to the court's purposes and responsibilities, ability to inspire, motivate, and guide others toward strategic goals and objectives, ability to empower and collaborate with judges and staff at all levels of the institution, and a visionary who establishes and fosters the tone for a high-performance court.	• 360 Degree Feedback Assessments • Professional Development Plan and Assessments • Succession Plan

(*Continued*)

Table 3.7 (Continued)

Fundamental Area	***Competency Summary***	***Operationalization***
Strategic and Long-Term Planning	Identifies key issues affecting the work of the court and develops and implements short- and long-term strategies to address the critical challenges in achieving the goals and realizing the mission and vision of the institution.	• CourTool 1 • Multi-Year Strategic Plan
Community Engagement	Advocates and represents the court and its work to external stakeholders. Builds networks with the communities and interest groups most impacted by the work of the judiciary.	• CourTool 1 • Ombudsman Office or PIO Program Development and Assessments
Stakeholder Collaboration	Fosters and sustains cooperative working relationships with justice system partners and groups. Ability to create a work environment that encourages innovation, exchange of ideas, and insight into the ongoing challenges that mutually affect justice system stakeholders.	• CourTool 1 • Committee and Subcommittee Formalization
Human Resources Management and Consultation	Effectively recruits, trains, develops and assesses employees across the wide spectrum of levels and positions in the court in accordance with local, state, and federal laws and regulations governing personnel and management.	• CourTool 9 • Workload Assessments • Bi-Annual Performance Advisories and Reviews (SMART Goals) • Job Aids / Training Assessments
Funding and Budget Management	Demonstrates a broad understanding of and appropriately applies the financial management practices in executing the purposes and responsibilities of the court.	• CourTool 7 • CourTool 10

(*Continued*)

Table 3.7 (Continued)

Fundamental Area	***Competency Summary***	***Operationalization***
Information Technology	Understands the impact and latest trends of technological innovations in society on the court organization and utilizes those technologies where appropriate to enhance decision making and improve organizational effectiveness.	• Hardware and Software Testing and Assessment
Operations Management	Maintains a high level of proficiency in the technical array of units and functions, which extends to managing courthouse tasks and processes, including jury management, records management, court reporters, interpreters, court security, business continuity, and other related court services to ensure effective court operations.	• CourTool 6 • CourTool 8 • Court Security Audits/ Assessments • Job Aids / Training Assessments • Quality Assurance Audits/ Assessments • COOP Planning/ Assessments • Formal Record of Agendas, Minutes, and Action Lists
Caseflow Management	Ability to manage all aspects of caseflow processes and institutionalize best practices and standards that promote the fair and timely resolution of all cases	• CourTool 2 • CourTool 3 • CourTool 4 • CourTool 5 • Backlog per 100

To highlight the operationalization of a quality assurance assessment that affected caseflow and workflow processes, consider, for instance, a business processing re-engineering (BPR) project administered in a civil docket. This initiative was spearheaded by the court administrator's office as part of the larger initiative to shift the court's culture. While the data specifics of the project are important because they enabled the court to significantly improve in several performance metrics, the project's success involved overcoming the larger prevailing culture that frustrated previous attempts to improve the division's document management. The purpose of BPR is to evaluate and redesign (when appropriate) the methods by which work is done to better support an organization's mission and reduce costs. In so doing, there exists a binary rationale in putting BPR into practice: first, to further the efficiencies and effectiveness of processes so that the administration of justice in service to the public is improved on a regular basis, and second, to evaluate operational expenditures to reduce costs, when appropriate, particularly those related to human capital. Ideally, the greater part of this second objective is likely accomplished if the first part is appropriately administered.

BPR is essentially a building process, wherein the organizational mission, values, and strategy serve as foundational elements. The primary goals and objectives of applying the BPR quality assurance method were to first, ensure the compliance of all business operations so that they adhered to all legal requirements, including court rules, statutes, and administrative directives, and second, to ensure that business operations were performed so that efficiencies were maximized. During the 24-month period of the project, the court sought to evaluate and assess practices and procedures within its civil part, and where necessary to modify its business practices to achieve compliance, efficiency, or both (Fazari & Holandez, 2014).

As our modern court administration paradigm demonstrates, the purposes and responsibilities serve as the foundational basis for each of the foregoing nine fundamental areas of court administration – all of which are overlaid by the court's culture. Instituting and ensuring the effective operationalization of these fundamentals requires a well-balanced and forward-thinking organizational culture. Effective organizations – whether private or public – are shaped by an institutional culture which delivers results and trial courts should not be managed any differently. The connection between highly effective organizations and superior performance has been observed in our experience and is well-documented in court administration literature. Given the link between the two, it is critically important for court leadership to assess its organization's effectiveness and to be purposeful in improvements shifting its culture toward those ends.

To illustrate these points (and in line with our organizational experiences and research), a fully effective court culture demonstrates strength along our three-pillar model (three Ps) noted in Figure 3.3 to achieve the following five core objectives:

1. Public Service: Streamline processes to deliver quality service to the public and mitigate the number of complaints and overall internal and external frustration.
2. Efficiency: Abridge the time without comprising the integrity of the process it takes to complete a task for key court management functions and practices.
3. Productivity: Maximize the return on stakeholder performance output.

4. Cost Reduction: Reduce the expense of operations and human capital throughout the court management value chain for each division's end product.
5. Innovation: Adapt current court management processes and structures to ensure that improvements can be continuously instituted.

The Three Pillars model was developed and implemented in two courts (a large urban court and a mid-sized urban court) and later used in the consultation of practices for several other court systems. The model is centered on the three Ps (people, process, and place) to develop a court culture that supports the institutionalization of criteria used to assess the performance of the nine fundamentals.

Figure 3.3 Three Pillar Court Culture Model

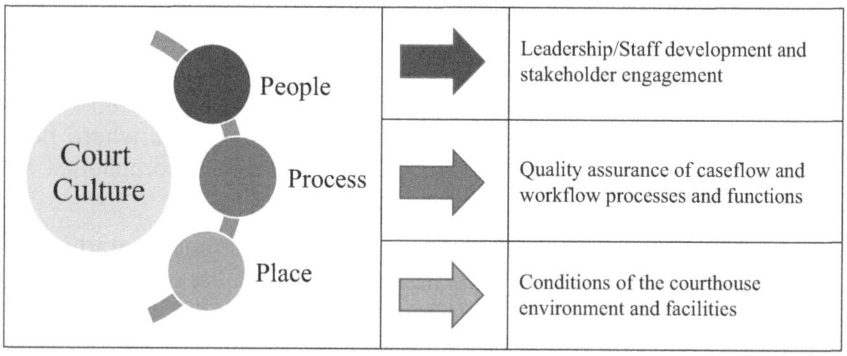

The "people" pillar incorporates the ability of court leadership to create an inspiring vision of the future, motivates and inspires people to engage with that vision, manages the institutionalization of the vision through the recruitment, training, and building of a network of teams, and continually engages with the variety of stakeholders who are impacted by the service delivery of the vision. The "process" pillar constitutes the perpetual evaluation of business processes of the courts so that they make the best use of judge and staff time, while ensuring the stability of key processes by identifying and improving mechanisms, procedures, and practices that a well-functioning court consistently uses to manage its end products. The "place" pillar comprises a physical and cultural environment that is safe, secure, and accessible where court professionals come together to work in the pursuit of a common vision to administer the efficient delivery of justice. Together, the three pillars are supported and guided by a court culture of "high-performing" values, which has the willingness and capacity to perpetually assess each fundamental area of managing the court, instituting the appropriate level of change as needed.

Notes

1 Pseudonym.

2 Pseudonym.

[3] The National Association for Court Management (NACM) has a mentorship program, wherein senior court administrators serve as mentors to early career court management professionals.

References

Church, T. W., Jr. (1982). *Examining local legal culture: Practitioner attitudes in four criminal courts* (Report No. NCJ 84047). U.S. Department of Justice, National Institute of Justice. https://ojp.gov/library/publications/examining-local-legal-culture-practitioner-attitudes-four-criminal-courts.

Craig, W. (2014, October 24). What is company culture, and how do you change it? *Forbes*. www.forbes.com/sites/williamcraig/2014/10/24/what-is-company-culture-and-how-do-you-change-it/#7889e28e3e4a.

Fazari, G. M. (2015). A 360° of the first 365 as trial court administrator: Developing a perspective. *Court Manager, 30*(1), 26–42.

Fazari, G. M. (2022). *Courthouse confidential: Unveiling lessons learned in leading and managing trial court organizations*. Kendall Hunt.

Fazari, G. M., & Holandez, P. J. (2014). Reassessing the wheel: Outcomes of a BPR initiative on civil case management. *Court Manager, 29*(1), 5–11.

Gladwell, M. (2008). *Outliers: The story of success*. Little, Brown and Company.

Greenleaf, R. K. (1970). *The servant as leader*. Robert K. Greenleaf Center for Servant Leadership.

Highet, G. (1950). *The art of teaching*. Knopf.

Jacobellis v. Ohio, 378 U.S. 184 (1964).

Knoster, T., Villa, R., & Thousand, J. (2000). A framework for thinking about systems change. In R. Villa & J. Thousand (Eds.), *Restructuring for caring and effective education: Piecing the puzzle together* (pp. 93–128). Paul H. Brookes Publishing.

Kotter, J. P. (1995). Leading change: Why transformation efforts fail. *Harvard Business Review, 73*(2), 59–67.

Lindblom, C. E. (1959). The science of muddling through. *Public Administration Review, 19*(2), 79–88.

Mahoney, B., & Bakke, H. C. (1995). *Criminal caseflow management improvement in Essex County (Newark, New Jersey), 1990–1994*. The Justice Management Institute.

May, D. R., Gilson, R. L., & Harter, L. M. (2004). The psychological conditions of meaningfulness, safety, and availability and the engagement of the human spirit at work. *Journal of Occupational and Organizational Psychology, 77*(1), 11–37.

Merrill, D., & Reid, R. (1981). *Personal styles and effective performance.* University Associates.

National Association for Court Management. (2004). *Core competency curriculum guidelines: What court leaders need to know and be able to do.*

National Association for Court Management. (2015). *The core.* https://nacmnet.org/nacm-core/.

National Association for Court Management. (2016). *Court administration: A guide to the profession.*

National Center for State Courts. (2005). *CourTools: Trial court measures.* www.ncsc.org/our-centers-projects/courtools.

Ostrom, B. J. (2008, October 6). *Understanding and changing court culture* [Conference presentation]. Mid-Atlantic Association for Court Management Annual Conference, Atlantic City, NJ.

Ostrom, B. J., & Hanson, R. A. (2010). *Achieving high performance: A framework for courts* (Research Division working paper). National Center for State Courts.

Ostrom, B. J., Hanson, R. A., Ostrom, C. W., & Kleiman, M. (2005). Court cultures and their consequences. *Court Manager, 20*(1), 14–23.

Ostrom, B. J., Ostrom, C. W., Hanson, R. A., & Kleiman, M. (2007). *Trial courts as organizations.* Temple University Press.

Quinn, R. E. (1988). *Beyond rational management: Mastering the paradoxes and competing demands of high performance.* Jossey-Bass.

Schein, E. H. (1992). *Organizational culture and leadership: A dynamic view* (2nd ed.). Jossey-Bass.

Schein, E. H. (2004). *Organizational culture and leadership* (3rd ed.). John Wiley & Sons.

Shakespeare, W. (2009). *Hamlet.* In *The complete works of William Shakespeare.* Oxford University Press. (Original work published 1603)

Spencer, J., & Watkins, M. (2019). *Why organizational change fails.* ERE.net.

4 Court Leadership

Leadership is the third element of court administration that impacts all the other aspects of the court management profession discussed in this book. A Google search for "leadership" in 2026 produced more than 2.5 billion results. The numbers have grown almost exponentially over time. One item in particular produced by the search was an internet article, "100 Answers to the Question: What Is Leadership?" by Lolly Daskal (2016), President and CEO of Lead From Within. She doubtless was challenged to limit the list to 100. Daskal introduces her article with a succinct: "It's a difficult concept to define, perhaps because it means so many things to different people." Stogdill (1974) addressed leadership similarly and defined it in numerous ways, reflecting the wide range of perspectives held by those who have attempted to conceptualize it. To that end, we aim to focus on areas of consensus, rather than analyzing the myriad of definitions.

A court with people capable of exercising leadership who are consistently allowed to do so operates at a high level; incidentally, these same institutions are also those that continually seek out innovation in their process and practice. These courts often are early adapters in their states and, sometimes, nationally; as a result, other, aspiring courts look to leadership courts for best practices and a vision of their own potential. Conversely, a court lacking leadership may be unable to sustain operational effectiveness, and either resists modernizations or adopts them only slowly after many of its peer courts.

Courts share the challenge of all organizations: to identify potential leaders, to foster their development and to place them where they can best serve the institution, to embrace leaders and their leadership, and to build a culture that is not dependent on the personality or skill of one person in a leadership role. Too often, someone with a leadership title will improve operations, access, transparency, structure, and/or other aspects of court operations, only to see those innovations or operational changes atrophy or disappear when the leader departs from the court. We are aware

DOI: 10.4324/9781003686804-4

of states and individual courts where advancements instituted by a strong leader over many years have disappeared within a year or two after that person left the court. These situations sometimes occur because the person did not exercise collaborative leadership, but relied, instead, on their title, personality, and use of positional power. Another possible contributor to the loss of sustainable organizational change is that toward the end of long tenures, some judges and staff start to chafe under the long-term leader, so they either consciously abandon innovative thinking, or the transformation weakens for lack of attention. It is a challenge to achieve an organizational change initially, which often requires strong leadership, but an even greater challenge to sustain it over the long-term during a leadership transition. Consequently, making longstanding organizational change frequently requires even more effective leadership than initiating it. This is regarded as institutionalizing change – a herculean task given the structure and culture of courts. A court will prosper with leadership that understands the need to institutionalize the acceptance of change and the need for continual improvement. This acceptance comes from building staff competence, a team- and court-focused commitment amongst staff, and guiding judges to accept that their personal values and needs are best served by a quality institution that looks beyond personal preferences of individual judges and administrators.

If courts depend on individuals with leadership qualities which randomly surface, they normally will see positive changes ebb and flow depending on the happenstance of who fills the leader role at any given time. A court's vision and goals are insufficient to assure sustained excellence; paying attention to selecting leaders with demonstrated leadership skills is also needed. Those judges and administrators with a leader's title but with limited to no leadership skills will continually be challenged by a varying cadre of judges – and, sometimes, other stakeholders – who may rank their professional status, their "independence," and their preference for doing it their way above institutional needs on a wide range of issues. This chapter explores what "leadership" means, both generally and its application in the courts, whether and to what extent court administrators or administrator-presiding judge teams can exercise leadership, and how courts can effectively develop people to *be* leaders, as opposed to simply occupying the designated leadership role.

What Is "Leadership"?

Given myriad views of leadership, it is not surprising that the National Association for Court Management (NACM) has long focused on defining and clearly describing what it means by leadership in a court setting. We explore the judiciary's challenges after looking at the general concept.

General Literature About Leadership

We will not reproduce the scores of statements discussing leadership selected by Daskal (2016), but instead share a sampling that, when combined, offers a helpful composite of the elements of leadership found in much of the literature:

- The art of leadership is saying no, not saying yes. It is very easy to say yes. – *Tony Blair*
- The task of leadership is not to put greatness into people, but to elicit it, for the greatness is there already. – *John Buchan*
- Leadership is the art of getting someone else to do something you want done because he [she] wants to do it. – *Dwight Eisenhower*
- Leadership is the process of persuasion or example by which an individual (or leadership team) induces a group to pursue objectives held by the leader or shared by the leader and his or her followers. – *John W. Gardner*
- A good leader takes a little more than his [or her] share of the blame, a little less than his [or her] share of the credit. – *Arnold Glasow*
- Leadership is the ability to guide others without force into a direction or decision that leaves them still feeling empowered and accomplished. – *Lisa Cash Hanson*
- To get others to come into our ways of thinking, we must go over to theirs; and it is necessary to follow, in order to lead. – *William Hazlitt*
- I start with the premise that the function of leadership is to produce more leaders, not more followers. – *Ralph Nader*
- The greatest leader is not necessarily the one who does the greatest things. He [She] is the one that gets the people to do the greatest things. – *Ronald Reagan*
- Leadership is a potent combination of strategy and character. But if you must be without one, be without the strategy. – *Norman Schwarzkopf*

Management author and expert Ken Blanchard (2000) echoes Eisenhower, Gardner, and Hanson, emphasizing that contemporary leadership is primarily based on the ability to influence others, rather than on exercising formal authority. Leaders at Emergenetics International (2026) offer a different perspective on leadership:

> I don't actually think that the definition is the issue... **it is the action of leadership that is the hardest part.** Inherently, defining leadership means understanding yourself from an inward perspective as well as translating your own tendencies, strengths and approaches into the way you interact, communicate and influence others. [Emphasis in original.]

In *How to Think Like Leonardo da Vinci*, Gelb (1998) answers the question whether da Vinci's method of learning and fostering intelligence can be operationalized by individuals to attain personal fulfillment or if it is reserved only for "geniuses." da Vinci articulated seven principles and qualities he thought would lead individuals to enhance their state of being. They are not, per se, a list of characteristics of leaders, but factors which people aspiring to lead others should consider and embrace. More simply, these apply to the "action of leadership" (Brown, 2016):

1) *Curiosità* – (Curiosity) An insatiably curious approach to life and an unrelenting quest for continuous learning
2) *Dimostrazione* – (Independent Thinking) A commitment to test knowledge through experience, persistence, and a willingness to learn from mistakes
3) *Sensazione* – (Refine Your Senses) The continual refinement of the senses, especially sight, as the means to clarify experience
4) *Sfumato* – (Embrace Uncertainty, translated as "Going Up in Smoke") A willingness to embrace ambiguity, paradox, and uncertainty
5) *Arte/Scienza* – (Art and Science, Whole Brain Thinking) The development of the balance between science and art, logic and imagination
6) *Corporalità* – (Mind-Body Care) The cultivation of grace, ambidexterity, fitness, and poise
7) *Connessione* – (Interconnectedness, Systems Thinking) A recognition and appreciation for the connectedness of all things and phenomena

This list overlaps modern leadership writings, but from the perspective of how someone aspiring to be a leader should approach life in general. The importance of life experience and growth is cited by many scholars and business leaders, as noted in the extensive search we mentioned. It goes directly to the question of whether leadership can be taught, which we discuss at the end of this chapter.

These lists were generated from the perspective of the private sector, not the public sector. Stupak (1999) wrote a short piece for the membership newsletter of the NACM that contrasts leaders and managers. Stupak offered a list of qualities he observed in effective public sector leaders. His list together with the foregoing lists overlap in many respects, but he added some elements of leadership that reflect government's unique role in society:

- Is value anchored
- Is opportunity driven
- Is an option generator
- Uses positive power
- Is performance anchored
- Communicates meaning
- Is a boundary crosser
- Cultivates networks

The Army War College offers an interesting perspective on leadership. It surveyed subordinates of highly regarded major generals in the Iraq War on "what makes a good leader?" The responses, in order of importance, were (What makes a good leader?, 2005):

- Keeps cool under pressure
- Clearly explains missions, standards and priorities
- Sees the big picture; provides context and perspective
- Makes tough, sound decisions on time

The military context for these responses is obvious, but the answers nonetheless are relevant for all leaders, including presiding judges and court administrators.

Welch and Welch (2006) remarked: "When you become a leader... nothing you do anymore as an individual matters except how you nurture and support your team and help its members increase their self-confidence." It is a leader's responsibility to ensure that staff have the training and tools needed to complete their assigned responsibilities. Further, a leader must ensure that the assigned responsibilities fit a person's strengths. A good manager should do likewise, which often seems to lead to some of the confusion regarding what is meant by "leaders."

Drucker (1973) reminded us that:

> no two people have the same configuration of strengths and weaknesses. And no one has only strengths... It is the manager's job [also a leader's job] to optimize resources. And placement is the way to optimize the most expensive resource of them all: the human being.

Harris Collingwood (2001), editor and writer specializing in business, finance, and economics, discussed the importance for a leader to place staff where their skills are optimized: "Leaders [and managers] must help their followers discover what they are good at. Leaders enable self-knowledge." Curiosity, a key quality for da Vinci, is not commonly put on lists of leadership qualities today. Bennis (2003), a leading evaluator and commentator on leadership, agreed with the importance da Vinci placed in curiosity, stating: "Leaders wonder about everything, want to learn as much as they can, are willing to take risks, experiment, try new things."[1]

There is a profusion of leadership quality lists that could be provided here. Some merely refer to the same characteristics with a different label. Some contain a new thought or two. Rather than provide more lists, we focus on one additional key quality or attribute that seems to be seminal for court leaders: emotional intelligence (EQ). This quality is the ability to match values and needs of leaders and followers so that followers come to see the leader's values as consistent with theirs and thus work with them for positive change.[2]

One of the most important characteristics exhibited by leaders involves strong people skills. The term "emotional intelligence" is widely noted in the leadership literature in conjunction with this concept. Emotional intelligence is not the same as empathy, but empathy overlaps a leader's ability to identify and then reinforce another's values and needs so they become a partner in organizational change. The terms previously characterized the components of emotional intelligence as varied and multifaceted in their levels of functioning, rather than one-dimensional. Nonetheless, the need for these qualities is almost universally recognized.

Goleman (1998) was one of the first to identify and explain emotional intelligence and why it is particularly important for those in leadership positions. He identified five components of emotional intelligence: self-awareness, self-regulation, motivation, empathy, and social skill. A self-aware person displays candor with others and an ability to assess one's self realistically. Effective leadership is often characterized by a well-developed ability to engage in self-observation and critical self-analysis. Self-regulation is an ability to say "no" to impulsive urges to act, but it also includes a propensity for reflection, thoughtfulness, a comfort with ambiguity and change, and integrity. Motivation is the drive within a leader to achieve beyond expectations, including their own, and a desire to achieve for achievement's sake. Socially skilled individuals demonstrate an aptitude for developing wide-ranging relationships and for building rapport by establishing shared understanding among diverse stakeholders.

Mayer and Salovey (1997) observed that emotional intelligence is understood as an ability-based construct involving the perception, understanding, and management of emotions in oneself and in others, rather than a collection of dispositional traits such as optimism or self-confidence.

In the *Harvard Business Review* article "Leading by feel" (2004), William George, former chairman and CEO of Medtronic, Inc., a medical device manufacturer, denoted self-awareness as follows:[3]

> Authentic leadership begins with self-awareness, a knowing yourself deeply. Self-awareness is not a trait you are born with, but a capacity you develop throughout your lifetime. It's your understanding of your strengths and weaknesses, your purpose in life, your values and motivations, and how and why you respond to situations in a particular way. It requires a great deal of introspection and the ability to internalize feedback from others.

Why is it important to understand emotional intelligence? Goleman (1998) explained:

> When I analyzed all this data [from the efforts of 188 companies to identify leaders and ingredients that make good leaders,] I found dramatic results. To be sure, intellect was a driver of outstanding performance. Cognitive skills such as big-picture thinking and long-term vision were particularly important. But when I calculated the ratio of technical skills, IQ, and emotional

> intelligence as ingredients of excellent performance, emotional intelligence proved to be twice as important as the others for jobs at all levels.

Emotional intelligence is highly personal and highly internal. The lists above and the factors discussed in this book describe the results of being a leader, not as often the traits that enable one to achieve those results. Importantly, emotional intelligence provides insight into the factors and traits that lead one to effective, sustainable leadership.

Burns (1978) authored one of the first books on leadership. Burns noted many insights, but one of the most important is the relationship between leaders and followers. Many people, even today, think of leaders as people who can make others do what the leader wants them to do. Burns refers to these people as exercising "headship," not leadership. He defined leadership as:

> Leaders inducing followers to act for certain goals that represent the values and the motivation – the wants and needs, the aspirations and expectations – *of both leaders and followers*. And the genius of leadership lies in the manner in which leaders see and act in their own and their followers' values and motivations.

Burns identified three types of leadership:

> The relations of most leaders and followers are *transactional* – leaders approach followers with an eye to exchanging one thing for another: jobs for votes, or subsidies for campaign contributions. [Note that this balancing and compromising is a feature attributed by some to managers today]. *Transforming* leadership, while more complex, is more potent. The transforming leader recognizes and exploits an existing need or demand of a potential follower. But, beyond that, the transforming leader looks for potential motives in followers, seeks to satisfy higher needs, and engages the full person of the follower. The result of transforming leadership is a relationship of mutual stimulation and elevation that converts followers into leaders and may convert leaders into moral agents. The last concept, *moral leadership*, concerns me the most. By this term I mean, first, that leaders and [those who are] led have a relationship not only of power but of mutual needs, aspirations, and values; second, that in responding to leaders, followers have adequate knowledge of alternative leaders and programs and the capacity to choose among those alternatives, and, third, that leaders take responsibility for their commitments... Moral leadership emerges from, and always returns to, the fundamental wants and needs, aspirations, and values of the followers.

People may prefer one approach to another when discussing a change, or believe that a proposed solution will not achieve the stated goals; that is where leadership takes hold. Leadership seeks needs, motivations, and aspirations that lie below the shared values and affect how people see proposals, either as threatening or as compatible and desirable with the organization. Leaders listen – another skill ascribed to those at the helm by almost all observers – and address these underlying factors so that others see the congruence between what they desire and what the leader wants. At that point, change is possible, and it is often transformational.

True leaders also are secure enough to understand and seek out multiple viewpoints, including those that challenge the leader's proposals. In other words, "You should no more expect others to agree with your every opinion than you should agree with theirs."[4] It is difficult to build an environment in which people feel free to challenge and test ideas for the purpose of strengthening the final result or avoiding solutions that lack merit. We all would like to be right all of the time and to have people always agree with us. In reality, neither desire can be realized. If the court administrator is surrounded by sycophants (sometimes by design), they are probably more a tyrant than a leader; they certainly are not an effective leader and the organization will ultimately suffer.

Much of the literature on leadership makes a point about needing dissenters to improve decision making. Welch and Welch (2005) emphasized that effective leaders intentionally foster a culture of candor within their organizations. Martin Winterkorn, a former CEO of automaker, Audi, remarked in the "On a roll at Audi" (2005) article:

> Audi's culture... endorses internal debate and argument. As a manager you have to be able to fight with colleagues on an intellectual plane without feeling attacked personally. This is especially important when it comes to discussing mistakes that are made. Everyone makes mistakes, even me.

Court-Based Leadership

The NACM has identified leadership as a critically important, key competency for a court administrator. We discuss in this section the similarities and differences between discussions of leadership generally and leadership specific to the courts. We also contrast leadership to management in courts. Further, we suggest the limits of "leadership" in a court context.

In 1999, the NACM published its first effort to define the competencies that court administrators and leadership judges should possess or understand: *Core Competency Curriculum Guidelines: What Court Leaders Need to Know and Be Able to Do* (2004). "Leadership" was one of the ten competencies identified in that document. These "Core Competencies" made important contributions to the professionalization of court administration, helping both senior managers and judges understand the multiple needs and demands associated with court leadership positions. Considerable discussion about each competency amongst the NACM membership followed over several years. Beginning in the mid-2000s, the NACM (2016a) decided to update the *Core Competencies* with what is known, as of 2016, as *The CORE*. The NACM (2015) explained its fresh look at administrators' competencies as follows:

> The field of court management has become increasingly professionalized and diverse. With increasing responsibilities, new demands, and changes in the environment in which court administrators work (e.g., political, economic, and technological), NACM recognized a need to review and update the original competencies.

The CORE is composed of 13 competencies organized into three modules and further refined by more than a dozen components. Leadership remains as a competency, but it now is part of the "Vision" module along with strategic planning and court governance. The concept and components of leadership are addressed in two of the competencies within the Vision module: Leadership and Strategic Planning. The introduction to the Leadership discussion in *The CORE* states:

> Leadership is an energetic process of creating vision resulting in commitment to a common course and preferred future. Just as there is no one best way to manage courts, there is no best way to be a court leader. Leadership is highly personal.

Immediately thereafter, when discussing the "relevance" of leadership, the NACM (2015) notes:

> Effective court managers/leaders create, implement, and nurture a clear and compelling vision for the court, bringing a strategic perspective to their work, while staying attuned to daily operations. The combination of *leadership* and *proactive management* enable the court to fulfill the public's trust in the judiciary through service and adherence to the rule of law. The effective court leader is ultimately measured by the judiciary's performance in the key areas [of] procedural due process, the protection of rights, transparency, accessibility, the stewardship of scarce resources, and the achievement of timely justice in individual cases.

Leadership also is described more broadly in the discussion of the "strategic planning" competency. There, *The CORE* says:

> The court leader not only manages the court but also must provide "leadership." Whereas management is primarily about directing how the organization accomplishes its mission, leadership is about establishing a strategic course for an organization, communicating that direction to internal and external stakeholders and engaging them to work collaboratively toward achieving the organization's mission... To fulfill this role, the court leader needs to focus on creating and sustaining a strategic vision for the court. This requires the court leader to demonstrate creativity, stamina, drive, conceptual and analytic skills as well as the ability to execute. A court leader who is competent in these areas is well-position [sic] to work as a

> leadership partner with judicial officers, to assess and respond to trends, to promote overall court capacity, and to guide the court in achieving its mission.

Each statement highlights different aspects of and views about "leadership." It is unspecified in these statements and from other references in *The CORE* whether the NACM (2015) is referring to a presiding judge-administrator team needing leadership skills or only to functional needs of the administrator. Ideally, the guidance will be applicable to both.

Each competency in *The CORE* had different authors. It is not surprising, therefore, that two competencies would highlight different aspects of leadership. A related NACM (2016b) guide, *The Court Administrator, Court Administration: A Guide to the Profession*, also addresses leadership and management in combination. The divergence of statements about leadership within the NACM documents reflects the difficulty of discussing leadership in general, but also reflects that in court literature, the terms "leader" and "leadership" include tasks, responsibilities, and aspirations that are clearly managerial and others that normally are attributed to leaders. That might be expected because the qualities of good managers and of good leaders overlap and the competencies desired by a specific court vary from court to court. This dual vision of "leadership" is explicitly acknowledged by the NACM in parts of the Leadership competency by references to "court managers/leaders."

In *The Court Administrator*, the NACM (2016b) puts forth the following insights about serving as a court administrator:

> At any given time, a court administrator may provide supervision, management, or leadership. It is leadership however, that is the hallmark of a professional and of the modern court administrator. These leadership abilities allow the court administrator to effectively partner with the chief judge and all judges as well as their staff, to respond to the growing demands upon a court and the increasing expectations for performance. Court administrators may also be called upon to be innovators, "out of the box" thinkers, change agents, or even entrepreneurs... The court administrator typically functions in administrative areas, rather than legal areas, and therefore requires the specialized skills of any professional position with managerial responsibility. One chief judge stated, "We have plenty of lawyers in the court. What we need is someone who has a managerial background and knows what management is."

This latter statement reflects the challenge of being a court administrator without being explicit: Court administrators see themselves, and want to be seen by others, especially judges, as professionals with the skills and qualities ordinarily associated with "leaders." Yet, some judges may think of their administrators – and want their administrators to be *only* – strong managers.[5] The NACM's ongoing efforts to define and articulate "leadership" as a critical competency of a court administrator reflects the world at large, while also highlighting the challenges of being an administrator in an acknowledged court leadership role.

There are limits to what even the best leader can achieve in courts, because all judges are organizationally equal, "loosely coupled,"[6] and usually see themselves as independent professionals irrespective of lines of formal administrative authority.[7] Therefore, the art of persuasive influence can be effective to get a critical mass of judges, and, following that, all judges, on board with an initiative or significant administrative change (Bureau of Justice Assistance & American University, 2005). That is best achieved by someone (or a team of several people) with high emotional intelligence and credibility. Persuasion must almost always be achieved judge-to-judge, and not directly by the administrator. Once judges are amenable with a change, other stakeholders who are *in* courts, but not *of* them (e.g., prosecutors, private attorneys, and, in some courts, law enforcement security personnel), must likewise be convinced. Occasionally, influence can be augmented by mandates about what a stakeholder must file with the court or what its representative must do in court during a hearing or trial, but dubious collaborators often circumvent mandates they find onerous or with which they disagree. This may occur even after pre-implementation discussions. Again, emotional intelligence and a high degree of situational awareness are critical in navigating these realities.

In terms of organizational mission, courts arguably have an advantage over virtually all of the private sector because the values of our legal framework and structure – due process, fairness, doing justice, the appearance of doing justice, access, even-handedness, preserving public order while protecting individuals from arbitrary government power – are ingrained in all judges and most stakeholders; certainly all the key collaborators (public and private attorneys and law enforcement) and the general citizenry. Courts do not necessarily have to seek or create new shared institutional values to which both leaders and followers can ascribe. These jointly held and widely accepted principles already exist and are built into courts as institutions.

The concept of emotional intelligence is not unknown in court administration, but it is not well known or widely explored in the court context (NACM, 2015). Emotional intelligence may now be seen by some as a cliché, but it still provides valuable insight into the kind of person who is an effective court leader. It may also be largely overlooked (at its own peril) when courts seek new administrators. Typical job interviews for a court administrator involve asking about accomplishments in one's current and recent job positions. They ask about how an applicant overcame a difficult situation or dealt with a difficult employee. The court may pose a hypothetical and ask how the applicant would deal with the facts presented (behavioral interviewing). If an applicant says they would talk to affected people, there may not be follow-up questions to coax whether the substance of the conversation suggests a high level of emotional intelligence.

Tobin (1999) spoke of the early pioneers in court administration as having "the ability to state a vision in simple and compelling terms. Their greatness did not lie in dreaming up visions, but rather in their ability to apprehend and mobilize support for ideas whose time had come." As courts speak of needing leadership, it is important to remember the previously noted James MacGregor Burns' concepts of leadership and realize that in an institution of loosely coupled peers who highly value their professionalism and independence, only transformative moral-based leadership can be effective. The wide array of court stakeholders involved, plus the element of judicial independence, make transactional leadership virtually ineffective in the long term. Presiding judges and court administrators who possess the emotional intelligence and moral leadership to reach and authentically communicate with their peers are the leaders who move courts forward. They may or may not have a leadership title, particularly in courts that do not place a premium on administrative judicial roles, experience, and skill when selecting a presiding judge. *Any* judge can be the true leader of a court – or several can be, serving in a leadership team with the court administrator. In some circumstances, a middle manager or staff member may have stronger leadership credibility than the court administrator. In those courts, effective presiding judge/administrator teams may expand their executive team scope, by recognizing and inspiring others to help achieve desired goals.[8]

Leaders are change agents. Leaders change and guide an institution's direction. In the private sector they often see the present context for an organization, modify or reject it, and create a new set of conditions and, sometimes, an entirely new business model. Then, the leaders persuade others to adopt the new paradigm and proceed to institute associated processes. They often reinvent organizations, just as IBM left the mainframe computer business and today is largely a consulting and information integration company, and just as Western Union used to deliver telegrams and is now a retail personal finance company (Associated Press, 2006). Drucker (1973), who is recognized as creating many modern concepts of "management," spoke of "managers," but often talked about tasks or qualities that today are ascribed to leaders. He discussed leadership in these terms: "The foundation of innovative strategy is planned and systematic sloughing off of the old, the dying, the obsolete. Innovating organizations spend neither time nor resources on defending yesterday." Drucker further remarked that an innovative strategy focuses on building an entirely new business model rather than introducing another product within an existing portfolio. Instead of incremental enhancements, it seeks to develop fundamentally new capabilities and redefine how value is understood and delivered. The purpose of such innovation is to produce meaningful, transformative systemic change rather than modest improvement.

Courts need effective organizational functioning and institutional integrity. Courts need to continuously define and improve their services. Courts also need new concepts of service delivery value and how to measure it. "Leadership," as Drucker (1973) and others consider it for the private sector, is not a perfect fit for the judicial branch governance model, however. Courts do not necessarily need to create new lines of businesses and in many important ways this is not feasible. Problem-solving "courts" – specialized calendars for particular judges that started in the late 1980s, followed more recently with what are called "therapeutic courts" – challenge this statement, but only in some limited ways. They are new methods of delivering court services, but not a new line of business per se. Problem-solving courts have created a novel way of *thinking* about what judges do and how they do it. Even if, as recently evidenced, application of problem-solving court approaches continues to expand, the judicial system must still adhere to established norms: due process, lack of bias and favoritism, integrity of the process and its participant collaborators, transparency, and full access to the institution for those affected. Even with the growing use of "problem-solving" methods, the number of cases to which these approaches apply is a small percentage of all cases adjudicated by a court. These specialized calendars also require substantially more resources and human capital to establish and maintain than calendars involving "regular" cases. Moreover, some courts continue to operate without "problem-solving" calendars. No matter how many cases are addressed by "problem-solving courts," the judicial branch cannot wholly negate the adversarial process or slough off constitutional and statutory limits in lieu of these alternative programs. Courts cannot (and should not) disregard their core "business" responsibilities of dispute resolution, public order, and ensuring the integrity and lawfulness of government. Of course, the courts can modify or expand strategies in fulfilling these roles and thus will continue to reinvent themselves in accordance with societal demand and technology, but those changes are delimited to their constitutionally defined function and roles. Consequently, some of the qualities of leadership identified and discussed above, particularly Drucker's (1973) idea of reinventing the institution, are not directly applicable to courts without a fuller comprehension of judicial branch nuances and the roles that these complex institutions serve in government.

The Tension in Courts Between Leadership and Management

In order to understand the tension between leadership and management, we further discuss briefly the concept of "management." As noted earlier, one of the difficulties in identifying the skills and knowledge required of a leader is that the qualities of competent managers and good leaders intersect. In Drucker's writings, the qualities and skills identified with management mirror those competencies desired in leadership today. Drucker (1973) characterizes management as a universal function that confronts fundamentally similar responsibilities across nations and societies. Central to this role is providing direction to the organization by defining its mission, establishing objectives, and arranging resources to achieve intended outcomes. Management is therefore charged with aligning vision and organizational capacity to maximize results and meaningful contributions.

Zaleznik (2004) offered one of the clearest and most complete descriptions of managers:

> A manager is a problem solver. The manager asks: What problems have to be solved and what are the best ways to achieve results so that people can contribute to this organization? To be a manager, [requires] persistence, tough-mindedness, hard work, intelligence, analytical ability, and perhaps most important, tolerance and good will...

Managers tend to view work as an enabling process involving some combination of people and ideas interacting to establish strategies and make decisions. They help the process along by calculating the interests in opposition, planning when controversial issues should surface, and reducing tensions. In this enabling process, managers' tactics appear flexible...

[What a manager does includes] reconciling differences, seeking compromises, and establishing a balance of power...

Managers relate to people according to the role they play in a sequence of events or in a decision-making process, while leaders, who are concerned with ideas, relate in more intuitive and empathetic ways. The distinction is simply between a manager's attention to *how* things get done and a leader to *what* the events and decisions mean to participants...

Managers see themselves as conservators and regulators of an existing order of affairs with which they personally identify and from which they gain rewards. A manager's sense of self-worth is enhanced by perpetuating and strengthening existing institutions. He or she is performing a role that is in harmony with the ideals of duty and responsibility.

Stupak's (1999) description of the qualities required of managers, discussed earlier in this chapter, reflects many of the same elements identified by Zaleznik:

- Maintains the present
- Is crisis driven
- Monitors progress
- Uses negative power
- Does things right
- Communicates rules
- Plans from memory
- Is activity anchored
- Manages things
- Is a stability protector
- Is tactically driven
- Is an "SOP" regulator

- Is technically anchored
- Protects hierarchies
- Is a boundary protector

A key difference amongst the lists of Drucker, Zaleznik, and Stupak is the fact many court administrators can relate immediately to the latter descriptions as being close to what they do. Drucker's list is less recognizable to court administration and in some respects is perhaps beyond what any court can conceivably do. Warren Bennis observed, "Managers do things right. Leaders do the right thing" (Covey, 1989). Although memorable and perhaps in isolated matters even factually descriptive, Bennis's one-liner is often repeated by an array of professional development trainers; it does not, however help create a court-related job description given the specific knowledge, skills, and abilities of these work environments. Two professors at the McLaren School of Business, University of San Francisco, succinctly talk about what managers do in contrast to what leaders do in terms that supplement Zaleznik and Stupak: "A manager controls, a leader builds commitment; a manager sanctions, a leader inspires; a manager administers, a leader creates; a manager focuses on the routine, a leader focuses on vision" (Imparato & Harari, 1994). The difficulty with this statement is that it sounds pejorative when describing managers. The description of a manager's role suffers by comparison to a leader's role, yet strong management is integral to modern court administration, whichever label is applied.

Part of the tension being discussed here was previously noted: there is significant divergence among judges about whether the ideal administrator is a strong manager or a "leader." Without question, successful managers not only share some tasks and techniques with leaders, but also some qualities. Examples would be a vision of "what might and should be," people skills, credibility, curiosity, and flexibility in approach but not necessarily in setting strategic goals and priorities.

Whether leadership judges believe their administrator is primarily a leader or primarily a manager, the job involves almost constant interacting with independent-minded judges, impactful and concurrently independent stakeholders, state and local government and private agencies, and the public on the court's behalf. The relative effectiveness of a court administrator is invariably linked to a high emotional quotient, which among other sensibilities, encompasses the skill of communicating ideas and concerns so that they are conveyed intelligibly, but without a tone that can be perceived as forbidding, disparaging, or indifferent. Lists of qualities that assign these competencies to "leaders" but not to "managers" are too narrow, at least in a court context. The NACM's multiple perspectives concerning the right label for a court administrator are understandable. Even so, we posit that strong leadership skills and qualities are central to being a successful court administrator for the reasons addressed below.

A full understanding of courts requires understanding that administrators seldom can be leaders in the full sense discussed to this point. Or, perhaps more accurately, it is incredibly challenging for court administrators to be the sole "face" of change or the main source of a vision of a new future. Administrators can have their own vision of how things should be and they can generate ideas for improvements, but unless they can convince leadership judges – and sometimes a critical mass of the entire bench – that their vision or system improvement should be pursued, it often is not approved and implemented. The independence and decision-making authority of leaders normally assumed and found in the private sector and in many government executive-branch agencies is lacking in the court setting. Particularly when dealing with stakeholders, when a court administrator proposes a new practice, stakeholders will seek assurance that the judges have reached consensus on the idea. Stakeholders may inquire with the administrator about the initiative or, in some instances go through the "back door" directly to judges. The administrator's statements often are not taken as the final word.[9] Even a small organizational change that some judges see as unnecessary or disruptive of the court's established process(es) can be rejected or may require other judges to intervene on behalf of the change before it can be implemented court-wide. The imprimatur of the presiding judge and other leadership judges often needs to be seen by the rest of the bench for the judges to be committed and involved before they agree to the suggested change.

Normally, for any change of major consequence, it is leadership judges who must lead their peers to be willing followers. To that end, court administrators can be leaders in the following ways: having and sharing a vision; articulating the need for and nature of a change; demonstrating high emotional intelligence and articulating effectively the core court values that will move early-adapting judges to sign on; and having the character, integrity, and emotional intelligence to bring staff along in realization of a shared vision. These are critically important qualities; a court with an administrator possessing these qualities is significantly advantaged. When a court's only leader with a particular vision is the administrator, however, it will not achieve whatever vision the administrator may have, particularly if a group of judges do not share the same vision. An administrator may nudge a court toward desired changes by exercising leadership qualities, but the efforts will inevitably fall short without the support of at least some of the leadership judges and, often, a critical core of additional judicial support.

There is no doubt that there are courts across the nation with judges who have strong leadership skills, visions of an improved judiciary, and the will to constantly improve court services. These courts are more likely to seek and hire an administrator who possesses both strong leadership and management competencies. When that happens, it becomes a symbiotic relationship that then attracts other leaders and proficient managers, who collectively build a dedicated and skillful staff. Together, the court leaders, managers, and staff continually improve the institution and over time ultimately create what are viewed as leadership courts from a nationwide perspective.

Some judges may fear that a court administrator exercising strong leadership may challenge their prerogatives or not accede to their conception of the court. These judges believe that they properly fill the policy-making role, defined very broadly by some judges, and that the court is best served by an experienced manager who will implement their policies, but not independently develop policies. To proactively resolve the inherent tension between administrators serving as leaders or managers, judges should directly address among themselves the role, skills, and qualities desired of their administrator – including leadership qualities – and adhere to their consensus thereafter.[10] Until then, the administrator's leadership role will be ambiguous, thus subject to redefinition from issue to issue, circumstance to circumstance, and presiding judge to presiding judge. To be successful, a court administrator must have a clearly defined leadership role, including delineation of decision-making authority vis-à-vis that of the presiding judge and the bench.

For purposes of this discussion, two dimensions of courts are noteworthy: the adjudicative one that provides fair, prompt, and impartial resolution of cases to all and the administrative one that provides operational support so judges can fulfill their adjudicative mission. The focus of all judges is properly on their adjudicative role. The administrative dimension of courts comprises two principal components: the extent to which judges retain or delegate authority over policy and rulemaking – including, in some instances, final authority over budgets and personnel policies – and, in many jurisdictions, authority over operational procedures. As part of an organization, however, judges also can be (or should be) subject to administrative policies and procedures once the policies are set. Most judges understand that both efficiency and effectiveness, available and accurate records, full public access, and transparency provide the operational foundation for them to fulfill their adjudicative mission, but that does not necessarily translate, in a given matter, into support for a specific new idea. This is the case even for smaller scale organizational changes. If a judge does not observe or personally experience problems on the administrative side, they may also not find any need for change or system improvement. If judges recognize an issue as a problem, they normally support addressing that specific element and they may agree on the need for a change, but challenge the solution the administrator proposes. The judge may focus on how they perceive a change affecting them and the staff with whom they work daily, and not necessarily on the operational needs of the entire institution. A varying number of judges who do not like a new procedure or process may modify or ignore it, in some situations without consequence. Fortunately, for the most part this number is small, but it seldom is zero, particularly in larger courts with 20 or more judges.[11]

A system improvement that everyone might see as falling squarely within a manager's job description may require keen leadership skills to become operational. That may explain why the NACM's *Core* offers multiple perspectives on the role of a court administrator as a leader, manager, or some generally defined combination. A key feature of courts from an administrator's perspective, as previously noted, is that judges have final authority over "policy." The challenge is that the concept of "policy" is fluid in many courts. Thus, many administrators may choose to bring changes they believe to be fully within their authority to the court's judicial executive committee (when there is one) or to the full bench to resolve a debate about whether it is or is not "policy." There are instances when an administrator believes something must be immediately resolved, but a final decision may be deferred by the judges. There are other circumstances when an administrator believes strongly in the need for a specific program, rule, or procedure which may be rejected by the judges. The judges may approve an alternative that only partially addresses the problem. Other situations involve matters when an administrator has made and announced a decision, almost always with the presiding judge's approval, that thereafter will have to be modified or withdrawn because a critical mass of judges insist on it.[12] Still, other predicaments draw in those "loosely coupled" entities when the judges and the administrator agree on a resolution, but the implementation fully or partially depends on the independent clerk of court, the sheriff, or others involved *with*, but administratively autonomous *from* the court, who will reject or ignore the change rendering it moot.

The key to understanding these constraints is that they may halt or modify large projects and changes, which is understandable in a complex, multifaceted organization, but they also may stifle a small change – at least one that is small from the court operations perspective but large from the perspective of one or more judges. A court administrator must have a sense of self and situational awareness that is strong enough to maintain the course, sustaining faith in one's basic strengths and abilities. This necessarily requires a high threshold for ambiguity and competing priorities. These are vital court leadership qualities.

There are copious factors and many critical personnel in the justice system that courts do not have authority over and often cannot control. Thus, it is essential to understand the constitutional and statutory limits of judicial branch power and governance, particularly as it relates to its impact on the management of the courts. Notwithstanding the absence of full administrative control, these realities do not abdicate the court institution's responsibility to seek and institute system improvement. Rather, it means that one must keep the long view in mind while working on what may be only small incremental steps toward achieving the long-term goal(s). Again, this is what effective court leaders do.

Most seasoned court administrators are well informed about the institutional, political, and personality factors that create the environment – the "court culture" – in which they operate. There also often are court budget and staffing limitations that, outside of the Great Recession and other fiscal downturns, may not impact the budgets of other criminal justice agencies to the same degree.[13] Understanding the local court environment requires perspective on both the court as an institution and of oneself to assure the proper functioning of daily operations, while continuing to work for long-term judicial system improvement. Leadership and management approaches overlap in significant ways in these circumstances.

There is another tension between a desire for leaders and a need for managers. Zaleznik (2004) noted correctly that the process of ensuring that people can assume practical responsibility – tasks associated with managers – may inhibit the development of leaders. This is because the vision of the leader and subsequent changes may not seem viable at the outset. The presence of great leaders can also undermine the development of managers. Leaders, by definition, are not primarily maintaining the organization but rather are focused on changing it. Paradoxically, some managers and judges may have trouble dealing with the disorder created by a dynamic, far reaching court leader.

We remarked on the general views of leadership, citing the need for "dissenters." Some of the more appropriate phrasing of this necessity could be identified as: challenge and test ideas for the purpose of strengthening the final result or avoiding solutions that lack merit and a culture of candor. The need to consider divergent perspectives is as important in courts as that of other organizations. Indeed, the complex court organizational environment makes it important to invite broad-scoped feedback on plans for change and the overall strategic direction of the court. Judges are generally not accustomed to their opinions being challenged openly and vigorously by people other than fellow judges. In a courtroom, judges always render final rulings, albeit their decisions are subject to appeal. In administrative matters, staff and subordinate managers can be reluctant to speak up after a judge indicates they have made up their mind or even have an opinion about a matter.[14] Leadership administrators can help foster communications by respectfully helping judges to understand this dynamic, explaining the apprehension some staff and subordinate managers have about offering input contrary to the stated views of judges. Administrators may need to cultivate honest and fuller discussions when staff or subordinate managers are part of a planning group with judges. Administrators can also encourage staff to address judges in a respectful, positive way while modeling the suggested approach to communication. Within areas that an administrator controls and in meetings led by administrators, staff should be invited to express diverse views to help shape and implement decisions.

The fact that some people do not want to be positive contributors or do not know how to present ideas constructively does not lessen the need for alternative views. Manfred Kits de Vries argued that leaders need some people to fill the classic role of "a King's fool" (Contu, 2004).

> The fool... is a foil for the leader – and every leader needs one... The fool shows the leader his reflection and reminds him of the transience of power... To be effective, organizations need people with a healthy disrespect for the boss – people who feel free to express emotions and opinions openly, who can engage in active give-and-take.

Ironically, leadership includes seeking and embracing these people. One need not think in terms of disrespect, nay-sayers, or difficult people. Diversity of opinion is a better held perspective and ultimately the goal. John Scully, a former CEO of Apple, remarked (Bennis, 2003):

> One of the biggest mistakes a person can make is to put together a team that reflects only him [or her]. I find it's better to put teams together of people who have different skills and then make all those disparate skills function together. The real role of the leader is to figure out how you make diverse people and elements work together.

Contingency planning is part of organizational maintenance, so normally it is considered a manager's responsibility. It involves thinking about things that might go wrong and how the organization is prepared to respond if there is no preventative option, such as a natural disaster. Some of the management literature suggests that individuals with more pessimistic outlooks may be effective managers in this context. This is attributed to their tendency to anticipate potential system failures and proactively develop contingency strategies. To that end, managers with more optimistic dispositions may benefit from deliberately identifying possible risks associated with new initiatives, ideas, or personnel decisions, thereby enhancing their preparedness to respond effectively should adverse outcomes occur (Briefly, 2005).

Managers can be pessimists – always thinking of worst-case scenarios – and *also* successful. Leaders cannot effectively lead from this negative perspective. Pessimists cannot sustain a vision to a better future or convince others that the years ahead will be more enriching if a new path is followed. If a court administrator is expected to be both leader and manager, there is an inherent tension. A leader can and should hire strong managers who may be pessimists at least insofar as to anticipate potential problems and to develop contingency plans. As indicated, however, positive forward thinking leadership capabilities are needed almost daily for a court administrator to succeed. On balance, leadership qualities are more important than day-to-day operational skills for an executive-level court administrator. Leadership judges should be aware of these considerations when seeking a new administrator and in delineation of the administrator's leadership role.

Teaching Leadership

In explaining why leadership is important, the NACM (2004) stated in its original *Core Competencies*:

> Leadership is the energy behind every court system and court accomplishment... Absent leadership excellence, courts and court systems cannot take or maintain effective action.

We concur with the NACM that courts need administrators with highly developed leadership skills and qualities. But how can the courts find them? Can courts train people to be leaders?

Leadership capacity is determined by a leader's worldview, their engagement with ideas and people, and their ongoing evolution by virtue of their experiences, knowledge, skills, and abilities. The NACM (2004) in its *Core Competencies*, which is supported by its wide network of court professionals, contends that leadership abilities can be developed to a substantial degree. In the more recent *Core*, it asserts that effective leadership techniques are broadly teachable (NACM, 2015). Our position is that while people can learn some techniques, there are many dimensions of a fully developed court leader. Techniques alone do not make leaders but can contribute to leadership growth. Leadership qualities are learnable only to the extent that one learns from living; the lessons gained from life are not learnable from a book or by following a prescribed curriculum in a classroom, or through learning a few tactics.

Leaders do not fully emerge merely from training. Gloria Anderson, a newspaper executive and editor, stated, "You can't make being a leader your principal goal, any more than you can make being happy your goal. In both cases, it has to be the result, not the cause" (Bennis, 2003). Bennis (2003) remarked similarly: "I am surer now than ever that the process of becoming a leader is the same process that makes a person a healthy, fully-integrated human being. And it is the same process that allows one to age successfully." Interestingly, the leaders interviewed by Bennis (2003) about leadership agreed on two basic points. First, there is broad agreement that leadership is developed rather than innate, and that it is shaped more through individual agency than through external forces. Second, leadership is not typically pursued as an end in itself. There may not necessarily be an explicit desire to lead. The process of becoming a leader occurred naturally while they sought to authentically express themselves through their work. Leaders, as a result, are not motivated by a need for self-validation, but rather by a desire to immerse themselves in meaningful work and life experiences. This distinction is very important because it separates personal ambition from genuine leadership. When such self-expression proves valuable to others, leadership naturally follows. Ultimately, the objective is never about becoming a leader. Instead, the goal is to come full circle using one's knowledge, skills, and abilities to become the best version of oneself.[15]

With respect to training people to be leaders, Bennis (2003) further noted, "I would argue that more leaders have been made by accident, circumstance, sheer grit, or will than have been made by all the leadership courses put together... Leadership courses can only teach skills. They can't teach character or vision – and indeed they don't even try. Developing character and vision is the way leaders invent themselves." Regarding the central role of personal character in leadership, Bennis echoed Drucker's (1973) sentiment, "What a manager does can be analyzed systematically. What a manager has to do can be learned... But one quality cannot be learned, one qualification that the manager cannot acquire but must bring with him. It is not genius, it is character."[16]

Goleman (1998) rejects as ineffective the practice of many large, contemporary companies in employing trained psychologists to develop "competency models" to aid them in identifying, training, and promoting likely stars in the leadership firmament. One of the co-authors of the report on the Army War College's study of highly regarded major generals noted, "One thing we found is that it's still easier to teach technical skills than to teach people how to gain trust and build teams" (What makes a good leader?, 2005). Richard Ferry, co-founder of Korn/Ferry International, an executive search firm, observed similarly, "You can't really create leaders. How do you teach people to make decisions, for example? All you can do is develop the talents people have" (Bennis, 2003).

The court cannot teach intellect, although it certainly can improve knowledge levels of judges, administrators, and staff. The court cannot teach how to imagine long-term vision, although techniques and planning strategies can facilitate big-picture thinking. Most importantly, the court cannot teach emotional intelligence insofar as it is based on the factors identified by Goleman (1998) and discussed earlier in this chapter. Leaders in many ways are discovered, not trained. Zaleznik (2004) indicated that managers are forged through socialization efforts over the course of one's life. Many of these socialization skills can certainly be taught, but leaders "emerge" from this process of self-mastery, through which individuals are driven to pursue psychological and social transformation.

Without doubt, technical skills and knowledge can be imparted through training. And that is the guiding objective underlying the statement in the NACM's (2015) *Core*. The qualities and experiences that result in the emergence of truly effective court leaders, however, cannot be captured and presented in tests, workshops, and similar formats. Leadership is a personal quality gained over time by people who possess qualities that make them open to life's lessons and who relate to others in a particular collaborative way, neither of which can be captured in a lesson plan.

Courts need to seriously consider these dynamics to more fully understand and recognize judicial branch leadership qualities. Courts can nurture and provide those with leadership capacity the broad range of work and life experiences for their leadership qualities to grow and coalesce with their training-based technical skills. To this extent, people can be trained to be leaders, but the court cannot take someone without leadership qualities and train them to be leaders (Kasparek, 2005). Nor should the court take good, even outstanding managers and expect them, necessarily, to be effective court leaders. Finding leaders in a court can be very helpful for several reasons, but it is necessarily a thorough search, not only a series of training workshops or education courses.

The fact that leadership is a convoluted construct is not exclusive to the courts – it is a thorny issue that all organizations must grapple with to remain relevant and to chart a course forward. If it were otherwise, there would not be more than 2.5 billion Google search results for the term "leadership." In the context of courts, the leadership concept presents unique challenges that are even more difficult to fully address. Courts as administrative entities are hydras; in some instances, the presiding judge and court administrator are unable to control many of the heads, some of which view themselves as *in* but not *of* the court. Most every significant organizational change in courts requires genuine broad-scoped collaboration and at times extensive negotiation, both internally and with critical stakeholders. Our experience suggests that most judges understand this reality and intellectually endorse the need for both their presiding judge and court administrator to embody the traits and skills that characterize a leader. In some courts, however, chasms may exist, between this understanding and that held by individuals in "leadership" positions. Robust, fully developed leadership qualities and accompanying strategies are critical for the presiding judge–court administrator team, if the gap is to be narrowed, however daunting the challenges.

Notes

1 Albert Einstein also attributed his "genius" more to curiosity and constantly asking questions than to a unique ability to think or analyze. He may have been unduly modest with this assessment, yet at the same time one can understand his perspective.

2 See also, Eisenhower's, Hanson's, and Hazlitt's quotes, above.

3 This article contains statements by 18 business leaders and scholars about emotional intelligence.

4 Quote is not attributable to any one person and was drawn from Daily Inspirations "quote of the day" publication.

5 In a few cases, judges do not want strong managers, but instead prefer administrators who work more as administrative assistants in a support role. This view of a limited court administrator role has become increasingly rare as the profession of court administration has evolved with a leadership focus in recent decades.

6 Judges are appointed by an executive branch official – normally the governor – or by the legislative branch, or they are elected directly by citizens. No one on a court can remove a judge for any unjust reason. Therefore, some judges may see their responsibility to be only to "the people," as opposed to the institution of the court or to those currently holding leadership positions. For a more detailed explanation of "loosely coupled," see McQueen, M. C. (2013). *Governance: The final frontier*. National Center for State Courts.

7 It also may be noted that some judges consider these same factors when determining whether to follow statewide court rules and, rarely, some statutes.

8 In truth, leaders in the private sector also are not limited to those individuals who have the highest titles. The difference between most courts and most businesses is that the latter actively seek leadership qualities in those given the highest titles. Some presiding judges gain that position with little attention paid to whether they have leadership qualities unless there are two or more judges seeking the position (not common) and enough judges think change is needed so seek out a leader to be the "presiding" judge. As noted above, leadership qualities are not always key factors in choosing a court administrator in some courts either, particularly among those judges who believe the most important quality in a court administrator is management expertise. Every court has its own mix of judges who seek someone with leadership qualities and those who want a good manager for the administrator position; the group with at least a plurality will determine the type of court administrator selected. The decision to seek and select an administrator with more leadership qualities or more management skills may or may not reflect the needs of the court at that moment.

9 Administrators who have been with a court and have gained independent credibility and trust with both the bench and stakeholders over several years may not be checked when they say X or Y will happen, but it takes time for an administrator to build that trust among stakeholders – and, sometimes, amongst court staff.

10 Boilerplate job announcements and set questions from the last time a court administrator was hired will not work. They should be rejected by judges at the outset. In effect, there needs to be a zero-based review each time the administrator is replaced.

11 In one large court to which one of the authors was a consultant, all 25 judges who were committed to implementing a three-year pilot project agreed to a new set of rules for managing civil cases. Within a year of the project's initiation, the judges made so many procedural changes in the rules that the project managers had to develop and distribute a 25-tab notebook for all attorneys showing the current procedures in each courtroom. While a somewhat extreme example of this challenge for all court administrators, this example is indicative of the observation that some judges may view uniform rules as suggestions, not requirements.

12 A "critical mass" in this context in a small court might be one judge. In a larger court, it might be three to six judges.

13 In some jurisdictions, when broad budget cuts are needed in multiple departments and agencies, law enforcement and prosecutors' budgets may be cut less than those of courts, public defense, and corrections, thus creating an imbalance in resources that can adversely affect a court's ability to resolve cases and create and maintain records.

14 Staff who work closely with a judge daily may be exceptions to this reality.

15 It is interesting to note that Bennis's view of leaders corresponds directly with Maslow's Hierarchy of Needs for humans. See also, the "Court Administration Hierarchy of Needs" (in Aikman, 2007).

16 See also General Schwarzkopf's quotation earlier in the chapter.

References

Aikman, A. B. (2007). *The art and practice of court administration.* Taylor & Francis Group.Associated Press. (2006, February 2). STOP – Telegram era over, Western Union says. *NBC News.* www.nbcnews.com/id/wbna11147506.Bennis, W. (2003). *On becoming a leader.* Basic Books.

Blanchard, K. (2000). *Leading at a higher level: Blanchard on leadership and creating high performing organizations.* FT Press.

Briefly. (2005, July 22). *Briefly, the newsletter of the Seventh Judicial District, New York* (Vol. 26, p. 3).

Brown, J. (2016, June 27). *Innovate like da Vinci.* Benedictine University. https://online.ben.edu/programs/business/mba/resources/innovate-like-davinci/.

Bureau of Justice Assistance, & American University. (2005). *Final report: Judicial System Leadership Forum (December 16–17, 2004).*

Burns, J. M. (1978). *Leadership.* Harper & Row.

Collingwood, H. (2001, December). Leadership's first commandment: Know thyself. *Harvard Business Review.*

Contu, D. L. (2004, January). Putting leaders on the couch: A conversation with Manfred F. R. Kets de Vries. *Harvard Business Review.*

Covey, S. R. (1989). *The 7 habits of highly effective people.* Simon & Schuster.

Daskal, L. (2016, March 28). 100 answers to the question: What is leadership? *Inc.* www.inc.com/lolly-daskal/100-answers-to-the-question-what-is-leadership.html.

Drucker, P. F. (1973). *Management: Tasks, responsibilities, practices.* Harper & Row.

Emergenetics. (2026). *The 5 ways to define leadership.* www.emergenetics.com/blog/5-ways-define-leadership/.

Gelb, M. J. (1998). *How to think like Leonardo da Vinci: Seven steps to genius every day.* Delacorte Press.

Goleman, D. (1998). What makes a leader? *Harvard Business Review, 76*(6), 93–102.

Imparato, N., & Harari, O. (1994). *Jumping the curve: Innovation and strategic choice in an age of transition.* Jossey-Bass.

Kasparek, F. D. (2005). *Leading the unfinished reform: The future of third branch administration*. Institute for Court Management, National Center for State Courts.

Leading by feel. (2004, January). *Harvard Business Review, 82*(1), 27–37.

Mayer, J. D., & Salovey, P. (1997). Emotional intelligence: Theory and implications. In P. Salovey & D. Sluyter (Eds.), *Emotional development and emotional intelligence: Educational implications* (pp. 3–31). Basic Books.

National Association for Court Management (NACM). (2004). *Core competency curriculum guidelines: What court leaders need to know and be able to do.*

National Association for Court Management (NACM). (2015). *The core*. https://nacmnet.org/nacm-core/.

National Association for Court Management (NACM). (2016a). *NACM core competencies, purposes and responsibilities*. https://nacmnet.org/nacm-core/.

National Association for Court Management (NACM). (2016b). *The court administrator, Court administration: A guide to the profession.*

On a roll at Audi. (2005, September). *BusinessWeek*. www.businessweek.com/print/innovate/content/sep2005/id20050916_2420.

Stogdill, R. M. (1974). *Handbook of leadership: A survey of theory and research*. Free Press.

Stupak, R. (1999, March). A turning point: From managers to leaders. *Court Communiqué, 1*(2), 1.

Tobin, R. W. (1999). *Creating the judicial branch: The unfinished reform*. National Center for State Courts.

Welch, J., & Welch, S. (2005). *Winning*. HarperBusiness.

Welch, J., & Welch, S. (2006, January 30). The leadership mindset. *Business Week*.

What makes a good leader? (2005, July 10). *Parade*. Intelligence Report.

Zaleznik, A. (2004). Managers and leaders, are they different? *Harvard Business Review, 82*(1), 75–79.

5 Caseflow Management

The Nucleus of Court Administration

Caseflow management is at the center of court administration and serves as the principal means by which the court carries out its purposes and responsibilities. Managing cases is of such critical importance to court administration that the entire profession can essentially be grouped into two general functions – case management and the support of that central function. Thus, although court professionals in these "support functions" may be recognized by virtue of their division's size, scope, and expertise, these entities – human resources, finance, operations – at bottom, exist to support the management and resolution of cases. We further submit that, to the extent these court management functions do not effectively or efficiently support this core responsibility, a re-evaluation of the division's purpose and objectives is warranted.

Caseflow management lies at the center of our model for an important reason: it must inform and permeate all aspects of the organization if the court's purposes and responsibilities are to be fully realized. Caseflow management and its importance to the court administration profession can generally be examined by addressing the following four questions (Fazari & Friesen, 2009): 1) What, precisely, is caseflow management? 2) How are cases "managed"? 3) What are some of the challenges in managing the caseload? 4) Why is caseflow management important to the field of court administration?

Viewed as a "business," the court's primary output is the adjudication of cases, and administrators must not lose sight of this fundamental point; accordingly, an organization exists because of the product it produces, not the functions that merely support it. Consider that, in a utopian scenario in which cases are no longer filed before an impartial, third-party arbitrator, courts would likewise cease to exist. Cases are the reason courts exist – not because they possess areas of expertise that support this function. Figure 5.1 illustrates that purposes and responsibilities encompass the mission and vision of the court, and the organizational culture

DOI: 10.4324/9781003686804-5

informs new and emerging leaders, who in turn shape the policies and practices in managing cases. Case management *is* at the core of what courts *do* (and should do well) in fulfilling their primary mandate – justice – to the public.

Figure 5.1 Nested Framework of Court Purposes, Culture, Leadership, and Caseflow Management

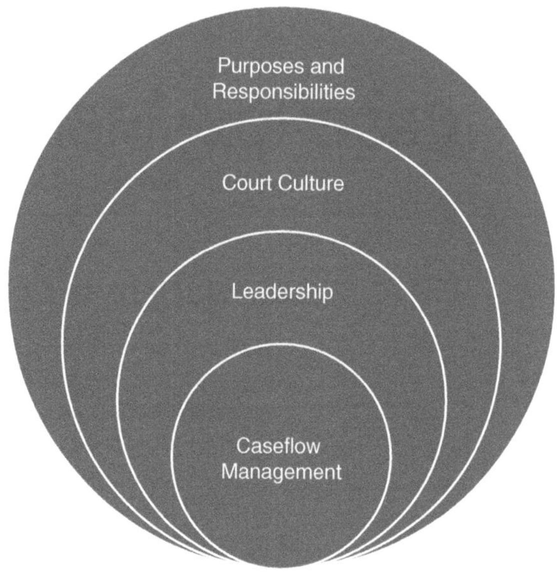

The National Association for Court Management (NACM, 2005) cited caseflow management as one of the core competencies for court leaders. Put succinctly, case management is "the process by which courts convert their inputs (cases) into outputs (dispositions)." The NACM Professional Development Advisory Committee remarked on its importance (Steelman et al., 2000):

> The quality of justice is enhanced when judicial administration is organized around the requirements of effective caseflow management. The quality of this process determines how well courts achieve their most fundamental and substantive objectives and purposes. Properly understood, caseflow management is the absolute heart of court management.

Solomon and associates (2002) defined caseflow management as "the coordinated management by the court of the processes and resources necessary to move each case from filing to disposition, whether that disposition ultimately is by settlement, guilty plea, dismissal, trial, or other method."

Ensuring that each case receives justice is the court's *raison d'etre*. Caseflow management coordinates activities and resources (including the human capital) so that this overarching responsibility is not impeded or otherwise compromised due to unnecessary delay. Delay, perhaps more than any other single factor, vitiates all other efforts made by the court to achieve justice. Hewitt et al. (1990) described delay as "a disease... and a symptom of unhealthy conditions." Indeed, developing methods to reduce and eliminate delay is a fundamental responsibility of a court's leadership, including its managers, because besides discrediting the purposes of the court, it is destructive to its very existence. In their discussion of caseflow management, Steelman and colleagues (2000) cited Ernest Friesen's explanation underscoring the importance of delay reduction:

> The study of delay is not the study of inefficiency, but is the study of the very purposes for which courts exist... Justice is lost with the passage of time... No matter how you look at it, whether it's a civil or a criminal matter, time destroys the purposes of the courts. We study case management because case management is the way we get rid of the waiting time, [by] which we control delay, [and by] which we enhance the purposes of courts. Case management is what we're about in controlling delay.

Delay is defined as the time lawyers and parties need to prepare for the next event that will advance a case closer to disposition that is "unnecessary." Much of what is involved in case management is distinguishing between what is "necessary" and what is "unnecessary." In so doing, managers are primarily responsible for proposing and implementing policy and procedure adopted by judges to mitigate unnecessary delay. As noted in the Trial Court Performance Standards, unnecessary delay "causes injustice and hardship... and is the primary cause of diminished public trust and confidence in the court" (Bureau of Justice Assistance [BJA], 1997). The American Bar Association (ABA, 1986) submitted that unnecessary delay constitutes any elapsed time that falls outside that which can be reasonably expected for court events to occur. While it is possible that processing cases expeditiously can have a negative impact on justice outcomes, research findings from several courts across the country show the opposite to be more likely. However infrequent, we have seen judges who get involved in moving cases "expeditiously," mainly in order to comply with existing case processing time standards – which are goals, not mandates. On those occasions, they neglect the function to provide justice in individual cases. No judge (and manager) should forget that case processing time standards are macro measures that apply to all cases; the need for due process and necessary preparation time in a particular case always should trump case processing time standards. We have had discussions with some judges where they thought administrators and senior managers care solely or primarily that data show that cases were disposed of within existing case processing standards. They know from handling many cases that the time standards need exceptions because of the special circumstances of specific cases. That experience, along with the perception that time standards may, in some cases, undermine judicial discretion – held by some judges as well as attorneys – can be used as a rationale by those who oppose all time standards or fear being judged unfairly if a standard is not met.

Solomon (1993) referenced one judge, who observed that, "while it may be true that 'faster' is not always better, 'slower' is almost always worse." Simply put, case management is not a numbers game, as some contend, but is rather about getting the same or better justice sooner. "The same," because justice remains the primary goal of courts; judges who seek more immediate dispositions at the expense of justice are not using best practices in case management. At the same time, in many courtrooms judges grant "standard" resets (continuances) that automatically include unnecessary time beyond the necessary time. Some judges may do so because they have a symbiotic relationship with the Bar, it is easier while calling a calendar, and calendars are easier to manage if everyone more-or-less follows a common schedule. Opposing attorneys do not object because they know they also will need similar accommodation, often sooner rather than later. No attorney wants to be perceived as the "obstructionist" who is unwilling to cooperate on continuances. Nonetheless, allowing needed time for a continuance but not unnecessary time is critical to achieving a case resolution sooner without adversely impacting justice.

We have experienced many instances where judges will "accommodate" lawyers asking for a continuance that extends well beyond what is needed. In some of these courts, it is seldom asked why a requested reset date (continuance) of X days is needed. They assume that if an attorney asks for X days, they require it. This illustrates the tendency to default to "standard" reset periods rather than case-specific needs. For example, continuance of a trial date for 30 or 60 days often is routine. Questioning the attorney about what remains to be done and why it has not yet been done could show that a week or two would be ample and/or that the attorney had been ill-prepared for justifiable reason. In our experience, most judges rarely wish to publicly identify an attorney as a procrastinator – even when the attorney's reputation suggests it. On the other hand, we have also found that an attorney needs to be so exposed only once for a point to be made. Additionally, word travels fast among the Bar that a judge is willing to ask "why" and will not automatically grant a 30- or 60-day extension. Attorneys generally adjust accordingly (and quickly) to the expectations of judges and will conform to a new reality. Judges are clearly aware that the possibility of a challenge by a disgruntled attorney in the next election presents a potential risk. Fortunately, we are not aware of any judge losing an election because they applied best practices of case management. We are aware, however, of several attorneys who appreciate and praise these judges who facilitate timely case resolution.

"Better" justice is likely when unnecessary delay is reduced because memories fade with time, often causing people to insert facts that did not occur, but that now make a narrative complete. Testimony that occurs closer to an event is more likely an accurate testament than assertions made months or years later. It is also considered superior justice because witnesses and some parties begin to lose interest and commitment when cases seem to be taking too long – or they leave the jurisdiction – risking a loss of justice for one or both parties. A higher quality of service to the public results, too, because businesses in contract and labor disputes are able to restore relationships with the other party when differences have been settled and are made aware of any costs or financial gains from the litigation. Finally, individual parties (and, sometimes, their families) are able to get on with their lives because they know the answers they have been seeking through the lawsuit and the anxiety of the unknown disappears.

The term "caseflow" is somewhat misleading, in that it insinuates cases moving through the judiciary at an uninterrupted set pace. Clearly, this is not what happens in reality. Rather than resembling a river running smoothly downstream, once filed, cases are in a "stop-and-go" pattern progressing through a series of "locks" until they reach their destination (resolution). The type of disposition reached sometimes governs the destination's distance, although too-often, all cases progress (or not) on the same schedule. Local factors such as resources, personnel, leadership, and court culture often explain differences in the pace of litigation in different courts. A factor contributing to delay may be acceptable in one jurisdiction, but not in another (Mahoney & Sipes, 1985). The life of a case thus consists of a series of events that are separated by varying lengths of time. Managing the caseflow involves an assurance that these events are meaningful; that is, the activity and preparation required for the event to take place on the scheduled date will enable the case to move closer to resolution and it is completed before that date by all involved stakeholders.

The idea of managing the courts, and specifically their cases, began shortly after World War II, when the Chief Justice of New Jersey (NJ), Arthur Vanderbilt, established an administrative office to carry out the court's policy. In 1948, he appointed Edward B. McConnell to head the organization. McConnell, the nation's first state court administrator chosen to be a manager,[1] later went on to become the president of the National Center for State Courts (NCSC) in 1973 and served in that capacity until 1990 (Tobin, 1997). The NJ model that began during the late 1940s, however, did not catch on in other states until the 1960s. Court administration, therefore, remained a largely emerging profession for many years (Friesen, 2002). During that time, 26 states followed NJ's lead and established administrative offices (Steelman et al., 2000). Between 1970 and 1980, the number of court administrators with management training grew from 50 to more than 500 (Solomon, 1987). Relative to other areas of study, caseflow management is still in its infancy, although with the pioneering efforts of the NCSC and professional court associations, progress has been rapid. Today, while many internal stakeholders are educated in the lexicon and methods of case management, administrators will find it a perpetual challenge to impress upon many of them the importance of this central function. Consequently, training in and knowledge of good caseflow management remains paramount to a court's success.

Our experiences at this juncture continue to support the earlier conjecture, that there is "some slippage across the nation toward a more passive role regarding caseflow management" (Aikman, 2007), shifting away from robust, proactive caseflow management and toward a court role focused primarily on managing calendars rather than actively directing the pace of litigation. As this pattern becomes evident across the trial courts, it reflects a corresponding widening of the gap in achieving the *ne plus ultra* of case management envisioned by administrators and judicial leadership. Chief among our findings is that for all the progress that researchers and experts have made in studying caseflow management, much work remains to be done. We will delve more specifically into the principles of leadership, stakeholder collaboration, and strategic management in those respective chapters, but insofar as these principles relate to fundamentals of caseflow management, we provide a scholarly overview and couple it with our experiential relevance.

Leadership and Vision

There exist several techniques to manage the caseflow; however, a few concepts have been universally accepted and proven to be successful. We refer to them as the "fundamentals of caseflow management" and integral to the archetype is the court's leadership and the vision it conveys for the organization. The ten essential ingredients were first identified by Mahoney and colleagues (1988) and include: leadership, goals, information, communication, caseflow management procedures, judicial responsibility and commitment, administrative staff involvement, education and training, mechanisms for accountability, and backlog reduction/inventory control. More recently, Solomon et al. (2002) highlighted the following seven fundamentals (and outlined heretofore) of an effective caseflow management system:

1) Judicial leadership and commitment to court management of the pace of litigation.
2) Consultation by the court with the organized bar and criminal justice agencies regarding caseflow policies, procedures, and performance.
3) Court supervision of case progress from filing to final disposition.
4) Time standards and operational goals for case processing.
5) Court control of continuances.

6) A credible scheduling system that assures that court events occur on the first scheduled date.
7) A case monitoring and information system to monitor the caseload and to identify any cases that are in danger of exceeding established time limits and goals.

The ABA (1986) described effective case management systems similarly purporting that the court must have early and continuous control of the case, events must be predictable and scheduled over short timeframes, and case processing time standards should be established and maintained through a performance monitoring system. Ostrom and Hanson (1999) submitted that in order to achieve efficiency, timeliness, and quality, a court should adopt a three-step strategy comprised of self-diagnosis (processes are examined and goals are set), communication (goals and their basis are explained), and education (training programs for judges, court personnel, and stakeholders emphasizing efficiency, rather than delay reduction).

Aspects of these recommendations, however, also rely on silver tongued leaders to impress and motivate internal and external stakeholders in doing their part to achieve the court's vision. Ultimately, what the literature and practical experience demonstrates is that much of the difference between successful and unsuccessful courts has to do with its leadership and the culture that shapes their organizational environments. In this respect (and perhaps only in this regard), the court is not unlike any other organization, public or private.

The NACM (2005) enumerated the following factors impacting the court's ability to process both simple and complex case types (emphasis added):

- Court system and trial court organization and authority relationships, including the *management of judges by judges*
- The identification, development, selection, and succession of chief judges and court managers, *chief judge/court manager executive leadership teams*, and the best use of these and other multi-disciplinary executive teams
- *Allocation of court resources*: judges, managerial, technical and administrative staff; budgets; technology; and courthouses, courtrooms, and other facilities across courts, court divisions, case types, and particular types of hearings
- *Application of court technology* and the court's research, data, and analytic capability
- *Coordination* with the judiciary's justice system partners

The concept and principles of caseflow management are well researched and while the literature admittedly shows that no universal approach can be applied by the courts in managing their filings, successful courts are characterized by the noted fundamentals, which are incidentally proven to work in practice. Differences in backlog and overall efficiency are assessed in parallel with the values and norms of each court; that is, its court culture – the tone and tenor of which is often established before the administrator's arrival, and which altogether cannot be entirely controlled. On several levels, therefore, caseflow management is an inherently complex undertaking which presents a host of challenges that can elude the administrator, given their limited span of control and influence. Those intangibles aside, there are concrete aspects of case management within the administrator's purview, such as the collection, monitoring, and evaluation of performance data, which can, albeit slowly, shape the culture to be more efficient and accountable with respect to its processes.

Peak (2004) examined court administrators' perceptions of the sources of conflict within their profession and found that caseflow management was a major contributor. Participants in the study mentioned, among other things, backlogs and judges' calendaring and adjournments of matters as critical areas of concern. These findings are in accord with results of other studies and our experience working in a variety of courts. Many judges viewed caseflow management as judicial in nature and were consequently reticent in delegating it to an administrator. Some even question why administrators should show any concern about case management and data related to it. Research supports this experience, showing that caseflow management is one of the ten *least*-delegated responsibilities among judges. Research cited by Dubois and Boyum (1993) proposed that the presiding judge take a more assertive role in handling cases to induce their disposition. A clear paradox thus exists, wherein, while caseflow management is typically identified as one of the primary duties of court administrators, it is generally not an area over which they have complete, or in some cases even partial, control.

Administrators' range of caseflow authority and their ability to therefore lead the court can vary from one court to another. This suggests in obvious ways that the court's leadership and organizational culture can profoundly affect administrator functions, including those fundamental to the position. Indeed, this can be taken a step further in stating that the "cultures" and expectations of individual courts within the same district can operate in very different ways, and unless the presiding judge has the willingness and influence to get the judges to support activity aligned with the vision, there could be a broad range of "working styles." For instance, one judge expected the case management supervisor to be a proactive manager, meaning preparing and summarizing a daily report that included recommendations on priority of scheduling based on backlog measures, to present it in the court each day to staff, and to collaborating with attorneys on trial readiness of pending matters. Another judge in the same district (and same division) directed his team's supervisor: "don't come to the courtroom unless I call you."

Stakeholder Consultation

There are profound differences among courts impacting their management of cases (some of which are beyond the reach of the court), some of which include resources, personnel, organizational policies and procedures, legislative mandates, external politics, and relationships with local stakeholders of those agencies that are loosely coupled to the courts. Studies have shown that cases are generally disposed of by attorneys – not judges or juries. Tobin (1999) found that while factors such as indiscriminate scheduling, relaxed continuance standards, and lack of accountability and case information contribute to delay, the most significant cause was the court's lack of control over *actual* case processing. Previous research also found that with regard to criminal matters, the procedures employed by the prosecutor's office and police department have a significant impact on case processing time (Mahoney et al., 1988).

The collection and analysis of data must be centered on the need to compare perceptions of case processing to actual performance and experience to appropriately develop and target policy and procedure for adherence to established guidelines and to meet year-end goals. Therefore, while the formulation of policy and procedure should be grounded on caseflow management principles, it must (in reality) bring to bear and not discount the experiences of local stakeholders, who can impact policy and practice outcomes. Ultimately, the success of case management rests with them. Sipes and associates (1980) observed:

> Case processing statistics should be supplemented by information obtained from judges and lawyers concerning actual operation of the litigation process. This qualitative information when combined with the quantitative information produces a profile of the local legal culture. More specifically, what is learned from participants in the litigation process often explains the pace of litigation, particularly between important events, and helps the court to assess where improvement is needed and feasible.

Because of differences in influence and resources, the local conditions and culture of the court must be considered when formulating case management policy and procedure. Gallas (1976) argued that in light of varying dynamics and factors that pervade the court from one district to another, there is no single approach in managing all court environments. Trial courts are unique and at the same time very complex because, inter alia, they operate with limited control over individuals (jurors, law enforcement, attorneys, witnesses, corrections, etc.), who can significantly influence the caseflow direction. This loosely coupled system incorporates individuals and groups whose competing interests and objectives do not necessarily correlate with efficient caseflow. Fetter (1993) described the structure as a fragmented one. These divisions make prospective analysis (policy futures) especially challenging because of interagency reliance on resources. Etzioni (1964) denoted the trial court as a "large, complex social unit in which many social groups interact. While these groups share some interests, they also have incompatible interests."

Court Supervision

In accordance with the prior fundamental, the courts cannot force case resolutions to occur. Cases are resolved when stakeholders have what they believe is adequate information upon which to act. Supervising the court entails setting clear expectations for attorneys so that they are understood and communicated to their clients. To that end, there are four axioms associated with this fundamental (Institute for Court Management [ICM], 2016):

1) Lawyers settle cases, not judges
2) Lawyers settle cases when prepared
3) Lawyers prepare for significant events
4) Decision-makers decide when they have sufficient information to act

These axioms apply fully to self-represented litigants, too, but possibly not with the same force as they apply to lawyers. Along this vein, there are four principles in overseeing the progress of a case that engender a culture of expectation (ICM, 2016):

1) Early court control
2) Continuous court control
3) On a schedule that incorporates enough time to prepare, but short enough so that it encourages preparation
4) Create the expectation and reality that events will occur when scheduled[2]

Case management is about controlling time such that "any elapsed time beyond what is reasonably required for pleadings, motions, and court events is eliminated" and thus, managing the caseflow effectively is important because it is critical to reducing delay (ABA, 1986). Despite claims by some stakeholders to the contrary, delay is not inevitable and research in support of this statement is clear. Moving a case from filing to disposition is a robust test of the court's effectiveness. Quite simply, the prevalence of delay relates directly to a court's commitment to reduce it.

Church and associates (1978) concluded that the pace of litigation is associated with the way a court manages its cases. Two important findings substantiate this argument. First, the best predictor in efficient disposition was the court's early and continuous control of events. Incidentally, caseload size per judge was inconsequential to the speed of disposition. This was echoed by Goerdt et al. (1987), who found that criminal case delay is generally not caused by large caseloads or a limited number of judges. There was, however, a threshold to this initial point whereby the caseload per judge cannot grow indefinitely without impacting even the best-managed courts. At some point, increases in caseload must be addressed by adding judgeships.[3] Second, effective screening and monitoring of criminal cases was associated with efficient caseflow management. These findings are encouraging because unlike court size and caseload, establishing and maintaining a protocol for moving cases through the system is within the court's control.

In an ongoing effort to manage their caseloads more effectively, courts have experimented with different types of calendaring systems including individual, master, and hybrid.[4] Church et al. (1978) found that data do not support one method of calendaring over another. Likewise, research found no analogous relationship between a type of calendaring system and the pace of litigation for criminal cases (Goerdt et al., 1987; Mahoney et al., 1988). Goerdt and associates (1987) favored individual over master calendaring because the former compares individual judge activity. Generally speaking, given the competitive nature of judges, the researchers argued that it served as an incentive for judges to be more productive in their day-to-day activity, thereby reducing delay. Having said that, we have seen instances where the competitive nature of some judges has had a negative effect on parties and the case management process. In these instances, highly competitive judges have put being "first" on the list and keeping processing time low at times ahead of individual justice in individual cases. We also have seen clerks chastised and held accountable for not keeping the judge's statistics up to date or entering case information incorrectly, so the judge does not continue to be first or second on the list of dispositions and the time to disposition. These responses are obviously inconsistent with "the same or better justice sooner" and are not part of sound case management.

Zorza (2002) also preferred individual calendaring, particularly for self-represented clients in family cases, because of the continuity that it establishes in the process. When cases are assigned to individual judges for the life of the case, individuals become more acquainted with the court, the personnel, and their practices. This familiarity makes court participants feel less isolated and the process less ambiguous. It also provides the judge with familiarity with the case and its litigants, and the parties with continuity in rulings. Tobin (1999) showed support for the individual scheduling method, but mentioned that a master calendar system gives the presiding judge the most latitude in matching cases with the strengths and expertise of particular judges. The drawback is obviously overburdening the most efficient judges, who may feel that they are being punished for meeting performance goals. Because evidence does not support one system over another, the most successful approach (again) may have more to do with what works best in a particular court, given the preferences of the individual judges and specific conditions.

Delay results when the process of moving the case from filing to disposition is protracted by the assigned attorney (not the court). Research indicates that the pace of case processing and backlog are influenced by the expectations, practices, and informal behavioral norms of judges and attorneys (Goerdt et al., 1987). The suggestion here is that disparities in backlog and pending cases may have more to do with the court's culture than differences in resources (Mahoney et al., 1988). This finding is supported by research in both domestic and foreign courts (Weatherburn & Baker, 2000). In particular, the literature emphasized "norms, relationships, and incentives of criminal court participants" as having the most significant impact on case processing (Goerdt et al., 1987). Ostrom and Hanson (1999) concluded that caseflow rate was the end product of the attitudes and expectations of judges and attorneys.

In some instances, a professional courtesy develops among adversaries, resulting in a high tolerance for continuances such that motions to disallow adjournments are less frequent or taken less seriously in courts with an elevated continuance rate. Abadinsky (2008) purported that lawyers and judges become socialized into the traditions of the organization. Once comfort settles in, attorneys, in particular, have a stake in the status quo because of the advantages reaped from an organization with which they have rapport and familiarity. Therefore, to make significant progress toward reducing delay, the behavior patterns of both the court and attorneys must be analyzed (Sipes et al., 1980). Once problem areas have been uncovered, reform measures to enhance efficiency do not come effortlessly. One particular judge who had overseen a variety of case types throughout his tenure admitted to one of us with respect to camaraderie that, "the criminal division is the best division to work in because it's generally the same people and lawyers that you're dealing with every day." While this can make the environment more hospitable, it can create a communal atmosphere where the judge seeks to build consensus around stakeholders, which can set a low expectation bar and dilute management efforts to increase accountability and enhance performance.

Standards and Goals (the Same or Better Justice Sooner)

Active caseflow management is fundamental to a successful program. This relies in part on research including generic caseload statistics, impact studies, and longitudinal reports, from which the manager can juxtapose to established standards and goals to make informed decisions and recommendations to the court (Saari et al., 1993). It is important to note that even in districts where case management was successful, there was chronic pressure from some attorneys to relax standards (Mahoney et al., 1988). Table 5.1

illustrates the Model Time Standards for State Trial Courts for selected case types (NCSC, 2011). Prior to the adoption of model standards in August, 2011, separate sets of time standards were promulgated by the Conference of State Court Administrators (COSCA) and the ABA.[5] Information systems from which reports are generated provide a framework by which administrators can operationalize goals and assess the court's performance with respect to those objectives.

Table 5.1 Model Time Standards for State Courts

Case Category	***Case Type***	***Model Standard***
Criminal	Felony	75% within 90 days 90% within 180 days 98% within 365 days
Criminal	Misdemeanor	75% with 60 days 90% within 90 days 98% within 180 days
Civil	General Civil	75% within 180 days 90% within 365 days 98% within 540 days
Family	Dissolution/Divorce	75% within 120 days 90% within 180 days 98% within 365 days
Juvenile	Delinquency and Status Offense: Youth Not in Detention	75% within 60 days 90% within 90 days 98% within 150 days
Juvenile	Neglect and Abuse	98% within 90 days of removal
Probate	Administration of Estates	75% within 360 days 90% within 540 days 98% within 720 days
Probate	Guardianship/ Conservatorship	98% within 90 days
Probate	Civil Commitment	98% within 15 days

Control Continuances

Solomon (1973) described the "continuance conundrum" as a self-reinforcing cycle in which attorney lack of readiness repeatedly generates requests for continuances. When courts routinely grant such requests, an insufficient number of cases are available for resolution to sustain judges' workload. To compensate for the low workload, courts schedule an unrealistically high volume of cases. Cases positioned low on the trial list are then not reached, reinforcing attorneys' expectations that preparation is unnecessary. This lack of readiness, in turn, results in further continuance requests, perpetuating the cycle of delay.

Although the importance of controlling continuances is a well-established research finding and a standard recommendation of effective case management, limiting the number of continuances generally proves to be more complicated in practice. When not adequately managed, however, continuances devolve into a cycle that may disproportionately advantage one side over the other and erodes the public's trust and confidence.[6] Other costs include the increased burden on staff, witnesses, victims, and other stakeholders, additional resources that are needed to reschedule the same events, jail overcrowding impacted by custody defendants awaiting disposition, and the multiplier effect when relatively simple matters become more complex with the passage of time.

Adjournments are an enduring feature of court operations. Effectively moderating their impact is still all the same important requiring courts to establish an "atmosphere of expectation" and then operationalizing that expectation in their day-to-day practices. To reiterate, adjournments on the whole cannot be eliminated, however, successful courts understand the distinction (and implications of the conundrum) of time that should be granted for *this* case on *this* occasion, as opposed to time regularly afforded to an ill-prepared party. Successful courts are good at making these expectations clear to stakeholders, and more importantly, enforced.

Courts that operationalize the atmosphere of expectation do so through a variety of practices. In our experience, the courts that manage continuances optimally always required attorneys (and pro se litigants) to document their request in a motion and submit it to the court at least two (sometimes three) business days prior to the event, so that the judge has ample time to review. Attorneys, in particular, may be more inclined to reconsider requests for adjournment when such requests require the submission of a documented justification and when the stated grounds for postponement become part of the public record.[7] This is especially true if, historically, the court has mostly denied requests for continuances. We say "mostly" because circumstances will inevitably arise when the court will (and should) grant an adjournment in the interest of justice to reasonably accommodate the party.[8] Having said that, when allowing a postponement for good cause, these courts document the finding on the record for two reasons: First, to ensure individual justice in individual cases (including the perception of fairness), and second, to solidify expectations of the caseflow process.

Continuances can have extraordinary consequences for the court and are a force to be reckoned with, particularly in those districts where the Bar wields considerable influence and power. Consider the master calendar system in one court, where the lead judge routinely granted adjournments to most attorneys. The resulting volume of adjournments exacerbated the backlog and adversely affected the caseload of each judge in the division. Costs increased to manage the growing workload, and the additional administrative tasks associated with each continuance negatively affected the morale of court staff and administrators. Centralizing requests to adjourn cases or extend plea cutoff dates can be effective only if the judge deciding those requests adheres to fundamental caseflow principles. In this particular court, the judge managing the calendar was highly popular among attorneys due to his willingness to grant most requests, to the extent that the political influence of the State Bar Association prevented the presiding judge from either implementing meaningful changes to the calendar system or (more simply) reassigning the judge to a different division. Consequently, for many years, efforts to address backlog issues in the division were only partially effective, as the day-to-day actions of the calendar-managing judge were not aligned with the broader caseflow plan.

In another court operating under an individual calendar system, attorneys granted an adjournment, along with their clients, were required to complete the appropriate paperwork documenting the rescheduled date and time.[9] These courts also employed "green sheets," stapled to the cover of each case jacket. The conspicuously colored document recorded all case events, including any adjournments granted and their reasons. Calendar clerks reviewed the green sheets and consulted with the judge prior to the day's calendar. In this high-volume court, the system created the impression that the judge had the "memory of an elephant," when in reality they were relying on this simple yet effective method to refresh their recall.[10] Assigned personnel kept judges informed both at the micro level – tracking the progress of individual cases – and at the macro level – ensuring that the daily calendar did not exceed the number of cases that could reasonably be reached. Courts employing these practices were empirically more efficient, as cases tended to settle sooner rather than later while progressing toward a trial date.

Mahoney and colleagues (1988) found that delays are mitigated when judges establish reasonable expectations for attorneys to follow in scheduling court events and trials. Delay most often occurs when the judge and attorneys accept "standard" continuance timeframes and multiple adjournments are unchallenged and granted as an ordinary expectation of case processing. While the court is charged with controlling the pace of litigation, the consensus among judges and attorneys must be that unnecessary delay is first, a problem, and second, unacceptable before any strategy to reduce it will have long-term effects (ABA, 1986). Aikman (2007) asserted that the judge is responsible for managing cases and thus controlling continuances. Staff and administration, albeit essential, are ancillary role players:[11]

> Caseflow management consumes a significant portion of a court's resources... and those responsible for generating statistical reports to advise judges about the status of their caseloads should be deemed mission critical to the caseflow management function.

While delay corrodes the purposes of courts, it is not always viewed as detrimental by attorneys. Glick (1982) asserted that justice delayed is not necessarily justice denied in the perspective of attorneys, who use delay strategically to reach a settlement, prepare more meticulously for the case, and to acquire more clients than they would otherwise have time to represent.[12] This can be especially advantageous for the defense attorney whose client is not in custody. Consider, for instance, that memories fade, victims may become less inclined to testify, and witnesses are more likely to relocate with the passage of time – all of which can contribute to an argument of "reasonable doubt." Munsterman and associates (1998) indicated that adjournments, particularly in criminal cases, tend to benefit the defendant. Apart from this, they contended that repeated postponements cause the court to lose its ability to manage the case. Defense attorneys also resist speedy dispositions in some cases because expediting the matter results in not being fully compensated by their client. Some prosecutors refer to cases where they did not seek a speedy disposition as "dogs," indicative of those matters which lack the necessary evidence from which a jury would likely convict the defendant. They were especially unmotivated when defendants were in custody awaiting trial. While the case could ultimately get dismissed, the defendant spends an indeterminate period of time in jail providing the state its "pound of flesh."[13]

There is an alternative perspective among attorneys regarding delay. Prosecutors generally favor the absence of delay because "bad guys" will plead guilty or be found guilty sooner and begin serving their sentences. The testimony of the state's witnesses is more likely to be accurate when the case is resolved more quickly. Criminal defendants also benefit from reduced delay. While it is generally accepted that memories fade, it is less often recognized that over time human nature tends to fill those gaps with experiences that, while they may "feel" or "sound" right, are not entirely accurate reflections of what actually occurred. Witnesses' accounts that they believe to be "true" may, in fact, be more detrimental to a defendant than a more accurate rendition. The same principle applies in civil matters. In some instances, defendants in corporate and civil litigation can use delay strategically to exert financial pressure while simultaneously increasing the overall emotional toll on plaintiffs. They calculate that the additional cost of these delays is less than the potential loss in a more expedited settlement. Tobin (1999) noted that, although attorneys may publicly endorse caseflow management, their private views of the practices – and of those who implement them – are often ambivalent. Many attorneys harbor significant reservations about caseflow management because of its impact on their ability to control the pace of litigation; in some cases, the degree of control over pacing determines whether their objectives are achieved.[14] There are numerous anecdotes from practitioners with whom we have interacted and consulted supporting these perspectives, but we are not aware of any empirical study that provides broad evidence of these realities. The point is that, as with most complex issues, there is rarely a single answer, including regarding the value of delay to attorneys and their clients.

Early Resolutions

The notion of efficient case management which court leaders employ is probably best understood within the context of differentiated case management (DCM). In its simplest terms, a DCM program tracks cases in accordance with relative level of complexity. This implies that all cases are not managed the same with respect to the rate at which and procedures through which they are resolved (BJA, 1993). DCM involves the court and attorneys addressing three questions (Solomon et al., 2002). First, approximately how much calendar time will this type of case normally and fairly require to reach disposition? Second, how much effort will the attorney need to invest in resolving the case? Third, how much judicial supervision will be needed for a just and timely resolution? These three questions are designed to maximize the availability of the court's two most valuable resources: judicial time and attention, ensuring that cases which require (or would benefit most from) such focus can receive it. DCM preserves justice because groups of cases, irrespective of case type, resolve with little or no judicial attention. Indeed, most cases can be resolved with modest judicial attention (one or two conferences with a judge, a limited number of hearings, and, in most instances, settlement or a plea); a relatively small number and percent of cases deserve and require significant judicial time because of their factual complexity, significant and/or new legal issues, or some other unique factor(s) such as a murder charge, a class action, or a multifaceted divorce matter. Lists of variables used to examine case complexity are not exhaustive. Other, unexamined factors identified in the literature may also influence the pace of litigation. While court administrators are encouraged to consider such intangible criteria, research typically focuses on factors that are more readily definable within the scope of a given study (Fazari & Ijoma, 2009).

Before DCM, many courts operated under a "FIFO" (first in, first out) approach. Under this approach, all cases are treated alike, and disposition is generally driven by both filing date and level of complexity (Bakke & Solomon, 1989). Solomon and Somerlot (1987) suggested that while all cases must be managed, the amount of time afforded in managing the case should be centered on its characteristics. Henderson et al. (1990) noted that DCM has potential cost savings for the court, but were careful in drawing cost–benefit conclusions because the expenses that were directly attributable to DCM were difficult to quantify.

In most courts, DCM includes three case management tracks, albeit research has supported the position that the number of tracks should reflect the requirements of the individual court rather than some arbitrary model.[15] The first level is often referred to as *expedited* because cases tend to be the most simple, meaning the facts and law normally are not as contentious as other cases so they can be resolved by the attorneys without a lot of discovery (and discovery disputes), motions, and, therefore, judicial attention. These cases often move through the system with relative ease, require minimal judicial intervention, and should not be expected to go into backlog.[16] The second level of cases, often termed *standard*, are more difficult than expedited cases. While they rarely involve unique circumstances or pose challenging legal questions, and the typical pattern of facts seldom raises unusual discovery issues, they nonetheless demand more of the court's time for motions and conferences to resolve disputes. The third level is commonly referred to as the *complex* track. For various reasons, cases are assigned to this category because of the time and difficulty that the matter is expected to engender, normally because of complex fact scenarios, challenging legal issues, other special circumstances, and/or multiple parties (Steelman et al., 2000).[17]

Complex cases typically require intensive judicial oversight and a greater amount of court resources and time. Solomon and Somerlot (1987) contended that these case types should be assigned to a judge once the determination has been made that the case is complex so that a disposition plan can be developed as soon after filing as possible. Expected disposition time should be based on its level of complexity (the track to be determined early in the process), rather than its filing date.

Notorious or high-profile cases tend to be complex, but setting a reasonable (but firm) trial date is a critical factor in managing the case. Together with the other fundamentals, the trial date sets the tone from which attorneys are expected to schedule and complete all other events leading up to the trial (Munsterman et al., 1998). Research by Goerdt and associates (1987) was consistent with this finding in that "a firm trial date policy (i.e., a high percentage of jury trial cases starting on the first scheduled trial date) was the best predictor of faster case processing times." While some judges and attorneys may agree with this approach, others disagree, asserting that at least for civil cases, a trial date should be scheduled two to three months from the filing date, after discovery so attorneys can assess the strength of their case and decide if a trial is in the best interest of their clients. Setting a trial date 18 to 24 months in the future, and ensuring that the date is feasible for both the court and the parties, can present a significant challenge. Similar considerations apply in criminal cases. A trial date scheduled 30 to 45 days out conveys a tangible sense of urgency to the defendant, only surpassed by the moment jurors enter the courtroom. In contrast, a date set 6–12 months ahead exerts little pressure on either the attorneys or the defendant to move toward resolution.

Apart from high-profile cases, studies have suggested that designating cases into a complex track is a highly individualized process; that is, there are no formulas that can be universally applied in making this distinction.[18] Steelman and associates (2000) stated that "a court might determine that its cases need even further differentiation than can be accommodated within this simple three-part scheme."

Bakke and Solomon (1989) believed that no case is presumptively complex. They posited that attorneys have the burden of distinguishing the case as complex and must justify the classification to the court before additional time is granted. This was the process that we observed in a variety of courts, wherein attorneys were responsible for specifying the appropriate track after which administrators would review and approve in consultation with the court. Heise (2004) posited that criminal cases generally *become* complex for three reasons: 1) evidence is technical in nature or difficult to obtain; 2) legislation relevant to the case is unclear; and 3) characteristics of the case (multiple defendants, gang involvement of defendant(s), victim, and/or witnesses) complicates the matter. Aside from this, there is occasionally a "scaling effect" in what constitutes a complex case based on the attorney's experience. While judges cannot prevent all errors that an attorney may make due to inexperience, they can help moderate the learning curve by providing impartial guidance on the record.

The methods that courts have used to institute DCM have varied because, among other reasons, joint assessments in the need and desire to incorporate the practice are based on local court conditions. For instance, when DCM was first introduced in one trial court, administrators used a pre-indictment disposition conference event to determine whether the case would be pleaded, diverted, or assigned to one of three tracks. In another county, DCM was originally used only for drug cases. Screening guidelines were developed in classifying each drug case to a specific track (Bakke & Solomon, 1989). Zorza (2002) noted a triage model for cases with self-represented litigants. The model defined complex cases as those "more likely to cause delay and injustice." These cases would be tracked separately and supervised more intensively. The criteria used to determine the level of complexity included: number of claims and counterclaims, number of parties, type of case, prior history of litigation, quality of pleadings, amount of money at stake, interpersonal history between the litigants, and the likelihood that the relationship will continue into the future.

Tobin (1999) asserted that differentiating cases based on complexity has been one of the greatest contributions of caseflow management. He found, however, that tracking cases as simply a misdemeanor or felony was not conducive to effective management. Other categories in differentiating criminal cases included: seriousness of charges, likelihood of plea, diversion alternatives, drug involvement, case complexity with regard to parties, issues, and witnesses, jail status of defendant, and constitutional issues such as search-and-seizure. Analyzing the length of criminal jury trials in nine jurisdictions, Sipes and Oram (1988) compared the complexity of cases using the following indicators: number of defendants, number and type of attorneys, number of and time for witnesses, and quantity of exhibits. Table 5.2 illustrates the complexity criteria considered by the Berrien County Court, Michigan, in tracking its criminal cases (Cooper et al., 1993).

Table 5.2 Criminal DCM Tracking Criteria in Berrien County, Michigan

Complexity Criteria		
Low Complexity Factors	***Medium Complexity Factors***	***High Complexity Factors***
• Police witness only • Simple motions (two or fewer) • Motions requiring evidence hearing of less than a half day • Less than five or six witnesses (total prosecution and defense)	• Multiple motions (three or more) • Expert witnesses necessary (other than drug analyst) • Out-of-state witnesses • Motion(s) requiring evidence hearing of a half day or longer	• Psychiatric defense / issue of competency to stand trial • Multiple motions involving complex legal issues • Extraordinary number of witnesses to be called • Defendant under interstate complaint or in prison

Cooper et al. (1993) suggested that tracking cases by their composition is important because complexity is not always determined by case type alone. For instance, a drug case, which is ostensibly simple and can be readily disposed, can be delayed given the characteristics of the case. A buy-and-bust drug case with a single defendant, a single buyer, and a police witness are relatively routine matters. Conversely, a drug kingpin case with several defendants and that involves wiretapping is quite different and requires considerably more time to dispose. Research into nine criminal trial courts showed that all the courts took a longer period of time to resolve complex cases, as compared to resolution times for simpler cases. In particular, murder and rape cases took longer to adjudicate than other case types. The time to disposition was, nonetheless, shorter in efficient courts.

Keilitz (1993) found that some civil courts use summary jury trials. The approach, which can help to decrease the burden on court resources while eliciting a timelier resolution, allows attorneys to synthesize evidence and reduce witness testimony. Verdicts are only advisory and provide the parties with an objective evaluation of the strengths and weaknesses of the case to compel them to be more flexible in their plea negotiations (ABA, 1986). Judges in another study overwhelmingly believed that it was the responsibility of the bench to control the length of the trial. In courts where trials were the longest, both judges and lawyers were more likely than in venues where it was shorter to report that trial time was, in fact, too long (Sipes & Oram, 1988). Overall, both research findings and practical experience indicate that a court's trial management policies and practices play a critical role in its handling of the caseload. Determining the appropriate course of action should not elude the bench, despite the numerous impediments that all courts encounter. In the rarest of cases, however, some courts fail to meet performance standards due to the institution's limited commitment to controlling delay and its insufficient efforts to develop an effective case management program.

The DCM model is also central to the civil justice reform initiative spearheaded several years ago by the Conference of Chief Justices (CCJ, 2016). This initiative recommends that courts establish early case triage, "mandatory pathway" assignment systems, and placement of cases in one of three flexible pathways: streamlined, complex, or general. The initiative also calls for use of alternative dispute resolution mechanisms for each pathway. The report states, in part (CCJ, 2016):

> For right-size case management to become the norm, not the exception, courts must provide judges and court staff with training that specifically supports and empowers right sized case management. Courts should partner with bar leaders to create programs that educate lawyers about the requirements of newly instituted case management practices.

Information Systems

Case management exists in all courts; the difference is how cases are managed. This variation is inherently tied to the extent to which courts adhere to the purposes and responsibilities – the mission and foundational elements of the judiciary – and to the ongoing commitment of judges to accept and implement policies and procedures grounded in best practices. Information is critical to any case management system.[19] The NCSC's CourTools' (2005) case management measures (clearance rate, time to disposition, age of active pending caseload, and trial date certainty) represent a good starting point, which should be collected, analyzed, and promulgated on a monthly basis to all judges. In general, the measures provide guidance for where the court should look to for more depth.[20] If for no other purpose, it provides the courts with the necessary information to gauge performance and to identify trends in caseload data. For the administrator, it is critical that any failure by the judge occurs despite the information provided, rather than as a result of insufficient information. Other reports that are reviewed on a daily or weekly basis should be reviewed to determine applicability to current processing realities. The court may conclude that while some reports are no longer needed or used by judges' teams, others may need to be created.[21]

The CourTools

The NCSC (2005) promulgated ten trial court performance measures, referred to as CourTools. The NCSC highlighted five reasons why managers should utilize CourTools in evaluating the court's performance. First, the empirical data offered by the measurements allows the court to develop policy and procedure based on outcomes that are consistent with reality, rather than perceptions or anecdotal information, which may not be entirely accurate and factually representative. Second, the measurements focus on aspects of the operation that have the greatest impact on court users, thereby ensuring that resources are directed to these areas. Third, given that the measures focus on outcomes, they foster creativity among court staff in developing innovative means to achieve desired ends. Fourth, the CourTools allow the court to articulate its resource and budgetary needs, while maintaining accountability through evidence-based data. Lastly, since courts operate largely from a budget funded by taxpayers, the public is entitled to objective data by which they can evaluate performance (NCSC, 2006). When the court assesses its own performance and acknowledges its accomplishments and areas of needed improvement, its ability to autonomously govern the role and responsibilities of the third branch of government is strengthened.

The second (clearance rate), third (time to disposition), fourth (age of active pending), and fifth (trial date certainty) measures in CourTools provide a methodology by which judges and court managers can examine their case management system performance. Clearance rate is defined as the number of concluded cases as a percentage of the number of incoming cases. The purpose of the measure is to determine (NCSC, 2005):

> Whether the court is keeping up with its incoming caseload. If cases are not disposed in a timely manner, a backlog of cases awaiting disposition will grow. This measure is a single number that can be compared within the court for any and all case types, from month to month and year to year, or between one court and another. Knowledge of clearance rates by case type can help a court pinpoint emerging problems and indicate where improvements may be made. Courts should aspire to clear (i.e., dispose of) at least as many cases as have been filed/reopened/reactivated in a period by having a clearance rate of 100 percent or higher.

Time to disposition is defined as the calendar time between filing of a matter (in criminal cases, often from the date of first appearance in court) and final disposition of a case. The time of all dispositions is measured against a standard of the percentage of cases that should be disposed within established timeframes. The measure is intended to be used in conjunction with clearance rates and age of active pending caseload, to assess the length of time it takes a court to process cases. These measures provide "a framework for meaningful measurement across all case types" (NCSC, 2005). Age of active pending caseload refers to the cases that are filed, but not yet disposed. It is measured as the number of days from filing until the time of measurement; the cases often are grouped into standards that either are the same as the standards for disposed cases or at least are related to those standards. The NCSC (2005) states:

> Having a complete and accurate inventory of active pending cases as well as tracking their number and age is important because this pool of cases potentially requires court action [or, at least, attention]. Examining the age of pending cases makes

> clear, for example, the number and type of cases drawing near or about to surpass the court's case processing time standards. Once the age spectrum of cases is determined, the court can focus attention on what is required to ensure cases are brought to completion within reasonable timeframes [or understands legitimate reasons why cases might be older than a standard].

Finally, the NCSC (2005) defines trial date certainty as:

> The number of times cases disposed by trial are scheduled for trial. Specifically, the measure evaluates... the effectiveness of calendaring and continuance practices for both jury and non-jury trials. Timely case disposition is correlated with the... court's ability to hold trials on the first date they are scheduled to be heard.

Ostrom and Kauder (2007) suggested that, although achieving success in the court can be elusive given the lofty goals of justice and equality, the CourTools can be used to assess a court's effectiveness in meeting its fundamental, broad objectives. Luskin (1981) recommended that, in order for a case manager to examine the effects of delay, the manager must first define and measure case processing time. While some tailoring of the CourTools may be necessary for individual courts – because, as noted, idiosyncrasies can affect the collection and analysis of data – it provides a relatively straightforward model for evaluating court performance. Our analysis indicated that, although the CourTools establish a foundation for more in-depth evaluation, steadfast leadership remains essential.

Backlog Per 100

The central court performance benchmark in New Jersey is referred to as the Backlog Per 100 measure, which allows judges and administrators to evaluate performance across its disparate districts. New Jersey is a unified court structure that comprises 21 general jurisdiction trial courts organized into 15 vicinages (districts). Although an obscure calculation relative to other case management measures, it allows the court to compare the backlog levels of different courts, notwithstanding vast differences in their population and caseload. The measure assesses backlog while controlling for the number of filings; thus backlog in small, medium, and large courts can be compared, despite caseload distinctions. Consider the application of the formula [Backlog / (Most Recent 12 Months of Filings / 12) * 100] to a criminal docket:

[June 2025 Backlog / (Filings between July 2024 and June 2025 / 12) * 100]

[7,372 / (51,504 / 12) * 100] = 172

This indicates that there were 172 backlogged cases in June 2025, per every 100 average monthly filings between July 2024 and June 2025 – a ratio of 1.72 backlogged cases for every filing. The "Most Recent 12 Months of Filings" is a rolling number that corresponds with the current month. In June 2025, for example, backlog per 100 monthly filings consists of July 2024 through June 2025 filings as the denominator.

Table 5.3 shows the number of criminal filings for select districts ranked by backlog per 100 cases. The data illustrate that the number and percentage of backlogged cases is not conclusive unless the number of filings is also considered. When all of these variables are considered, judges and administrators can more accurately compare performance. For instance, Urban County A had the second largest number of backlogged cases in the sample, yet it had the best backlog per 100 score when controlling for the number of filings. Conversely, Suburban County B was on the lower end of the backlog spectrum, but it was ranked last in its backlog per 100. This suggests that given the volume of cases over the most recent 12 months, the backlog should be lower when compared to the other counties.

Table 5.3 Selected Counties Ranked by Backlog per 100

County Setting	***Criminal Filings Year to Date***	***Active Pending***	***Backlog***		
			N	***%***	***Per 100***
Urban A	4,271	1,275	443	35	124
Rural A	533	107	58	54	131
Suburban A	1,600	383	208	54	156
Rural B	1,256	505	177	35	169
Urban B	4,786	1,724	781	45	196
Suburban B	1,038	476	196	41	227

Is backlog per 100 the quintessential measure for comparing districts within a unified system? Perhaps, but the measure is not without limitations. Two important aspects of the caseload are not captured by this metric. First, not all backlogged cases are equivalent. Backlog per 100 does not convey the relative age or complexity of cases that exceed established time-to-disposition standards. These factors are critical to assessing the overall "health" of the backlog and enable judges and administrators to diagnose specific problems and develop informed policy responses. Second, while a spirit of competition – particularly within unified court structures – can promote favorable outcomes, clearly defined goals must remain paramount. The backlog per 100 measure merely facilitates comparisons across jurisdictions and fails to account for system-level deficiencies in the absence of an articulated standard, such as those reflected in the ABA, the COSCA, and Model Time standards. A target ratio of no more than one-to-one – meaning fewer than one backlogged case for every filing – may be appropriate. Without an established benchmark, systemic deficiencies may reduce comparisons to distinctions in mediocrity at best, and at worst, to assessments of which districts are performing poorly versus more poorly.

Notes

1 McConnell had both a law degree and an MBA.

2 No court can schedule well enough that it will never adjourn a case or continue an event. What is critical, however, is that attorneys believe events will occur as scheduled. We have interviewed many attorneys in different jurisdictions who prepare for events, particularly trials, as if they will occur even though they know intellectually and the data show that that is not the case. The exceptions are sufficient to create the needed expectation.

3 Technically, judges could be added from another division / case area, however this relates to judgeships we would want added, not reassigning judges already on the court – although that is what sometimes happens in the short term.

4 Some of the literature notes that the system preferred by the judges is the most effective calendaring system – so long as the case management principles are applied in that favored system.

5 The Model Time Standards were formally approved by the COSCA, the CCJ, the ABA, and the NACM.

6 Based on our experience, we submit that a failure to control continuances disadvantages both parties because any advantage apparent at an early stage may later evaporate. Moreover, the passage of time erodes the memories of witnesses for both parties. In some cases, we have found that the only parties who may benefit are civil litigants with weak substantive positions and criminal defendants who, knowing their guilt, remain at liberty longer (if released on bail) or whose cases are advantaged by the erosion of witness memory, thereby undermining testimonial reliability.

7 Variations of adjournment requests such as, "I need to be paid before I can proceed," may have to be initially accommodated in the interest of justice to enable a criminal defendant to be represented by an attorney of their choice, but the need for a private attorney to be compensated cannot be an "open sesame" for delay. The defendant should be advised directly that if they are unable to make satisfactory financial arrangements with the attorney within the allowed time, the court will be prepared to appoint a public defender to represent the defendant at the next scheduled appearance. If a second continuance request is made and additional time is granted, both counsel and the defendant should understand there will be no more time granted at the end of this second extension and a public defender should be appointed following the second adjournment.

8 Circumstances that justify a continuance can arise unexpectedly within those two to three days. Those circumstances should be considered by the judge even if presented orally at

the scheduled hearing, but it also is fair for the judge to assure themselves that the circumstances were, in fact, something that could not have been anticipated. For example, an inability to serve a subpoena on a witness should not be something suddenly discovered the day before or the day of an appearance.

9 In one instance, the judge asked the attorney how much additional time he required and when he stated, "two weeks," the judge (knowing through experience that for the issue at hand, he would need more time) responded, "I'm going to give you four weeks because you'll need it," and then cautioned, "but please don't return to my court in four weeks asking for another adjournment because you'll already know the answer."

10 In one of the rare instances when an attorney defied the judge's directive to be prepared for a status conference, the judge consulted with operations and assessed the attorney $358 for the "system's cost" including the expenditure to transport his client, a custodial defendant, to the court.

11 We know of courts in which staff working with a judge or central calendar staff understand the principles of case management so well that they are critical gatekeepers and "enforcers" for their judges. In the end, though, these staff are effective only because a judge (or all judges) allow them to be.

12 Some criminal attorneys market their ability to keep clients on the street and delay trial as key reasons why they are "good" attorneys.

13 We have had informal interactions with prosecutors and police where they are aware that the defendant committed the crime but do not have the evidence to support it such as when a victim or witness is unwilling to testify because of fear of reprisal or some technicality the defense counsel has benefitted from. In other instances, the defendant is a reputed criminal and the prosecutor is seeking to keep them off the street for as long as possible.

14 One of those objectives may be their own compensation when they are paid by the hour. Research shows that delay increases costs for both the court and the parties. Costs for the parties include out-of-pocket expenses and the time of attorneys. Even contingent-fee attorneys are hurt financially by delay – assuming they conscientiously put the time in to prepare – because they have to go to court more often and, normally, prepare more documents when cases are delayed, thus reducing their hourly compensation.

15 DCM also can be applied to only some of the cases, such as high-volume cases, contract, tort, or complex cases. The goal always is to provide the amount and quality of judicial attention that particular categories of cases normally require and, within each category, each case requires.

16 "Backlog" is not all of a court's pending inventory, but the cases that exceed existing time standards without being disposed. If a court does not have or ignores case processing time standards, the concept of "backlog" has little to no meaning except to the litigants. Regrettably, litigants' needs for timely dispositions may not be factored into some attorneys' and courts' calculations of what is "timely."

17 Research shows that multiple parties, in both criminal and civil cases, is strongly correlated to additional processing time because of discovery challenges, including scheduling depositions and hearings, often more court hearings, and multiple attorneys whose clients may have conflicting interests.

18 We have found that if the court creates a set of circumstances that are shown to be associated with complexity, it can be relatively easy to identify complex cases. This can be more difficult by simply assigning case types to expedited, standard, and complex. Some "complex" cases can be resolved quickly while a few expedited and standard cases turn out to be complex. The court therefore also requires a process to transfer cases between tracks, even if the number of cases that must be retracked is limited.

19 The phrase, "If you can't measure it, you can't manage it," is attributed to Peter Drucker, one of the best-known and most influential thinkers on the matter of management theory and practices. www.thefamouspeople.com/profiles/peter-drucker-132.php

20 The CourTools do not include the micro data that is needed by each judge about the cases on their calendar and macro data such as the number of trial dates for cases set for trial and when cases settle relative to the scheduling of typical key events such as status conferences and trial scheduling conferences.

21 In the California Civil Delay Reduction Project, it was found that judges did not know how to use the reports in nine of the most delay-impacted courts in the state. To the extent this holds true in other jurisdictions, it is incumbent on the administrator to ask why and change the report or provide training.

References

Abadinsky, H. (2008). *Law and justice: An introduction to the American legal system* (6th ed.). Pearson Education.

Aikman, A. B. (2007). *The art and practice of court administration.* Taylor & Francis Group.

American Bar Association. (1986). *Defeating delay: Developing and implementing a court delay reduction program.*

Bakke, H. C., & Solomon, M. (1989). Case differentiation: An approach to individualized case management. *Judicature, 73*(1), 17–21.

Bureau of Justice Assistance. (1993). *Differentiated case management: Program brief.* U.S. Department of Justice, Office of Justice Programs.

Bureau of Justice Assistance. (1997). *Trial court performance standards with commentary.* U.S. Department of Justice, Office of Justice Programs.

Church, T. W., Jr., Carlson, A., Lee, J., & Tan, T. (1978). *Justice delayed: The pace of litigation in urban trial courts.* National Center for State Courts.

Conference of Chief Justices. (2016). *Call to action: Achieving civil justice for all.* National Center for State Courts.

Cooper, C., Bakke, H., & Solomon, M. (1993). *Differentiated case management: Implementation manual.* Bureau of Justice Assistance.

Dubois, P. L., & Boyum, K. O. (1993). Court reform: The politics of institutional change. In S. W. Hays & C. B. Graham, Jr. (Eds.), *Handbook of court administration and management* (pp. 27–51). Marcel Dekker.

Etzioni, A. (1964). *Modern organizations.* Prentice-Hall.

Fazari, G. M., & Friesen, E. C. (2009). Caseflow management: A review of the literature. *Court Manager, 24*(1), 41–47.

Fazari, G. M., & Ijoma, C. E. (2009). Squaring a definition for the complex[2] criminal case. *Court Manager, 24*(4), 10–21.

Fetter, T. J. (1993). Planning for court management. In S. W. Hays & C. B. Graham, Jr. (Eds.), *Handbook of court administration and management* (pp. 483–496). Marcel Dekker.

Friesen, E. C. (2002). Court leaders: Survivors or agents of change? In G. M. Griller, E. K. Stott Jr., & J. Fallahay (Eds.), *The improvement of the administration of justice* (7th ed., pp. 31–47). American Bar Association, Judicial Division.

Gallas, G. (1976). The conventional wisdom of state court administration: A critical assessment and an alternative approach. *The Justice System Journal, 2*(1), 35–55.

Glick, H. R. (1982). The politics of state-court reforms. In P. L. Dubois (Ed.), *The politics of judicial reform* (pp. 17–33). D.C. Heath & Co.

Goerdt, J., Lomvardias, C., Gallas, G., & Mahoney, B. (1987). *Examining court delay: The pace of litigation in 26 urban trial courts.* National Center for State Courts.

Heise, M. (2004). Criminal case complexity: An empirical perspective. *Journal of Empirical Legal Studies, 1*(2), 331–369.

Henderson, T. A., Munsterman, J., & Tobin, R. W. (1990). *Differentiated case management: Final report.* U.S. Department of Justice, Office of Justice Programs.

Hewitt, W., Gallas, G., & Mahoney, B. (1990). *Courts that succeed.* National Center for State Courts.

Institute for Court Management. (2016). *Fundamentals of caseflow management* [Seminar notes]. National Center for State Courts.

Keilitz, S. L. (1993). Alternative dispute resolution in the courts. In S. W. Hays & C. B. Graham, Jr. (Eds.), *Handbook of court administration and management* (pp. 383–403). Marcel Dekker.

Luskin, M. L. (1981). *Describing and analyzing case processing time in criminal cases: Suggestions for administrators.* U.S. Department of Justice, National Institute of Justice.

Mahoney, B., & Sipes, L. (1985). Zeroing in on court delay: The powerful tools of time standards and managed information. *Court Management Journal, 8*, 8–13.

Mahoney, B., Aikman, A. B., Casey, P., Flango, V. E., Gallas, G., Henderson, T. A., Ito, J. A., Steelman, D. C., & Weller, S. (1988). *Changing times in trial courts: Caseflow management and delay reduction in urban trial courts.* National Center for State Courts.

Munsterman, G. T., Loveland, G. K., Hannaford, P. L., & Murphy, T. R. (1998). *Managing notorious cases.* National Center for State Courts.

National Association for Court Management (NACM). (2005). *Core competency curriculum guidelines: What court leaders need to know and be able to do.*

National Center for State Courts. (2005). *CourTools: Trial court performance measures.*

National Center for State Courts. (2006). *Future trends in state courts: Performance measurement gains momentum through CourTools.*

National Center for State Courts. (2011). *Model time standards for state trial courts.*

Ostrom, B. J., & Hanson, R. A. (1999). *Efficiency, timeliness, and quality: A new perspective from nine state criminal trial courts.* National Center for State Courts.

Ostrom, B. J., & Kauder, N. (2007). Measuring court performance. In *Ten trends impacting state courts* (pp. 20–21). National Center for State Courts.

Peak, K. J. (2004). *Justice administration: Police, courts, and corrections management.* Pearson Education.

Saari, D. J., Planet, M. D., & Reinkensmeyer, M. W. (1993). The modern court managers: Who they are and what they do in the United States. In S. W. Hays & C. B. Graham, Jr. (Eds.), *Handbook of court administration and management* (pp. 237–261). Marcel Dekker.

Sipes, D. A., & Oram, M. E. (1988). *On trial: The length of civil and criminal trials.* National Center for State Courts.

Sipes, L. L., Carlson, A. M., Tan, T., Aikman, A. B., & Page, R. W., Jr. (1980). *Managing to reduce delay.* National Center for State Courts.

Solomon, H. E. (1987). The training of court managers. In C. R. Swanson & S. M. Talarico (Eds.), *Court administration: Issues and responses* (pp. 15–20). University of Georgia.

Solomon, M. (1973). *Caseflow management in the trial court: Support studies – 2.* American Bar Association Commission on Standards of Judicial Administration.

Solomon, M. (1993). Fundamental issues in caseflow management. In S. W. Hays & C. B. Graham, Jr. (Eds.), *Handbook of court administration and management* (pp. 369–381). Marcel Dekker.

Solomon, M., & Somerlot, D. K. (1987). *Caseflow management in the trial court: Now and for the future.* American Bar Association.

Solomon, M., Cooper, C. S., & Bakke, H. (2002). Building public trust and confidence through effective caseflow management. In G. M. Griller, E. K. Stott Jr., & J. Fallahay (Eds.), *The improvement of the administration of justice* (7th ed., pp. 111–129). American Bar Association.

Steelman, D. C., Goerdt, J. A., & McMillan, J. E. (2000). *Caseflow management: The heart of court management in the new millennium.* National Center for State Courts.

Tobin, R. W. (1997). *An overview of court administration in the United States.* National Center for State Courts.

Tobin, R. W. (1999). *Creating the judicial branch: The unfinished reform.* National Center for State Courts.

Weatherburn, D., & Baker, J. (2000). Delays in trial case processing: An empirical analysis of delay in the New South Wales District Criminal Court. *Journal of Judicial Administration, 10*(1), 6–24.

Zorza, R. (2002). *The self-help friendly court: Designed from the ground up to work for people without lawyers.* National Center for State Courts.

6 Judicial Branch Human Resources Management and Consultation

Benchmarking, Culture, and Accountability in Modern Court Administration

Individuals seek to understand their own performance. Their work performance must be objectively assessed to evaluate the degree of success or failure, allowing for modifications when necessary. Benchmarking is the process of establishing a standard and subsequently assessing the relative performance of an individual or the organization against that goal. Benchmarking possesses significant organizational value, serving as the foundation for the implementation of specific policies, practices, and procedures. Similarly, the distribution of human capital resources should be re-evaluated to ascertain how staff positions and expertise might optimally align with the court's mission, objectives, and purposes.

In conventional institutions like the courts, which Mintzberg (1979) classified as a "professional bureaucracy," the effectiveness of measurement instruments and the significance of benchmarking might become ambiguous when first implemented. In these organizations, professionals – referred to as "indoctrinated specialists" – are employed for the operational core and are granted substantial autonomy over their assigned tasks. In contrast to machine bureaucracy, which establishes its own productivity standards, the criteria of professional bureaucracy primarily derive from external sources. Authority in a professional bureaucracy originates from the profession itself – "the power of expertise." Therefore, it is crucial to establish performance criteria and hold subject-matter experts accountable for their actions. These experts possess considerable autonomy due to their professional expertise and current appointment (or election). The reality of

DOI: 10.4324/9781003686804-6

these interactions can hinder benchmarking endeavors. Consequently, conflict may emerge when judges, who rely on criteria established by the legal profession, endeavor to fulfill the dual roles of manager and jurist, or, more succinctly, when their work culture is composed of a divergent framework of performance standards and expectations.

A fundamental contradiction exists between the judicial and managerial cultures within the court environment due to their differing perspectives. Given the influence of their respective professional perspectives, the methods judges and administrators employ to assess performance vary. Lefever (2005) delineates the stark contrast between the two cultures: the legal culture is characterized by abstract goals, diffuse authority, low interdependence, and internal performance metrics, whereas the managerial culture emphasizes concrete goals, formal authority, task interdependence, and external performance metrics. The training and experience of judges and administrators, which inform their decision making, frequently differ significantly. Lawyers are educated to examine exceptions and construct arguments accordingly, while managers focus on the overall facts (the rule) to formulate conclusions and establish forward moving processes. In this respect, the courts face obstacles analogous to those found in diverse organizational cultures such as medical and university administrations. Similarly, although professors and administrators are dedicated to their craft to support the education of students, the organization's culture reveals divergent value systems when academics and practitioners collaborate to formulate strategy.

The presence of conflicting cultures that must coexist in the court, each dependent on the other, complicates the process of establishing and disseminating benchmarks more than one might expect. Failure to acknowledge or comprehend this essential principle will result in the court's inability to realize its goals. Judges are legal authorities designated to oversee and resolve contentious court cases. They are anticipated to be resolute and equitable authority figures who should maintain an even temperament and control of the courtroom. Judicial personnel, especially managers and supervisors, are urged to collaborate as a team in accordance with fundamental management principles such as cooperation, compromise, and (in some instances) concession. When judges and staff interact, it is essential to cohesively integrate these differing perspectives. The presiding judge and court administrator must effectively collaborate to serve as intermediaries, bridging the chasm between their respective professional cultures, irrespective of how wide that gap may be, given the culture of that *specific* court. Thus, a presiding judge who is capable of effectively managing the court is irreplaceable; this competency is not inherently derived from seniority or personal appeal.

Friesen (1991) examined how delays in case resolution undermine each of the eight purposes of courts, which are fundamental to their existence in a free and democratic society. The significance of benchmarking measurable aspects influenced by judges, particularly in case management, cannot be overstated in the daily management of the court. As a long-time presiding judge observed, "everyone deserves their day in court, but not necessarily the whole day."[1] This perspective is indicative of establishing the tone and emphasizing the significance of managing the court's resources and time. It is insufficient for the court to merely ascertain its output levels; it is equally imperative to juxtapose these measures against reasonable, mutually accepted benchmarks. Advocating for this approach necessitates substantial backing, empirical evidence, and persuasive skills on the part of the court leadership team.

There is, of course, the opposing aspect of management. The maxim, "you can't manage what you don't measure," does not universally apply to all aspects of management. Even the respected statistician and academic W. E. Deming (1986) contended that numerous significant management factors are immeasurable. For instance, when queried about the potential advantage of investing $20,000 to train ten individuals in a specialized field, Deming (2005) noted the importance of theory, observing that one could never know because it would be impossible to quantify it. What motivated the organization's actions? Was it because the organization was convinced that it would yield some kind of benefit? The answers to these and other questions could never be known for certain; thus, managers must rely on theory to explain and guide actions when causal relationships cannot be directly measured. Like Deming, court administrators should identify which elements of the court are quantifiable against those that are not, while also having the capacity to know when such a distinction is relevant.

Because the court is ultimately accountable to the public, its objectives should be framed so that they are quantifiable. It is not enough to simply state that the court is responsible for administering justice and therefore court performance is not measurable. The court must, as a matter of principle, concern itself with the measurement of time. The court must consider its limited resources and determine how effectively it is achieving justice.

Functions and Essential Qualities of the Modern Court Administrator

Debates continue regarding the proper scope of responsibilities of court administrators and, by extension, the competencies and characteristics they must possess to effectively execute those responsibilities. Understandably, the perceptions of practitioners are shaped by their institutional experiences – whether within small rural courts or large, complex urban systems. Judges, in particular, may conceptualize the role through the lens of their experiences with previous administrators or in response to immediate operational challenges. Because the administration of justice is fundamentally a human-centered enterprise, the question of what a court administrator "does" and "should do" lies at the core of understanding the profession and its evolving demands.

Although the National Association for Court Management (NACM, 2005) Core Competencies emphasize "knowledge, skills, and abilities" (KSAs), the present discussion extends to the broader personal qualities and dispositional traits that enable an administrator to effectively deploy those KSAs. Modern court administrator job descriptions often enumerate extensive responsibilities mirroring the NACM framework, yet the association itself acknowledges that few, if any, professionals can master every competency or perform all of the duties enumerated in a typical description. Consequently, courts must seek the "right fit" – an administrator capable of executing the most consequential functions with acumen, while thoughtfully delegating other tasks. No job description, however exhaustive, can fully anticipate the breadth of situations court administrators will encounter. For this reason, articulating a clear understanding of the role and the qualities that enable success in the local court setting is indispensable to sound hiring and performance evaluation.

Judgment, Critical Thinking, and Institutional Awareness

Above all, effective court administrators must possess the capacity for rigorous critical thinking and sound, evidence-based judgment. Judgment is more than the act of deciding; it entails the ability to discern when to defer executive decisions, whom to consult, what to delegate and to whom, and how to assess whether proposed actions are sufficiently supported by data and aligned with institutional goals. It also requires enterprise-level strategic awareness – understanding the timing of proposals, anticipating institutional "land mines," and recognizing when modifications are necessary to secure the support of key stakeholders or avoid unnecessary opposition. Judgment is notoriously difficult to evaluate in a hiring process. Yet, failing to assess it is a significant organizational risk.

Professional Backgrounds and the Value of Non-Court Experience

In the private sector, executives frequently ascend based on demonstrable competencies and leadership qualities, even when their prior experience lies outside the industry. The judicial branch, however, often defaults to requiring prior court experience, given the judiciary's distinct professional culture, loosely coupled organizational structure, and the specialized nature of court operations. While direct experience in court operations is undeniably beneficial, it should not be treated as an absolute prerequisite for every court management position. Doing so may unduly narrow the court's applicant pool by disregarding candidates who possess strong managerial, analytical, or leadership credentials developed outside the judiciary. Indeed, individuals with substantial experience in information technology, human resources, finance, budgeting, or organizational management may bring innovative perspectives and valuable skill sets. Provided they demonstrate an ability to understand and adapt to the judiciary's unique environment, such candidates can enhance the administrative capacity of courts. In some cases, inviting a qualified external manager to participate in resume screening or interview evaluation may help ensure that promising non-court applicants are not prematurely excluded. Having said that, we submit that there are critical management and administrative-level positions such as the executive-level court administrator or chief probation officer, where prior experience in the courts (or at the very least judicial branch) should not be substituted.

Adaptability, Openness, and a Problem-Solving Orientation

In a domain characterized by continual change – whether in statutory mandates, caseload dynamics, technological expectations, or public accountability – adaptability is indispensable. Court administrators must be open to new ideas, willing to reassess their assumptions and capable of integrating input from a diverse range of stakeholders. Excessive confidence in one's own correctness, or a tendency to consult only a narrow circle of voices, ultimately constrains institutional learning. As former General Motors Chairman and CEO Daniel Akerson observed, "Darwin said you have to be strong, fast, and smart. Everyone forgets the fourth one: you have to be adaptable" (Welch, 2011). Adaptability, understood as cognitive flexibility and institutional responsiveness, should therefore be regarded as a core professional asset in court administration.

Initiative, Accountability, and Organizational Contribution

Courts, like all organizations, benefit from personnel who take initiative, assume responsibility, and contribute positively to the workplace environment. These qualities are no less essential in a court administrator than in any court staff member. In medium-sized to large courts, administrators need not be proficient in frontline operational tasks; instead, they must excel in planning, monitoring implementation, identifying deviations from expected performance, and ensuring that managers and staff have the necessary resources to accomplish their work. Court administrators serve as critically positioned liaisons amongst judges, staff, and external stakeholders, synthesizing information across organizational boundaries and supporting coherent, system-wide functioning.

Commitment to Learning, Curiosity, and Innovation

An effective court administrator must demonstrate a commitment to continuous professional development, both for themselves and for their staff. Budget fluctuations may influence training modalities, but the underlying commitment to professional development should not waver. Courts can foster professional development of key staff by encouraging and supporting their participation in tiered, credentialing programs such as those offered by the Institute for Court Management (ICM), including the internationally recognized ICM Fellows Program.[2] Curiosity – particularly curiosity directed toward how other courts, government agencies, non-profit organizations, and private-sector entities solve analogous problems – frequently stimulates imaginative solutions. The relevant question becomes: *"Can this innovation be adapted to our environment, and who must be involved to determine its feasibility?"*

Technological Literacy and Strategic Technology Management

While administrators need not be technical experts, they must possess sufficient technological literacy to make informed decisions, supervise skilled IT staff, and appreciate technology's role as an instrument – not an end in itself – in advancing court performance and access to justice. Court leaders must ensure that technological innovation is grounded in mission-driven goals and that staff remain vigilant in assessing emerging tools, without succumbing to the allure of untested "next big things." Effective administrators do not need to be hands-on technologists, but they must know how to hire, support, and evaluate those who are. Contract administration is also critically important in today's world of cloud-based technology services, software as a service, and outsourcing. Modern court administration requires executive-level oversight of contracts and vendor services, with clear delineation of related staffing.

A Commitment to Justice as an Institutional Guiding Principle

High-performing court administrators share a deep, internalized commitment to justice as the ultimate purpose of the court institution. Courts do not merely seek to meet deadlines, complete paperwork, or implement programs; they aspire to produce fair, equitable outcomes consistent with community values and constitutional principles. Administrators driven by a passion for justice focus on system efficacy and outcomes, rather than bureaucratic maintenance. They test court programs both empirically and qualitatively, welcome ideas from diverse sources, and pursue continuous improvement as facilitated in the High Performance Court Framework (National Center for State Court [NCSC], 2010) – not for its own sake, but to advance the court's foundational mission.

Administrators must cultivate an organizational environment that facilitates the comprehensive flow of information across the organization. Valuable ideas can arise from any tier of the judiciary, ranging from court executives to frontline clerks. The court administrator must stay open to hearing such information, and when warranted, take action accordingly. Promoting open communication instills trust in staff that their viewpoints are acknowledged and considered in court planning efforts. It also acts as a protection against managerial insularity or the establishment of departmental fiefdoms. When a clerk or employee presents an issue directly to the administrator, the administrator should not first question whether the employee adhered to the official chain of command; instead, the administrator must initially assess the most effective way to address the information. This may entail taking direct action or, alternatively, advising the employee on the appropriate course of action and requesting a follow-up on the results. A restructuring and re-engineering initiative inside a court's civil division, for instance, was prompted by information from a unit supervisor who requested permission to create a training manual, a request that was initially denied by the division head. The sitting judge of the division provided further motivation by regularly visiting the mailroom to verify that motions were being efficiently and accurately directed to the relevant judges. These interactions, originating from different levels of the organization, are ultimately what guided a significant operational improvement effort.

Integrity, Candor, and Ethical Leadership

Integrity is not negotiable. Administrators must be prepared to provide forthright, evidence-based counsel even in the face of expected court dissent. Simultaneously, they must honor the authority of judges when decisions pertain to judicial prerogative, executing those decisions properly provided they do not contravene law or ethics. Assessing outcomes – regardless of whether they pertain to endorsed or contested policies – is an essential aspect of accountable administrative leadership. In this context, court administrators are held to the highest level of ethical standards (NACM, 2016; American Society of Public Administration, 2013). Given the increasingly rapid pace of societal change and emerging ethical considerations, court administrators and management staff must stay abreast of current ethical issues and related governing provisions.[3]

Court leaders will likely face lawsuits and formal complaints in their administrative roles, particularly in unionized environments. This danger cannot be eliminated entirely. Administrators must ensure that their actions consistently adhere to established judicial branch policies and procedures. When an administrator complies with ethical standards and organizational protocols, they can maintain confidence in the integrity of their decisions and stay impervious to fabricated allegations or legal intimidation. With time, an administrator will demonstrate their professionalism and compliance with organizational practice and policy. Conversely, an administrator who harbors persistent fear of litigation undermines the decision-making capacity of the court administrator position. This, in turn, creates apprehension to enforce rules and progressive discipline, which then perpetuates undesirable conduct and organizational dysfunction.

No combination of qualifications or attributes can ensure success as a court administrator. Without a comprehensive examination of the court administrator's job functions, the qualities that contribute to professional effectiveness, and the organizational culture in which administrators operate, courts may make erroneous decisions and set unrealistic expectations. A comprehensive understanding of the administration role is crucial – not only for making the appropriate hiring choices, but also for guaranteeing that courts fulfill their objective of administering justice with integrity and efficiency.

Typologies of Employees Misaligned with Organizational Purpose

This book began by likening the purposes and responsibilities of the court to a foundation upon which all administrative meaning and activity are grounded. A strong, clearly articulated, and well-understood foundation sustains the organization; conversely, a weak or ambiguous grounding in the court's mission leaves the institution vulnerable. At best, such a court becomes ineffective; at worst, it devolves into a dysfunctional bureaucracy whose inefficiencies erode public trust in ways so diffuse and systemic that they defy precise measurement.

An essential question for any court administrator, therefore, is how to determine whether the organization is purposeful; that is, whether its operations, culture, and personnel behaviors are meaningfully aligned with the court's mission. Consider, for instance, a recurring case management problem. While it may first appear as a technical or procedural issue, closer examination may reveal the problem to be symptomatic of a deeper misunderstanding or neglect of the court's foundational purposes and responsibilities. In essence, a deficiency in the "why" will inevitably compromise the "how."

Failures in the "how" principles such as poor leadership, inconsistent human resource practices, or inadequate case management can certainly hinder performance. However, these failures do not always originate from a misunderstanding of the "why." Over time, though, persistent weaknesses in leadership or an entrenched, counterproductive organizational culture can indoctrinate new employees into patterns of disengagement, thereby transforming the court into the very type of bureaucracy that fuels public cynicism toward government institutions.

The following typologies represent patterns of employee behavior observed in court organizations that exhibit varying degrees of misalignment with institutional purpose and mission. The initial five typologies – Clockwatcher, Conflict Artisan, Institutional Fatalist, Crown Chaser, and Sleepwalker – emerged from collective experience and organizational observation. These typologies capture overt and familiar manifestations of disengagement, cynicism, and self-interest within the court workforce. To complement and extend this framework, nine additional typologies are presented that describe more nuanced or covert expressions of purpose misalignment. Together, these models provide administrators with a conceptual tool for recognizing behavioral archetypes that impede organizational cohesion and performance, and ultimately the fulfillment of the courts' responsibilities to the public:

1. *Clockwatcher* (passive detractor) – Clockwatchers exhibit minimal engagement and enthusiasm for the work of their division or the court as a whole. They view their role as a mere "nine-to-five job," demonstrating rigid adherence to schedules and a lack of initiative beyond narrowly defined responsibilities. These employees frequently exhaust all available leave, openly anticipate retirement, and disclaim responsibility for issues that fall outside their immediate duties – often with the refrain, "That's above my pay grade." Their demeanor is typically lethargic, and their disinterest in process improvement or service enhancement signals an absence of professional investment. For them, the courthouse is simply a place to occupy time between weekends and holidays.
2. *Conflict Artisan* (active detractor) – Conflict artisans derive satisfaction from organizational discord. They are often catalysts for conflict, engaging in rumor propagation, political maneuvering, and alliance-building to advance their personal interests. These individuals are opportunistic and self-serving, viewing court employment less as public service and more as a venue for social or positional gain. Their presence can be especially corrosive in collaborative environments where trust and collegiality are critical.
3. *Institutional Fatalist* (reactive detractor) – Institutional fatalists embody resignation and skepticism. While they may possess deep institutional knowledge, their outlook is characterized by defeatism and passive resistance. Their frequent invocations of "we tried that before, and it didn't work" illustrate a fundamental unwillingness to embrace change. Such employees often remain in the organization not out of commitment but because they see few alternatives elsewhere. Their longevity within the institution may allow them to outlast reform efforts, effectively neutralizing new initiatives through inertia or subtle obstruction.
4. *Crown Chaser* (proactive detractor) – Crown chasers are driven by competition rather than collaboration. They pursue personal victories without regard for organizational

impact or the morale of their colleagues. Confrontational and argumentative, they often resist authority and demonstrate low emotional intelligence. Their behavior – marked by blame-shifting, mood volatility, and an insistence on "winning" – can destabilize teams and undermine leadership. For these individuals, the motivation to work in the court system is rooted less in public service and more in personal advancement.

5. *Sleepwalker* (inactive detractor) – Sleepwalkers represent the "retired in place" cohort. They possess institutional knowledge but are unwilling to share it, either from apathy or as a means of maintaining influence. Although eligible to retire, they remain in the organization, contributing minimally and resisting change. Content with mediocrity, they fulfill only the bare minimum expectations of their role. For them, continued employment provides structure and familiarity rather than purpose or engagement.

Building upon the five foundational typologies, the following nine classifications in Table 6.1 further illustrate the diverse ways in which court employees may become misaligned from the court's mission. While these categories are not rigidly delineated, they provide a framework for understanding how misalignment manifests in the court workforce and how administrators might recognize and address it.

Table 6.1 Profiles of Purpose Misalignment in Court Organizations

Typology	*Defining Characteristics*	*Behavioral Markers*	*Organizational Impact*	*Administrative Response*
Red-Tape Sentinel	Prioritizes rules and procedures over mission or purpose	Rigid adherence to policy; resistance to innovation or discretion	Reinforces a compliance culture that values form over justice	Reconnect rules to purpose; emphasize judgment, context, and mission-based decision making
Backroom Diplomat	Uses informal influence and political maneuvering to maintain control	Builds alliances, mediates selectively, or manipulates relationships for advantage	Creates unofficial hierarchies and undermines transparency	Promote open communication, rotate leadership roles, and equalize access to information
Judiciary Romantic	Idealizes the past and resists modernization	Defends legacy practices; skeptical of reform or technology; appeals to "how things used to be"	Slows organizational learning and frames change as decline	Link reform to tradition; engage as mentors to bridge institutional history with modernization
Spotlight Chaser	Motivated by recognition and visibility rather than contribution	Pursues high-profile tasks; avoids essential but unglamorous work	Encourages performative rather than substantive productivity	Establish balanced recognition systems; reward impact and teamwork, not optics

(*Continued*)

Table 6.1 (Continued)

Typology	*Defining Characteristics*	*Behavioral Markers*	*Organizational Impact*	*Administrative Response*
Division Driftwood	Remains in the organization out of habit, not purpose. Sustained by the momentum of work accomplished by the respective court unit or division	Minimal effort; disengagement; limited contribution or initiative	Normalizes mediocrity and drains morale	Use purpose-centered evaluations; offer development or dignified exit options
Courthouse Gadfly[4]	Asserts personal moral authority over institutional direction, rules, policies, and procedures	Selective compliance; challenges leadership under the guise of ethics	Fragments mission alignment for the purposes of undermining authority	Reinforce shared ethical standards; engage constructively in policy and practice
Workplace Nomad	Engages energetically in new initiatives but avoids sustained follow-through	Enthusiastic at project onset; disengages once novelty fades	Produces incomplete reforms and disrupts program continuity	Define end-stage accountability; pair with detail-oriented staff; reward completion
Bean Counter	Values efficiency and measurable outputs over substantive justice	Focused on volume, speed, and metrics; overlooks fairness and access	Promotes a technocratic culture disconnected from mission	Balance quantitative and qualitative performance indicators; reframe success around purpose
Institutional Insulator	Seeks to protect the court by insulating it from external influence	Frames external engagement as risk rather than legitimacy; restricts public access and information flow	Fosters institutional isolation, reduces public trust, and weakens accountability	Redefine protection as stewardship through openness; engage in community partnerships

These typologies demonstrate the various ways in which employees can become misaligned with an organization's mission, thereby weakening institutional purpose and morale. This phenomenon was empirically illustrated by Felps and associates (2006) in their seminal study on group dynamics and team performance. Students were divided into small teams tasked with solving management problems, unknowingly including embedded actors who were instructed to display disruptive behavioral roles: the indifferent participant, the cynic, and the pessimist. The findings revealed that the presence of even a single "bad apple" – an individual who persistently exhibited disengagement, hostility, or negativity – diminished the team's overall effectiveness by 30 to 40 percent, regardless of the capability or motivation levels of other members. The researchers concluded that "bad apples" not only reduce productivity, but they also adversely impact group norms, leading otherwise high-performing members to mirror counterproductive attitudes and behaviors (Felps et al., 2006). For court administrators and judicial leaders, the implication is profound: the overall health of a court organization depends not only on the number of exceptional performers, but also on its capacity to prevent, contain, or rectify dysfunctional behavior before it weakens the court culture.

Despite the obstacles presented by the noted archetypes, judicial leaders can mitigate their impacts by meticulously assessing and (when necessary) altering the direction of the court's culture. Administrators, in partnership with leadership judges, can ensure that the actions of staff and the daily supervision of work assignments are aligned with the purposes and responsibilities of the court. We emphasize this as a critical issue in the long-term health of the court institution precisely because the court is a "people-based" organization. Investing in the court's human capital is not a luxury, but rather it is vital to the basic functioning of the judicial branch. Therefore, strategic planning vis-à-vis recruitment, training and development, advancement, and progressive discipline standards are what will ultimately preserve and strengthen the court, as well as guaranteeing greater levels of continuity during leadership or structural transitions. An effective court strategic plan integrates these elements so that individual employee job descriptions and annual advisories are aligned with the overarching goals and objectives of the court. This is integral to the planning that is at the same time focused on court infrastructure. Safe and well-maintained facilities make judicial processes more efficient because the physical environment impacts the morale and productivity of court employees.

These points also demonstrate the importance of forging robust collaborations with external agencies and the community, thus creating a critical pathway to enhance court operations and public service. Maintaining good caseflow management and associated operations is inextricably linked to the existence of the court and central to its primary duties. This focus on operations management must be balanced with ensuring that the court culture fosters an environment of transparency and accountability. This means that no individual is above the organization, and that the genuine concerns of every court employee must be taken seriously, even if they initially shed a negative light on the organization. When all of these interconnected activities are effectively managed, court leaders can more easily overcome workplace challenges, regardless of their source.

A court's ability to fulfill its mission depends as much on the alignment of its people as on the design of its business processes. Misalignment – whether born of inertia, ego, rumination, or misplaced loyalty – erodes the integrity of the court institution from within. By identifying and addressing the foregoing behavioral archetypes, court administrators can cultivate a workforce and organizational culture that not only maximizes court performance, but also embodies the judiciary's enduring commitment to justice and public service.

Training Judges in Caseflow Management and Related Administrative Functions

Nearly every state provides judicial education programs and some include specific training in court administration for newly appointed presiding judges, as well as assistant presiding judges in larger courts. Notwithstanding these endeavors, we have interacted with numerous court administrators who recount instances where one or more judges exceeded their administrative authority, or enacted decisions that, while aimed at resolving an immediate problem, inadvertently compromised the court administrator's role or engendered persistent long-term difficulties. These anecdotes highlight persistent disparities between optimal enterprise-level governance practices and unaligned, ad hoc administrative decisions.

Kevin Burke, a former judge of the District Court of Minnesota, remarked that courts are comprised of judges who perceive themselves not as an institution, but as individuals united by necessity in a shared office environment within the courthouse (Griller, 2010). We have recognized the related difficulties of judicial management for decades. Saari (1970) addressed the difficulties associated with administering a loosely coupled court, an organization with a professional role orientation. Understanding the origins of our loosely coupled courts and the professional culture of the judiciary does not imply that no improvements can be made. Rather, this recognition underscores the pressing need for court leaders – both judges and administrators – to squarely address institutional requirements, thus focusing administrative decisions on the betterment of the court as a whole.

Some judges may ascend to the bench with the understanding that their achievement is in some ways largely self-derived. No judge, however, is an island. Over time, most judges acknowledge that their tenure on the bench is sustained by the contributions of their chambers staff and other court personnel. The most astute judges understand that all court personnel can influence their long-term service on the bench. Their fellow judges can also affect how they are perceived during re-election or retention, as the conduct of each judge contributes to the public's overall assessment of the judiciary and its members – this may not be fair, but is nonetheless the case. Judges who make the kind of error which garners national attention might also influence the political perception of other judges and the court institution. Dale Lefever observed that a cooperative and collaborative approach in court administration among judges benefits both individual judges and the court institution as a whole (Griller, 2010). Cooperation is also more likely to facilitate the court's work in achieving its essential objectives; that is, access to justice, equitable treatment, and due process. The court (as a whole), in other words, surpasses the sum of its individually positioned judges. John Gardner (1990), a former presidential advisor and founder of Common Cause, coined the phrase "The

War of the Parts Against the Whole." Although this phrase was not used in relation to the courts per se, it can be readily applied. Given this knowledge, administrators and judges who are invested in the institution must collaborate to enhance the recognition and acceptance of the institution's inherent value among all judges.

Administrative decisions are not exclusively the responsibility of the presiding judge or other leadership judges. All judges are influenced by court budgets, personnel regulations, and applicable state and municipal administration policies. Leadership judges and administrators are frequently required to make important policy choices in these administrative governance domains. In addition, judges will be requested to participate in judicial committees and bench–Bar workgroups to address various subjects. Court administrators have consistently acknowledged that all judges ought to contribute to policy formulation for a court, rather than limiting this responsibility to the presiding judge, or, in larger, urban courts, the executive committee. The question is not whether judges should participate in administration (they should), but rather to delineate the boundary between court policy determinations and policy execution, as well as between administration and adjudication. More simply, where does judicial independence, which is necessary for adjudication, end, and where does non-adjudicative administration, for which such independence is not inherently granted, begin? The existence and location of that line bifurcating these two "worlds" remains a focal point in court administration.

Nearly all of the literature authored by court administrators discusses the "partnership" between the presiding judge and the court administrator. Judges who are also good leaders of their courts embrace and cultivate this executive team partnership model. Delaying discussions regarding the administrative aspects of courts until judges have taken on a leadership role, or are on the verge of doing so, is an unacceptable postponement of the necessary. At that point, habits and expectations are established and/or validated. We argue that it is imperative to address, from the inception of a judge's career, the concept of the court as an institution that transcends mere office-sharing, and to maintain this discourse throughout their tenure on the bench. We also contend that sustained interaction between administrators and judges is essential to enhance the perception that the court institution itself possesses a status that warrants respect and support. The collective advantages of using this approach far outweigh the "extra time" which may be required in judicial education programs, onboarding of new judges, and collaboration with the full bench on policy formulation.

Prior to training, a consensus must be established regarding the information to convey to incoming judges. Reaching an agreement necessitates re-evaluation and candid discussions among judges and administrators. Unanimity will never be attained. However, fostering an open dialogue that values both judicial and administrative perspectives will likely facilitate greater consensus. Should these conversations occur and an accord is achieved, an "administration" module can be incorporated into the training for incoming judges. In the absence of an organization-wide consensus, we argue that it is at least imperative that the court leadership issues and roles be identified and deliberated among the newly appointed judges and their more experienced judicial faculty. Granting administrators comparable roles as faculty in training modules can generate some progress in determining those instances when judicial independence is warranted and appropriate.

Court administrators contribute distinct perspectives and potential solutions to discussions with judges. Neither of the perspectives of judges or administrators are inherently "correct" or "incorrect." They simply have different vantage points, concerns, and priorities. The optimal solutions will consider all perspectives and ideas. When committees consist solely of judges or when administrators' perspectives are undervalued, significant insights are forfeited, resulting in a decline in the quality of decisions. We believe that the partnership model valued by administrators is increasingly perceived by a growing number of judges as more like the "executive component" structure referenced in the court administration literature. This is in part due to the contemporary challenges which show that both judges and courts are positively impacted through collaborative decision making in the administrative realm. Incorporating court administration into judicial training will enhance judges' appreciation of the collaboration and fortify their roles as collaborators. Support of this executive component model is further evidenced by the creation of the National Association for Presiding Judges and Court Executives (2016), which has strongly embraced the productive pairs paradigm of court leadership.

Our empirical observations and practical experience indicate that judges' assessments of caseflow performance consistently affirm the need for sustained, structured training in case management practices. Although attorneys exert significant influence over the pace of litigation, the ultimate responsibility for the progression and resolution of cases resides with the judiciary, supported by administrators and staff. When judicial control over case processing is clearly defined and consistently exercised, the process is far more likely to yield outcomes that are both timely and substantively just. Conversely, when the process lacks direction or is unduly influenced by external stakeholders, the likelihood of achieving just outcomes diminishes – even if such conditions may inadvertently serve the tactical interests of counsel. Accordingly, meaningful accountability for caseflow performance must begin with judicial leaders and extend to all judges who manage active dockets. Performance benchmarks can only be achieved and the intended purposes of procedural frameworks realized through clear expectations and accountability mechanisms.

Achieving a cultural shift toward stronger caseflow oversight also requires the strategic engagement of frontline supervisory court personnel. These individuals, who work closely with judges on a daily basis, should be empowered to participate actively in case management rather than being constrained to narrowly defined, task-oriented roles. When administrative staff are relegated to such limited functions, backlogs are often perceived as the sole responsibility of the judge, thereby obscuring shared accountability. To mitigate these unintended consequences, court supervisors should be delegated appropriate authority – such as the discretion to approve or deny routine adjournment requests lacking compelling justification.

Stott (1982) discussed the span of control within the court and clarifies the collaborative interface between judges and administrators that continues to resonate in modern court structures. Except for responsibilities that involve substantive legal determinations, such as adjudication of cases, an effective court governance structure relies on continuous consultation between administrative leaders and the presiding judge. Stott's (1982) consultative model ensures that both administrative and judicial activities are aligned, reinforcing a cohesive and well-coordinated approach to caseflow management and overall court performance.

Stott's (1982) model further substantiates the need for judges and court administrators to receive comprehensive education in case management principles and practices. At the outset, newly appointed judges and recently hired administrators must be introduced to the organization's performance standards to acquire a foundational understanding of institutional values and the metrics used to assess performance. Beyond this initial exposure, courts should ensure that ongoing professional development opportunities are available in ways that do not impede daily operations. Although most newly appointed judges are required to participate in some form of judicial orientation, such programs do not always address administrative best practices – particularly those related to caseflow management. Furthermore, judges may be insufficiently informed about the distinct functions of court administrators and supervisory personnel. Consequently, for many new judges, the administrative processes and standards associated with caseflow management remain largely opaque.

Expecting judges to grasp and apply caseflow management techniques without structured instruction is impractical. Most new judges transition directly from legal practice, where the professional culture and operational expectations differ markedly from those of the judiciary. Attorneys – especially those in criminal defense – tend to frame arguments around exceptions and illustrative anecdotes. In contrast, court managers, drawing upon data analysis, focus on developing procedures that address the more typical and predominant categories of cases, rather than the rare anomalies that often dominate anecdotal memory. Given the managerial responsibilities inherent in judicial office, structured education is essential to ease the transition and to ensure that judges can effectively administer strong case management practices.

Following initial orientation, newly appointed judges should be paired with a mentor judge who has demonstrated proficiency in case management – a skill set not necessarily tied to seniority. Mentor judges can offer guidance not only on handling high-volume dockets, but also on understanding and navigating administrative procedures. Supplemental training on emerging technologies for monitoring case progression should be jointly provided to judges and supervisory court staff. Although these groups are sometimes trained separately, joint sessions can facilitate shared understanding and improve coordination, generating benefits that might otherwise go unrealized. Workshops focusing on core court functions and responsibilities should also be offered regularly, with mandatory participation to ensure consistent professional development across the bench and administrative leadership. Table 6.2 synthesizes the principal recommendations outlined above and incorporates key elements identified by Friesen and associates (1991), which are characteristic of effective delay-reduction programs in criminal courts.

Table 6.2 Summary of Case Management Recommendations

Element	***Recommendations***
Leadership	The executive component structure of the court should take an active role in forging collaborative partnerships with all lead representatives from affected agencies. The partnership should work to ensure that the following caseflow techniques are being conducted: • Early prosecutorial screening and charge decision making • Early and appropriate assignment of defense counsel • Early exchange of discovery • Early resolution of possible motions • Meaningful events (including strict enforcement of plea cutoff and firm trial dates). Attorneys should be fully prepared at the arraignment conference meaning that judges must ensure that diversion program eligibility has been assessed, discovery was exchanged and reviewed, and that a plea offer was offered and discussed.
Goals	Time standards and goals should be promulgated with the intention that it will be received and understood by affected stakeholders.
Information	Select reports should be developed by management and shared with stakeholders to assess the caseflow along the four main performance metrics including clearance rate, time to disposition, active pending caseload, and trial date certainty.
Communications	Select supervisory and staff personnel should be added to speedy trial or district-wide caseflow committees. Subcommittees should also be developed in accordance with case management needs and new or evolving policy and procedure. In particular, a strong working relationship should be emphasized between judges and respective trial court team members with trial readiness meetings scheduled and attended on a weekly basis. Supervisory personnel should be empowered to increase their span of authority so that they can take ownership of performance outcomes.
Commitment	Commitment should be demonstrated through action-orientated behavior (i.e., active attendance at committee meetings, meeting deadlines for court-imposed initiatives, etc.).

(*Continued*)

Table 6.2 (Continued)

Element	***Recommendations***
Case management procedures	Procedures should be assessed to determine how cases are processed to determine problems with filing, exchange of discovery, scheduling, attorney assignment, and capacity to meet goals. A case-tracking consortium should be established to explore the feasibility of implementing the tenets of differentiated case management. Complex cases should be explored to determine the relative impact the full range of variables have on the rate and speed of resolution.
Mechanisms for accountability	Meetings between executive personnel of the division together with individual judges and supervisory staff should be attended on an ongoing, individual basis to evaluate case management performance. Supervisors should be charged with knowing the status of cases on their list, monitoring time between events, and assisting the judge in setting future dates. Together, they should evaluate cases early to determine complex and most probable backlog cases. Attorneys who are habitually unprepared should be required to return to court sooner than the normal adjournment period.
Attention to detail	The work performance of judiciary clerks and probation officers should be evaluated to ensure that the work product is in accordance with policy and procedure. The district should institute a data entry quality assurance program to monitor the accuracy and consistency of information. The total number of events and the lapse of time between events should be monitored closely and controlled based on individual case elements.
Education and training	A case management training course should be made available to judges and supervisory personnel with an emphasis on calendar management.
Backlog reduction	The feasibility of reducing the backlog should be determined in accordance with empirical-based data. Problem-centered policy analysis should be utilized to substantiate where additional or temporary resources are needed for the purposes of backlog reduction.

Judges – rather than administrators – exercise primary authority over their judicial colleagues. This reality underscores a broader organizational principle: individuals tend to place a high degree of credence in guidance received from peers who share similar professional backgrounds and experiences. And this dynamic is particularly salient in judicial settings, where the scope of the administrator's influence over judges is necessarily limited. For this reason, the paradigm at the center of the text identifies this chapter's discussion as "Human Resources Management *and* Consultation" (emphasis added). We add "consultation" to clearly delineate the difference between what court administrators *do* in "managing" staff and "consulting" with judges.

Apart from the other points of a working relationship made in this text, the partnership between a court administrator and a leadership judge brings to bear a consultant–client dynamic. The role of the court administrator is remarkably complex in this regard and must be carefully navigated, particularly for the neophyte who comes to the job without the benefit of knowing the range of judge personalities. For instance, when a judge makes an inquiry or requests clarification or guidance on a management issue, the administrator must view what is being asked (information gathering, diagnosis of an operational issue, or a proposed solution) in tandem with an awareness of deeper organizational factors that may influence judicial decision making. For the court administrator to be genuinely effective in this collaborative partnership, yet another "hat must be worn" – that of a consultant; they must be clear about the true purpose of the engagement and understand how the information they provide will be used.

In any courthouse setting, judges (some more than others) will request information about caseloads (clearance rates, backlogs, etc.), staffing models, workflow procedures, policy parameters, among a host of other matters. When these inquiries are made, the court administrator's responsibility extends beyond simply providing the information that is being requested (most anyone can do that). Instead, the administrator must identify the fundamental issues underlying the judge's inquiry. The judge may be inquiring because of internal or external pressures to more effectively manage the caseload, justifying budget demands, or navigating a difficult human resource issue that has not yet been formally reported. Functioning in this capacity requires that the court administrator respond diplomatically and gently probe the judge's line of questioning to assist the judge in pinpointing the problem so that the true cause, and more importantly the best solution, can be determined. Similar to the engagement process that is undertaken by a proficient consultant, the administrator should seek to increase the likelihood that any proposed action will be both acceptable (in theory) *and* workable (in practice). The administrator, akin to a consultant, achieves success not only by making sound recommendations that are documented and compensated for, but also by cultivating understanding and consensus. They also demonstrate a willingness to implement the suggested changes through evaluation and reassessment. But, unlike the consultant, failures under such circumstances for a court administrator are much more dire because they cannot simply move on to the next consulting job. Instead, they must "live with" the decisions that are ultimately made by the presiding judge or the bench en banc.

A court administrator regularly advises a leadership judge in this consultant-like role, bridging communications between chambers staff, administrative units, county agencies, the judiciary's central office, and other entities. Skilled court administrators will identify sources of problems and loci of resistance. The administrator/consultant will collaborate with the bench and shape processes that develop from those discussions so that judges perceive "ownership" of solutions, rather than feeling subjected to management's bureaucratic directives. This higher-level work and executive functioning should be conducted in a manner that enables judges (clients) to develop the ability to analyze and resolve similar issues in the future, just as an experienced court manager would do, even if it is not explicitly stated. The consultation should be carried out with the ultimate aim of strengthening the judge's administrative acumen and decision making, thus ensuring that the court is successfully managed in the long term.

Employee Satisfaction

The workload for court personnel is substantial and is oftentimes emotionally taxing because it entails exposure to the case narratives, testimony of traumatic incidents and crimes. And in some instances, these workplace experiences can result in vicarious trauma; as a result, repeated exposure can heighten the likelihood of burnout. Workforce studies demonstrate that these experiences, however indirect, reduce productivity while increasing absenteeism and staff turnover rates (American Psychological Association, 2023). Other, less dire circumstances can also psychologically impact judges and staff. For instance, the adoption of new technology, while often perceived to be positive, is not without a downside. Some employees, particularly those with longer tenure, may experience higher levels of anxiety or frustration when required to learn new systems. At the same time employees of a younger generation may hold the court to the same expectations that one would expect of a private entity; that is, resources should be allocated to make processes more rapid and seamless. The NACM (2024) found – perhaps unsurprisingly given the importance of court culture – that the primary obstacle in implementing new technologies is not the technology itself, but in getting employees to make the change and *use* it as intended. But, for court leadership to get people to do such things requires that it is both trusted and persuasive. Human resource departments are critical in this regard because they are responsible for supporting staff throughout these transitions, providing creative training opportunities that should clearly (and convincingly) articulate the rationale for the ongoing organizational and technological change.

Another notable challenge for the courts relates to matters of diversity. Given that courts engage with individuals from a variety of cultural, language, and socioeconomic backgrounds, it is essential for court officials to have the social competence required for effective interaction with represented populations. Bell (2022) underscored the necessity for courts to implement continuous training aimed at mitigating implicit bias and promoting equal treatment of stakeholders in the legal process, regardless of their background. Court personnel must also embody the diverse experiences of the populace they serve. A varied team of judges, administrators, and personnel enables close community relations, hence improving service delivery quality. At the same time, it reinforces the community's perceptions of representativeness and institutional validity. Conversely, a lack of diversity can lead to inequities in treatment and erode public trust and confidence in the judicial system.

It is widely acknowledged across the nation that court cases need ample time for resolution. Courts, as public institutions, are governed by laws, regulations, technologies, among other methods for case adjudication. Each of these factors influences public perception regarding the duration of a court case. However, "court administration" functions on a different clock. Few, if any, court administrators can complete their daily "to do" during any given day. The administrator's "representative" role is a significant factor contributing to this shortcoming. An administrator may regularly represent one or two judges or "the court" in various meetings with local government agencies or officials, in coordination and informational meetings with local law enforcement leaders, in local Bar Association meetings, or occasionally on a committee with local educators. Most administrators additionally convene court management committee sessions. The administrator also represents the court at other statewide meetings, including those with the state court administrative office. Numerous hours are expended or disrupted by various meetings, essential telephone calls, staff contacts, and a multitude of other activities. The prevailing circumstances for most administrators underscore the significance of diversity within the personnel and management. The administrator requires assurance in the competencies and expertise of personnel and management, as both staff and managers must possess the aforementioned skills to effectively *represent* the administrator (and by virtue of that – the court) when necessary and with minimal notice.

The concept of diversity and the related discourse do not imply the pursuit or employment of individuals based on their race, ethnicity, family background, past experiences, or educational qualifications. It necessitates something far more complex and beneficial; that is, a variety of experiences, talents, and management strategies to address the extensive difficulties and challenges faced by the courts, as demonstrated in prior roles. Courts require these attributes (among others) in their administration and personnel to fulfill their purposes and responsibilities. More simply, it pertains to how results are achieved and obligations to society are meted out. Diversity in courts entails empowering court administrators and their staff to enhance the court through beneficial contributions from myriad perspectives. Diversity in courts is essential as it facilitates the fulfillment of their mandate to ensure justice for all parties and to be viewed as doing so, irrespective of the case type. Few people comprehend or contemplate the administrative aspects influencing the quality of justice administered in the courthouse. Most people presume that the staff will exhibit the same commitment to an impartial and equitable procedure as that of the judges. For judges to effectively fulfill their roles, courts require public acceptance of the judicial rulings issued in the courtroom – an aspect for which staff and management bear little responsibility. A well-organized support structure comprised of personnel and managers equipped with the requisite skills, knowledge, and attributes is therefore fundamental to modern court systems. Furthermore, all personnel within the courthouse require access to resources that enhance their efficiency, as well as tools that judges can utilize to streamline the judicial process and improve access to justice.

The modern court is one which is dedicated to a wide range of diversity, encompassing skills, knowledge, experience, and empathy.

It also ensures that the organization instills confidence in the community that entering the courthouse will lead to a fully committed staff and management team, dedicated to upholding justice alongside the judges. To ensure that impartial, proficient, and informed personnel assist judges between scores and thousands of individuals daily (depending on the court size), non-judicial staff and leaders must provide extensive support that the public often overlooks or considers unnecessary. A court's commitment to the defined diversity is vital for attaining these objectives.

Employee retention constitutes a crucial and interconnected issue. Even when courts succeed in hiring competent professionals, many may resign prematurely. Research conducted by Walsh and Williams (2025) reveals that employee turnover is often influenced by a host of factors including occupational stress, limited advancement opportunities, and comparatively low compensation structures. Not unlike other organizations, high turnover rates put significant administrative and financial strain on the courts due to the sunk costs associated with hiring, onboarding, and training new personnel. To enhance retention, courts may adopt tactics including acknowledging employee achievements, creating explicit pathways for professional progression (succession planning), and fostering supportive and collaborative work environments.

To address the aforementioned points, and to the extent they have not already been done, the courts must expand and modernize their recruitment and outreach efforts to ensure a broad and diverse applicant pool. This pool should intentionally include individuals from various backgrounds, experiences, and perspectives, including those who have overcome significant hardships or faced systemic disadvantages. These efforts must be undertaken by human resource departments in a manner consistent with the applicable laws and policies that guard against discrimination, based on protected categories including race, sex, age, ethnicity, religion, national origin, color, sexual orientation, gender identity, pregnancy, disability status, or political affiliation (Administrative Office of the U.S. Courts, 2025).

Similar to other management and operational domains within the court, human resource departments should collect and then leverage data to ensure that decisions are empirically grounded. These data points will assist judges and administrators in formulating strategies to ensure stability in the court workforce, both in the short and long term. Judicial bodies that monitor and evaluate employee metrics, including the duration of the hiring process, inputs, activities, outputs, outcomes, and impacts of employee training, levels of employee satisfaction, and attrition rates, can render more informed staffing decisions. Human resource data analytics allow judicial leaders to identify the most difficult positions to fill, assess the effectiveness and sense of purpose associated with employment in the courts, and uncover areas of workforce misalignment.

With respect to employee satisfaction, the NCSC (2005) provides a framework for this in CourTool 9, the definition and purpose of which is as follows:

> Ratings of court employees assessing the quality of the work environment and relations between staff and management. Committed and loyal employees have a direct impact on a court's performance. This measure is a powerful tool for surveying employee opinion on whether staff have the materials, motivation, direction, sense of mission, and commitment to do quality work. Knowing how employees perceive the workplace is essential to facilitate organizational development and change, assess teamwork and management style, enhance job satisfaction, and thus improve service to the public.

Employee satisfaction is a vital element in the efficient running of the courts, influencing both daily activities and long-term outcomes related to organizational stability, public trust, and succession planning. The significance of "workplace happiness" can be understood for several reasons. The first relates to perhaps the most obvious, which is service delivery. As we noted in this chapter and throughout this text, courts operate within strict procedural frameworks – the work of which is constrained by substantial caseloads, limited resources, reduced budgets, and complex administrative demands. A court employee who is "happy" will be more likely to work accurately, quickly, and meticulously. This, in turn, improves case processing, lowers errors, and streamlines judicial proceedings. Second, high rates of satisfaction boost employee retention rates. Maintaining a cadre of competent professionals is crucial, given the court's need for specialized knowledge, experience, and skill. Frequent turnover increases recruitment and training costs, disrupts workflow, and reduces the court's ability to preserve its institutional memory. Third, court staff often function and are perceived as gatekeepers to the institution, meaning that the public's first interaction with justice is generally with clerks, probation officers, interpreters, IT staff, and other administrative staff. Employees who feel respected and supported are more likely to provide respectful, accurate, and timely assistance, improving procedural fairness and public trust in the court. Fourth, employee satisfaction reduces ethical misconduct. Employees who believe they are supported and valued are more likely to follow the court's ethical standards, laws, policies, and internal controls. Finally, a court with a content workforce will have a healthy organizational culture that is generally more professional, collaborative, and respectful. This level and kind of atmosphere is then more adaptable to new technologies, legislative changes, or crises that compel courts to change (and sometimes quickly). Courts with satisfied staff and management are more open to change, training, and innovation – all of which are vital for modernizing court operations.

Ensuring that the judiciary's most valuable commodity – its people – are supported requires that the court prioritize the physical and psychological welfare of its personnel. Transforming organizational structures in the courts – specifically how stakeholders communicate, collaborate, and complete their work – creates opportunities to better serve the public and fulfill the courts' purposes and responsibilities. It is not without a unique set of challenges. Shifts in work modes allow the judiciary to diminish its spatial needs and related infrastructure expenses, while concurrently promoting a more efficient and supportive organization. To make the best use of these advancements, the judiciary must continue investing in new technologies and institute procedures that enable a competent and efficient workforce. Such efforts enhance operational resilience, promote employee satisfaction, and underpin the long-term viability of court operations.

U.S. Government Accountability Office (2024) reports indicate that the judiciary requires more stringent regulations than other branches to avert harassment, discrimination, and retaliation. Human resource units must aim to cultivate an environment where court employees feel empowered to report misconduct. We have found that if employees are afforded respect and dignity in those processes, this will mitigate any apprehension they may otherwise have about communicating unethical information to leadership. Routine workplace climate assessments, confidential reporting policy and procedure, and supervisor training in trauma-informed management are all essential. A workplace that fosters safety and professionalism will at the same time enhance employee retention and performance. And, just as importantly, it will substantiate what court leaders are "saying" through their actions.

Succession Planning

The collapse of the Roman Empire in the 5th century resulted in the loss of its institutional knowledge of concrete for almost 1,500 years. Concrete during this historical period, however, was an exceptional building material. Roman concrete facilitated the creation of architectural masterpieces that remained unparalleled for generations, including harbor constructions, expansive vaults, monumental domes (the Parthenon in particular), and resilient submerged structures. Eventually (a millennium and a half later), it was discovered that the concrete was manufactured using pozzolana – a volcanic ash whose chemical qualities, in conjunction with lime, generated a building material of remarkable durability (Pruitt, 2025). With the dispersal of skilled laborers who had actual knowledge of concrete coupled with the disintegration of trade networks supplying the volcanic ash, what was lost was not only a recipe, but also tacit knowledge (Farmer, 2025). The art of creating the amalgamation could not be conveyed merely through communication because it required *actual* practice, supported by specific guidance.

This historical episode underscores a central truth about complex institutions; that is, when the transfer of knowledge is not deliberately cultivated, essential competencies can disappear within a relatively short period of time. The courts are not an exception to this reality. Instead, circumstances surrounding court administration make it quite the contrary. Consider that managing the courts depends on layers of institutional knowledge. Included in that range of "insider information" are caseflow management strategies, fiscal processes, and the ability to forge and maintain (oftentimes subtle) collaborative relationships among internal and external stakeholders. Much of this knowledge exists not in manuals or organizational charts, but also in the long-term, professional experience of judges, administration, and staff. Without an intentional and structured succession plan, courts risk a gradual erosion of institutional memory that could impair administrative capacity and diminish the quality of justice delivered to the public. Succession planning in the courts is, therefore, not an optional administrative exercise, but instead a strategic imperative essential to organizational continuity and long-term excellence.

Any substantive discussion of succession planning in the judicial branch must commence with an exploration of the structural and operational patterns that have developed over the last 20 years. This enables the court to foresee the difficulties and opportunities that will likely influence the judicial landscape in the future. This proactive perspective establishes the basis for judges and court administrators to formulate cohesive strategies for recruiting, training, and retaining future court leaders. Since the onset of the 2008 Great Recession, American society has experienced heightened division along demographic, economic, and ideological dimensions. The divisions are seen in the politicization of judicial selection processes, when party and ideological factors increasingly influence the appointment or election of judges. The trend has been intensified by the impact of social media platforms and the algorithmic reinforcement of preconceived notions about criminal justice, civil litigation, family relations, and the overarching prescribed roles of the courts in modern society.

These developments have occurred concurrently with significant impacts on judicial operations. Despite a long-term reduction in aggregate caseloads across numerous jurisdictions, the complexity of legal conflicts has intensified, alongside a growing population of self-represented litigants and increasing per-case costs. Nonetheless, court budgets have remained relatively static, even as facilities, technological equipment, and infrastructure continue to age. The COVID-19 epidemic catalyzed innovations, especially in the use of remote-access technology, but the degree and sustainability of these developments vary by jurisdiction. These advances were primarily motivated by increased public expectations concerning the online accessibility and responsiveness of the courts in the midst of the pandemic. Another important point to bear in mind is that while video/remote court hearings may enhance convenience for some, research indicates that it can also compromise accessibility and fairness for others (LaGratta et al., 2024). This factor can be particularly salient for self-represented litigants, individuals with disabilities, or those lacking reliable internet connectivity. Consequently, for human resource departments, the implementation of novel training methodologies is crucial. Employees must receive training in utilizing video platforms and operating case management systems, while also ensuring that data privacy is maintained. In addition, human resources must ensure that communication training is tailored to online settings to guarantee clarity and empathy in virtual public service interactions (Bannon & Adelstein, 2020).

Judges and court professionals must simultaneously manage limited and closely monitored budgets, while addressing the increasing public demand for culturally responsive services, therapeutic and problem-solving adjudication methods, and institutional proficiency in tackling various social issues, including shifts in family structures, community norms, and social needs. And all of this must be managed in light of the significant strain caused by staffing shortages and system inefficiencies (Thomson Reuters Institute, 2025). Shortages are particularly severe in positions necessitating specialized expertise, including those designated in IT, interpretation, finance, cybersecurity, and data analytics, since courts must contend with private-sector compensation and remote employment opportunities. Moreover, the hiring process in the courts is generally highly protracted and possibilities for court job advancements are comparatively more limited than those of the private sector. One of the ways the courts *can* compete is to engage those committed to public service by providing flexible employment opportunities, assisting with tuition or debt repayments, and establishing programs that facilitate career advancement for employees (Klaversma, 2021).

Notwithstanding those points, courts should prioritize paying higher, market-based competitive salaries for newly hired and incumbent staff when resources allow. Consider the instance when a deputy court administrator was promoted, and the court administrator approved the salary in accordance with the applicable compensation scale, resulting in an annual wage equivalent to that of the court administrator. The Administrative Office of the Courts cautioned against this decision, citing concerns regarding internal compensation equity; however, the court administrator asserted that newly hired or promoted employees should not be penalized due to the structural deficiencies in the compensation of current staff, including that of the court administrator. The court administrator contended that when funding is available, it ought to be utilized to fortify the organization instead of allowing it to be diverted for other purposes. A comparable strategy was employed when the same court administrator appointed a jury manager at 15 percent above the base compensation. These decisions, made individually, ultimately enhanced salary advancement across the board, yielding positive organizational impact.

Internships, visitations, and other partnerships between the courts and universities can also be used to draw on a more diverse and technologically proficient generation of employees. Collaborations can begin with visitation programs linked to pertinent course curricula offered by faculty at local universities and colleges. These experiences have been shown to broaden students' understanding of court administration, as they encompass an irreplaceable experiential learning opportunity beyond the classroom. Moreover, results demonstrate remarkable potential in shaping cognitive and affective learning outcomes by expanding students' understanding and appreciation for the work of the courts; in some instances, inspiring them to become the next generation of leaders (Fazari, 2024). These dynamics highlight the necessity of strategic succession planning, which is based on a comprehensive grasp of historical trends, present challenges, and the skills needed to manage courts effectively in a progressively complex environment.

Some courts have integrated AI tools to bolster their human capital capacity and mitigate the pressures associated with persistent staffing shortages and increasing caseloads. These technologies function as force multipliers. Among other things, AI can help alleviate the burden of limited human resources without compromising the quality of judicial services. By embedding AI-driven processes into routine operations, courts can preserve institutional knowledge and maintain the continuity of their operations and service delivery to the public. This can be particularly important during periods of transition (hiring freezes) or crises (pandemic or natural disaster including hurricanes or wildfires), when large segments of the workforce are unable to physically report to work at the courthouse. According to a recent report by the TRI/NCSC AI Policy Consortium for Law & Courts (2025), some potential applications of AI in the judicial environment include:

- Automating document summarization and redaction to reduce the time demands placed on court personnel
- Streamlining scheduling and case-processing workflows to promote efficiency and reduce backlogs
- Offering self-service tools for the public, such as automated jury-duty rescheduling, thereby decreasing administrative workload
- Providing real-time translation and transcription for virtual proceedings, which supports accessibility while minimizing reliance on scarce specialized staff

The foregoing points highlight the urgency with which the courts must safeguard the quality of their services, regardless of the precariousness or ambiguity of financial resources. In the absence of intentional organizational advancements, courts risk developing a workforce largely consisting of individuals who occupy these roles not due to professional dedication, but because they recognize limited viable alternatives. This possibility reinforces the need for courts to develop innovative strategies capable of attracting highly qualified young professionals to the administration of justice.

Meeting this challenge requires court systems to broaden the range of competencies they cultivate and to demonstrate that the profession demands a sophisticated, multi-dimensional skill set. Today's administrators must be proficient in collaborating effectively with various institutional partners, including local and state legislative bodies, executive-branch officials, justice-system agencies, and the media, while also addressing the concerns of the general public and the needs of culturally diverse communities. Their work increasingly entails the utilization of evidence-based approaches, incorporating validated risk-assessment instruments and data-driven decision-making tools that guide policy and operational decisions.

The administrator's role in directing the progression of cases within the court system is equally significant. Efficient case management and caseflow coordination increasingly necessitates proactive supervision and collaboration among judges, attorneys, law enforcement, and associated service providers. These responsibilities are accompanied by the expectation that administrators will facilitate system governance, enhance interagency coherence, and develop work processes that ensure institutional efficiency.

As judicial systems progress, the provision of services must similarly adjust. Numerous court jurisdictions are exploring decentralized models that utilize local, regional, and global resources to broaden access, increase responsiveness, and augment public engagement with the judiciary. Such innovations necessitate a workforce that not only values the proposition of enhanced court service, but also acknowledges that the knowledge, skills, and abilities acquired in this context are widely transferable. Court administration may represent a long-term career for some, while for others, it may serve as a significant phase within a broader professional journey. Together, these considerations illuminate the central challenge facing modern courts: cultivating a professional environment capable of attracting talented individuals, equipping them with the competencies demanded by the contemporary justice system, administration demands, and ensuring that the quality of court services remains optimal, despite persistent fiscal constraints.

Effective succession planning in the judiciary acknowledges that being a diligent protégé is as crucial as being a competent mentor. Aspiring court administrators must develop both technical expertise and a capacity characterized by curiosity, humility, and dedication to lifelong learning. Court administration requires not just procedural expertise, but also the cultivation of strong professional character and collaborative leadership skills. The court employee's "involvement" is crucial to institutional continuity. The perpetual difficulty, however, resides in getting proficient leaders who are both adept administrators and eager mentors – individuals capable of conveying the implicit knowledge that cannot be encapsulated in manuals, strategy plans, or competency frameworks.

Historical comparisons highlight the importance of rigorous apprenticeship. Alexander the Great is frequently lauded for his exceptional leadership and administrative skills. His accomplishments were not solely the result of inherent genius; they were rooted in the developmental phase he experienced as a student and assistant to King Philip of Macedon. By meticulously analyzing his father's strategies, diplomatic methods, and comprehension of human psychology, he gained insight over a relatively short period of time that would ordinarily have taken decades to cultivate (Worthington, 2014). His achievement exemplifies a bigger guiding principle: successful leadership is developed via experiential proximity, deliberate observation, and continuous interaction with a proficient mentor.

The courtroom setting underscores the significance of this principle. Judicial administration is a multifaceted and frequently ambiguous domain characterized by intricate organizational cultures, overlapping responsibilities, and unique professional standards of judges and court personnel. Managing these dynamics necessitates competencies – collaboration on policy and procedure, clarity in role definition, effective communication and negotiation, trust maintenance, and combined strategy planning – that can pose challenges even for experienced executives from other sectors. In this context, the ongoing dissemination of institutional information and court performance data is essential.

Succession planning within the judiciary must emphasize not only the identification of prospective leaders, but also the provision of substantial chances for mentorship under seasoned court managers. Similar to Alexander's mentorship, the efficacy of forthcoming court administrators will hinge on their capacity to assimilate, analyze, and eventually leverage the teachings of their teachers. In a system as complex as the judiciary, the ability to learn may be the most dependable indicator of enduring leadership success.

Tactics and Resistance

An administrator can employ various strategies to implement succession planning, both inside and outside the court. Simultaneously, emerging court leaders must be prepared for the inherent resistance that may come from personnel. Prior to implementing any of the recommended strategies, and in alignment with the preceding discussion, the administrator should consider the following inquiries to facilitate those endeavors:

- What are the notable changes that have transpired in the court over the last 10 to 20 years?
- What are the most significant crises encountered by the court?
- How did the court address such crises, and to what degree was it effective?

- How were the consequent modifications implemented and overseen?
- What insights were gained from the transformation?
- What methods were employed to complete individual tasks?
- Who were the stakeholders involved, and whose facets of the process did they influence?

Our experience shows that succession planning in the courts can be tricky. In almost every respect that we have discussed, the nature of managing the courts is both unique and complex. Planning for the next generation of court leaders is not an excluded rule to that process. Succession planning in the courts requires deliberate, methodical strategies to preserve institutional memory so that the continuity of administrative competence is preserved. Because courts rely heavily on tacit knowledge – much of which is held by those staff we earlier described as Lipsky's (1980) "street-level bureaucrats" – succession planning requires an assessment of the court that goes beyond formal documentation. This is critically important because *all* of the pertinent information is rarely captured in those artifacts.

We have found that conducting a survey of the court system allows administrators to identify critical positions and the essential competencies required in those service areas. Survey findings also reveal potential vulnerabilities in the court's operations and can pinpoint those areas of practice where institutional knowledge is at risk of being lost. An assessment that goes into the core of each of the court's operational units can also reveal the informal practices, historical precedents, and unwritten norms that define the court's internal culture, but are not documented in any new employee training manual. These kinds of "deep dive" assessments are indicative of high-performance courts.

One tactic that has been used for both judges and staff to capture institutional knowledge involves pairing potential successors with experienced employees through structured mentorship programs or "shadowing" opportunities. Observing how individuals manage their daily tasks and responsibilities affords emerging leaders with insight into the subtle competencies that formal training seldom provides. Among other factors, these experiences reveal how the court manager goes about interpreting policy, negotiating intra- and inter-departmental relationships, and resolving administrative problems of which there is no readily apparent definitive answer. Mentorship programs are particularly valuable because they make space for experiential learning. With this approach, one's management perspective and judgment calls are based on the reality of circumstances that exist in that particular court.

Institutionalizing the organization's history is another critical dimension of succession planning. Courts can benefit from systematically documenting the experiences of key personnel through formal oral history interviews. These interviews can be documented through the use of court reporters or audio recording.

Creating a "court history" not only preserves information about past practices and the court's evolution, but it also demonstrates how the values of the court have been communicated and maintained. In one district, the "court historian" responsibilities were assigned to the Ombudsman Office. In other instances, the role of collecting, organizing, and preserving material deemed critical to institutional knowledge was given to court operations (specifically to the librarian or records manager). Some courts provide oversight of such functions to human resources, which asks retiring employees to document their work processes during the last year of employment as a part of their career transitions. However the institutional knowledge is documented, it is important to distinguish how the work is accomplished. In those instances when the work is process driven, such as grand jury scheduling, video documentation can accurately depict how tasks are completed. These videos can provide future clerks and administrative personnel with concrete, replicable demonstrations. For higher managerial positions, structured interviews may be more appropriate. Positions that require more complex decision making would not be captured by following a court manager around with a camera. Interviewing the court manager would be more effective, allowing them to articulate their rationale and judgment calls based on experience and intuition.

The quality of these interviews depends heavily on the techniques employed. Skilled interviewers draw upon a variety of question formats. The nature and complexity of the administrator's work will dictate the best type of instrument for collection of information. Open-ended questions can serve as prompts to elicit reflection on the part of the interviewee about a court's process, procedure, or decision. Fill-in-the-blank questions should provide specific information and clarity regarding tasks or dilemmas. Multiple-choice items can provide future leaders and staff with decision pathways. Finally, true-false statements help to verify understanding of critical facts and issues. The interviewer's approach is equally important to the selected format. Court historians or other assigned practitioners who seek to document institutional knowledge can benefit from the "Columbo Method" of interviewing. This particular technique refers to an interviewing strategy modeled after the television detective Lieutenant Columbo, who was known for his disarming, humble, and seemingly absent-minded style (Levinson & Link, 1971–2003). Although he appeared confused or ineffectual, his approach consistently encouraged people to relax and volunteer valuable information they otherwise might withhold. Likewise, a court historian could utilize the same interviewing tactic. When executed correctly, the tactic can create a conversational environment that enhances candor and facilitates deeper knowledge extraction.

Despite the administrator's best efforts, various forms of resistance can undermine succession planning. This resistance, however, is a natural reaction of staff who may fear potentially losing their jobs. The fear of being marginalized by giving up their only source of power (their institutional knowledge) is felt acutely by these employees. And this is especially salient in the courts, where this "authority" was accrued only after many years of service. To share their knowledge, then, is to diminish the only leverage on the organization and influence that they have among peers. Knowing that employees may be naturally oppositional to succession plans, court leadership must incentivize them so the transfer of knowledge is more appealing. Whatever the incentive, leadership must know the basis of staff motivations so that consideration can be tailored to personal preferences.

Succession planning initiatives can commence with personnel who have formally declared their retirement or transition schedules. For positions designated as an essential function, or those with executive-level, administrative responsibility, the process may need to start earlier. In these instances, the court can run data related to years of service, projected retirement eligibility, and related indicators, and incorporate these data into long-term planning initiatives. This emphasis guarantees immediate knowledge acquisition, while exemplifying the process for other employees, alleviating concern, and illustrating that the program prioritizes organizational continuity rather than personnel displacement. Succession planning is inherently connected to and facilitated by court leadership, as it relies on their ability to implement these changes.

The presiding judge and court administrator must underscore the importance of preserving institutional knowledge and incorporate it into the court's long-term strategic planning. Absent ongoing support from court leadership, succession planning may be perceived as intrusive and inconsistent with the judiciary's objectives. Conversely, when leaders endorse transition planning, they validate the process, diminish opposition, and cultivate a court culture that prioritizes the transmission of the intergenerational knowledge as a vital component of the administration of justice.

Notes

1 Personal communication with a tenured presiding judge.

2 The ICM, NCSC, offers three levels of professional certification: Certified Court Executive, Certified Court Manager, and ICM Fellows.

3 NACM offers guidance on current and emerging ethical issues through "Question of Ethics" podcasts and articles in *The Court Manager*, https://nacmnet.org/question-of-ethics-podcasts.

4 Socrates famously likened himself to a "gadfly," whose purpose was to provoke reflection and challenge complacency in Athens. We use the term differently here – to describe an employee who acts as an "irritant" to court leadership by resisting or challenging efforts to manage the judiciary in accordance with agreed-upon policies and legal requirements.

References

Administrative Office of the U.S. Courts. (2025). Priority 4: Maintaining an exemplary judiciary workforce and workplace. In *Strategic plan for the federal judiciary*. www.uscourts.gov/data-news/reports/strategic-planning/strategic-plan-federal-judiciary/priority-4-maintaining-exemplary-judiciary-workforce-and-workplace.

American Psychological Association. (2023). *Work in America™ survey: Workplaces as engines of psychological health and well-being*. www.apa.org/pubs/reports/work-in-america/2023-workplace-health-well-being.

American Society of Public Administration. (2013). *Code of ethics*. www.aspanet.org/ASPA/ASPA/Code-of-Ethics/Code-of-Ethics.aspx.

Bannon, A., & Adelstein, J. (2020). *The impact of video proceedings on fairness and access to justice in court*. Brennan Center for Justice. www.brennancenter.org/our-work/research-reports/impact-video-proceedings-fairness-and-access-justice-court.

Bell, E. (2022). Helping courts address diversity, equity, and inclusion. *Judicature, 106*(2). https://judicature.duke.edu/articles/helping-courts-address-diversity-equity-and-inclusion/.

Deming, W. E. (1986). *Out of the crisis*. MIT Press.

Deming, W. E. (2005). *Critical evaluations in business and management* (J. C. Wood & M. C. Wood, Eds.). Routledge.

Farmer, J. P. (2025, July 21). The lost secret of Roman concrete: How 2,000-year-old buildings are outlasting modern skyscrapers. *Men of Pompeii*. www.menofpompeii.com/the-lost-secret-of-roman-concrete-how-2000-year-old-buildings-are-outlasting-modern-skyscrapers/.

Fazari, G. M. (2024). From classroom to courtroom: Engaging today's students to become tomorrow's court professionals. *Trends in State Courts*, 72–83.

Felps, W., Mitchell, T. R., & Byington, E. (2006). How, when, and why bad apples spoil the barrel: Negative group members and dysfunctional groups. *Research in Organizational Behavior, 27*, 175–222.

Friesen, E. C. (1991). *Caseflow management principles and practices: How to succeed in justice.* National Center for State Courts.

Friesen, E. C., Mahoney, B., & Solomon, M. (1991). *Caseflow management, principles and practices: How to succeed in justice* [Videotape]. National Center for State Courts.

Gardner, J. W. (1990). *On leadership: Chapter 9: Fragmentation and the common good.* Free Press.

Griller, G. A. (2010). Governing loosely coupled courts in times of economic stress. *Trends in State Courts*, 28–34.

Klaversma, L. G. (2021). *Recruitment, selection, and retention of IT staff.* National Center for State Courts. https://ncsc.contentdm.oclc.org/digital/collection/hr/id/209/.

LaGratta, E., Danser, R., & Greiner, D. J. (2024). Litigant empowerment through choice? Insights from an ongoing study of remote versus in-person family court hearings. *Trends in State Courts*, 30–39.

Lefever, D. (2005, October 20). The integration of the managerial and judicial cultures of the court. Paper presented at the Mid-Atlantic Association for Court Management Annual Conference, Ocean City, MD.

Levinson, R., & Link, W. (Creators). (1971–2003). *Columbo* [Television series]. NBC; ABC.

Lipsky, M. (1980). *Street-level bureaucracy: Dilemmas of the individual in public services.* Russell Sage Foundation.

Mintzberg, H. (1979). *The structuring of organizations: A synthesis of the research.* Prentice Hall.

National Association for Court Management (NACM). (2005). *Core competency curriculum guidelines: What court leaders need to know and be able to do.*

National Association for Court Management (NACM). (2016). *The court administrator, Court administration: A guide to the profession.*

National Association for Court Management (NACM). (2024). *Courting AI: Understanding artificial intelligence in courts.*

National Association for Presiding Judges and Court Executives. (2016). *Leadership guide 1: Building and maintaining productive pairs.*

National Center for State Courts. (2005). *CourTools: Trial court measures.* www.ncsc.org/our-centers-projects/courtools.

National Center for State Courts. (2010). *High performance court framework: A road map for improving court management.* www.ncsc.org/_media/Files/PDF/Services%20and%20Experts/Areas%20of%20expertise/High-Performance-Courts/High-Performance-Court-Framework.ashx.

Pruitt, S. (2025). The secrets of ancient Roman concrete. *History.* www.history.com/articles/the-secrets-of-ancient-roman-concrete.

Saari, D. J. (1970). *Modern court management: Trends in the role of the court executive* (U.S. Law Enforcement Assistance Administration Report). U.S. Government Printing Office.

Stott, E. K., Jr. (1982). The judicial executive: Toward greater congruence in an emerging profession. *The Justice System Journal*, *7*(2), 152–179.

Thomson Reuters Institute. (2025, June). *Staffing, operations and technology: A 2025 survey of state courts*. www.thomsonreuters.com/en-us/posts/wp-content/uploads/sites/20/2025/06/Staffing-Operations-and-Technology_2025-survey-of-State-Courts.pdf.

TRI/NCSC AI Policy Consortium for Law & Courts. (2025, August 11). *Preparing for future workforce needs*. National Center for State Courts. www.ncsc.org/resources-courts/preparing-future-workforce-needs.

U.S. Government Accountability Office. (2024). *Federal judiciary: Additional actions would strengthen efforts to prevent and address workplace misconduct* (Report No. GAO-24–105638). www.gao.gov/products/gao-24-105638.

Walsh, J., & Williams, A. R. (2025). *Opportunities for rewarding work vary widely within and across counties*. Urban Institute. www.urban.org/urban-wire/opportunities-rewarding-work-vary-widely-within-and-across-counties.

Welch, D. (2011, August 25). General Motors CEO Dan Akerson is not a car guy. *Bloomberg*. www.bloomberg.com/news/articles/2011-08-25/general-motors-ceo-dan-akerson-is-not-a-car-guy.

Worthington, I. (2014). *By the spear: Philip II, Alexander the Great, and the rise and fall of the Macedonian Empire*. Oxford University Press.

7 Court Funding and Budget Management

Funding for and of the judiciary has been a matter of contention and, to some extent, subject to local political forces since the founding of the United States. It is linked to the multiple layers of courts that existed in the new country and continues as part of the debate about whether and to what extent trial courts should be funded by the state, local government (counties or cities), or some combination of both. Decisions by the legislative and executive branches regarding funding and how a state structures its court system impact almost all aspects of court operations, organization, and support by the public. It is difficult to overstate how funding decisions in the two other branches of government either facilitate or hinder the effectiveness of the entire judicial branch, but especially that of trial courts.

Once courts are given a budget by local or state authorities, management of those funds is critical to how leaders of the two other branches of government and the public perceive the court. Management of the court budget can influence how judges and court staff view the competency of court administrators. A lack of demonstrated competence, accountability, and transparency in fiscal domains leads to negative perceptions, and those views directly impact a court's ability to maintain adequate funding and to obtain additional resources needed to improve services to the public and stakeholders.

Sound fiscal management also is required to deal with budget increases and decreases that follow the normal fluctuations of the national and/or local economy – putting aside the Great Recession and Great Depression. The Great Recession of 2008–2009 and its aftermath for public-sector revenue demonstrated two things: 1) it is very difficult to anticipate major cuts in budgets (15 percent or more in a year) that occur with little or no warning and to respond in a timely manner; and 2) notwithstanding this near unprecedented challenge, each court needs to

DOI: 10.4324/9781003686804-7

have, in advance, a clear understanding of its priorities should a significant budget cut (10 percent or more) occur, just as it should have a "continuity of operations" plan for a response to major natural and man-made disasters (fires, floods, acts of terrorism, and firearm attacks and/or hostage situations in or near a courthouse).[1]

These two aspects of judicial administration are, on one level, among the most complex challenges for a court leadership team. They are challenging because they demand a clear understanding of and commitment to the court's strategic priorities by institutional leaders and, hopefully, by the full bench and staff. Complexity is also introduced by both internal and external political considerations, and the varying levels of leadership skills of court administrators for these kinds of negotiations. Internal political considerations and the need to negotiate terms often arise in setting priorities for the next budget and when some stakeholders seek funding for preferred priorities that are not accorded the same level of import by the bench and/or the court's leadership.

At the same time, some aspects of funding and budgeting are largely "mechanical" and, thus, "simple." In budgeting, the process involves allocating most of this year's budget numbers to the next year's budget with numeric or percentage adjustments up or down as required by the funding authority, predicated on fiscal projections. For budgetary management, the "simple" aspects include keeping track of revenue and expenditures, allocating and reporting those monies fully and properly to appropriate authorities; paying invoices fully and on time; ensuring the timely collection of court-ordered financial obligations (e.g., restitution, fines, and fees); and ensuring that expenses do not exceed the allocated budget. There is also a need to monitor and pursue bail forfeitures so the court remains current regarding that account. These tasks normally are performed by court staff. Ideally, at least one of the staff has accounting skills and knowledge, even in small courts, but these functions must be overseen by court leadership. At times, administrators need to understand the details of these processes to properly oversee them and to make systemic improvements. When any of the processes break down (and they inevitably do), finding the reason(s) and correcting it/them is neither mechanical nor simple. The following sections address each of these topics and challenges.

Funding

Sources of Funding

In Federalist Paper 78, Alexander Hamilton described the judicial branch of the federal government under the proposed Constitution as "the least dangerous branch... because [federal courts] had neither soldiers nor money to enforce their decrees" (Rosen, n.d., citing Hamilton, 1788). Today, all states are structured like the U.S. Constitution's model of three branches of government: the judicial branch incorporates similar powers, however, it lacks the "power of the purse." Hamilton's description was a political assessment. Most of those now serving in the judicial branches of both federal and state governments would argue that courts do not have sufficient money to operate effectively, much less to fully enforce their decrees.

For most of this country's history, the host government unit responsible for funding courts has a paralleled local court structure. That is, cities funded city courts – where they exist – counties funded counties' limited and general courts, and the states funded appellate courts.[2] The contemporary national picture is less clear. For the past 50 or so years there has been a movement to consolidate limited and general jurisdiction trial courts into respective counties, thereby reducing the number of limited jurisdiction courts. Policy drives funding requests and in those instances when necessary monies are not provided, it compels the court to reassess its priorities. Bearing this general process in mind, trends show the reassigning of local court funding to the state. As this book goes to press, there are at least 20 states that have assumed full responsibility for funding the operations of all county trial courts.[3] Addressing the debate between state and local court funding, Carlson et al. (2008) note the following espoused benefits of the state court funding model:

> The state level judiciary sees an opportunity to achieve higher levels of trial court funding, greater equity of funding and services across the state's trial courts, and greater uniformity of practice.

A few of these states have also assumed responsibility for the maintenance and construction of local courthouses. These latter costs are so significant, however, that only eight states have accepted facility costs as a state obligation; all other states continue to require counties to fund some or all courthouse construction and building maintenance costs.[4] Regardless of which government level funds trial courts, the judicial branch virtually everywhere struggles to obtain the funding that the legal community, judges, and administrators generally regard as sufficient.

The adequacy of court funding depends on one's perspective. For instance, many state court systems desire the staff levels and facilities characteristic of federal courts. Most rural courts covet the funding levels found in more affluent counties. Even after a shift to state court funding, smaller, previously underfunded courts may not necessarily obtain funding equivalent to the level of larger urban courts as determined by cost per-judge, per-case filing, per-staffing member, or other basis.

Viewed externally, most court systems have been strained by funding pressures for decades, most notably during the Great Recession of 2008. Budget cuts in some courts during this period alone were 20 percent or more. Courts' budgets have been reduced in virtually every business cycle, but the decreases during the two-year period of the Great Recession were the most remarkable since the Great Depression. Consequently, funding level reductions following the Great Recession have since been dubbed the "new normal" (Schauffler & Kleiman, 2010).

Some aspects of trial court funding are determined by its source of those monies. When trial courts are funded locally, a court's budget competes for funds with other county departments and agencies. Budget levels are impacted by local politics and existing priorities that can transmute year to year, depending on shifts of power and personal relationships between the judges/administrators and elected local officials. This latter point can be a powerful and instrumental factor with respect to court requests for new funds or, at minimum, to limit budget cuts commensurate with local government funding reductions. The outcome of all budget requests is relegated by the quality of the justification and empirically based data in support of the budgetary item. Having said that, local politics and personal influence can be more compelling in some jurisdictions than the evidence provided in a budget justification.

When referencing personal influence, it is not to suggest being socially active with leaders of the other branches or having a long-term relationship with those persons is necessarily unacceptable. In some instances that may be the case, but court leaders cannot count on those types of personal relationships or despair if they lack them. More important is transparency regarding each court's visible system improvements (some requiring funds and others made without more funds), where and why the court is struggling operationally, and why current funding is insufficient to meet the court's critical needs. Transparency thus builds trust. And trust is essential if leaders of the other branches are to take statements about the court's resource needs seriously. Arguments such as "we're the third branch and have to be funded to the level we say we need," if they ever worked, are simply not heeded today. This is particularly true now, given the tight fiscal climate in which governments at all levels must contend; courts are not exempt from these pressures because they are providing "justice." Incomplete answers to legitimate questions from the other branches' budget staff are imprudent and will in many instances result in the request being denied, but moreover, set a poor precedent in building trust to cooperate and collaborate in the future. Court leaders also have to create and accept opportunities to meet with leaders of the other branches to develop those relationships so that mutual understanding and trust is fostered.[5]

Finally, the willingness of courts to engage the community to draw insight and support among citizens impacts how budget requests are viewed by elected officials of other branches. Community engagement can facilitate multiple interactions with the public, from judges' appearances before community groups (not for election purposes), judicial and staff participation in community activities (county fairs, helping with managing events and other local fundraising affairs, etc.), various "judge in the classroom" programs, student tours of courthouses and observing trials, and ethically appropriate involvement with charitable organizations and other civic activities. The administrator – or public information officer in larger courts – can issue press releases regarding court job promotions, significant hires, retirements, and technological and operational improvements that benefit court users. These efforts, among others, will humanize the court in unique ways so that it remains relevant in the public consciousness, and help garner public support for its programs and services.

No leader in the two other branches – especially no finance director – believes there is enough revenue to meet all budget needs. This reality is also true with respect to each level of government funding the courts. States have more gross revenue than local jurisdictions and, generally, more flexibility in the sources of income, but the resource demands are greater too. When trial court funding shifts to the state, the key difference is that each trial court now competes with all of the other state-funded courts in the state, not only with local government agencies and associated priorities.[6] When the judicial branch budget is consolidated, it must compete with all other state programs and funding needs. Generally, in this process, no individual court needs are discussed in detail during the judicial branch's budget presentation. Rather, statewide needs are combined into a single summary and advocated for as needs of *all* trial courts. In some respects, the above discussion about how to sell a budget locally may seem irrelevant. Except that data (performance measures compared to best practices) and cogent statements about the consequences of not getting new funding or losing existing funding remain essential, along with cost–benefit analysis for major new investments in the court. When it comes to state funding, requests are submitted to judicial branch reviewers, who are generally knowledgeable about how courts work as well as how they *should* work. State-level judicial branch specialists are also normally more demanding than those at the local government level. Public support from local citizens or groups may be helpful at the margins, once a budget is addressed in a public hearing at the state legislature, but it is generally not as compelling at the state level.

There are advantages and challenges with both court funding models. The decision about how a state's trial courts will be funded is more political than fiscal, although the financial element is often very important to city and county leaders. Shifting to state court funding may save local authorities significant money for other needs. However, court-generated revenues (fine and fees) are generally shifted from the local court government entity to the state, as a quid pro quo in the state court funding model. The concerns that the courts and some provincial leaders voice about losing "local control" are generally not enough to outweigh the fiscal relief that the state provides in taking on overall costs. Another consequence, sometimes overlooked, is that citizens in the county or city still perceive the court as their local court, which can adversely impact local politicians and the court. On the other hand, local courts are often told that because the state has more money than local government, the shift will make them more adequately funded. Sometimes state court funding works, sometimes it does not (depending on who is asked).[7] The key is that the needs of individual courts are merged into the needs of all courts, statewide.[8] It is then incumbent on the legislature to consider the collective needs of the courts and how many total dollars will be allocated to the judicial branch. State legislators usually leave the specifics of how those dollars will be allocated to the various courts and distributed among assorted programs to the state-level judicial branch authorities, e.g., the chief justice, judicial council, administrative director, and the administrative office of the courts.

This dynamic – the allocation of funds within the statewide court budget – introduces another level of complexity in most state-funded states. Local courts, particularly larger courts and judges and/or administrators who have developed good political relations with their local state legislators, may continue to lobby for the funding needs of their individual courts. These local needs may or may not match the priorities of the state judicial leaders.[9] Organizational turmoil and miscommunication can set in because legislators become uncertain about whether to seriously consider requests made by state leaders or those proposed by local constituents. If local courts are particularly effective politically, they may get the legislature to earmark funds that other courts also might need, but are not afforded because there is only so much money available and each court generally prioritizes its own needs first. The remedy, however draconian, is for state judicial leaders to prohibit lobbying by local leaders or to designate spokespersons in the respective counties who they know will support the state-level priorities. These efforts create better assurances that the judiciary speaks with "one voice." That said, neither approach necessarily ends "back-door" deals that are sometimes struck, but a singular judicial branch message can reduce prevalence and relative impact of unsanctioned communications (Durham & Becker, 2011; Mundell & Jefferson, 2011).

Another way that the state's leadership can skew the allocation of funds is to set aside a "fund" for grants to support a specific item (e.g., security enhancements, jury improvements) and/or for pilot efforts to test new procedures or changes in rules that require monetary support (e.g., new process for juvenile cases or better handling of conservatorship and guardianship cases). Grants for specific programs may benefit smaller courts that could not otherwise obtain the funding, but pilots tend to favor larger courts because they have specialized staff and a greater number of jurists who are able to support the initiative. Smaller courts may not have the resources to administer a pilot effort and participation is more easily vetoed by a smaller contingent of judges who think that the pilot may fail. Consequently, resources can accrue at a faster pace for the better-endowed courts than those made available to their smaller counterparts.

Even if the aggregate funds for trial courts are increased (which is not assured) in state-funded court states, so too are the resource demands. Larger courts – normally in counties that are relatively richer than smaller counties – will not willingly relinquish previous levels of funding to help upgrade the budgets of nominal-sized courts that have been historically underfunded.[10] Larger courts do not object to underfunded courts being given more funds, *provided* the funds these larger courts receive are not curtailed and continue to cover their continuingly increasing costs, such as negotiated raises for staff, increased technology maintenance costs, increased costs for facility rent and maintenance, and other "essential" expenses. Smaller courts in lower-resourced counties are disadvantaged when competing with courts in traditionally affluent counties at the state level for a share of the state legislature's budget allocation, as richer courts normally also have greater political clout within the judicial branch.

In short, there is no "magic bullet" regarding which government entity funds the trial courts. There are only advantages and disadvantages that each state together with their respective courts must weigh. The type of funding authority notwithstanding, the need for data-driven performance measures and evidence-based budget justifications remain essential to funding and budget management because those metrics demonstrate the objective impact of funding levels on litigants and the general public.

Non-Fiscal Challenges

There are three non-fiscal issues that affect court funding at the local and state levels. First, prior to the advent of professional court administrators, many legislators and budget professionals in the executive branch disregarded the courts' ability to effectively manage existing capital and human resources, to create compelling justifications for new funds, and, sometimes, to prudently manage the budget funds. There have been at least two generations of legislators and executive-branch officials since appointment of the first state-level and trial court professional administrators. The other branches' view of courts and their budget management skills, and the skills brought by their professional managers, have improved materially over the years. Yet, some executive-branch budget professionals and legislators still rank the judiciary third in budget justifications and management skills, behind the legislative and executive branches.

The second factor can be broadly characterized as "politics." Negative views about an appellate court decision or trial-court result (usually a criminal verdict or sentence), whether in one's hometown or state or, occasionally, someplace else, if intense enough, can affect – and have affected – budget decisions by the two other branches. When this occurs, the concepts of the adjudicative independence of the judiciary and separation of powers are ignored or flatly rejected. In these instances, no argument using statistical performance measures will dissuade the efforts of politicians to reprimand the court for some perceived malfeasance in decision making.[11]

Lest readers think it is only judicial rulings that can negatively affect a court budget, a significant shortfall or failure on the administrative side of a trial court or state administrative office will have similar outcomes. Examples of administrative failures include the poor implementation and high costs of new case management information systems, undetected theft by a court employee that spanned years, bribery of a staff member to alter or delete records, disagreements between legislators or executive-branch fiscal officers and the court administrator that become personal, a failure to pursue aggressively enough (in the eyes of the other branches) the collection of bail forfeitures and fine payments, and significant mismanagement of budgeted funds. Serious administrative lapses can impair the relationship between a court or the branch and the two other branches for several years.[12] If the court's management of its funds is believed to be or is shown to be misleading, any budget request for new resources or maintaining the same funding levels will almost certainly be jeopardized, even if the miscreant(s) is ultimately dismissed.

Related to this point is the divergence in perspectives between judicial branch leaders and budget authorities in the two other branches. Judges and administrators see the judicial branch as equal to the other two branches – whether state or local. Thus, they believe the judiciary's budget should be afforded the same deference legislators accord that of their branch and the governor (or the budgets of the city or county). Unfortunately, those with decision-making authority in the two other branches may view funding levels of the courts proportionate to those of any executive branch agency or department, as opposed to those of an entirely separate and co-equal branch of government, requiring equal inter-branch treatment. Most budget analysts in the other branches deny this perception, but many court budget decisions suggest otherwise. This can obviously frustrate efforts of judicial branch leaders who work to ensure that the courts are adequately funded.

Even when the judiciary's best budget efforts are to no avail, we recommend against abandoning the argument that the judicial branch is a constitutionally created branch that benefits all of society and it is as critical to the operation of government as the other branches. Treating the judicial branch's budget as equivalent to that of an agency or department undermines the essence of the nation's three-branch form of government. The constitution of the state does not require a welfare or road department, or even a police department and a prosecutor's office per se. It does require a judiciary. This argument may be too abstract in the frenzied days before the final court budget is approved, but it should not be abandoned or recognized as a "technical" footnote when the budget is being reviewed and considered. Instead, it should be a regular part of a court's communication with leaders of the other branches, reinforced by open communication, transparency, and the performance measurement approaches suggested heretofore.

There is one crude aspect of "politics" that courts cannot overcome: Arguably, no elected official at the local or state level has gained or lost votes because of the size of a court's budget. Ethical restraints on judges (and derivatively, administrative staff) mean that court representatives cannot promise to deliver votes or threaten to shift votes to another person or party. The currency of politics, especially local politics, has been and always will be votes. Courts have none of that currency. Judges cannot even endorse or give a speech in support of those seeking office in the other branches. Over time, judges also lose whatever access to that currency they may have possessed when appointed or elected. This makes it more difficult on courts than on some other budgetary units and agency heads in the days prior to finalizing the budget.

Many presiding judges and administrators are also "politically" challenged by legislators and executive-branch leaders who ask why the court should get more funds "at the expense of – single mothers, children, the sick and addicted, and/or other at-risk populations, not to mention fixing potholes and police protection." Implicit in the message is that the court cannot effectively meet the assigned burden. Court leaders often have difficulty showing how at-risk populations and public safety benefit from an effective court system that is fully staffed, has sufficient facilities and equipment, and has the technology needed for its operations and the public's need for access, transparency, and accountability. Providing resources such as food, housing, and clothing for needy children is a relatively straightforward argument that can be articulated in one sentence; whereas courts resource arguments are more nuanced and multi-dimensional, thus not as easily captured. In times of limited funding – a seeming constant in many jurisdictions – meeting the resource needs of the courts is generally not a good use of time for politicians because it does not yield a sizable bloc of votes.

Courts should accept objective scrutiny of their budgets and performance standards – to the extent that performance of the justice function can be quantified – particularly for requested budget increases, but not if the scrutiny is ill-considered and the court is regarded as inferior to the two other branches. Court leaders may also need to comport themselves in a more business-like fashion in assessing individual judges' requests. This means being pragmatic when evaluating judges' proposals – such as staffing, scheduling, or resources – by weighing those preferences and desires against organizational priorities, fiscal constraints, and measurable performance goals, rather than giving those requests default approval. There is no easy or short-term answer to this challenge, but data, transparency, accountability, having court users make the case in writing or in person at budget hearings, and strong working relationships with leaders of the two other branches are some of the key elements of a long-term strategy.

The third factor relates to data, which is both within a court's control and beyond it. Data are critical to support budget requests, but their use in court budget justification is inhibited by four restrictions: 1) the lack of any data supporting a specific budget request; 2) incomplete or incorrect data the court itself does not trust; 3) using easily obtained summary data – i.e., case filing and disposition data – in convoluted arguments that the legislature and executive recognize as not supporting the requested funds; or 4) the court not persuasively using the performance data it collects. There are two primary reasons for each of these challenges. The first and most important is often limitations of the court's information system. An outdated system that does not capture needed data elements in its "standard" reports with limited report customization is the principal problem in many courts. The inability of courts to obtain funds to upgrade or replace outdated systems is a key factor. Generally, these costs are considered to be capital investments and legislators and executive-branch budget officials typically fund ongoing operational costs ahead of capital costs. Capital items are often only allocated in a limited, set amount of funds despite the fact that these "capital" funding needs far exceed amount of the funds made available each year.[13] Courts, therefore, need to more effectively compete for these capital funds. Unless the two other branches recognize that these needs are interconnected with the direct interests of the state or voting public, capital investment into other entities are often given higher priority.

Courts do not choose to have ineffective or limited information systems, but are often instead saddled with these antiquated systems because they are unable to secure the necessary funding to replace or improve the technological infrastructure. More than a decade ago, most court software development companies did not understand all of the data requirements and myriad business functions of courts. Today's information systems and "standard" reports are vastly better. Ad hoc reports can be created more readily and with greater ease. Reports can be customized with little difficulty. The ability of individual courts to obtain customization of "off the shelf" software remains a significant issue, but the capacity to produce useful reports and create graphs and charts is far superior to the limited reporting capabilities that burdened courts for generations.

Even with good sources of data, court administrators and court budget staff often lack training on how to effectively present the data. Tables, for instance, must be simple: no more than four or five rows and columns and preferably fewer. Short paragraphs describing the key point(s) of the tables and charts are also needed for those who learn best through words rather than figures and depictions. The performance data should focus on core court needs and impacts of various funding levels, including budget reduction scenarios for mandated functions. It is incumbent on court administrators and budget managers to explore all available information sources to gain insights and enhance their budget presentations. The court can leverage the approach it takes to garner a more competitive advantage in the arena with executive and legislative departments, agencies, boards, and commissions.

Finally, on the import of data, too often courts only cite increases in case filings and dispositions as evidence that they need more judges and/or more staff. Several states now have weighting systems to determine the number of required judges and associated staff; that is, they evaluate workload compared to the number of judges as opposed to caseload alone (Tallarico, 2010). Among other factors that are applied to staffing models, these systems also assess how much time (on average per judge for each case type) is used to resolve each case handled by the court. This figure is multiplied by the number of cases in each category to determine total judicial resources demand. The amount of time each judge must devote to disposing of cases is multiplied by the number of judges on the court. The total amount of time required for all cases documents the demand, which is then compared to the total number of judges. This methodology, in turn, demonstrates whether a court has enough judges or needs more. In rare instances, the calculation shows a court or a particular court department has more judges than what the demand justifies. In this situation, judicial branch leaders may determine that it is necessary to reassign existing judgeships, say from the civil department to the criminal department or from one county to another.

A few courts and states have developed similar workload-based assessments for court staffing levels (Supreme Court of New Jersey, Administrative Office of the Courts, 2003). Such calculations are difficult to apply to court staff on a statewide basis (judicial workload typically is determined statewide) because of differences in technology and the methods for allocation of work among staff. Therefore, some courts develop a system of separate workload numbers for court staff positions. Even without a formal study, individual courts can use an ad hoc study[14] of the amount of time a clerk needs to complete certain tasks for particular case types or functions, assess the workload based on the number of cases vis-à-vis that case type to be processed per clerk, and the staff time available to process those cases – i.e., the same approach as with weighted caseload systems for judges – and thus document workload statistically to determine if the current contingent of staff is reasonable given the workload.

These types of analyses and presentations are far more compelling than arguing that "filings have increased from X to Y in the last three years, staff has not increased in that time, so we need two more staff positions." Justifying one or more judge or staff positions based on workload does not guarantee that new positions will be funded, but it offers a more persuasive argument than using caseload alone.[15]

General Fund

Historically, courts have been seen as a general obligation of government, akin to the funding model for the legislative and executive branches. They are "general obligations" because the constitutions of the nation and every state provide that the branches exist and essential services are assigned to each. All citizens benefit in some respect from each institution, directly or indirectly, and, therefore, all citizens should contribute to the institution's existence by way of the operational budget. This concept was reaffirmed by the Conference of Chief Justices (CCJ) and Conference of State Court Administrators (COSCA) (2018):

> Courts should be entirely and sufficiently funded from general governmental revenue sources to enable them to fulfill their mandate. Core court functions should generally not be supported by revenues generated from court-ordered fines, fees, or surcharges.

This history remains relevant, as affirmed by the said conferences, but it has often been deemphasized by the two other branches in the last few decades. Today, the budget needs of most courts continue to be met through the general fund of the host funding authority. The concept of a general benefit to all remains, but it has been tempered in some respects. In many jurisdictions, the demands on the general fund exceed the money available annually. Once funds are committed from the general fund in one year, they often become ongoing annual expenses that press the capacity to meet other financial needs in later years. There are two modifications that mitigate the impact of the subsequent-year commitments: growth in the revenue sources that comprise the general fund (e.g., real estate, sales, and income taxes and fees) and cutbacks in expenses – either mandated cuts by the funding authority or expenditure reductions due to operational efficiencies and/or technology improvements. Each year, courts must compete for these general funds. There are no assurances that court budgets will increase to meet increases in expenses. As noted above, the ability of courts to compete with executive branch counterparts funded from the general fund is inherently more limited than that of these other entities.

There is an unspoken but recognized aspect of the general fund's annual gap between available revenue, requests, and needs: legislators have the authority to take all or part of unspent monies or reserves held by any agency or department, including that of courts, previously designated as dedicated for specific and often-important needs. The legislature exercises this power when its current priorities are deemed important enough to do so, often in absence of overarching policy or rules. This happened in many local court jurisdictions and states during the Great Recession. Courts were not the only budgetary domain affected by these cash "seizures," or "sweeps," but the reserves of courts were more likely than other agencies to incur fund sweeps. Monies garnered through funding sweeps may be earmarked for future capital needs (Baar et al., 2010). Given that courts often have difficulty obtaining needed capital funds and software upgrades, the loss of these funds can be particularly difficult to absorb. In some state-funded court systems, judiciary budget authorities did the same thing with reserves held by trial courts during the Great Recession. This feature of government funding becomes a budget-management crisis as soon as it happens, making court funding exceedingly challenging and, sometimes, tenuous at best.

There is a parallel feature of funding and budget creation in some states that is even more invidious. It is the failure to fund statutorily or contractually required accounts, sometimes year after year. Some states, counties, and cities across the nation have not fulfilled their obligation to fund employee retirement funds, for example, so they can spend those funds on the needs for the current year rather than increase taxes.[16] Illinois is one of the most notorious of these government units, but it is not an anomaly. Court employees can be adversely impacted by this practice if their pension accounts are shorted in this way. The distinction between failing to fund contractual or statutory obligations, such as retirement accounts, and diverting money from dedicated court funds lies primarily in which category of government employee is affected.

In an attempt to guard against being underfunded by the legislature, some state court systems have sought legislation mandating that the judiciary receive a specific percentage of each year's budget or revenue. The constitution of West Virginia, for instance, stipulates that the judiciary's budget cannot be reduced, but the courts are not in the practice of enforcing the provision; instead, the judiciary adheres to the regular budget process including reductions (Raftery, 2018). To our knowledge, similar efforts to ensure that the state judiciary has some kind of "guaranteed" minimum funding level have not been successful. Legislators in most instances view their authority over each budget entity as sacrosanct and unlimited. Dedicated funds for specific purposes are therefore generally considered "just another" source of revenue for the host government's budget managers. Although funds for an exclusive court purpose are not ordinarily reallocated, judicial-branch leaders are occasionally challenged by these budgetary circumstances.

The general fund is normally derived from various tax revenues and some fees imposed by the jurisdiction. For courts, these funds are supplemented by a portion of the fines, fees, and penalties imposed by judges in their sentences or through filing fees. When filing fees were first instituted for court cases, they were considered a limited source of supplemental income returned, *de facto*, to courts by the funding authority. In some localities fees were given to – and still are reserved for – the clerk of court in order to reduce the impact of that office on the general fund. Court filing fees also were seen by some as a partial barrier to entry (i.e., the fee for initial filing of cases), so the courts would not be inundated by inappropriate and frivolous civil cases. Fines were considered to be appropriate penalties included in criminal court cases, but these revenues are normally deposited in the general fund for whatever use the legislative body deems appropriate.

Legislators generally prefer to generate revenue through the use and creation of court "fees" and/or "penalties" rather than raising taxes. These assessed charges are rationalized as "user fees" so the cost of individuals who use government services is not borne by the general population. In the world of courts, end users are not nearly as "few" as some believe. In one of the courts in which one of us worked, the estimated number of people entering the courthouse each year represented about one-quarter of the county's total population. Other courts have done similar estimates, reflecting an even higher percentage of the total county population visiting the courthouse.[17] The users of courts go well beyond those who violate various laws and become parties to the full range of non-criminal and non-traffic cases. They include military representatives checking on potential recruits, credit companies and representatives of local businesses reviewing court records for information affecting credit worthiness, local media outlets pursuing information about cases (particularly criminal cases and trials), real estate developers seeking to confirm ownership of real property, and, in much greater volume, potential and selected jurors, law enforcement and civilian witnesses, family members of those involved in cases, students learning about courts (particularly elementary school students), and citizens who simply are curious about a case. Courts that recognize the justice needs of these other users reinforce the policy argument that courts, indeed, serve the entire community and thus should not need to rely on user fees for a significant portion of their funding.

Penalties, of course, are created to induce compliance with the payment of fees or fines and as a punishment for those who fail to comply. In many respects, the effect is the same as a tax, but because fees and penalties appear to apply only to the "direct users" of government services, the labels make a difference politically. However labeled, these fee-generated income streams have become a significant source of revenue, both for local and state legislative bodies when they consider how much funding to give the judicial branch.

North Carolina is a remarkable example regarding the impact of fees and penalties on the general fund. Half of the judiciary's budget is based on fees charged in court cases (Neff, 2017). Fees have an outsized effect on the courts' budgets, as well as those of "jails, law enforcement, counties, and the school system," who rely on the court fee income each year. Judges can and do waive the payment of some or all fees for indigent defendants, almost always in cases in which the total to be paid is beyond the means of a person. The practice, however, is scrutinized by the legislature, which attempts to restrict the waivers of fees by auditing the practices of individual judges.

North Carolina is not alone, although its legislature's efforts appear to be among the most extreme. We are personally familiar with jurisdictions, primarily local court jurisdictions, where audits have been conducted by the legislative or executive branch to document waivers of fees or penalties, the collection rate for imposed fines, fees, and penalties, or the failure to pursue bail forfeitures from bail agencies and others. Such audits are undertaken because some in those branches believe strongly the courts are "leaving tens (or hundreds) of thousands on the table" that the city or county needs for its budget purposes. All of these audits are directed to pressure judges and staff to collect more money, normally for the general fund that is shared with other departments, agencies, or programs. Some counties and cities also require the courts to turn over any account that has been unpaid more than X days to their own executive branch collection apparatus because they believe the courts are not sufficiently committed to or sufficiently skilled to collect these funds. It is, however, in part because judges seek to facilitate compliance with court orders, that they grant installment payments to low-income defendants.[18] It also is why judges sometimes waive or defer court fees and/or penalties, taking into account the party's ability to pay. It is also often the case, however, that some judges think their judgments are self-executing, so if they order payment, it will be made timely. Some judges and administrators conclude that it is not the courts' responsibility to raise money for the two other branches, despite the evidence to the contrary. However, United States law is well established that people cannot be imprisoned unless their failure to make payment is "willful," and not because they cannot afford to pay (*Bearden v. Georgia*, 1983). Nonetheless, many who are unable to pay are arrested and jailed. The North Carolina example – among the myriad of others across the nation – demonstrates three points. First, it documents that court fees are increasingly being used to fund government services unrelated to court capital and operations expenses. Second, it shows the dilution of the concept that government is to be funded by all, but is now instead subsidized in large part by "direct" users. And third, it illustrates the concerted, ongoing effort by some legislators to avoid general fund tax increases.

Fines, Fees, and Penalties

The principles regarding the use and number of fines, fees, and penalties are understood and longstanding. While situations occur where user fees and surcharges are necessary, such charges should always be kept to a minimum and should generally not fund operational expenditures outside the justice system. Assessments should be established only for the express purposes of the "administration of justice," so that monies levied do not exceed the actual cost of providing the service (CCJ & COSCA, 2018).

The CCJ and the COSCA have endorsed this principle. Yet, fines, fees, and penalties as a means of paying for government are a widespread, antiquated technique. For instance, before it was ruled unconstitutional by the United States Supreme Court (USSC) in 1927, local governments were in the practice of using fines imposed on convicted defendants to pay sentencing judges' salaries (*Turney v. Ohio*, 1927). Notwithstanding the ruling almost a century old, the idea of using fines to generally fund the courts remains in some jurisdictions. Many court leaders have been pressured by budget directors and/or executive-branch auditors to collect a higher percentage of unpaid fines and/or bail forfeitures for the benefit of the general fund and, sometimes, to support an increase in the court's budget. In some instances, court administrators and leadership judges have been challenged to identify a court-based funding source to offset costs for new staff, technologies, or programs. In these scenarios, funding was tied to those new sources of revenue and the burden to find the funding was shouldered by the court, not the legislative branch. The simplest and sometimes the only way to fund the expense was to add a new court fee or increase an existing one. If the fee(s) and increased budget were approved, executive- or legislative-branch budget staff then monitored the revenue to assure that monies collected aligned with the court's projection. If it did not, added pressure was applied to the court to increase its collection efforts or, somehow, to increase case filings or court events to bolster revenue.

Legislators and budget directors turned increasingly to fees and penalties to fund courts in the 1960s. The idea of "users" paying for the services provided became an article of faith for some legislators. The absence of choice for those in the criminal courts was grounded on a dual basis: 1) they "chose" to commit the traffic violation or crime; and 2) thus, they "chose" to use the court and are liable for the accrued costs to the system. Several jurisdictions require a fee payment for each day a convicted person spends in jail. And even in those instances where there is a dedicated fund for victims, there are implementation gaps. Hospitals in New York, for example, improperly billed sexual assault survivors for forensic rape exams, despite state law requiring that these costs be covered through victims' services (Wamsley, 2017). In some jurisdictions, persons convicted of drug use must pay a fee to cover the cost of their drug tests. The reasoning here being that non-narcotic users should not have to pay for the tests which addicts "require." The underlying rationale is that society needs to have assurances that addicts are "clean" while on probation, so the addicts should pay to demonstrate compliance in lieu of a custodial term of incarceration. Of course, there is a universal benefit when probationers are compelled to remain sober including their families, friends, and co-workers. The public, in particular, also benefits by ensuring greater levels of employability, while also reducing recidivism-associated costs.

A considerable faction of the population believe individuals make a rational choice to commit a crime based on hedonistic calculus of costs and benefits; a significant fine, thus, adds to those costs while reducing or eliminating the cost of their bad choices for "good people."[19] The "general benefit" argument often buttresses antipathy to both the criminal and crime. As a result, fees, fines, and penalties are legitimized without regard to the validity of the "rational choice" argument or whether another approach would be as equally effective for those who are unable to pay. While courts are required to impose these monetary sanctions, often they see no improvement in their budgets as a result. Notwithstanding the evidence to the contrary, the premise that all citizens benefit from the work of courts, so courts should not be supported through "user" fees has been largely ignored.

There is a growing irony in the use of fees and penalties: they now raise as much or more – at least on paper – than basic criminal and traffic fines and filing fees in civil cases.[20] For example, in California, a basic fine of $100 becomes $490 because of added fees. Failure to pay by the prescribed deadline or appear in court further increases the amount owed to $815 (Ewing, 2017).[21] In 2016, a $35 fine for running a stop sign cost $283 once surcharges and fees were added. Revenue generated from fines in California may be distributed among scores of state and local funds established by law to support various initiatives (Watts, 2016). The difference in both illustrations is comprised of fees (almost incredulously) for 80 "funds," depending on the offense(s), including funds for rabies enforcement and eradication, emergency services, the Veterinary Medical Board, abalone restoration and preservation, and the "county general fund." Only a modest portion of the added fee revenue is invested into the courts: only 7 of the 80 funds directly benefit the judiciary (Lowrey, 2012). The movement to use fees and penalties imposed by courts to fund several entities other than courts has created a policy conundrum for the legislature and judiciary.[22] It may yet be possible to reach consensus among the varied stakeholders in the fees and penalties arrangement, but this too is not without significant challenge. Many state legislatures, as well as the judiciary, have trapped themselves into relying on these monetary sanctions to fund operational expenditures that are outside the scope of the purposes and responsibilities of the courts.

It remains to be seen whether the timing is right to address head-on the substitution of fees and penalties for general taxes to fund multiple commitments deemed to be important, but not imperative enough for legislators to admit that such obligations can be adequately funded with only general funds and dedicated fees.[23]

It also remains to be seen if the two other branches of government will accept the argument that the judiciary should not be treated for budget purposes as if it is just another department, agency, or board.

The insidiousness nature of onerous court fees has created a fiscal "death spiral" for the poor and others who cannot afford the initial payment or who miss a timely payment. Consider the following opinion piece (Sibilla, 2016):

> Pagedale, Missouri saw the number of non-traffic tickets issued skyrocket by 495 percent between 2010 and 2014. In this small suburb of St. Louis, residents have been ticketed for saggy pants, uncut grass and fallen trees. The city also managed to outlaw holding a front-yard barbecue on days that aren't national holidays. In 2013, almost one-fifth of Pagedale's revenue came from court fines and fees.

The sizable totals that are attributable to fees and compounded by penalties result in a large number of unpaid fines. In 2016, Californians owed the state $9.7 billion in traffic debt (Ewing, 2017). People who can afford the fines normally pay; thus, much of that $9.7 billion likely is owed by those who cannot afford to pay.[24] For those unable to pay, the frustration is compounded in 43 states that suspend the licenses of drivers who do not pay.

Two examples from news reports highlight the issue in more personal terms. Ashley Sprague, a resident of Tennessee, was making $2.13 an hour plus tips as a waitress when she was cited for speeding and not having insurance. The fine totaled $477.50. Unable to afford the sanction, she did not pay, which led to her being cited twice over the next 13 months for administrative violations, including driving on a suspended license (Schwartzapfel, 2017). Tennessee is one of the 43 states that suspends licenses for non-payment of fines. The rationale behind suspending an individual's license is that it eventually compels the person to pay what is owed, either shortly after they learn of the suspension or when they seek to renew their license or their car registration, which also is denied until the fine(s) is paid in some states. Ergo, because most people *need* to drive, they inevitably pay all their fines. Sprague was a co-plaintiff in a class action suit challenging the suspension of her license, claiming it punishes people for being poor. This occurred after the USSC ruled that having a driver's license is a property right that cannot be taken away without due process (*Goldberg v. Kelly*, 1970). The federal judge overseeing the class action suit agreed, ruling, "no person can be threatened or coerced into paying money that she does not have and cannot get."

The second case involves Graham Gore who was serving in the military in southern California. He made a rolling stop before turning right at a red light at an intersection equipped with a camera that recorded him. Gore received a $465 ticket in the mail. Because he was attending his military training, he missed the payment deadline and the added fees and penalties increased the fine to $703. The fine for the same violation in his home state of North Carolina would have been $50 (Lowrey, 2012).

This book does not examine all the intricacies of money as a punishment in the criminal justice system, but the more recent and extensive debate about bail and its disproportionate impact on the poor and destitute is equally applicable to fines – and, certainly, fees and penalties (Bains, 2017). From the perspective of court funding, there are two consequences. First, some of the fee proceeds are supposed to be returned and reinvested into the courts, which affects expected revenue and available funding. When the proceeds are not collected, courts are held responsible and, on occasion, penalized because the estimated revenue did not meet projections. Second, as unpaid balances increase, legislative and executive branch auditors often negatively report on the court's efforts to collect imposed fines, fees, and penalties. These same reports will cast the general fund and "taxpayers" as the victims of these failed attempts. There is occasionally a press release or budget hearing chastising the court, which perpetuates the public and legislative perception that courts are not well managed and do not uphold their obligation to support the revenue needs of the city, county, or state. In some locales, the predicament also fortifies the view that judges are indifferent about enforcing the court's orders.

There is an overlooked burden of multiple fees and penalties: the burden on court staff. Today, most courts have computerized information and accounting systems to distribute the funds received to the various recipients, but someone must still ensure transfer of the funds to the proper accounts and the auditing function becomes much more complex. In small(er) courts that have not fully computerized their accounting functions, staff must manually distribute these fees, which can be very time-consuming and subject to a high likelihood of error. Some funds can be grouped together into one check, but that varies by case type and the reason for imposing the fines, fees, and penalties. The learning curve for staff (or computer programmers) is concomitantly substantial and steep. In a court administered by one of the authors several years ago, each traffic ticket required disbursing the fee revenue funds across 13 accounts; the number of accounts since that time has increased.

In the 1990s, "day fines" which are used in all criminal cases in Sweden and Brazil received some attention in the United States. The model is based upon a person's income, wherein the dollar value of a fine is different for different people, but the financial impact on disposable income is the same (or almost the same) for all. Uniform monetary fines impose unequal burdens on individuals at opposite ends of the income spectrum, as the same financial penalty represents a negligible cost for a billionaire, but a substantial hardship for a minimum-wage earner. In Sweden, for instance, there is no limit to what a billionaire can pay (one person paid

$67,000 in 2015 for going 14 miles over the speed limit), but other governments have capped fines (Schierenbeck, 2018).

Day fines were piloted in several courts in the United States during the 1990s with mixed results. The consensus of the initiative was that it worked well in some courts, but generally it was too cumbersome to administer, presented political problems when the fines for the very rich were calculated, and it was too difficult to reach agreement about how many days particular criminal and traffic violations were "worth," such that the dollar total would be broadly fair yet still generate revenue comparable to the current fine structure. The latter factor was not determined in the evaluations of these projects. Theoretically, if a fine is "fair" to the poor as well as those with sufficient resources, the payment rate for all would increase and total revenue also should increase. As the issues involving bail continue to be debated, the challenges presented by the day fines model should be re-evaluated for potential solutions.

Budget Creation and Management

Budget Creation

Creating an annual or biennial court budget is as much art as it is math. Budgets also must be created twice: once when submitting the court's request to the funding authority and again when the funding authority decides on the final budget. Our focus here is on developing the proposed budget, as that is where policy and sometimes tactical choices must be made and the justifications for increases or limiting decreases must be developed. The funding authority decides on a finalized total (and ideally only a total, leaving the court with the decisions on how to allocate the "lump sum") or on the amount to be spent in each line item category (personnel, equipment maintenance, capital items, counsel for indigents, etc.). Adjustments in each budget line may be needed with some items withdrawn, but the foundational policy decisions made by judicial leadership should guide those changes, including whatever concessions are warranted.

The funding authority will occasionally mandate one or more expenses that were anticipated when the court prepared its budget request. These obligations normally apply to all funding units, but sometimes they are limited to the court because of something the funding authority thinks the court should (must) do that the court has not requested, nor even wants to include. There is generally no appeal from a budget requirement imposed by the host governmental unit. Far worse, however, is that the final budget total is seldom increased to accommodate the new mandate(s). The funding authority expects the new expense(s) to be covered within the final total court budget by decreasing how much is spent on other items – normally at the court's discretion. Again, the priorities of the court when the original budget was prepared should guide these decisions.

The "art" part of budget development and management comes from a detailed review of the court's resource needs, determining priorities, including whether to seek all of the funds needed for an expense in one year or to distribute the new expenditure over multiple years, and developing data-based and performance-based justifications to support policy decisions. There also are some tactical decisions for the proposed budget, including how much to request for constitutionally required disbursements, such as indigent defense expenses and whether to include an item desired by a key member of the funding authority's budget committee, a judge, or the local Bar.

Mathematical Process

Government accounting methods and the budgeting process make some facets of budget creation relatively straightforward. Typically, funding for court staff positions is approved and continues year-to-year, unless there are revenue shortfalls (mostly in recessions) that require that positions be left vacant or eliminated. For approved positions that continue, next year's budget is a mathematical exercise. The city, county, or state budgeting authority advises the court of contractually required salary increases (i.e., normally, union-negotiated pay increases), changes in the cost of fringe benefits (usually increased and most-affected by health insurance costs), any changes in inter-department charges for services from other departments, and any targets for the percentage increase or decrease in total spending decided upon by the funding authority. Increases in inter-department charges may include the cost of building and equipment maintenance by staff in other budget units and monies for central data processing support, if any. The cost factors used to adjust personnel expenditures often vary by the different salary levels of staff and managers and, at times for managers, more generous fringe benefits or leave policies than accorded to line staff. Policy decisions by a court about reorganizing staff, re-engineering operations, or adding staff, technology, and possibly whether there should be a change in the jury management process are generally not considerations in these routine budget processes. Consequently, the court accounting staff's work is to apply the various budget increase or decrease multipliers to existing numbers. These calculations can be complex and time-consuming because budget factors for different levels and types of staff require computation. For the most part this is largely a mathematical exercise, nonetheless.

The fact that budget creation is partly a mathematical exercise does not diminish its importance. Mistakes can still be made in developing the formulas for personnel funding spreadsheets, or in data entry. Accounting software and spreadsheets minimize the likelihood for error (other than creating the wrong formulas), but all of the aggregate totals must still be reviewed thoroughly before the court's final budget request is submitted. If the funding authority finds an oversight or inaccuracies, the validity of the entire court budget proposal is potentially put at risk and the court's credibility is diminished.

Recessions that occur in the normal business cycles of the United States often require either leaving court positions vacant during the budget year or permanently eliminating positions. The latter normally occurs when the recession is deep or extended, for example, and most dramatically during the Great Recession of 2008–2009. In lesser or shorter recessions, courts are ordinarily required or opt to temporarily institute a hiring freeze, leaving some positions vacant ("elimination by attrition"). Assuming proper justification, when a recession concludes and government revenue restabilizes, reinstating the court's aggregate budget is typically delayed until the first or second budget following the economy's recovery. In "modest" recessions, government revenue loss and recovery normally lags the general economy by 18–24 months. Reestablishing eliminated job positions is a greater challenge, however, and often not possible for several years, if at all. Funding authorities may predictably conclude that if the court functioned without the staff position for as long a period of time, the position is no longer warranted. There are circumstances where that might be true, particularly if the court was able to institute technology to mitigate the impact of staff shortages or re-engineered business processes to create greater efficiencies. However, if the funding authority resists reestablishing eliminated but still needed positions, the court will need to develop and articulate a well-grounded operational justification.

The "Art" of Budget Creation

Judicial branch budget creation depends on the funding authority setting target increases or decreases before the finances are completed by a court. Independent of any established budget targets, there clearly are important aspects of court budget creation that involve strategic decision making. Central to this process is to set priorities that account for the formulation and execution of strategic objectives in accordance with the court's status quo, vision, reassessment of its goals and mission. There are at least four ways in which this can be accomplished. The methods are not independent and exclusive options; each of the first three should be part of budget development, considered in parallel, as each adds value to the budget planning process.

Yogi Berra, the longtime catcher for the New York Yankees, was widely known for his distinctive aphorisms that blended humor with practical insight. A member of the National Baseball Hall of Fame, he famously observed, "You've got to be careful if you don't know where you're going 'cause you might not get there" (Berra, 1999). Along this vein, the first step is to have a strategic plan for the court's future that has already been developed. Berra's observation is most germane to having a strategic plan for the court's future, but it is derivatively a caution about creating budgets in a vacuum. An existing strategic plan for the next three to five years should guide budget policy decisions each year and create continuity in program development. The plan sets forth the court's vision, mission, and goals, as well as illustrating the procedure it will undertake to improve operations, facilities, technology, and other aspects of court administration; thus, these plans should be a starting point when the budget is developed to incorporate new items or to address potential reductions.

As a court commences its budget development, it should review the priorities and the timeline set in the strategic plan. The court leadership should then juxtapose its "status quo" this year against its "vision" in forthcoming years together with the relevant plans to accomplish each respective goal. If the court has not yet reached the goals in the plan for this year, the subsequent year's budget should incorporate a plan to bridge the shortfall. Inevitably, the plan priorities that were developed two or more years ago may need to be reconsidered in light of more recent ideas, changes in law, or delays in implementing previous projects. Any proposed court budget established without reference to an existing strategic plan and a commitment to achieve its goals, however, undermines the planning effort and raises questions in the two other branches about the court's management and commitment.

The second approach to budgeting is to evaluate court improvement projects initiated over the last three to five years, ideally with baseline and data collected as the projects are implemented. These evaluations serve as the basis for the necessary resources to continue the effort, for mid-course correction to bring a project or program closer to achieving its goals, to extend the effort in those instances when it was a pilot project, or to expand the benefits already achieved. Evaluations of previous and ongoing projects can also demonstrate the success achieved as evidence that the new project would likewise be a fruitful undertaking. Assessments show that the court is nimble, as circumstances emerge modifying procedures and processes to improve the project's effectiveness. In those instances, when the court had no recourse, program appraisals validate the cost-saving efforts the court took to terminate operations when reliable forecasts showed that the project would be unsuccessful. Accordingly, evaluations are an important part of modern court administration, bolstering accountability for the use of public funds, transparency, and credibility of the court management team.

The third approach to developing the subsequent year's budget should be administered notwithstanding the existence of a strategic plan: inquire of judges, management, line staff, and other judiciary stakeholders for input about what is needed during the development phase of the budget plan. This line of inquiry conveys management's genuine interest in both internal and external stakeholders' considerations and adds relevance and context to the court budget, assuring judicial branch leadership that critical resource needs are not overlooked. Moreover, bringing representatives into the fold of the discussion ultimately helps to create buy-in from the various contingent groups, who can impact how efficiently dollars are spent on approved programs. Input should always be requested regardless of the kinds of proposals that have historically been presented. It is incumbent on court leadership to make clear that ideas are sought with the caveat that they may not necessarily be included in the final budget. So long as court leaders provide reasonable explanation why particular items are excluded, stakeholders are generally pleased to contribute to the process.

The final approach, and the one least likely to move the court closer to achieving its overall goals is to forgo requesting any new funds. Submitting a budget with zero requests for increases may reflect responsible "citizenship" so far as the funding authority is concerned and suggests that the status quo is exemplary without needed improvement. Absent a reduction mandate by the funding authority, our study and experience have shown that no court is consistently so remarkably well resourced that it cannot benefit from investments – however nominal they may be – in technological advancements, a new program, general operation enhancements, or additional staff in critical areas such as interpreters or self-represented litigant services. A status quo budget is generally indicative of a lack of imagination or a false sense of accomplishment that should be resisted by the court leadership team. To that end, in a year for which cuts have been mandated by the funding authority, the court should still consider requesting targeted funding to support business process re-engineering, helping to optimize court operations. Although this type of budget proposal may be less than that of the current year, the court must still seek to do its due diligence to maintain service, transparency, and access (Reinkensmeyer, 2004).

Leaders facing a "zero increase" budget or mandated cuts should be prepared for a situation in which some judges or stakeholders may insist that the next court budget allocate funds that are only of particular interest to them and that the budget be cut elsewhere. Including only the items driven by the most assertive cadre of judge(s) or stakeholders at the expense of other mutually agreed upon initiatives is a reckless use of administrative power. A prudent administrator, however, can neutralize these efforts if they build strong support from the leadership judges. Absent that support, an administrator who resists such demands may jeopardize their job position. It is worth mentioning that requests for new funds not aligned with the strategic plan may involve unconvincing justifications or data that are suspect, both of which can undermine valid budget requests. Although the full representative spectrum of stakeholders deserves consideration, requests should not be given higher priority based on *who* is making the demand and without reference to an existing aspect of the strategic plan. To do so places those who will speak on behalf of the court in an unenviable position that lacks credibility, along with bringing into question the leadership competence of those acceding to the request(s).

Other Factors

There are two highly important elements of court budgets that pose challenges most every fiscal year because they fluctuate annually and are very difficult to predict: constitutionally and statutorily mandated expenses, and new case inventory (case filings) – that being, demand for court services. Mandates include criminal defense attorneys for indigents, prospective jurors who must be summoned and used in trials, and, in some general jurisdiction courts, psychiatrists and psychologists for mental health exams, other experts and, occasionally, hiring investigators for indigent criminal defendants. Almost all courts forecast these expenses based on the trends of prior years; however, these projections may be over- or underestimated. When the funding entity needs to fund non-court needs that exceed the projected general fund revenue, courts are often compelled to reduce the estimates of mandated costs. Reductions of these budget lines transmutes in a kind of unsustainable "budgeting game." The budget lines for these costs are reduced at the beginning of the fiscal year, even though everyone realizes that if the reduced figure proves to be inadequate, sometime during the last two or three months of the fiscal year these lines will be augmented because the items are constitutionally mandated. Occasionally, the funding authority may request a review to find less costly, alternative ways to provide these services, particularly for the largest of these expenses, defense attorney services. Irrespective of whether changes are made, the alternative approach seldom removes the year-to-year uncertainty and, usually, does not reduce total costs in the long term. At best, modifications in the delivery system for defense services may reduce or contain the total cost on a short-term basis.

The impact of the court's inventory (volume of case filings) on the budget may be less clear year-to-year, but it is an important factor in budget planning and resource allocation. Three factors affecting the number of filings per year can produce an increase in these resource needs: 1) law enforcement and prosecutorial discretion about priorities in the short term (one year) or over a longer term (term of present chief prosecutor, sheriff, or police chief), as these often are not shared with the court until after case filings noticeably increase; 2) economic factors that produce increased case filings that carry a heavy workload; and 3) a new statute or constitutional interpretation that leads to either a new type of case that courts must hear, an unexpected increase in filings in an existing case type, or additional court functions which increase the workload of judges and/or staff.[25]

Although the scratch rate by prosecutors varies by state and county, decisions by one or more police departments or a sheriff about enforcement priorities for the coming year are the variable that most often impacts criminal case filings, both in the way of increases and decreases. For instance, decisions to emphasize (or deemphasize) drug enforcement or "quality-of-life" violations (the latter almost always being misdemeanors) or to target a gang problem can lead to substantial increases in case filings for months or, in some jurisdictions, several years. These changes have a lesser impact on the workload of general jurisdiction judges if they result in misdemeanor charges (traffic and quality-of-life charges such as loitering, graffiti, shoplifting, etc.) rather than felony charges. However, such changes can produce a significant burden on limited jurisdiction court judges and court staff, if filings increase by 5 percent or more. Case processing times also may increase as judges' calendars expand. If staff capacity is extended to the limit, overtime work might be needed, which has a direct budget impact.

A cross-state study of civil case filing trends has revealed broad-scoped declines in the volume of civil case filings amidst population growth, disparities in per capita case filings, and other counterintuitive findings (Carlson & Grecean, 2024). This study has given rise to a number of unanswered questions regarding case filing dynamics, measures of caseload versus workload, and case resolution through private alternative dispute resolution. With these intriguing findings in mind, we explore some of the factors which may impact litigation rates, based on our collective observations working in state courts.

The state of the general economy may impact the volume of case filings more than is generally recognized. If the economy booms, a court can expect the following between 9 and 18 months: the volume of traffic cases will likely increase as gasoline and travel become more affordable; the volume of a few misdemeanor case types associated with lack of income will decrease (e.g., shoplifting); the volume of contract disputes may increase because businesses can better afford to hire attorneys and pursue disputes; the volume of small claims cases may decrease, as businesses are in an improved position to absorb small losses; and the volume of civil suits associated with an increase in housing and commercial developments often increases. The latter category of cases normally constitutes a heavy workload for both judges and staff, which should be part of the budget presentation, even if additional staffing is not immediately requested. Conversely, when the economy is in a recession, the volume of small claims cases may increase, some misdemeanor case types increase, domestic violence cases often increase, traffic cases may decrease (less driving), self-represented divorce filings increase, and contract filings may decrease. In severe economic situations, such as the Great Recession, the volume of mortgage foreclosure and collection cases can markedly increase. These are general trends associated with the state and local economy, but each court should carefully track its filings, so it will have a clear understanding of how these variables impact the court's workload and, in turn, affect funding needs. Of particular note are mass-tort case filings or many individual case filings resulting from a natural disaster, wherein plaintiffs argue that the aftermath could have been averted or diminished by a defendant. These types of litigation create an additional, normally unexpected, burden on judicial workload and on staff assisting the assigned judge(s).[26]

Elements of Sound Budget Management

Several factors are fundamental to sound budget management:

- Accurate data entry and tabulation of court performance results; if possible, build in automatic checks on typical errors such as dates, position of the decimal point, and numbers that do not make sense for each category of income and expense, usually because they are much too large or too small.
- Timely production of month-end statistical and financial reports, which for budget management should be ten days or less after the end of the month, preferably seven days.
- Revenue is as important to review as expenses, including management of time payments and bail forfeitures.
- Accurate allocation of paid fines, fees, penalties, and special charges to various accounts.
- Administrators should personally review each month's report and then discuss any issues as soon as possible with the presiding judge.
- Reports that help the administrator to manage do not simply show one-twelfth of the annual total in their appropriate lines. Rather, reports that aid management show the projected budget for the month and year-to-date based on when variable expenses are expected to occur including encumbrance reports.
- Reports that aid management do not only show every line but provide views with category totals for most cost centers, in addition to the most-variable lines and those lines most likely to impact the court in meeting or exceeding its budget at the end of the year.
- Reports that show both the dollar and percentage variance from the budget for both the current month and year-to-date.[27]
- There should be an initiating point for percentage and/or dollar variances that will lead to the accounting staff and managers determining the cause of a variance.
- The leadership team, including the chief budget official, reviews the budget quarterly and makes any needed adjustments for the balance of the fiscal year.
- Manage the budget to a level between 97 and 98 percent of the allocated amounts, allowing flexibility for unexpected but tolerable expenditure increases.
- Significant shortfalls in expenditures should be checked to ensure figures are accurate, review upcoming expenses, and

determine if the funds can be transferred to another line or deferred until later in the fiscal year.

- Significant shortfalls of revenue also should be checked for accuracy and acted on to enable the judges and funding authority to understand the reason(s) for the deficit.
- Advise the funding authority as soon as practicable of any spending increases that may jeopardize compliance with the overall budget. If the court has the authority to independently reallocate funds among budget lines, it should do so. If such authority is lacking, the court should initiate discussions with the funding authority regarding proposed solutions to address the projected deficit.

Two notes are offered here for managing expenses to a target of 97 or 98 percent of the total budget and for each significant category in the budget. First, there is a risk in doing this, because if the court ends the fiscal year with 2 percent of its budget unexpended, the funding authority is likely to reduce the subsequent year's budget by the same amount. The budget authority will have deduced that the court was able to operate at 98 percent of the budget. Most government entities, including courts, manage the budget surplus by having a list of one-time expenses they would like to purchase and do so before the end of the fiscal year, thus having spent all or almost all of their annual budget allocation. Some administrators prefer these "budget safeguards" because they enable the court to purchase capital items such as computers, security equipment, vehicles, and furniture that were not originally funded. Moreover, this practice facilitates passage of a balanced budget at the start of the fiscal year, while providing for limited and largely acceptable expenses. If some budget units can meet their needs with unspent funds, this permits other departments that have a genuine need to tap into these fund reserves. Although more seldom, a court may not have enough of these one-time expenses to absorb the budget surplus and so it might be challenged with a budget reduction the subsequent year. The most important resource needs often are in the area of personnel, which cannot generally be met with unexpended funds.[28] The best solution may be an agreement with the funding entity to allow either an unlimited reserve account funded by surplus funds or one with a cap that makes sense to both the court and the funding authority.[29]

Second, if the funding authority allows the court to carry over unspent funds, this option cannot be relied on during a significant recession. Reserve accounts were largely re-appropriated ("swept") by most funding authorities during the Great Recession, even if the reserve account was for an important dedicated purpose. If this happens in a court and the option is not restored, the court should seek restoration of reserve accounts when the fiscal climate is vastly improved. Reserve funds encourage prudent fiscal management by the court, as the court can retain and use the surplus funds rather than return them to the city, county, or state general fund.

Dealing with the Funding Authority

If the funding authority is local, accuracy in reporting, restraint in articulating resource needs, avoidance of exaggeration regarding the consequences of insufficient funding, and transparency about budgetary needs and status at any given time are critical. Not all court leaders agree with these four prescriptions, some preferring to manage the budget without external intrusion or presumptions about their decisions. One reason for this perspective is a tradition that judges' adjudicative work is often considered to be confidential; that attitude may carry over to administrative matters, however unintentional. Another stated reason is that courts are not subject to close review by the executive or legislative branches. Courts do, in fact, constitute an independent branch of government, but they are a public entity that is not above accountability and thus one that should be transparent in its use of public funds. It is also important to build trust and positive personal relationships with leaders of the two other branches.

Practice suggests that courts do better in budget acquisition using these guidelines, rather than withholding budget information until there is a serious need or problem. In our experience, a lack of transparency regarding public resources is precariously replete with pitfalls. Sometimes, the court gets what it wants, largely because local authorities respect the judiciary's position in government and the court budget is a relatively small portion of the total host government budget, so only a limited number of dollars are at risk in approving the request. It is not because the funding authority approves of the lack of transparency or the discussions that result in utilizing this approach. Given today's focus on performance-based budgeting, this scenario is becoming more the exception. When critical needs require trust from the funding authority, budget negotiations require collaborative, open discussions. Transparency also responds to the growing recognition among courts across the country of the need for accountability. Courts are a vitally important part of government; judges are visible and generally respected members of the community. The public expects judges and court administrators to act ethically, with good stewardship of public resources. Courts cannot be accountable and openly manage their budgets without also being candid about the basis for their budget proposals.

For instance, while one of us was a trial court administrator, the county's budget analyst was invited to a few management committee meetings prior to a new budget request being submitted. These joint meetings were held so that the analyst would better understand the issues with which the court was dealing, why budget increases were being sought, and how they would be used. This approach successfully built understanding and support with the county's budget-review process, leading to several important increases in the court's budget. Likewise, this strategy proved successful in garnering support for capital funding requests, both for renovation and expansion of court facilities. To that end, we have also found it very helpful to have county budget analysts and other county officials tour court facilities in need of restoration.

If the court funding entity is the state legislature, the "funding authority" for trial courts is in some dimensions subject to the state judiciary's budget process, not only the legislature per se. The guidelines suggested for court funding from a local unit of government apply equally for state funding, but possibly with even more direct impact, as the budget reviewers at the state level are court personnel – sometimes with judges as the final authority. Thus, budget justifications that are embellished, unconvincing, or altogether invalid can be even less successful than they might be at the local level.

Creating and managing a structurally sound court budget involves multiple elements and paying close attention throughout the fiscal year. Courts cannot control the general economy or general fund revenues. But, if they manage their budget well, build strong arguments for increases, and prepare for unexpected funding reductions, the courts should be able to weather the inevitable fluctuations in available funds. Courts that follow the approaches suggested here should experience few critical resource problems, while also leveraging the proven funding strategies within their control.

Notes

1 The continuity of operations plan also should include priorities for restoring services, staff, courtroom and/or courthouses, facilities management, and restoring and/or upgrading technology.

2 Within this structure a number of states assumed responsibility for the salaries and benefits of trial judges, while all other expense items were a local responsibility.

3 We are unaware of any state that has city or municipal courts that have assumed the cost of those courts. Data on state funding can be found at www.ncsc.org/resources-courts/data.

4 Normally, states that have assumed the cost of trial courts to include daily upkeep and minor repairs.

5 A number of courts have invited local and state legislators to sit on the bench with a judge for a day. These are good programs, but outreach should not end when the courtroom day is over; it should extend to operations. These programs should be ongoing and extend to non-elected local officials too.

[6] Locally funded courts sometimes can use their unique status as being bound by state and national constitutional requirements in support of their budget requests with more effect than they can when competing at the state level with other courts.

[7] Some regard this as having inevitable "winners and losers." For instance, when the system underwent state funding in the mid-1990s in NJ, urban counties "won" because they were able to draw on the entire pot of funding. The other, more affluent counties were frustrated and "lost" because all their funding could no longer be used for the sole purpose of the county but instead had to be pooled.

[8] Based on a review of state funding budgets by the National Center for State Courts, communicated by William Raftery via email, January 3, 2018.

[9] In some instances, these funding requests are designated as "pilot initiatives" wherein funding is provided to an individual court for a particular model project.

[10] Large counties are not always the "rich" ones. Sometimes, there is a geographically small county that has wealthy residents who can drive state policy by virtue of that affluence from which the state draws on.

[11] There are some elected officials who also want to show constituents how strongly they disagree with the court decision, particularly if it was in a criminal case. They may believe that such opposition will be helpful in their next election.

[12] One example of legislative punishment comes from California. In a case about the budget, the Supreme Court added a footnote – i.e., something not necessary to its decision – that the legislature probably did not need as many staff positions as it had. The Supreme Court's budget did not change for the next three years.

[13] Alternatives strategies in lieu of large capital funding requests for information technology systems include ongoing funding for lease-purchase of equipment, software as a service, and cloud computing.

[14] Such a study can be conducted by clerks for a few weeks using timesheets or a Delphi group to estimate the time needed for each task, which then is combined to determine total time for a case start to finish. Either approach will provide the court enough data to support a basis for a requested increase in staff.

[15] For a number of reasons, led by the cost of a judge and the supporting staff and complications in determining judicial workload, obtaining new judgeships is an entirely different process that is outside the normal budget process.

16 Some state legislatures and the federal government in recent years have cut taxes, sometimes dramatically, but increasing taxes ordinarily is anathema to legislators and governors/presidents.

17 We recognize that these numbers are artificial in a sense, because they include individuals who might enter a courthouse multiple times a week or year. Nonetheless, the numbers indicate a level of use and demand for service that few outside courts recognize – and do not include the large volume of telephone calls, email inquiries, social media updates, and items of mail received at a courthouse daily, much of which relates to persons only seeking information.

18 With the size of some fines today, time payments also may be necessary for middle-income defendants.

19 Obviously, for more serious crimes, jail or prison is another heavily used "cost."

20 This phenomenon is similar to the use of fees by airlines in order to compete through "low fares." Fees now represent billions in revenue to the airline industry and seem unlikely to be abandoned.

21 California has the highest total fines in the country.

22 There are a number of instances across the country where voters have supported increased taxes for specific purposes following an education program by tax supporters about why the purpose was important and assurances that the increased taxes would be used for the purpose indicated.

23 Facing this issue may require re-examining which functions, tasks, and programs warrant government support in contrast to government oversight and monitoring. We also must acknowledge that the role and ability of government to perform competently and effectively in almost all areas have been under constant, vociferous attack for over 30 years.

24 Some also is owed by those who can afford to pay but think they can "game" the system or get lost in the court's bureaucracy and end up paying nothing.

25 For instance, in the mid-1980s the California Supreme Court interpreted a statute to allow citizens to sue insurance companies directly if they did not pay for an injury caused by a policy holder. It led to a double-digit increase in civil filings directly against insurance companies by injured parties. Toward the end of the decade, the Supreme Court reversed its ruling. Filings, in turn, dropped dramatically.

26 We have experienced a mass tort so complex that it essentially took one judge out of the rotation of receiving case assignments for an entire year. X number of unassigned cases were

distributed to the other judges. In another instance, a "complex cases task force" of federal and state judges was created.

27 For instance, a 10 percent variance in a $2,000 budget for the year is irrelevant almost every time because the dollar variance is only $200. Two hundred dollars is de minimus in most courts' budgets. A 10 percent variance in a $200,000 line, however, is considerable and warrants further review.

28 As a general proposition, personnel are the largest expense category. In courts of limited jurisdiction, personnel costs may be 75 percent or more of the total budget. In courts of general jurisdiction, personnel may be a smaller percentage of the total if indigent defense costs are included in the budget.

29 Some court leaders do not want reserve accounts because they fear they will be told by the funding body to use them for general expenses.

References

Baar, C., Friesen, E., Hall, D., Reinkensmeyer, M., & Cooper, C. S. (2010, March). *Financing the third branch in lean times: Putting the present fiscal crisis in perspective* (Final draft). BJA Criminal Courts Technical Assistance Project, American University; National Association for Court Management.

Bains, C. (2017, October 28). Sessions says to courts: Go ahead, jail people because they're poor. *The New York Times*. www.nytimes.com/2017/12/28/opinion/sessions-says-to-courts-go-ahead-jail-people-because-theyre-poor.html.

Bearden v. Georgia, 461 U.S. 660 (1983).

Berra, Y. (1999). *The Yogi book: I really didn't say everything I said.* Workman Publishing.

Carlson, A., & Grecean, J. (2024). *What is happening with state trial court civil filings: The unresolved riddles.* American Bar Association.

Carlson, A., Harrison, K., & Hudzik, J. K. (2008). *Adequate, stable, equitable, and responsible trial court funding: Reframing the state vs. local debate.* Judicial Management Institute.

Conference of Chief Justices, & Conference of State Court Administrators. (2018). *Principles on fines, fees, and bail practices.* National Center for State Courts.

Durham, C. M., & Becker, D. J. (2011). *A case for court governance principles.* National Center for State Courts.

Ewing, M. (2017, May 13). Should states charge low-income residents less for traffic tickets? *The Atlantic.* www.theatlantic.com/politics/archive/2017/05/traffic-debt-california-brown/526491/.

Goldberg v. Kelly, 397 U.S. 254, 262 n.8 (1970).

Lowrey, B. (2012, August 18). Courts: How your $35 speeding ticket becomes a $235 fine. *The San Diego Union-Tribune*. www.sandiegouniontribune.com/2016/09/04/courts-how-your-35-speeding-ticket-becomes-a-235-fine/.

Mundell, B. R., & Jefferson, W. B. (2011). *Herding lions: Shared leadership of the state trial courts*. National Center for State Courts.

Neff, J. (2017, November 29). No mercy for judges who show mercy. *The Marshall Project*. www.themarshallproject.org/2017/11/29/no-mercy-for-judges-who-show-mercy.

Raftery, W. E. (2018, March 16). *Gavel to Gavel: Volume 12, Issue 7* [Newsletter]. National Center for State Courts.

Reinkensmeyer, M. W. (2004). Court budget strategies: Stewardship, accountability, and partnership in Maricopa County. *Judges' Journal, 43*(3), 38–42.

Rosen, J. (n.d.). *The court and democracy: Court history* (citing Alexander Hamilton, *Federalist No. 78*, 1788). PBS. www.pbs.org/wnet/supremecourt/democracy/history.html.

Schauffler, R. Y., & Kleiman, M. (2010). *State courts and the budget crisis: Rethinking court services*. National Center for State Courts.

Schierenbeck, A. (2018, March 15). A billionaire and a nurse shouldn't pay the same fine for speeding. *The New York Times*. www.nytimes.com/2018/03/15/opinion/flat-fines-wealthy-poor.html.

Schwartzapfel, B. (2017, November 21). 43 states suspend licenses for unpaid court debt, but that could change. *The Marshall Project*. www.themarshallproject.org/2017/11/21/43-states-suspend-licenses-for-unpaid-court-debt-but-that-could-change.

Sibilla, N. (2016, August 11). Los Angeles County suspended thousands of driver's licenses for people too poor to pay court fines. *Forbes*. www.forbes.com/sites/instituteforjustice/2016/08/11/los-angeles-county-suspended-thousands-of-drivers-licenses-for-people-too-poor-to-pay-court-fines/.

Supreme Court of New Jersey, Administrative Office of the Courts. (2003). *Staffing models: Court administration directive no. 2–03*. State of New Jersey. www.njcourts.gov/sites/default/files/administrative-directives/2003/06/dir_02_03.pdf?

Tallarico, S. (2010). *Making the most out of a weighted caseload model: The varied uses of weighted caseload studies, models and data*. National Center for State Courts.

Turney v. Ohio, 273 U.S. 510 (1927). https://supreme.justia.com/cases/federal/us/273/510/.

Wamsley, L. (2017, November 28). Hospital improperly billed patients for rape exams, says New York attorney general. *NPR*.

Watts, J. (2016, January 5). California could review complicated and costly traffic ticket fee structure. *CBS Sacramento*. www.cbsnews.com/sacramento/news/california-could-review-complicated-and-costly-traffic-ticket-fee-structure/.

8 Court Operations Management

At first glance, operations management may appear to represent one of the more routine or even "mundane" aspects of contemporary court administration. The term often evokes an image of a static, internally oriented environment governed by entrenched rules and standardized procedures. Upon closer examination, however, court operations are found to be highly dynamic, publicly visible, and integral to the daily functioning of the judicial system. These interrelated service functions require proactive and strategic leadership capable of balancing administrative efficiency with the judiciary's broader mission of justice. Operational activities within the courts are fast-paced and resource-intensive, demanding both a strong customer service orientation and agile managerial oversight to ensure the consistent delivery of high-quality service to court users, legal professionals, and the public.

Operations management may be conceptualized as the organizational "catchment area" of the courts – a domain that integrates numerous specialized areas of technical and administrative expertise. Although distinct in their individual purposes, these operational functions (and the management thereof) can be broadly grouped into four principal categories: courtroom support, court operations support, customer service, and infrastructure. Each component represents a critical element of the court's overall functionality and requires competent managerial supervision to effectively coordinate personnel, processes, and technology. As illustrated in Figure 8.1, these domains collectively underpin the day-to-day continuity of court services. Given the breadth and technical complexity of these areas, the present chapter offers a high-level overview of their key features and management considerations, rather than an exhaustive treatment of each specialized field.

DOI: 10.4324/9781003686804-8

Figure 8.1 Fundamental Domains of Operations Management

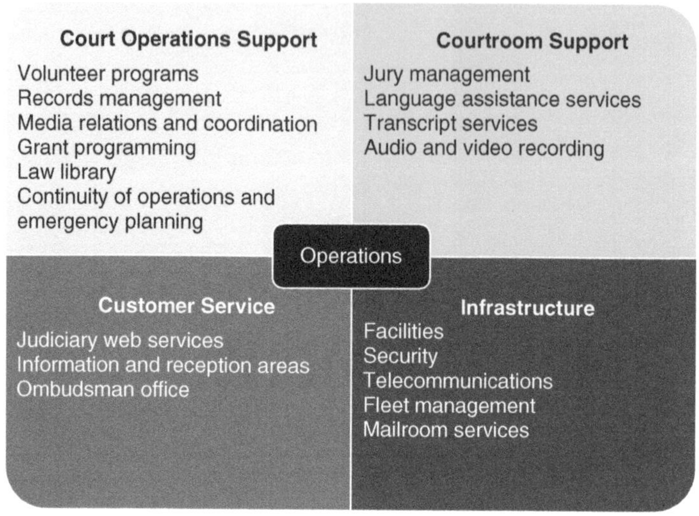

Operations define how tasks are accomplished. Court management incorporates clearly defined best practices to optimize accomplishment of diverse tasks. As depicted in our Fundamental Areas of Court Administration model (Figure 1.1), operations management is linked with each of the elements of court management, particularly with those functions and services related to caseflow management and human resources management. High functioning, mission-based court operations are integral to the provision of court access, procedural fairness, and the timely administration of justice. Operations management is incorporated in the "Practice Competency" of the National Association for Court Management (NACM, 2015) *Core*, together with caseflow management, workforce management, accountability and court performance, and other related functions. The NACM (2015) describes operations management as follows:

> Courts are complex organizations, which are comprised of an array of departments, units and functions that need to be maintained on an on-going basis to support court operations. Although court leaders may not need to perform all the various functions, organizational and management competencies should be developed to support whatever functions may be required.

One of the most daunting challenges for court leadership teams is to bring court operations into alignment with the court's long range strategic agenda. To this end, presiding judges and court administrators must facilitate ongoing communications, both amongst the various court operations functional units and the full court workforce. When communication – necessarily a two-way dialogue – is accessible and transparent, the court leadership team prompts institutional progress that is synchronized and holistic in nature. It is through these critical pathways that the court's strategic agenda is broadened and advanced. Porter (n.d.) found that "continuity of strategic direction and continuous improvement in how you do things are absolutely consistent with each other. In fact, they're mutually reinforcing."

Our discussion here addresses the main specialized areas of court operations management, some of which are truly unique to the judicial branch: support services, including court reporting, interpreting, records management, and collections; court infrastructure, comprising security, continuity of operations, facilities, and information technology (IT); jury management; probation and pre-trial services; and program management. As mentioned, our outline of operational areas is not intended to be universal or all inclusive; the management principles employed in this framework are equally applicable to other current and emerging specialized areas of court operations, such as alternative dispute resolution programs (including online dispute resolution), problem-solving courts, self service centers, and court navigators.

Organizational responsibility for the various areas of court operations management varies widely from jurisdiction to jurisdiction, based in part on governing authorities, which bring to bear the respective state constitution, statutes, and court rules. Local court culture and tradition also have pivotal roles in the assignment of court operations functions, either within court administration or closely annexed to the court. For example, in jurisdictions that employ an elected clerk of court, the records management and jury summonsing roles and responsibilities may rest entirely with the clerk or the court administrator's office, or the court may alternatively utilize a shared, hybrid work model.

From a public administration perspective, focus on efficiency of operations can be traced back to the systematic measurement of worker performance, which Taylor (1911) described as "scientific management." This early 1900s work explored organizational productivity assessed through time-motion studies, the role of workers, and relations between management and workers. The economic expansion which followed World War II ushered in an emphasis on workflow, systems optimization, and total quality management (Deming, 1982). In more recent years, end user needs and the demand to meet customer satisfaction metrics have revealed expanded and increasingly important dimensions of modern operations management.

In the contemporary world of judicial administration, opportunities for reassessing and restructuring practices and procedures and continuous improvement abound in the operations management arena. Proven strategies are readily available for business process re-engineering (Hammer & Champy, 1993) and periodic assessments to enhance services, perhaps most notably the National

Center for State Court's (NCSC) comprehensive High Performance Court Framework (Ostrom & Hanson, 2020).[1] Viewed from a "big picture" perspective, seemingly small improvements in court operations can result in a range of benefits, including marked improvements in system efficiency, customer engagement, and public confidence in the judicial branch.

Support Services

Court Reporting

The Court Reporting Unit fulfills a core function of the judiciary by ensuring the accurate creation and preservation of the official court record, specifically the verbatim record of court proceedings. Official Court Reporters (OCRs) are typically appointed pursuant to court order in accordance with governing statutes or procedural rules. Within the trial courts, the principal responsibility of an OCR is the production of a verbatim record of proceedings, which serves as the authoritative source for appellate review and other post-trial processes. OCRs contribute to the effective operation of the judicial branch not only through the creation of the court record, but by also providing transcription and "real time" captioning services for matters involving compliance with the ADA and by supporting a range of judicial functions, including training sessions, captioning of supreme court hearings, committee meetings, and live webcast events. In ADA-related cases, OCRs play a particularly vital role in facilitating accessibility for hearing-impaired litigants, witnesses, judges, court personnel, and other participants, such that the judiciary's commitment to equal access and procedural fairness is advanced.

The organizational structures and supervisory arrangements governing court reporters differ across jurisdictions. In unified court systems, however, these personnel are often placed under the purview of the state's Administrative Office of the Courts (AOC). In both centralized and decentralized systems, the assignment of OCRs should be informed by a systematic needs assessment. OCRs are most frequently assigned to criminal courts because proceedings are likely subject to appellate review. Determining the appropriate number, type, and feasibility of OCR positions requires an analysis of caseload volume in relation to the specific case types that necessitate real-time record production, together with the statutes and court rules that govern those caseflow procedures.

As with other specialized technical units, OCRs should report to a designated supervisor or manager responsible for monitoring judicial workload demands, managing assignments, and providing general administrative oversight of the reporting function. Supervision of OCRs can, however, pose distinct challenges in unified systems that employ a centralized management structure. In such contexts, OCRs typically report to a courthouse and perform their duties onsite, while supervisory oversight is conducted remotely by AOC management. Consequently, communication regarding performance issues, scheduling, or other operational matters must be facilitated through a liaison or operations manager, who serves as the intermediary between the local court and the central supervisory authority.

This centralized arrangement can complicate key personnel processes such as coordination of meetings, performance evaluations, and disciplinary actions, as the OCR does not technically report directly to the court where their services are being rendered. Based on our comparative observations of both supervisory models, the presence of an onsite supervisor offers notable advantages, including improved responsiveness, communication, and accountability. Nevertheless, practical considerations such as caseload volume and staffing resources often impact the feasibility of onsite supervision. In the absence of a local supervisor, the court should provide substantive input on performance assessments and court operational needs to ensure that oversight remains contextually informed and functionally effective.

When not actively engaged in courtroom proceedings and upon request, OCRs are responsible for producing verbatim transcriptions of their stenographic notes. OCRs are also tasked with completing and submitting the requisite documentation once a transcript is finalized and they may be required to upload their notes to a designated digital server. The rapid advancement of recording technologies, however, has made the demand for OCRs markedly decline. Beginning in the mid to late 2000s, as digital recording initiatives expanded from pilot programs in select jurisdictions to full implementation across many courts, OCR staffing levels decreased substantially (generally through attrition). Simultaneously, shortages in the court reporter workforce have necessitated a shift to electronic recording in many court jurisdictions (Gravely, 2019) – both at the state (Sabalow, 2025) and federal levels (United States Courts, 2024).

In New Jersey, the policy position was to employ only those OCRs capable of providing real-time transcription. Real-time court reporting technology enables the instantaneous display of testimony in readable text for courtroom participants and can be integrated with webcast proceedings. Importantly, real-time reporting remains essential for ensuring accessibility, as deaf and hearing-impaired individuals rely on this service to meaningfully participate in judicial processes. Within the courtroom, real-time reporting also affords judges and attorneys immediate access to the developing transcript, thus enhancing procedural efficiency and accuracy.

Despite significant technological advancements in digital recording, some judges continue to prefer the presence of an OCR in the courtroom. In certain cases, this preference persists due to longstanding organizational practices and institutional tradition. In others, the inclusion of an OCR is justified by the nature of the proceedings – particularly in complex, multi-attorney or multi-defendant trials, mass tort litigation, and high-profile cases – where the likelihood of inaudible recordings must be minimized. Moreover, when requested, OCRs may arguably provide prompter and more accurate readbacks of testimony than those provided by electronic recording systems.

Divergent perspectives often exist between judges and court administrators regarding judicial needs related to OCRs. Consequently, it is incumbent upon administrators to incorporate judicial viewpoints when determining how best to meet the operational requirements of the court. Administrators should conduct a comprehensive assessment of the organizational costs associated with OCR staffing that encompasses salaries, benefits, and related operational expenditures, as well as those of digital reporting platforms, with the goal of implementing an ideal combination of both options. These strategies should be explored (absent any other reason) to broaden the functional role of OCRs as a means of deploying a skilled reporting workforce that the court can continue to rely on to capture and maintain the official record. For instance, one court implemented a pilot program in which OCRs were tasked with digitally capturing exhibits to expedite the appellate process in response to a newly adopted court rule that imposed stricter filing deadlines. These and other expanded OCR responsibilities must be brought to bear by administrators, knowing that electronic recording systems are not without substantial costs, which include staffing, centralized records storage, backup systems, records distribution, and transcription services.

Language Assistance Services

Language assistance services within the judiciary extend well beyond oral interpretation and encompass a broad array of functions designed to ensure full and equitable access to justice for individuals with limited English proficiency (LEP) and for those who are deaf or hard of hearing. While court interpreting remains the cornerstone of linguistic accessibility and is the most visible component of such services, the Office of Interpreters plays a vital institutional role in guaranteeing linguistic access across all dimensions of court operations. Interpreting services represent a significant expenditure for most jurisdictions; however, they constitute an indispensable component of procedural fairness and due process. The judiciary's growing investment in these services underscores its constitutional and ethical commitment to ensuring that all court users, regardless of language ability, can participate fully and meaningfully in judicial proceedings.

Interpreter services should be supported and enhanced through a broad framework of supplemental measures that integrate language access into the daily operations of the court. These measures extend beyond the courtroom and are essential to fulfilling court's purposes and responsibilities. Key components of this framework include the following:

- Signage (Including Emergency and Directional Signage): Courts should engage in continuous evaluation of their physical and digital environments to ensure that signage adequately meets the needs of LEP users. This includes the provision and maintenance of bilingual or multilingual signs throughout courthouse facilities, encompassing routine directional markers, courtroom identifiers, and emergency exit instructions. Signage should be displayed both in hard-copy form and on digital platforms such as monitors or electronic information boards. Equally important are notices advising the public of the availability of interpreter services and encouraging individuals to communicate their language assistance needs to designated court personnel or administrative offices. Thoughtfully designed multilingual signage not only facilitates efficient navigation, but it also symbolizes the judiciary's commitment to accessibility and inclusivity as fundamental components of due process.
- Customer Service Training and Assistance: Frontline court personnel play a pivotal role in the accessibility of court services for LEP users. Courts should implement regular and structured training programs for staff, particularly those assigned to public service counters, information desks, and intake units, to ensure they are knowledgeable about language access protocols and capable of responding effectively to LEP individuals. Training should emphasize both procedural awareness – such as how to request interpreter services – and cultural competency so that the quality of interactions between court personnel and diverse court users is enhanced. The Ombudsman's Office or designated court liaison unit can serve as a centralized resource hub for LEP assistance. These offices should ensure that LEP users are informed of the full range of available services, including interpretation, translation, and procedural guidance. Additionally, these offices may provide multimedia resources – such as instructional videos or interactive tutorials – that visually explain court processes in a linguistically and culturally accessible manner. Such initiatives not only support user understanding but also reduce administrative inefficiencies by minimizing miscommunication and procedural errors.
- External Publications: Courts should ensure that public-facing materials – such as informational brochures, notices of rights, online resources, and educational outreach documents – are translated into the most frequently encountered languages within the jurisdiction. These materials function not only as instruments of communication, but as vehicles of civic education and trust-building between the courts and the respective communities they serve. A systematic process for reviewing,

translating, and updating external publications ensures consistency and accuracy while also reducing barriers that may prevent LEP individuals from understanding their obligations or rights when engaging with the court.

- Court Forms and Pleadings: Translation and adaptation of standard court forms, petitions, and pleadings are essential to meaningful access. LEP users must be able to navigate procedural requirements without reliance on ad hoc assistance or informal translation. Courts should maintain a centralized repository of standardized multilingual forms to ensure uniformity and to mitigate the frequency of errors. Moreover, translated materials should be reviewed periodically by both legal and linguistic experts to maintain the fidelity of these materials to original legal concepts and to reflect any statutory or rule changes. Providing translated court form templates for common filings – such as motions, responses, and applications – can also serve to expedite case processing and enhance administrative efficiency.
- Emergent Matter Translations: In addition to routine materials, courts must be prepared to translate emergent or time-sensitive communications, particularly in instances where immediate understanding is essential to the protection of rights or compliance with court orders. Examples include emergency protective orders, bail determinations, and urgent public notices issued during crises or natural disasters. The development of a rapid response translation protocol ensures that critical documents are accessible in real time. Such readiness reflects the court's ability to manage linguistic accessibility as an operational necessity rather than a reactive measure.

Together, these initiatives exemplify a holistic approach to language access embedding the importance of these practices in court administration.

Records Management

The administration of justice depends fundamentally on the accuracy, availability, and integrity of court records. The basic tenets outlined in our discussion of the court's purposes and responsibilities cannot be realized without reliable documentation of judicial proceedings, decisions, and case-related actions. Historically, legal accessibility has meant that members of the public may review laws, judicial opinions, and most case files without restriction. This principle reflects the understanding that government work products – especially those generated by the judiciary – constitute public property and therefore must remain open to examination (Dibble, 1986). Such openness not only reinforces constitutional guarantees of transparency, but it also sustains public trust and confidence in the judicial process. Within this framework, therefore, the creation, maintenance, and preservation of the official court record represent a foundational duty of the courts and a cornerstone of institutional legitimacy.

The management of records – whether paper-based or digital – falls squarely within the domain of court administration. In some jurisdictions, the responsibility for records management and fiscal records may rest, in part, with the clerk of court's office. Court records serve multiple legal and procedural functions: they document appeals, validate prior convictions and sentences, authenticate due process, establish enforceable civil judgments, and record family status determinations such as divorce, custody, and guardianship. The implications of record accuracy and accessibility extend to every stakeholder in the justice system, including litigants, victims, attorneys, judges, justice agencies, researchers, the media, and the broader public. Consequently, court administrators must address complex operational and managerial issues that include, inter alia, ensuring the reliability and integrity of case files, assigning appropriate personnel for record servicing, selecting suitable technologies for record collection and distribution, and developing comprehensive project plans for implementing records management systems.

The NCSC (2005) has articulated the importance of these functions through CourTool 6, Reliability and Integrity of Case Files. This performance measure emphasizes that all essential case documents – both paper and electronic – must be complete, accurate, and readily available for court and public use. A reliable record system is one in which the information contained in each case file can be trusted as a true and complete representation of judicial proceedings. Accordingly, CourTool 6 serves as a benchmark for assessing whether courts possess the necessary policies, procedures, and technologies required to ensure the dependability of case data over time. Integrating this measure into judicial operations reinforces accountability and establishes a standardized basis for evaluating the quality of case management practices across jurisdictions.

As detailed in the discussion of information technology in the courts, the evolution from analog to digital systems has profoundly transformed records management. From audio tape recording to digital repositories, and from in-person testimony to remote appearances, the recordkeeping tools of the courtroom have undergone a paradigm shift. These advancements have generated efficiencies in documentation and retrieval, yet they also impose ongoing expanded obligations for administrators and judges to periodically review and update recordkeeping standards.

Maintaining the reliability of case files within a digital ecosystem presents unique challenges. A court record is not an isolated document, but rather a composite of information drawn from multiple systems and agencies including law enforcement, corrections, probation, social services, and health authorities, among others. Ensuring the integrity of the court record requires coordinated policies that govern data entry, transfer, and verification across these interconnected entities. Moreover, administrators must continuously monitor the release and protection of sensitive information, balancing statutory mandates for transparency against privacy and confidentiality concerns – the improper disclosure or data inconsistency of which can undermine the public's trust and confidence in the courts.

When courts modernize or consolidate record systems, administrators should conduct a comprehensive analysis of existing manual and automated processes. This analysis should identify redundancies, inefficiencies, and opportunities for workflow integration. Early stages of system design (or intermediate enhancements) should include a detailed review of local court rules and definitions for the noted reasons. This is particularly important because data contained in the court's case management system should be considered the authoritative record of judicial activity. Akin to the other technology examples already mentioned, existing rules and standardized data definitions were likely developed to complement paper-based procedures, which will almost certainly need to be revised to accommodate digital functionalities.

Reiterating a key reality in the courts, the judiciary operates within a loosely coupled system comprised of numerous independent stakeholders – prosecutors, defense counsel, victims, social agencies, internal and external IT personnel, legal counsel, department heads, representatives of state archive repositories, and compliance officers – each of whom utilize court record systems differently. Effective records management requires administrators to understand and accommodate these diverse functional needs during system design, testing, and implementation. Early and continual stakeholder engagement, therefore, is critical to achieving broad-based acceptance of technologies and procedures related to records management. Of particular note, judiciary counsel should maintain oversight throughout the development and implementation phases, especially in matters concerning data retrieval, production, and evidentiary use (Conference of State Court Administrators [COSCA], 2013). This oversight is essential to ensure that court records are managed in accordance with established legal standards and procedural safeguards. Moreover, administrative oversight plays a critical role in verifying that practices comply with statutory requirements governing confidentiality, access, and retention.

In this vein, it is incumbent on court administration to assess existing workflows, identify potential redundancies or conflicts, and ensure that new systems do not disrupt the operations of partner agencies. Judiciary policy for record storage and retention must also be analyzed by the courts to anticipate future needs. We have found that consulting with other courts through their respective network of records managers can prove beneficial, because they will share their experience and recommendations about the maintenance, training, and policy enforcement of various systems.

Each caseflow process that generates data must be evaluated for how and when information enters the record. To enhance efficiency and reliability, court systems should be designed to capture data at the point of origin; that being, when a document is created or an event occurs prompting a court record to be generated. Administrators should also promote the use of standardized electronic forms and automated validation checks to ensure data accuracy at the time of case submission. E-filing mechanisms play a critical role in this regard by minimizing manual data entry and allowing parties to submit information through integrated, user-friendly platforms (NCSC, 2025).

The American Records Management Association (ARMA) developed the Generally Accepted Recordkeeping Principles (GARP) as a foundational framework for organizations seeking to implement sound information governance practices (ARMA, 2017). This model provides a valuable point of reference for courts to assess their own recordkeeping systems. Comprised of eight interrelated principles, GARP establishes a global standard for the effective management of information throughout its lifecycle described as follows:[2]

1) Accountability: A designated, senior executive should bear the overall responsibility for the recordkeeping program and ensure that specific duties are delegated to qualified personnel.
2) Integrity: Records must maintain authenticity and reliability, providing reasonable assurance of their accuracy and trustworthiness.
3) Protection: The recordkeeping framework must incorporate safeguards that ensure an appropriate level of security for sensitive or confidential information.
4) Compliance: The program must adhere to all relevant legal, regulatory, and professional requirements governing records and information management.
5) Availability: Records should be organized and maintained to enable their timely, efficient, and accurate retrieval when needed.
6) Retention: Records must be preserved for durations that satisfy legal, operational, and historical obligations, balancing institutional needs with regulatory requirements.
7) Disposition: Secure and systematic procedures must be established for the final disposition of records once their retention period has expired.
8) Transparency: The structure and operation of the recordkeeping program should be clearly documented and accessible to organizational personnel and other relevant stakeholders to promote accountability and trust.

Together, these eight principles form a coherent and adaptable framework that courts can employ to promote responsible information governance, ensure compliance with legal mandates, and strengthen institutional integrity in the management of judicial records. This would involve the court's critical decisions such as:

How should confidential or sealed records be protected? What constitutes the official docket? How should electronic service and digital signatures be incorporated into daily operations? What categories of information should be publicly accessible online, and under what conditions? Decisions in these areas shape not only the efficiency of recordkeeping, but also the perceived legitimacy of the court's information management practices.

Records management is not a discrete or ancillary administrative function, but rather a central pillar of judicial governance and more specifically to operations. The capacity of a court to administer justice depends as much on its procedural integrity as on the quality, consistency, and reliability of the information it maintains. As courts increasingly rely on cloud-based storage and third-party systems, information security and data retention have grown exponentially more complex. Many courts are also implementing cloud-based systems for evidence submission, storage, and presentation. Sound records management practices for making and preserving the official court record as a goal do not change, however. Selecting appropriate storage solutions requires both technical and legal expertise to ensure compliance with recordkeeping laws, cybersecurity standards, and privacy mandates. Ultimately, the success of any records management program lies in its capacity to uphold the principles of reliability, integrity, and accessibility – the very criteria embodied in CourTool 6 and the ARMA framework – which will sustain the public's confidence in the judiciary as a transparent and accountable institution.

Collections

As discussed in the Funding and Budgeting chapter, the collection of court-ordered financial obligations including fines, fees, surcharges, and restitution constitutes a critical administrative function within judicial governance and reflects the intersection of fiscal accountability, access to justice, and public trust in the courts. Organizationally, the management of collections varies considerably across jurisdictions. Some courts maintain internally administered collection units that operate under the direct supervision of court administration, ensuring close integration with judicial operations, affected case management divisions, and probation. Other jurisdictions delegate the collection function to external entities, such as executive branch agencies or outsourced contractors, as a means of leveraging resources or reducing the court's administrative burden.

These divergent organizational structures carry important implications for court administration. When collections are retained within the judiciary, administrators exercise direct control over policy implementation, staff supervision, and compliance monitoring, allowing for a highly cohesive approach to balancing enforcement with considerations of fairness and proportionality such as the points we noted related to the individual's "ability to pay."

Conversely, when collection responsibilities are transferred outside the judicial branch, the court's role shifts toward interagency coordination, contract oversight, and policy guidance, potentially reducing its capacity for day-to-day management, but increasing the need for accountability mechanisms.

The organizational locus of collections fundamentally shapes the administrator's ability to influence and carry out strategic decision making and ensure the type and category of enforcement practices. Measure 7 of the NCSC (2005) CourTools provides a framework for court collections, including performance metrics. Court administrators should regularly review performance data for collections programs, irrespective of whether they are managed in-house or are externally based, for the purposes of ensuring that the system is optimized and aligned with the court's strategic agenda.

Infrastructure

Court Security

The heightened emphasis on court security in recent decades is indicative of the vulnerability of government institutions and the judicial branch, in particular. Ensuring that the courthouse is safe is an absolute necessity for the preservation of constitutional rights and the rule of law (Zaruba, 2007). Yet, from a historical perspective, courts across the country continue to experience a wide range of security threats, many disrupting court operations and some resulting in fatalities. Modern-day threats to the judiciary come from an array of actors and groups, including international terrorist organizations, patriot assemblies and militias, hate groups, and workplace violence incidents involving terminated employees, disgruntled workers, or domestic partners, among others. Broadly speaking, court security breaches typically consist of the following types of incidents (United States Department of Justice, 2004):

- Contraband entering the courthouse, including handguns, knives, brass knuckles, incendiary devices, etc.
- Threats and attacks against judges, attorneys, and other court participants, at both onsite and offsite locations
- Protests resulting in infrastructure damage
- Inmate escapes
- Bomb attacks or bomb threats prompting a disruptive evacuation of the building
- Use of chemical agents, biological agents, or other toxins targeting court personnel and property
- Delivery of suspicious mail or packages that contain (or are suspected to contain) toxic powders or substances including those intentionally altered to mimic real toxins to provoke alarm and force building closure
- Unauthorized video recording and live-streaming of victims, jurors, or witnesses

- Cyberattacks on the court IT systems including ransomware, data breaches, and system outages
- Social media attacks and misinformation about the courts, some of which target specific judges or other government officials

A security plan and audit will provide an overview of the court along four areas or zones, including facility perimeter, facility exterior, public access areas, and restricted access areas. The facility perimeter encompasses the space between the property line and the courthouse. Architectural considerations in this area include landscaping, lighting, fencing, sidewalks, parking, and position of building on-site. Operational and technological considerations include the elements, types, and maintenance of alarm and camera systems. "Hardening the perimeter" is one of the bedrock, proven strategies for risk mitigation – the primary aim of which is to block the entry of weapons, bombs, toxins, and other dangerous materials and vehicles from entering the court environment. In order to better safeguard the court, many jurisdictions have instituted sophisticated entry screening equipment (magnetometers and x-ray machines), panic buttons, bollards, use of biometric device systems (e.g., face recognition, fingerprint readers, and retina scanners), and video monitoring systems using artificial intelligence, among other architectural and operational considerations, in their infrastructure (NCSC, 2022).

The facility exterior consists of the external portion of the court complex. Architectural considerations for this zone include entrances, windows, walls, fire escapes, and other openings such as manholes, sewers, skylights, grates, and HVAC vents, all of which can be used to gain access into the court. Operational and technological considerations include the implementation, use, maintenance, and upgrades of intrusion alarms, locks, surveillance systems, and weapon screening equipment.

Public access areas relate to the service areas and hallways that are open and accessible to the public. Architectural considerations include the use of barriers and signage to prevent the public from entering restricted areas. Operational and technological considerations include the use of mirrors and cameras to observe and monitor movement in the facility. This includes the routine inspection of false ceilings separating rooms, restrooms, elevators, and emergency stairways. In general, the key issues relate to limiting penetration (closing off non-public hallways and areas) and congestion (wide hallways and clear signage), while maximizing visibility (removing potential obstructions with clear and monitored hallways) in and around the public areas of the courthouse. The public areas of courtrooms must also be managed to control overcrowding and access, by ensuring that physical barriers separate the gallery from the space designated to judges, litigants, attorneys, and judicial staff. Courtrooms should be well lit with clear signage and always locked when in recess. Notwithstanding the hardening of the perimeter, the judge's bench, witness stand, and courtroom workstations should include ballistic shielding and, to the extent possible, the armored protection should also be installed in staff areas and chambers. Modern day synthetic fiber material made of Kevlar provides the court with cost-effective shielding that is durable relative to other products.

Restricted access zones relate to those areas reserved for only authorized personnel, including judges, court staff, and sheriff's officers. These spaces include those designated as private or employee-only corridors and entrances, detention floors, areas and rooms, chambers and staff offices, and cash or vault areas. Architectural considerations include the configuration of separate access to the courts that is limited and controlled for judges and court staff, jurors, witnesses, attorneys, and detained defendants. Operational and technological considerations include electronic locking mechanisms, duress alarms, and video surveillance systems to control, limit, and monitor access and movement in restricted spaces of the courthouse.

John McMahon, Project Director for an early court security guide, discussed some of the preventative measures that remain relevant today (National Sheriffs' Association, 1978):

> In court security, the emphasis is on prevention, containment, and control – directed towards the protection of life and property and the preservation of the judicial process.

Given the high stakes involved in providing a safe and secure court environment, responsibility for court security is no longer a task readily delegated to middle management or outside contract services. Rather, the court security function requires constant, prioritized attention on the part of presiding judges and senior court administrators. Fully engaged court management teams will spearhead continuous improvements in all facets of the court security plan. Addressing the key role of court administration vis-à-vis court security, Cooper (2007) noted:

> Court security is an integral part of the responsibilities of court administration, reflecting the increasing recognition that the issue of court security and the responsibility for ensuring continuity of operations are inextricably intertwined.

For the court management team, development and maintenance of a robust security program entails ongoing collaboration with the bench and court staff, law enforcement agencies, the jail system, and other justice partners (Campbell & Reinkensmeyer, 2007). The same dynamics hold true for continuity of operations (COOP) planning, an area which necessarily intersects with security and also engages many of the same organizations, including, among others, first responders, facilities management, and public information. Given the considerable interplay between these two dimensions of court administration, courts should have a joint Steering Committee on Court Security and Continuity of Operations as depicted in Figure 8.2 (Reinkensmeyer, 2011).

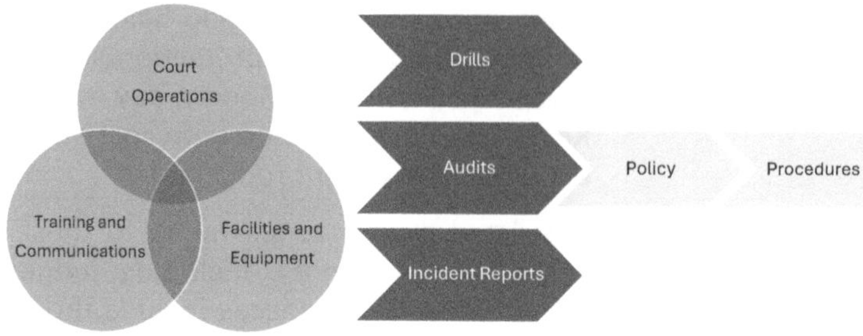

Figure 8.2 Court Security and Continuity of Operations – Continuous Improvement Process

Ideally, the steering committee should be established as a formal, standing body chaired by the presiding judge and staffed by court administration. At the outset, the court should clarify the roles and responsibilities of the committee, which may vary depending on the nature of the subject matter under consideration and the organizational culture of the locality. For instance, will the committee serve in an advisory role or is it expected to make policy decisions, and, if so, in what areas? Our experience has shown that some of the more controversial topics of initial policy formulation may include the following:

- Which, if any, group of individuals should be authorized to bypass entry screening?
- Should law enforcement officers or any other persons (e.g., judges or staff) be permitted to carry or house guns in the courthouse?
- Will court security personnel function under the administrative direction of the court or an executive branch law enforcement agency (e.g., the sheriff's office), or a combination thereof?
- Will the court's security officers be armed and, if so, under what authority?
- Which officials have the authority to order a building evacuation in the event of a bomb threat or other emergency situation?

Once established, the Steering Committee can establish an ongoing, iterative system of meetings and reviews for continuous improvements in security and continuity of operations. Periodic risk assessments, drills, and system audits will help the court identify vulnerabilities in infrastructure and operations. This kind of systematic "gap analysis" will generate a "to do" list of action items for court administration, while also providing the rationale for security- and facility-related budget requests.

Reference to a uniform set of court security criterion and best practices can serve as a reference point for periodic gap analyses (Fautsko et al., 2013). For example, the Arizona Supreme Court instituted statewide court security standards, phased in across the state over a three-year period. The standards-based policy and procedural requirements address governance and administration of local court security programs, entrances and screening, management of in-custody defendants, protocols for taking individuals into custody, facilities and equipment, and other related areas (Supreme Court of Arizona, 2020).

Our proposed continuous improvement model (Figure 8.2) identifies three intersecting spheres of work in the areas of security and business continuity: 1) Court operations; 2) Facilities and equipment; and 3) Training and communications. Depending on the size of the jurisdiction, the court may find it helpful to establish workgroups or subcommittees for each sphere and to structure the Steering Committee's meeting agendas accordingly. Likewise, project management and reporting can be organized within these three interrelated domains. To galvanize the prioritization of the security program, the Steering Committee should establish clear, widely distributed policies and procedures, and regularly debrief security incidents. Emphasizing the need for ongoing improvements in court security, Fautsko and associates (2013) observed:

> Security is not a one-time achievement. It is a serious and continuous goal and requires constant vigilance. Further, it must be a number one priority every single day for all those interested and involved in the process. The risks involved in court building operations are great and varied, and generally can never be eliminated. However, by exercising due diligence and devoting the appropriate attention, incidents can be both minimized and mitigated.

Continuity of Operations

Not unlike the existent vulnerabilities of other government entities, courts are subject to major business interruptions occasioned by natural disasters, technological accidents, and attack-related emergencies. While many such incidents cannot be impeded or otherwise eliminated, a business continuity plan can mitigate the extent to which a court is required to cease operations so that it can resume mission critical functions. Along this vein, courts with a comprehensive and current COOP plan offer an expedited pathway to full recovery of systems, data, and critical business records. Although it is difficult to quantify the timely restoration of judicial branch services, a workable, pretested business recovery plan inevitably reaps benefits.

As detailed in the Strategic and Long-Term Planning chapter, courts across the nation maintained essential services throughout the COVID-19 pandemic, quickly implementing remote video hearings and other online technologies including digital signatures, digital evidence, and off-site payment systems. Under similar circumstances, the judicial branch successfully instituted a range of measures to provide public access in the wake of the 9/11 terrorist attack (Birkland, 2004) and natural disasters such as Hurricane Sandy (United States Courts, 2012) and Hurricane Harvey (Birkland & Schneider, 2007; Raftery, 2017).

In anticipation of such crises, the American Bar Association (ABA) promulgated a Model Court Rule on Provision of Legal Services Following Determination of Major Disaster (Raftery, 2017). Relatedly, Tichy and Bennis (2007) provide insightful analysis of executive decision making during emergencies. Another invaluable resource regarding continuity of operations is the NCSC (2021a) COOP Planning Guide, which sets forth an extensive court planning framework. The guide was developed in collaboration with the Federal Emergency Management Agency (FEMA) and the CCJ/COSCA Joint Committee on Court Security and Emergency Preparedness, some of which occurred during the COVID-19 pandemic. Some of the online resources supported by the NCSC (2021a) and the NACM (2006) include templates for readiness and preparedness, activating the blueprint in the midst of a disaster, ongoing court operations, "reconstitution" and cost recovery, and plans for training and testing COOP plans.

FEMA (2023), in particular, urges the coordination of federal, state, and local executive agency functions, in tandem with private sector service providers. A parallel model generally exists on the judicial branch end, which brings together the trial court COOP plan with that of other local courts, first responders, the state supreme court (administrative office of the courts), federal courts, and private sector service providers. FEMA (2023) delineates the following foundational elements of a business continuity plan pertinent to federal executive branch agencies:

- Identification of essential business functions
- Provisions for leadership succession and delegation of authority
- Identification of alternative "continuity facilities," such as "sister" court locations or other government office spaces
- Continuity communication strategies
- Vital records management
- Human capital, including first responders and essential emergency staffing
- Testing, training, and exercises
- Shifting authority for certain functions from one entity to another ("devolution of control") and resumption of normal operations ("reconstitution")

Given all these considerations, we submit that responsibility for COOP planning rests with a standing, joint Steering Committee on Court Security and Continuity of Operations as depicted in Figure 8.2. Tabletop exercises, audits and drills administered by the Steering Committee should provide valuable feedback to the court leadership as it develops and regularly assesses its emergency contingency plans and ensures alignment with the long-term strategic agenda.

Facilities Management

Court facilities management is frequently discounted as a vital function to ensure high performance in modern court administration. Critical to this function is the development and periodic update of a comprehensive space master plan (Hardenbergh et al., 1998; NCSC, 2021b). The plan should encompass the courthouse, court-related office buildings such as probation facilities, inmate circulation, courtrooms integrated into the jail or mental health facility, movement and flow of jurors, and employee and public parking (Judicial Conference of the United States, 2021). Modern court facilities planning and management must also consider long-term sustainability and environmental impact, bearing in mind the full life-cycle of court buildings (Dibble & Cousins, 2009). A well-organized and executed master space plan will situate the court in the best possible position to attain capital funding for security-related facility enhancements and renovation of existing buildings, as well as new court facilities.

Apart from the development of a master space plan, several aspects of facility management are unique to courts. First, funding for construction and maintenance of most court facilities is generally provided by the "host" governmental entity (e.g., city, county, state or federal government), which often retains ownership ("title") of the facility and land. For instance, at the federal level, the General Services Administration (GSA) – an executive branch entity – provides all court facilities through a nationwide "Courthouse Program" (GSA, 2025). A notable exception here is the transfer of some 500 California court facilities from local to state court jurisdiction, as part of California's transition to full state funding of courts (Administrative Office of the Courts, 2009). Under the host government model, the court's leadership team must work closely with the funding body to ensure that adequate monies are provided to work within existing facilities or expand allocated space to fill emerging demands. The resulting concern, in many jurisdictions, is the extent to which space needs of the court will be timely met, given the inherent tensions which may develop between the court and the funding body. The competition for capital funding is ever-present in light of pressing space needs of other public units, including those related to law enforcement, jails, parks, libraries, transportation, and healthcare, which are financially supported by the host government.

Secondly, given the dependency of the court on the host government, the court leadership team may find it necessary to develop an intergovernmental agreement and/or and service-level agreement for facility maintenance, architectural work, and court expansion projects. A key decision related to this point involves management oversight and direct supervision of courthouse maintenance personnel. For instance, will this function be managed by the court or the host government, and after this matter is resolved, under what terms and conditions? Once these determinations are made, formal agreements must also be reached on the facilities staffing model, mainly delineating whether to use full-time staff, contract services, or a combination thereof. This particular collaborative effort must also consider the specific nature of the work at hand, whether it be for court cleaning services, HVAC maintenance, landscaping, or building repairs.

The third aspect which can further complicate matters involves whether the court operates under a shared government facility model, such that the courts are co-located in the same building with non-judicial-related offices (e.g., prosecutor's, public defense services, police department, city council meeting room, recorder's office, treasurer's office, etc.). These circumstances can present difficulties for the court because those other entities may not appreciate or otherwise support the court's need for robust security measures, separate circulation patterns for inmates, safety demands associated with jury trials and probation, among other considerations. Moreover, expansion of court facilities may be challenged, if not altogether blocked, due to the shared facility arrangements. Joint space management planning committees can help foster open communications between the court and other entities housed in the same location. The master plan can also serve as an impactful tool in these coordination efforts.

IT Infrastructure

The transition from local data centers to the cloud computing model may convey the false impression that management's attention to on-site IT infrastructure can be redirected to that of other facility needs. On the contrary, the decentralization of a court's IT systems necessitates a high degree of detailed long-term planning, substantial capital investment, and proactive ongoing maintenance. Court facilities planning, consequently, must provide for a stable, robust, and scalable broadband network, both for intra-court communications and for uninterrupted access to cloud applications and remote data storage; secure physical areas for programmable network routers and onsite servers; flexible courtroom technologies and bi-directional video transmission. Fully developed, the court's IT infrastructure will also include backup power systems, flexible data center space, remote "hot sites" for data recovery, water detection, and specialized fire suppressant systems. The court's IT infrastructure must also support the foregoing array of security technologies, including security cameras, panic buttons, motion detectors, card badge readers, etc. In today's increasingly volatile world of cyberattacks, a comprehensive court IT infrastructure necessarily requires substantial investments in network and data security, including a regimen of periodic vulnerability testing and remediation (Joint Technology Committee, 2021). Access to wiring closets and areas housing onsite computer equipment must also be incorporated into the security plan so that these spaces are restricted to designated IT staff.

Other strategies to garner financial support for facilities include the court administrator's participation in city/county planning bodies, court facility tours for government officials and other stakeholders, collection, analysis, and presentation of trend data on the usage and limitation of space. Additionally, court administrators can facilitate development of intergovernmental agreements with the host government and trusted agency partners in areas such as network expansion, joint systems maintenance (e.g., integrated criminal justice system), cybersecurity, IT staff development, and cross-sector facilities management.

Jury Management

The right to a jury trial was regarded by the Founding Fathers as a cornerstone of democratic governance, a belief reflected in its inclusion in both the Declaration of Independence and the United States Constitution. Thomas Jefferson described the trial by jury as "the only anchor ever yet imagined by man, by which a government can be held to the principles of its constitution" (ABA, 2005a). Although the tripartite system of government comprising the executive, legislative, and judicial branches was designed to balance power, it was nevertheless recognized as insufficient on its own to safeguard the individual rights of life, liberty, and property. The institution of the jury, composed of one's peers, thus served as an essential safeguard against potential governmental abuse and judicial overreach. Citizen participation in government proceedings was conceived not merely as a procedural formality, but as a central mechanism through which the people themselves could restrain the excesses and authority of the state. By integrating public judgment into the administration of justice, the Founders ensured that the law remained grounded in societal norms and moral sensibilities, while simultaneously curbing the arbitrary use of government power (Jost, 1995). Early colonial charters, including those in Virginia and New York, instituted functional jury trials, yet it was the operation of non-jury British Vice-Admiralty courts that most provoked colonial resentment and helped to catalyze the American Revolution (Levy et al., 2000).

The right to a trial by jury is explicitly guaranteed in the Sixth and Seventh Amendments to the Constitution. In accordance with these provisions, courts bear a constitutional and administrative obligation to uphold, evaluate, and continuously refine the processes by which this right is exercised. As Alexander Hamilton (1787/2003) observed, "The ordinary administration of criminal and civil justice... contributes more than any other circumstance to impressing upon the minds of the people affection, esteem, and reverence towards government." Similarly, in his 1906 address to the ABA, Pound (1906) emphasized the relationship between the effective administration of justice and public confidence in judicial institutions. The management of jury operations falls squarely within this "ordinary administration," as it represents one of the most visible and participatory aspects of the court's engagement with the public.

Given the jury's critical role in legitimizing the judicial process, courts are duty-bound to evaluate both their internal jury management practices and the public's perceptions of them. This assessment must be systematic and ongoing, encompassing the planning, implementation, evaluation, and reassessment of policies and programs that govern juror selection and service. Modern court management recognizes that jury administration is not a peripheral concern, but it is rather an essential component of justice delivery. Indeed, the functions performed by the jury are directly tied to at least four of the eight purposes and responsibilities of the courts: (1) assuring individual justice in individual cases; (2) assuring the appearance of justice in individual cases; (3) providing a forum for the resolution of legal disputes; and (4) protecting individuals from the arbitrary exercise of governmental power. Through the effective and principle-based management of jury operations, courts not only fulfill constitutional mandates, but they also reinforce the broader legitimacy and authority of the judicial branch itself.

For most citizens, the only direct interaction with the courts occurs through jury service. Relatively few individuals have experience with the courts as litigants, victims, or witnesses. Instead, for the vast majority of members of the public, their impressions of the judicial system are formed through the singular experience of being summoned as a prospective juror. This experience becomes the lens through which they evaluate the court's accessibility, fairness, and operational efficiency. The stakes, therefore, for jury system management are significant. Jury administration provides the court with a rare opportunity to advocate for itself. A negative juror experience may reinforce public stereotypes of courts as bureaucratic and inefficient, whereas positive, informative engagement is more likely to leave participants more knowledgeable and appreciative of the judiciary's vital role in safeguarding constitutional rights and upholding the rule of law.

From an administrative perspective, it is well understood that jury trials are the exception, rather than the norm in the resolution of court cases. Nonetheless, they remain a fundamental component of the American justice system, constitutionally mandated and symbolically central to the democratic process. Accordingly, court administrators must be prepared to effectively manage the human and material resources required to support the jury system. However episodic we know jury trials to be, the operational demands of jury management are considerable, underscoring the importance of strategic planning and best practices. Courts must maintain an adequate and representative pool of qualified jurors, ready for service when needed, while simultaneously managing costs and preserving institutional efficiency. Those courts that adopt evidence-based best practices in jury administration are best positioned to balance operational demands with administrative efficiency.

While practices necessarily vary by jurisdiction – depending on caseload volume, staffing, geography, and available technologies – certain fundamental principles remain universal. The ABA (2005b) articulates 19 such standards, providing a comprehensive framework for juror usage across all stages of the process. These principles emphasize, among other things, the preservation of the right to trial by jury, facilitation of citizen participation, protection of juror privacy, fairness in the selection process, the promotion of juror understanding, and the safeguarding of deliberative integrity. They further reinforce the judiciary's responsibility to uphold the rights of jurors and litigants alike, and to manage the jury system in ways that promote both justice and public confidence.

In practical terms, effective jury administration begins with the creation of a comprehensive and regularly updated master source list from which prospective jurors are drawn. This list should be constructed using multiple, broad-based sources and periodically reviewed to ensure accuracy and representativeness, with duplicate or ineligible entries removed through automated verification processes. Courts should also consult U.S. Census Bureau data to compare the demographic composition of the eligible population against that of the master source list, thereby ensuring inclusivity and adherence to principles of fair cross-section representation.

To enhance efficiency in the jury management process, the summons and qualification questionnaire should be systematically designed to collect relevant data that facilitate administrative review and analysis, while also serving the informational needs of other key stakeholders, including attorneys and judges. While some jurisdictions have combined these documents into a single mailing to reduce handling and postage costs, others have adopted a two-step process (often facilitated by web-based submission portals) to encourage public responsiveness. The cost-effectiveness of each approach should be periodically evaluated, weighing immediate expenditures against long-term efficiency gains and participation rates (Munsterman, 1996). Additionally, courts must assess the benefits and potential drawbacks of enforcing compliance among non-responding jurors. Enforcement initiatives – whether random or targeted – can be effective when paired with transparent communication and public awareness campaigns through local media (Fazari, 2013).

Accessibility and communication have long been known to be critical components of juror engagement (Hannaford-Agor, 2008). Courts should provide multiple channels for interaction – such as in-person service counters, online portals, and automated telephone systems – to accommodate varying user preferences and reduce operational burdens. Court websites should contain prominently displayed and regularly updated information, including directions to the courthouse, parking and public transportation options, juror compensation details, frequently asked questions, and policies governing jury service.

Upon reporting, jurors should encounter a well-organized check-in process with clear signage and staff assistance as needed. A comprehensive juror orientation session should be provided, covering key topics such as voir dire procedures, empanelment, trial structure, and fundamental legal concepts. Courts should also clearly communicate policies regarding electronic devices and appropriate use of technology during proceedings. The physical facilities provided to jurors should be comfortable, clean, and well maintained, with sufficient seating and designated areas for reading, eating, or completing work-related tasks (Munsterman et al., 1997).

At the conclusion of their service, all jurors – regardless of whether they were selected – should be thanked formally and invited to complete an evaluation survey, e.g., juror exit questionnaire. These surveys can provide valuable data for assessing procedural effectiveness, juror satisfaction, and opportunities for improvement. Collected data should be analyzed and summarized, including recommendations and implications of the findings, in periodic reports and provided to the presiding judge and court administrator.

Courts can further enhance efficiency by allowing flexible rescheduling of juror service dates, which can help to reduce failure-to-appear rates without undermining the annual juror yield. However, such flexibility must be managed to ensure the even distribution of prospective jurors among available pools. Service terms should be kept as brief as practicable (typically one day or one trial) to minimize individual burden while broadening community participation. Finally, coordination between juror call-in systems and trial calendar management should be utilized to align attendance with actual courtroom demand.

Effective Use of Jurors

Measure eight of the NCSC (2005) CourTools provides a methodology by which judges and administrators can examine how effectively their court utilizes jurors. The measure is comprised of two elements – juror utilization and juror yield. Juror usage is noted as "the rate at which prospective jurors are used at least once in trial or voir dire, expressed as the number of jurors selected as a percentage of the total number of prospective jurors qualified and available to serve." Juror yield is defined as "the number of citizens selected for jury duty who are qualified and report to serve, expressed as a percentage of the total number of prospective jurors available." The NCSC (2005) noted:

> The percentage of citizens available to serve relates to the integrity of source lists, the effectiveness of jury management practices, the willingness of citizens to serve, the efficacy of excuse and postponement policies, and the number of

exemptions allowed. The objective of this measure is to minimize the number of unused prospective jurors – the number of citizens who are summoned, qualified, report for jury service, and who are not needed.

Costs related to jury service are cumulative throughout the selection process. Cost savings from optimal juror utilization accrue to the courts, citizens (juror satisfaction), and employers. There are three categories of costs – direct, opportunity, and indirect. With respect to the courts, direct costs relate to printing, postage, juror fees, and court resources including staff and facility expenses. For jurors, these costs include uncompensated expenses such as transportation, parking, meals, childcare, and lost wages that they would have otherwise received if they were not required to report to the court. Employers also endure the costs of wages and benefits that are paid without the benefit of production. Opportunity costs relate to the loss of revenue to juror expenses that could have been diverted to other, more emergent, court needs. Indirect costs are linked to variables that are not necessarily quantifiable, yet have a significant impact on the administration of justice. These include public perceptions and levels of satisfaction with the judiciary (Munsterman & Hannaford-Agor, 2003).

The foregoing costs compel the courts to carefully consider the process of summoning and selecting prospective jurors so that resources are not squandered due to overestimates or mismanagement. Standards-based assessments such as these promulgated by the NCSC allow the court to measure some of the key causes of poor juror utilization including a deficient yield, inaccurate estimates of jury trials, and excessive panel sizes. The court's inability to secure a sufficient yield is typically due to inaccurate addresses, long terms of service, low rates of respondents, and an inadequate follow-up procedure on jurors failing to respond or appear. The failure to accurately predict the number of jury trials is primarily due to inaccurate calendaring and late cancellations due to plea agreements or settlements. Excessive panel sizes are frequently driven by judges, who request a larger number of jurors than that which is required to select the jury.

Improving juror utilization is grounded on two fundamental principles – the ability to predict jury trial activity and to maximize the use of jurors who report for service by assigning them to as many voir dires as possible. Making "good use" of jurors' time is an important and worthwhile objective for the court. As we previously mentioned, the court has few opportunities to make a good impression on its citizenry, given that many members of the public do not have contact with the court but for their intermittent jury service. The fact that perceptions about jury service are in some part shaped by the media makes the matter only more pressing. Unfortunately for the courts, the media's emphasis usually centers on notorious cases. Consequently, false impressions about the workings of the legal system and jury service often become widespread.

When jurors' time is managed efficiently it demonstrates that the court is not squandering taxpayer revenue, while concurrently giving the public an important lesson in the legal process. Munsterman (1996) noted the following in achieving good juror utilization: 1) adapt panel sizes to jurors needed, 2) do not call panels prematurely or unnecessarily, 3) make special arrangements for exceptionally large panels, 4) stagger trial starts, 5) maintain intensive operation when pool is used, 6) do not overcall jurors to the pool, and 7) dismiss and excuse jurors whenever possible. Some courts, such as those in Kansas, have long adopted the following juror usage guidelines (Kansas Supreme Court, 1983):

(a) Courts should employ the services of prospective jurors so as to achieve optimum use with a minimum of inconvenience to jurors.
(b) Courts should determine the minimally sufficient number of jurors needed to accommodate trial activity. This information and appropriate management techniques should be used to adjust both the number of individuals summoned for jury duty and the number assigned to jury panels.
(c) Courts should ensure that each prospective juror who has reported to the courthouse is assigned to a courtroom for voir dire before any prospective juror is assigned a second time.
(d) Courts should coordinate jury management and calendar management to make effective use of jurors.

Munsterman (1996) posited that yield analysis is critical in assessing the summoning and qualification of jurors. He found that the proportion of individuals selected who are both eligible and able to serve functions as a measure of several factors: the quality and comprehensiveness of the source lists, the community's readiness to fulfill jury service obligations, the effectiveness of the court's policies governing excuses and postponements, and the scope of statutory exemptions permitted. Table 8.1 illustrates the most common factors impacting yield and various tactics to improve it.

Table 8.1 Determinants of Juror Yield and Strategies for Improvement

Category	***Key Factors Influencing Yield***	***Recommended Actions***
Disqualifications	• Demographics of the population • Quality of source lists • Age of master or qualified lists • Eligibility criteria for source lists	• Enhance and diversify source lists • Increase frequency of selection • Combine qualification and summons processes
Exemptions (Class)	• Statutory exemptions • Locally determined exemptions	• Limit or remove non-essential exemptions

(*Continued*)

Table 8.1 (Continued)

Category	***Key Factors Influencing Yield***	***Recommended Actions***
Excused	• Court policies on excusals • Length of service required • Statutory excuse provisions	• Establish clear, uniform excusal policies • Shorten service periods where feasible • Restrict excusals to hardship cases • Offer postponement rather than excusal when possible
Postponed	• Court policies • Length of service	• Permit only limited postponements • Reduce required service periods
Failure to Appear/Report	• Public willingness or concern	• Implement juror education initiatives • Enforce attendance statutes • Conduct follow-ups for non-respondents
Undeliverable Notices	• Age and accuracy of mailing lists	• Regularly update and sample lists • Use reliable mailing methods such as first-class mail
Serving/ Availability	• Standby call-in systems or reporting mechanisms	• Improve forecasting of juror demand to optimize use

The NCSC (1998) found that stress factors relating to jury service included the lack of information about serving as a juror, past negative experience, loss of income, and the unanticipated arrival of the summons. Each of these factors may impact the yield, wherein prospective jurors will simply choose not to respond or appear for service. The analysis of the yield demonstrates which of these factors is contributing to the poor response rate and provides administrators with focus in knowing where to deploy resources to improve the yield. Boatright (1999) asserted that the non-response rate is a significant challenge that courts must address for three main reasons. First, it raises concerns about discrimination, as the pool of available jurors may fail to reflect the broader community if substantial differences exist between respondents and non-respondents. Second, non-response may be indicative of economic and social barriers. Beyond general disinterest in civic duties, some individuals may not respond due to the time commitment required, potential loss of income, or lack of employer compensation for jury service. Third, high non-response rates can undermine the legitimacy of the legal system. If those who fail to respond are demographically similar to those who do (including characteristics such as age, gender, race, income, education, and occupation), then non-response may be less symptomatic of accessibility gaps and more reflective of the court's perceived legitimacy and public reputation.

High-Profile and High-Juror-Volume Cases

Public interest in certain high-profile jury trials is not a new phenomenon. The 1954 Sam Shepard case, which later inspired the television series and movie *The Fugitive*, drew considerable publicity. Shepard's trial was one of the first cases of the modern communication era, which demonstrated the discord between the first amendment (freedom of the press) and sixth amendment (right to a fair and impartial jury) (*Sheppard v. Maxwell*, 1966). The challenges and conflicts which high-profile and high-juror-volume cases present remain unchanged for court managers and judges. In some instances, jury sequestration serves as a remedy to ensure that jurors are not exposed to the media's account of the trial, but in other circumstances, sequestering the jury could be futile despite the court's best efforts. For example, the Warren Commission investigating President John F. Kennedy's assassination reported that the "most difficult task" of the Lee Harvey Oswald case would have been to select an impartial jury in light of the publicity and the public's "intense feelings" about the crime (Jost, 1995).

Jurors selected for high-profile and high-volume cases are generally exposed to heightened media attention before, during, and after the trial. Trials requiring the jury to be isolated are often simultaneously notorious. These cases present a host of challenges for the court, including the substantial number of jurors that are required to be summoned, qualified, and questioned. Bearing this in mind, administrators must take the necessary precautions to safeguard the safety and objectivity of the jurors, as well as the integrity of the process, through each step of the caseflow. For example, in a northeastern court, a judge ordered the jury sequestered in a gang-related murder trial. The county sheriff subsequently informed reporters that sequestration was necessary "for their own protection," citing threats allegedly made by gang associates against the judge and jurors if the defendant was not acquitted. Apart from the potential risks, as a practical matter, the court should account for the costs whenever sequestration becomes necessary. The trial judge and court administrator should convene with the stakeholders identified in the relevant policies and procedures to coordinate and develop a workable plan. Court administrators must typically collaborate with the judge, sheriff, and relevant county personnel to address numerous logistical factors, including lodging; meals (and dietary needs); medical care and accommodations; management of media exposure (e.g., newspapers, television, and social media); family contact and visitation; transportation; laundry services; recreational opportunities; religious services; and employment-related concerns (Fazari & Holandez, 2012).

In the case described above, two noteworthy lessons were subsequently incorporated into the court's policy and procedural framework. The first concerned law enforcement partnerships. When appropriate, relevant agencies should be brought together to assess the nature, credibility, and potential for jury tampering. In this instance, the Sheriff's Office coordinated with the State Police to investigate and evaluate the threat, generating substantive leads that assisted them in identifying the responsible party. Establishing these partnerships enables the court to assess the credibility of threats and to take prompt, appropriate action, including sequestration when warranted. Importantly, the perceived likelihood of whether the person(s) will carry out the threat should not influence the decision to conduct a thorough investigation in pursuit of the appropriate action. The obligation to respond decisively to such incidents, however innocuous the threat may ostensibly be, is critical to deter both individual (specific) and broader (general) attempts to obstruct the judicial process.

The second lesson involved soliciting juror perceptions. Jurors may be reluctant to provide feedback to court personnel with whom they are unfamiliar and, depending on the nature of the threat that necessitated sequestration, may fear that responding to such inquiries could place them at risk. Prior to formally discharging the jury, the judge instructed jurors not to discuss the case with the public. Several days after the verdict was rendered, the jury manager began contacting jurors to survey them about their experience. When jurors were unavailable, a voicemail was left identifying the manager's name, court affiliation, contact information, and the purpose of the call. One juror, however, questioned the authenticity of the message and contacted the Sheriff's Office. Because the jury manager was relatively new to the court, their name was not immediately recognized by personnel at the Sheriff's Office, which caused temporary alarm and triggered additional protocol responses. To mitigate such concerns, judges should inform jurors prior to discharge of the name and role of the jury manager who will contact them following the trial. The jury manager should then initiate communication through official court letterhead, advising jurors that follow-up contact will occur in the coming days to solicit feedback regarding their service.

Policy and procedure regarding the adjudication of widely publicized cases have three interconnected purposes. First, is the purpose to safeguard the jury from inappropriate influences before, during, after the trial that could adversely affect the integrity of the justice system process; second, is the purpose to protect the jury from all forms of harm which results from their participation in the trial; and third, is the purpose to minimize the inherent burdens on the jury brought to bear by the sequestration order. In accordance with these purposes, procedures are generally divided into three segments: pre-trial (in cases when a high-profile or high-juror-volume case is anticipated and/or jury sequestration is decided beforehand), during the trial, and post-trial. On a related and equally important note with respect to policy and procedure, high-profile cases also provide the court with the unique opportunity to educate its constituents about the law and the judiciary as a co-equal and impartial third branch of government. Administrators should be prepared to take advantage of these circumstances to communicate the purposes and responsibilities of the courts as it pertains to the instant case, as well as cases in general.

Given the generally perceived burdensome nature of jury service, there exist limitations in reaching exceptional levels of juror satisfaction that would otherwise be more quantifiable and attainable in other areas of court administration. The process itself may, in some instances, never match juror expectations, despite the court's best efforts to improve it. Data collection and analysis of jury management should continually build on the court's findings and the methodologies employed in those studies to evaluate both the trends of satisfaction levels among jurors, as well as the relative performance of court management practices in meeting a wide range of objectives. Juror attributes and socially constructed aspects of the community should be assessed to determine if satisfaction and perceptions are impacted by demographic factors such as socioeconomic status, among other variables, such as juror type. This would be relevant for those states that summon grand jurors as the fact-finding body to determine if sufficient probable cause exists to issue an indictment. Greater or lesser levels of satisfaction on the basis of whether someone served as a grand juror or petit juror may be indicative of resources that are being allocated to specific areas of the operation. The amount of time spent in the court complex, for instance, may affect juror satisfaction with the facilities. These are important considerations because grand jurors or those who are sequestered will spend significantly more time in the courthouse than those who are summoned, but not selected, or those who serve on a typical trial not lasting more than a week or two. Other experiences can be evaluated denoting the differences between jurors who are selected to serve on a trial and prospective jurors who are not selected and conclude their service at different stages of the summoning and selection process.

The court is obliged to empirically test and analyze these and other kinds of questions and to incorporate policies, processes, and practices to address juror concerns and make the process generally more efficient. We believe we are far within the mark in stating that this is among the most important responsibilities judges and administrators can fulfill, given the jury's critical role in serving the community and upholding the democratic principles of our judicial system. While accommodation can and should be made to alleviate the burdens and hardships associated with jury service, administrators should recognize that jury service will always remain a sacrifice to citizens. In recognition of these realities, the goal for court administration must therefore be to maximize satisfaction with the overall experience so that the majority who are called to serve view it as a *worthy* forfeiture of time in fulfilling their civic duty.

The court must often balance the right of the public to know as much as possible about the case, the parties involved, and the judicial process against the need to keep that same process fair, lawful, and irreproachable. The demand for information to always be accessible requires that judges and administrators understand what the court can reasonably do without compromising the integrity of the juror selection process. The following discussion points address some of the general guidelines that the court should consider when managing cases that draw the public's attention:

1) Stakeholder Team Formation – The various entities should be identified based on whether they will be affected by the public and media interest in the case or have jurisdictional responsibilities regarding the media's presence in and around the courthouse. External groups generally include government agencies that have facilities inside or within the proximity of the courthouse, have enforcement or public safety jurisdiction, or represent the political interests of the district's constituency. Internal groups generally include representatives of the court and law enforcement agencies who have court security responsibilities. To develop a comprehensive action plan the team should include representatives from each affected group. A series of meetings among internal stakeholders is advisable in advance of meetings that include external representation. Among other related matters, these meetings should address security and jurisdictional questions, juror exposure as it relates to the media, as well as potential issues that were previously experienced with other high-profile cases. A recommended list of representatives is noted in Table 8.2.

Table 8.2 Suggested Stakeholder Team for Managing High-Profile Cases

Internal Representation	***External Representation***
• Judicial Leaders – includes the presiding and trial judge. Their presence will provide the opportunity to establish the framework and set the tone for cooperation in developing the action plan. • Court Leaders – includes the court administrators and assigned managers, who will have the overarching responsibility for court issues and logistics. Supervisors and appropriate staff can also be included such as the courtroom clerk, administrative assistant, law clerk, etc. to handle task-oriented matters. • Media Liaison – a court appointed person who has the subject-matter knowledge and expertise regarding media needs, expectations, and related issues should be assigned as a liaison between the court and media. As the court's official spokesperson, they will be the source of information for court-related issues and procedures. • Courthouse Law Enforcement – includes the law enforcement agency responsible for court security and safeguarding the jury. Among other responsibilities, representatives from the agency would coordinate the activities and roles of other law enforcement agencies.	• Media – select members of the media should be included so that they can plan and prepare for the logistical needs and issues that will impact their ability to cover the trial and associated court events. The projected level of media interest is linked directly to the scale and scope of the action plan. • Fire Department – local fire department should be represented on the group to provide oversight of policies and related public safety and building codes including ingress/egress, walkways, fire equipment, and occupancy levels and hazards. • Police Department – local police will generally be relied upon to coordinate with other public safety agencies on jurisdictional, parking, and code enforcement issues. • County Administration – representative who will serve as a liaison between the courts and county government. • Attorneys (Prosecution and Defense) – respective attorneys need to be aware of the action plan and corresponding procedures.

2) Plan of Action – Depending on the anticipated length of the trial, a pre-trial meeting that includes the court officials and leaders, affected agencies, media designees, and county representatives should be arranged. The meeting should be led by the court to confer with and advise stakeholders of policy and procedure and approved protocols, as well as respond to any questions and review logistics. Longer trials will generally require weekly status meetings involving assigned representatives of the agencies and groups to facilitate and update ongoing communication.
3) Staffing – The presiding judge together with the court administrator should communicate with staff the increased attention and scrutiny that can be expected given the public interest and media focus on the case. Staff should be guided in their discussions with media representatives and should avoid appearing to favor one party over the other. Such guidance can be accomplished through an orientation or training session prior to the trial commencing.
4) Courtroom Seating – Seating and any designated reserved seating in the courtroom may be allocated on a first come, first served basis to ensure that all available seats are used. If large groups of court observers are expected, it may be necessary for the court to limit seating to one representative per media outlet so that there is a balance of local and national press represented.
5) Media Collaboration – Administrators should expect and be prepared for media interest during each of the major stages of the case including arraignment, jury selection, and trial. A representative of the court should be assigned as the media liaison so that information flows from a single point of contact. Among other things, the spokesperson will provide information to the media and determine how often details will be updated on the approved mediums.
6) Media Pool Coverage – A single media outlet should be assigned to provide video and audio coverage of the trial. The selected outlet would be responsible for providing access to other interested media. The court should establish parameters, but the press is better equipped to determine who will provide pool coverage for the duration of the trial.
7) Media Space – To the extent that accommodations can be arranged, the court may consider providing the media with a designated room with a "live feed" from the courtroom to handle press overflow.
8) Media Orientation – An orientation meeting should be conducted with media representatives prior to the trial commencing to review courtroom seating, procedures for audio, video, and still cameras, as well as to introduce key contacts for media coordination.

A growing number of courts are establishing programs to address juror trauma, a condition resulting from viewing disturbing graphic evidence, exposure to descriptions of violent crimes, and the stress of jury duty in high-profile cases. The COSCA (2023) recommends several "in-trial mitigation" strategies, including limitations on the amount of disturbing testimony and images, warning jurors before displaying gruesome material, frequent breaks, post-verdict debriefings led by the judge, and contact with family members to address emotional issues, but without discussing the case per se.

Post-trial, some courts are providing trauma counseling services for jurors to address vicarious juror trauma and coping strategies. Through an intergovernmental agreement with the Federal Occupational Health Employee Assistance Program, federal court judges can authorize free counseling services for jurors who served in a traumatic trial (United States Courts, 2020). Coping strategies and counseling services for juror trauma are offered by the Court of Common Pleas in Philadelphia, Pennsylvania, Alaska, Massachusetts, North Dakota, and selected counties in California and Texas (Bedard, 2025).

Probation and Pre-Trial Services

Adult Probation

Community-based probation and parole services are an integral part of the criminal justice system, directly involving the courts among a host of other justice organizations. Since 1956, a probation supervision division exists in each of the 50 states (Hsieh et al., 2015) – a network that includes an estimated 2.693 million adults (Kaeble, 2023).[3] At the national level, probation and pre-trial services are administered by the federal courts. The following mission statement for the United States Probation and Pretrial Services, District of Arizona (2025) addresses the multifaceted roles of probation as a judicial branch function:

> Our Mission is to assist the Court in the fair administration of justice, providing unbiased, accurate information, facilitating lasting positive change in the people we assist and supervise, in order to protect and improve our community.

At the state and local levels, there is a strikingly diverse array of organizational structures vis-à-vis probation administration, some models of which combine these services with parole (New York City Department of Probation, 2025). A central difference is whether probation functions under the auspices of the judicial or executive branch of government. If administered by the judiciary, the court's leadership team will be tasked with actively overseeing the division, including associated responsibilities with setting and carrying out probation policies and procedures. To this end, court leaders will find that probation and pre-trial services can be promising areas to engage the community, collaborate with a variety of stakeholders, and develop the present and future workforce. When governed by the executive branch, the court will generally serve in a liaison role, representing the interests and position of the judiciary in relation to the management of probationers, including their rehabilitation and reintegration into society.

Probation-related policy and practice matters include the role of probation services and, by extension, those of probation officers, probation supervision levels, caseload sizes, centralized versus regional probation officers, probation officer firearms, personal safety equipment, discharge criteria (ahead of schedule or extended), revocation criteria, drug testing methodologies, and supervision of "re-entry" cases (e.g., persons placed under the court's probation supervision upon release from the state prison). While some of these policies are established at the state supreme court level, others may be rendered locally.

Although a fuller, more comprehensive discussion on divergent philosophical views of probation and the changing role of probation officers is beyond the scope of this publication, decisions in this realm directly shape the mission and character of court probation services. There exists an inherent tension in the dichotomy between the enforcement and reformatory features of working in probation. The law enforcement aspect of probation requires managing the caseload in a "surveillance style" and places emphasis on monitoring and enforcing compliance pursuant to the court's order and rules. Conversely, the rehabilitative dimension of probation necessitates a "casework style" of supervising clients where counseling and treatment are underscored. Given the bifurcated nature of the work, probation officers must be adept at performing the roles characterizing those in both law enforcement and social work fields. Some of the relevant literature supports a "balanced" approach, meeting the needs on both ends of the divide based on relative risk. Accordingly, Hsieh and associates (2015) concluded:

> Probation officers who balanced the law enforcement and rehabilitation role have been found to improve the effectiveness of supervision, reduce recidivism, and provide a promising prosocial life for offenders that includes sound coping mechanisms even under a complicated workout. Such a balanced approach is now acknowledged by scholars as a contemporary goal for probation officers.

Today, many probation departments use instruments to assess risk among probationers to determine the suitable level of supervision that accounts for the client's physiological, psychological, employment, educational/vocational, familial, and financial makeup apart from other specific needs (Bureau of Justice Assistance [BJA], 2025). Results from the evaluation also help the probation department determine the kinds of specialized services appropriate for each probationer (e.g., standard or intensive supervision), the need for electronic monitoring, as well as the applicability of other interventions (e.g., periodic drug testing, educational programs, vocational training, and counseling services) (BJA, 2025). This evidence-based practice (EBP) approach is designed to facilitate an effective supervision plan in monitoring and rehabilitating probationers, while also helping the court to efficiently leverage its finite resources (Webster & Bechtel, 2012).

From a planning standpoint, court administrators are responsible for developing long-term, sustainable funding models for basic probation services and specialized probation-related programs such as drug court.[4] These frameworks generally include various combinations drawn from the following sources:

- General fund appropriations
- State and federal grants funds distributed to local probation departments
- Court-generated revenues derived from fines, fees, and surcharges
- Monthly "probation supervision fees" and electronic monitoring fees payable by probationers/pre-trial releasees and collected by the probation department and/or the clerk of court's office

The other essential component of adult probation is the staffing of presentence investigations (PSI) and preparation of presentence reports for the court. Jurisdictions vary in the use of the PSI, but there are three main types: 1) Detailed written report on the defendant's personal and criminal history; 2) Abbreviated written report; and 3) Verbal report to the court. Typically, for the PSI, probation officers interview defendants convicted of felony offenses and are pending sentence. The PSI is a report detailing the background of the offender, comprised of information gathered during an interview that includes a chronology of the defendant's social, familial, and educational background, criminal case history, mental health condition, addiction issues, and a victim's impact statement, among other pertinent information. The PSI may also incorporate the probation officer's recommendations that are supported by the investigation's findings. The sources of information are drawn from an assortment of records and mainframe systems including the FBI's National Crime Information Center and individual jurisdictions' registers. Information proffered by the defendant is generally corroborated with another reliable source.

Prior to the sentencing hearing, the PSI is provided to the judge, prosecutor, and defense counsel for review. The judge will consider the implications of the report's findings and recommendations to determine the appropriate sentence range to the extent discretion is allowed by law. Once the defendant is sentenced, the PSI is made available to the probation department or, in the event of a prison sentence, to the department of corrections and parole board. Correctional officials may utilize the PSI to assign inmates to custody levels based on offense history, assessed dangerousness, criminal affiliation, among other factors enumerated in the report. In this context, the PSI is used for the purposes of external and internal classification of inmates. External classification determines *inter-institutional* placement of an offender in accordance with the facility's security level (i.e., minimum, medium, and maximum). Internal classification specifies the *intra-institutional* assignment of an inmate to a particular housing, unit, cell block, work detail, and program based on their background, risk, needs, and length of sentence.

Pre-Trial Services

Pre-trial services agencies generally have a dual function. The first function is administered following the arrest of a defendant, when court pre-trial personnel collect data and information on the defendant's criminal case history and conduct a standardized risk assessment. As a part of this process, defendants may also be interviewed while in custody. The information and statements are compiled into a report and provided to the judge for consideration prior to the initial appearance hearing. The principal aim of the evaluation is to aid the decision-making process of the court on whether to detain the defendant or release them into the community pending trial. Judges will also use the pre-trial assessment to consider discretionary conditions of release such as bond amounts, electronic supervision and travel restrictions, etc., as deemed necessary. To ensure compliance with procedures, court administration will periodically review and validate the risk assessment instrument, oversee and conduct training of staff on the use of the assessment, and maintain access to state and federal repositories of criminal case records.

The second function pertains to defendants released under pre-trial supervision. These circumstances dictate that pre-trial services officers monitor defendants to ensure compliance with an individualized supervision plan. Conditions of release may include home detention, electronic monitoring, home and work site visits, mental health evaluations, substance abuse treatment, and financial status reviews (ABA, 2007).

Juvenile Probation and Detention

Dating back to the juvenile court and probation services established in Cook County in 1899, courts designated to youth offenders have a rich history of community-based rehabilitation services (National Center for Juvenile Justice et al., 2019). In many jurisdictions, the juvenile court administers the detention facilities, which necessitate continuous and uninterrupted intake and screening services throughout the year, specialized educational programming, and other residential provisions. Juvenile detention centers also require amenities for medical care, parental visitation, transport for court hearings, emergency evacuation, and food services. Given the specialized care and rigid scheduling, staffing of these facilities with qualified personnel can be challenging. And this is apart from the unique issues involving security and capital planning that court leaders must consider for facilities housing minors.

Since the inception of these specialized courts, the philosophy and policies of juvenile courts has continued to evolve. For instance, several far-reaching reforms have occurred over the last several decades, including calls for greater accountability of youth ("zero tolerance policies" for violent crimes and weapons possession), increased use of community-based alternatives to incarceration, and extensive research on brain development in adolescents (National Center for Juvenile Justice et al., 2019). To that end, court leaders overseeing juvenile probation and detention services must become conversant with the ever-growing body of research and best practices that pertain to juvenile justice. And with respect to the recruitment and development of its workforce, administration must ensure that the court employs mission-oriented, professional staff with the subject matter expertise and the temperament required to responsibly lead and manage this specialized area of focus.

Program Management

Program management involves overseeing the operations that pertain to a particular court initiative together with the allocated resources and assigned staff who work across various divisions in the judiciary to achieve strategic goals. Key aspects to managing court administered programs are incorporated into each of the stages of policy and program analysis, and include problem analysis, setting goals and objectives, program design, action planning, implementation, evaluation, and reassessment (Welsh & Harris, 2016). In each of these stages, managers are responsible for initiating, developing, and implementing programs and systems to meet stated goals, coordinating technology and personnel, collaborating with a range of external stakeholders, analyzing data and project measurables, and developing and assessing training programs. Operations is the central clearinghouse for the courts to establish and maintain programs, bringing together what are otherwise disparate areas of work and expertise. Apart from having the relevant knowledgebase and experience to ensure compliance with policy and procedure, managers assigned to oversee these initiatives generally require exceptional organization, communication, and leadership skills and abilities because they must collaborate with various agencies and stakeholders, inspire others to act, and adapt to changing needs based on ongoing evaluation.

In accordance with the seven stages of program integration, Table 8.3 provides an outline of the five key responsibilities generally associated with judiciary programs.

Table 8.3 Key Management Responsibilities Associated with Judiciary Programs

Program Aspect	***Key Responsibilities***
1. Data Analysis and Presentation	• Collect and analyze program data related to court processing activities • Evaluate program inputs, activities, outputs, outcomes, and impacts and prepare and present summary analysis reports
2. Internal and External Communication and Collaboration	• Liaise with various agencies, government units and other divisions within the courts • Communicate and collaborate with internal and external stakeholders including the central office, law enforcement, and county governments • Address media requests and develop media releases in collaboration with leadership judges and counsel
3. Operations Management	• Monitor and manage program budget and spending plan • Track associated projects, duties, and assignments • Develop, implement, and evaluate procedures to maximize the efficiency and effectiveness of program units • Oversee program operations related to continuity of operations, security planning, and facility renovations
4. Personnel Management and Development	• Manage and direct the activities of staff, including supervisors and analysts • Develop and deliver training programs and provide technical assistance and guidance to court personnel, judges, and other stakeholders
5. System Development and Implementation	• Initiate and coordinate the development or reconfiguration of appropriate systems to implement the program • Collaborate with the appropriate technology departments, policy units, and stakeholders for planning and implementation • Develop and implement public access, media, and communication plans

These management responsibilities generally require program managers to have a mix of soft (interpersonal) skills for leadership and communication, as well as hard (technical) skills for procedural work and strategic management. With regard to interpersonal competencies, program managers must provide visionary leadership to inspire and guide project teams and staff. This involves the capacity to align individual projects with the broader judicial branch strategy, as well as the ability to motivate, coach, and mentor staff to foster a positive and productive work environment. Program managers must be able to effectively communicate and present the initiative's vision, goals, and progress to a wide range of stakeholders – including judges, court staff, municipal officials, and the public. Along the same lines, program managers are required to engage, negotiate, resolve conflict, and build consensus among stakeholders while making sound decisions under pressure. At the technical end, program management requires planning, organizing, and executing small-, mid-, and large-scale initiatives. Proficiency in creating project plans, managing schedules, and tracking performance against program goals is necessary, requiring expertise and knowledge in data collection and analysis, budgeting and resource management, information technology applications and networks, and regulatory and legal policy and practice.

Many judiciary programs and initiatives generally involve some aspect of technology and, as a result, program managers generally work closely with management and staff employed in the information technology division of the courts. Programs centered on technology will involve the development and implementation of technological systems and tools to keep pace with evolving and expanding advancements in today's market. Ensuring an updated technological framework is compulsory for modern-day courts, given the public's expectations and demands and the need to connect the loosely coupled system (e.g., prosecutor, public defender, law enforcement, jail, private counsel, pro se litigants, etc.) across the digital landscape. These initiatives aim to create efficiencies in human capital costs and enhance public safety by modernizing and streamlining a wide range of judicial processes. Examples of such programs include cloud technology migrations, case management and workflow systems, and eCourt services platforms across various case types, including civil, criminal, and family. Innovations that focus on migrating legacy systems to modern, cloud-based applications require an overhaul of not just the systems and their core components, but also of how the technology is used. This encompasses system programming, staff training, and online functions (including regular upgrades), requiring integration of both hardware and software in managing court operations.

Program managers also lead projects that enable the secure digital submission and access of court information such as those that provide around-the-clock access and a secure electronic system for the submission of online payments, court documents, exhibits, and court records. The NJMCDirect system based in New Jersey (2025), for instance, allows the public to pay traffic tickets and other municipal court complaints online. Another New Jersey system, the Judiciary Account Charge System (JACS), allows attorneys to electronically pay court filing fees and other charges. Other innovative systems overseen by program managers include automated networks such as those that allow petitioners, attorneys, prosecutors, and court staff to manage expungement petitions, orders, and responses online and those which support the computerized entry of court charges used by law enforcement and court personnel (New Jersey Judiciary, 2025).

These and other advanced systems will likely expand exponentially in the future – all of which require program managers with specialized knowledge, skills, and abilities. Since the COVID-19 pandemic, the judiciary's response has resulted in the acceleration of numerous system improvement projects that involve virtual operations. Program managers in this realm led the rapid transition of converting courtrooms into virtual forums so that court operations could continue remotely. Since then, projects have reconfigured how court services are delivered to the public to make them more accessible and efficient by supporting video conferencing hardware and software necessary for remote hearings and operations. Today, program managers are focusing on implementing advanced technology, including developing policies for the use of artificial intelligence and implementing cybersecurity measures such as multi-factor authentication (Administrative Office of the U.S. Courts, 2023; National Association for Court Management, 2024).

Program management also involves intra- and inter-divisional oversight such that assigned managers in specialized areas will oversee case management, budgetary issues, technological implementation, and personnel (recruiting, hiring, and training). Examples include the full range of problem-solving and specialized courts such as drug courts, veterans courts, mental health courts, and youth courts. Some programs are created to educate the public about court processes and procedures such as those that involve expungements and landlord–tenant issues. Other initiatives generally function under the auspices of community engagement initiatives and include courthouse tours, speaker's bureau, law day, court careers outreach, and community service projects to increase public trust and accessibility.

Courts will likely continue to institute job training and placement and other service-oriented programs to aid defendants and community members in need of such locally based services. In New Jersey (2025), for instance, the Judiciary Opportunities for Building Success (JOBS) program assists probation clients in gaining work and life skills. The Homeless Outreach Court in Orange County, California helps those who are displaced to resolve multiple overdue infractions and low-level misdemeanors (Orange County Public Defender, 2025). Integration of these and other innovative, far-reaching court-connected programs – which function under the purview of operations management – enhances the sustainability and accessibility of modern-day court services.

Notes

1 Included in this framework is a "quality cycle" for system improvement and a "balanced scorecard," reflecting both customer and internal perspectives.

2 ARMA originally released GARP in 2009, with subsequent updates.

3 This equates to approximately 1,143 adults under community supervision per 100,000 adult U.S. residents.

4 Other specialized courts having a probation supervision component include those for veterans, the homeless population, and individuals involved in the mental health system.

References

Administrative Office of the Courts. (2009, August). *Fact sheet: Transfer of court facilities*. Judicial Council of California. https://courts.ca.gov/system/files/file/fact-sheet-transfer-court-facilities.pdf.

Administrative Office of the U.S. Courts. (2023). *Information systems and cybersecurity* (Director's Annual Report 2023). United States Courts.

American Bar Association (ABA). (2005a). *Dialogue on the American jury: We the people in action*.

American Bar Association (ABA). (2005b). *Principles for juries and jury trials*. www.uscourts.gov/file/document/aba-principles-juries-and-jury-trials-2005.

American Bar Association (ABA). (2007). *Standards for criminal justice: Pretrial release* (Standards 10–1.4, 10–5.6). www.americanbar.org/content/dam/aba/publications/criminal_justice_standards/pretrial_release.authcheckdam.pdf.

American Records Management Association. (2017). *Generally accepted recordkeeping principles*.

Bedard, H. (2025, September 4). *Juror trauma: The added cost of capital cases*. Death Penalty Information Center. https://deathpenaltyinfo.org/juror-trauma-the-added-cost-of-capital-cases.

Birkland, T. A. (2004). *Emergency planning and the judiciary: Lessons from September 11*. Center for Court Innovation. www.courtinnovation.org/sites/default/files/emergencyplanning.pdf.

Birkland, T. A., & Schneider, C. A. (2007). Emergency management in the courts: Trends after September 11 and Hurricane Katrina. *Justice System Journal, 28*(1), 20–35.

Boatright, R. G. (1999). *Improving citizen response to jury summonses: A report with recommendations*. American Judicature Society.

Bureau of Justice Assistance. (2025). *What is risk assessment*. Public Safety Risk Assessment Clearinghouse. https://bja.ojp.gov/program/psrac/basics/what-is-risk-assessment.

Campbell, C. F., & Reinkensmeyer, M. W. (2007). The court security challenge: A judicial leadership perspective. *Justice System Journal, 28*(1), 49–53.

Conference of State Court Administrators. (2013). *To protect and preserve: Standards for maintaining and managing 21st century court records*.

Conference of State Court Administrators. (2023). *Citizens on call: Responding to the needs of the 21st century jurors.*

Cooper, C. (2007). The evolving concept of court security. *Justice System Journal, 28*(1), 40–45.

Deming, W. E. (1982). *Quality, productivity, and competitive position.* Massachusetts Institute of Technology, Center for Advanced Engineering Study.

Dibble, T. (1986). *A guide to court records management.* National Center for State Courts.

Dibble, T., & Cousins, F. (2009). Modern courthouses and the new green. *Court Manager, 22*(4), 30–41.

Fautsko, T. F., Berson, S. V., O'Neil, J. F., & Sheehan, K. W. (2013). *Steps to best practices for court building security* (Revised January 2013). National Center for State Courts.

Fazari, G. M. (2013). Targeting noncompliant jurors: Findings from a comprehensive enforcement program. *Trends in State Courts,* 71–77.

Fazari, G. M., & Holandez, P. J. (2012). The home away jury: A framework for managing sequestration. *Court Manager, 27*(2), 18–37.

Federal Emergency Management Agency. (2023). *Continuity of operations (COOP).* www.fema.gov/emergency-managers/national-preparedness/continuity.

General Services Administration. (2025, May 28). *Courthouse program.* www.gsa.gov/real-estate/gsa-properties/courthouse-program.

Gravely, A. (2019, July 28). The silent problem facing the nation's courtroom: Fewer people want to be court reporters, adding to delays. *The Wall Street Journal.* www.wsj.com/articles/the-silent-problem-facing-the-nations-courtrooms-11564315200.

Hamilton, A. (2003). Federalist No. 17. In C. Rossiter (Ed.), *The Federalist papers* (pp. 115–120). Signet Classics. (Original work published 1787)

Hammer, M., & Champy, J. (1993). *Reengineering the corporation: A manifesto for business revolution.* HarperBusiness.

Hannaford-Agor, P. (2008). Jury news: Getting the biggest bang for your buck from online qualification technologies. *Court Manager, 23*(1), 25–27.

Hardenbergh, D., Griebel, M. A., Tobin, R. W., & Yeh, C.-M. (Eds.). (1998). *The courthouse: A guide to planning & design.* National Center for State Courts.

Hsieh, M.-L., Hafoka, M., Woo, Y., van Wormer, J., Stohr, M. K., & Hemmens, C. (2015, December). Probation officer roles: A statutory analysis. *Federal Probation, 79*(3), 20–37.

Joint Technology Committee. (2021, September 15). *Cybersecurity basics for courts* (JTC Resource Bulletin No. 3.0). National Center for State Courts. www.ncsc.org/__data/assets/pdf_file/0037/68887/JTC-2021-05-Cybersecurity-QR_Final-Clean.pdf.

Jost, K. (1995, November 10). The jury system: Are major changes needed? *The CQ Researcher Online*. http://library.cqpress.com/cqresearcher/cqresrre1995111000.

Judicial Conference of the United States. (2021, March). *U.S. Courts design guide*. United States Courts. www.uscourts.gov/administration-policies/judiciary-policies/us-courts-design-guide

Kaeble, D. (2023). *Probation and parole in the United States* (Report No. NCJ 310118). U.S. Department of Justice, Office of Justice Programs, Bureau of Justice Statistics. https://bjs.ojp.gov/library/publications/probation-and-parole-united-states-2023.

Kansas Supreme Court. (1983). *Standards relating to jury use and management* (Supreme Court Rule; effective July 15, 1983). https://kscourts.gov/Rules-Orders/Rules/Standards-relating-to-Jury-Use-and-Management.

Levy, L. W., Karst, K. L., & Mahoney, D. J. (Eds.). (2000). *Encyclopedia of the American Constitution* (2nd ed.). Macmillan Reference.

Munsterman, G. T. (1996). *Jury system management*. National Center for State Courts.

Munsterman, G. T., & Hannaford-Agor, P. L. (2003). *The promise and challenges of jury system technology*. National Center for State Courts.

Munsterman, G. T., Hannaford-Agor, P. L., & Whitehead, G. M. (Eds.). (1997). *Jury trial innovations* (Publication R-193). National Center for State Courts.

National Association for Court Management (NACM). (2006). *Business continuity management mini guide*.

National Association for Court Management (NACM). (2015). *The core*. https://nacmnet.org/nacm-core/.

National Association for Court Management (NACM). (2024). *Courting AI: Understanding artificial intelligence in courts*.

National Center for Juvenile Justice, National Council of Juvenile and Family Court Judges, & Annie E. Casey Foundation. (2019). *Desktop guide to good juvenile probation practice: History of juvenile probation*.

National Center for State Courts (NCSC). (1998). *Through the eyes of the juror: A manual for addressing juror stress*.

National Center for State Courts (NCSC). (2005). *CourTools: Trial court measures*. www.ncsc.org/our-centers-projects/courtools.

National Center for State Courts (NCSC). (2021a). *Courts continuity of operations (COOP) planning guide and template.*

National Center for State Courts (NCSC). (2021b). *Retrospective of courthouse design, 2010–2020.*

National Center for State Courts (NCSC). (2022). *Steps to best practices for court building security.*

National Center for State Courts (NCSC). (2025). *Process automation guidance for courts* (TRI/NCSC AI Policy Consortium for Law & Courts).

National Sheriffs' Association. (1978). *Court security: A manual of guidelines and procedures* (Project No. NCJ-O supported by grant No. 77-DF-99-0023 from the Law Enforcement Assistance Administration, U.S. Department of Justice).

New Jersey Judiciary. (2025). *NJ Courts systems and services (including NJMCDirect and JACS information).* www.njcourts.gov/.

New York City Department of Probation. (2025). *History of probation.* www.nyc.gov/site/probation/about/history-of-probation.page.

Orange County Public Defender. (2025). *Homeless outreach court.* www.pubdef.ocgov.com/programs/post-conviction-services/homeless-outreach-court.

Ostrom, B. J., & Hanson, R. A. (2020, April). *Achieving high performance: A framework for courts.* National Center for State Courts.

Porter, M. E. (n.d.). The thing is, continuity of strategic direction and continuous improvement in how you do things are absolutely consistent with each other. In fact, they're mutually reinforcing. *BrainyQuote.* www.brainyquote.com/quotes/michael_porter_396281.

Pound, R. (1906). *The causes of popular dissatisfaction with the administration of justice* [Speech]. Speech delivered at the American Bar Association. https://law.unl.edu/RoscoePound.pdf.

Raftery, W. (2017). How state courts are preparing for continuity in disaster. *Judicature, 101*(4), 3–5.

Reinkensmeyer, M. W. (2011). Court security and business continuity in lean budget times. *Trends in State Courts*, 87–93.

Sabalow, R. (2025, June 30). California doesn't have enough court reporters. Their unions are fighting substitutes. *CalMatters.* https://calmatters.org/politics/2025/06/california-court-reporter-shortage.

Sheppard v. Maxwell, 384 U.S. 333 (1966).

Supreme Court of Arizona. (2020, January 8). *Arizona code of judicial administration § 5–301: Court security standards* (Administrative Order No. 2020–01). Arizona Supreme Court.

Taylor, F. W. (1911). *The principles of scientific management.* Harper & Brothers.

Tichy, N. M., & Bennis, W. G. (2007). *Judgment: How winning leaders make great calls.* Portfolio.

United States Courts. (2012, November 2). *After Hurricane Sandy, courts in New York struggle to restore operations.* www.uscourts.gov/after-hurricane-sandy-courts-new-york-struggle-restore-operations.

United States Courts. (2020, January 24). *How courts care for jurors in high profile cases.* www.uscourts.gov/data-news/judiciary-news/2020/01/24/how-courts-care-jurors-high-profile-cases.

United States Courts. (2024). *Court operations – Annual report 2024.* www.uscourts.gov/data-news/reports/annual-reports/directors-annual-report/annual-report-2024/court-operations-annual-report-2024.

United States Department of Justice. (2004, September). *Off-site security handbook for United States judges: Practices to employ when away from the courthouse* (No. 94).

United States Probation and Pretrial Services, District of Arizona. (2025). *Mission statement.* U.S. Courts. www.azp.uscourts.gov/mission-statement.

Webster, M., & Bechtel, K. (2012, August). *Evidence-based practices for assessing, supervising, and treating domestic violence offenders.* Crime and Justice Institute at Community Resources for Justice.

Welsh, W. N., & Harris, P. (2016). *Criminal justice policy and planning* (5th ed.). Routledge.

Zaruba, J. E. (2007). Courthouse security – A direction or a destination. *The Justice System Journal, 28*(1), 45–56.

9 Court Information Technology Management

In the 1960s, technology in courts was essentially comprised of court reporters using stenographic machines (sometimes audio recorders) and early-adopter courts use of stand-alone (i.e., seldom connected to others in the justice system) computerized case management information systems. Sixty years later, almost all courts rely heavily on multiple technologies and are looking to expand their use. This trend has been accelerated by the COVID-19 pandemic, which ushered in a relatively rapid adoption of remote (audio and video) court hearings and expanded use of online court services. The rapid emergence of artificial intelligence (AI) offers the prospect of more advanced court technologies, while also underscoring the need for strong IT governance and strategic planning.

New uses of technology seem to appear monthly in one court or another across the country. There are several categories of technologies currently in use in many, if not most, federal, state, and local courts:

- Case-related data and storage, often cloud-based: more sophisticated and useful computerized case management information systems (virtually all courts) and increasingly paperless (i.e., digital borne only) case-based records; digitally completed and filed court forms.
- The use of social media by courts and judges for case-related notices and reminders and communication with jurors and prospective jurors, in addition to general public information about the court and court procedures on social media outlets and on court websites.
- Video used in the presentation of evidence and in providing video connections between witnesses and litigants and the court; digital presentation of evidence and litigants' arguments; virtual hearings and, in some cases, trials using video.

DOI: 10.4324/9781003686804-9

- Court websites that are more user-friendly and informative about the court generally and the general processing of cases.
- Digital connections and data sharing with justice and social service agencies involved in and affected by cases.
- Digital creation and storage of the information and processing of most administrative functions, such as accounting and financial management, payroll, and human-resource functions, and video meetings among judges, managers, and others.
- Court reporters using computer-assisted transcription to reduce the time to produce transcripts and to provide attorneys and judges real-time draft transcripts[1] they can refer to during a hearing or trial, including the ability to make marginal notes on the drafts and electronic recording of court proceedings to make the official court record.

Promulgated by the Joint Technology Committee (2017), the prototype Application Component Model provides an excellent framework for courts to methodically inventory current technology solutions and to formulate plans for expanded use of technology. This approach is predicated upon the business needs of the court, seeking to match standards-based technology solutions with the functional needs of the court. This modular approach defines both fundamental case management features and "additional components" such as e-filing, public access, jury management, digital recording, notifications, and compliance monitoring. The model also includes a comprehensive set of enterprise-wide technology modules including search engines, reporting and analysis, workflow engines, knowledge management, integration engines, and system-wide security (Joint Technology Committee, 2017).

Transitions and Growth

As mentioned, technology in trial courts in the 1960s was mostly limited to creating and using some case records on software kept on the county's mainframe system. There also were often-contentious disputes about whether audio recordings and their resulting transcripts were "comparable" to, better than, or worse than the record and transcripts produced by stenographic reporters. These debates have lessened considerably in the 21st century for cases of "lesser significance,"[2] such as traffic, small claims, landlord–tenant, misdemeanors, many family law and juvenile matters, and, sometimes, preliminary matters in felony cases. In some states, audio or video recordings have replaced stenographers for almost all cases (Jaafari & Lewis, 2019). These changes have been driven more by budget considerations and a shrinking pool of stenographers than by the resolution of issues related to court technology, with the rate of adoption accelerating in the 1970s and 1980s.[3] Today, a wide variety of hardware and software technologies are available for the court's consideration and use (Greacen, 2018). Yet, many courts still lag considerably behind the private sector and some other government agencies in their use of smartphones, social media, and user-friendly software applications. This is particularly true in the use of AI and case management information systems that take advantage of advances in programming (e.g., "big data" analysis). Public expectations increasingly reflect the standards and practices of the private sector that are generally technologically savvy and offer digitally convenient end-user-focused applications – capabilities that are not nearly as common or fully implemented in the courts. Bear in mind, too, that starting with the millennial generation, a growing percentage of the population has only known a world with computers and the many conveniences provided by digital technology. This familiarity has also created an "instant gratification" expectation. These realities pose significant challenges that courts must address in keeping pace with technological advancements.

Case Management Information Systems

Case management information systems are essential for courts. The sophistication and the number of courts using software to align operations with "best practices" have increased considerably. Today's systems not only improve productivity within the court, but also provide a more seamless interface with litigants, attorneys, other government agencies, and the general public, thus enhancing service, access, transparency, and accountability. Electronic filing, delivery of court materials, text and email reminder notices of appearances, and online completion of intelligent court forms are becoming increasingly common. The importance and necessity of automated case management systems is clear and irrefutable. Having said that, substantial variation in system quality persists, particularly within states that do not operate unified statewide platforms and between states more broadly.

Case management information systems have gone through several generations. The first generation, except in a few instances, was software packages developed for individual courts by executive-branch computer programmers in the agency's IT department (this applies to state courts). Federal courts developed their software "in house" in Washington, DC. In some instances, the court or the IT department, specifically, hired private contractors who were then supervised by IT department personnel. Court officials and attorneys were consulted, but often the people doing the programming lacked knowledge of, and familiarity with, court functions and thus did not ask the questions needed to create effective software. Sometimes, they would ask a question and receive a response from the judges or key staff. The answer could be "we can't do that" either because the computers or software being used did not allow it, or because, even after the guidance they were given was ignored, the weaknesses in the programming did not become apparent until the software was actually implemented. Regrettably, these statements at times reflected that programmers knew only one software package and either lacked the desire and/or incentives within the IT department to learn new programming techniques and languages. The results were often better than the operation of the existing manual systems, but in that early period of automation, complaints from judges and court staff regarding court automation were common. Some of the more typical comments were directed to the inability of the case management system to perform the functions needed, or the absence of data about a case which resided in the manual system.

The next generation was state-funded statewide information systems that improved upon the functionality of the first generation, extended the availability of computerized information to all courts in the state regardless of their size, and transferred the fiscal burden of their locally funded systems to the state.[4] The statewide case management systems provided case-based information that facilitated the use of better case data for local courts, while supporting management needs statewide and documenting the judicial branch's achievements. State funding of these new systems also brought state officials the ability to obtain local court data. Some trial courts opposed development of a statewide system from the outset and objections were sometimes successful in delaying implementation, but they generally did not altogether halt them.

This second phase of software development also brought forth the entry of a few private-sector companies looking for new markets. In the initial period, the value of interfacing with other local criminal justice agencies became recognized. Thus, the second phase of software development also included information systems that could be used by law enforcement, prosecutors, and, sometimes, public defenders so that information (e.g., case data) could be readily shared among these local agencies, while allowing each of them and the court to operate their own, independent information systems. These "integrated" systems allowed electronic case filings with the court, electronic communications between the courts and other agencies, including court rulings, and, in a few instances, shared databases for information that should be made available to the public (management-related data and reports were not typically shared). Sometimes, the state bought the court-only systems and sometimes individual courts purchased these newer systems. Systems characterized as local "criminal justice information systems" were locally developed and funded.

The third generation saw private-sector companies coming to dominate the development and expansion of court case management software. Government programmers have not disappeared, but there are fewer instances of locally developed software.[5] The advantage for courts in this wave is the in-house expertise that the companies develop, based on not just one state or level of court, but rather on multiple states and courts with different jurisdictional parameters. These case management systems have been developed with input from hundreds, if not thousands, of judges, attorneys, administrators, and court staff. Companies providing case management software generally tend to keep up with state-of-the-art software development tools and features of robust case management systems and reports[6] better than local IT staffers and contractors, in part because the latter often are not provided with the same level of up-to-date training that private companies provide to their staff. The limited number of vendors also produces some economies of scale, as each vendor has an opportunity to have multiple clients. There are certainly downsides to this development, but comparative expertise and relative cost advantages have been key in this third generation of court software development.

Some court leaders would like to see a general-market software company develop a case management information system. The theory behind this desire is that the programmers of large IT companies are well resourced and highly skilled, so the software will more fully match court needs and use programming techniques that will maximize functionality and access. A large company also might create competition that would lower costs for the courts. However, courts represent a relatively much smaller market for any of the large technology companies from which court leaders would want help. Compared to the user numbers and profit potential that drive these companies, courts constitute a negligible share of the market for new revenue opportunities.

A number of issues exist for courts using locally developed software versus software to be used statewide, as well as software developed by private companies for courts across the country. Key advantages of software for individual courts are local control, responsiveness, and flexibility to customize. For a single court, these advantages normally outweigh programming expertise and broad input about how to address challenges shared by most courts.[7] For some courts, the advantages of local software creation and control offset economic issues; these courts do not see the possibly greater expertise of programmers as insurmountable.

Technology funding is generally difficult to obtain at both the local and state levels, often causing delays in system development. Decisions are ultimately driven by the funds available at a given point and, occasionally, local or state politics, rather than consideration of court needs (e.g., accountability, customer service, and system efficiency). There are numerous instances in which leaders in the other two branches have difficulty understanding (or accepting) the interrelationships among case types underpinning all court operations, and how new software that handles only a few case types reduces management flexibility and creates or perpetuates inefficiencies.[8] At the same time, we cannot ignore the responsibility of courts' leaders to effectively explain these interrelationships and the efficiencies that are offered by updated computerized information systems.

When an information management system is locally developed and controlled, the court advises the programmers on what the judges and staff want and need, sometimes supported by attorneys and stakeholders in the criminal justice system. In most instances, local programmers will accommodate a court's desires – subject to any fiscal constraints or lack of knowledge about how to do so. It may be difficult to get the funds needed for an entirely new court information system, but local courts sometimes have knowledgeable staff who can provide modern or new features at a limited cost that keep system functionality reasonably up-to-date. These features of local systems are lacking in some state-developed systems and in privately designed "national" software packages. The more general systems are designed to accommodate multiple courts within a state or, with the privately developed systems, across the country. They meet the needs of most courts, but accommodations must be made during development to cover most courts most of the time. Adjustments for individual courts are generally not allowed, typically for one of two reasons. First, they can affect other aspects of the standardized programming adversely and the adaptation would be too expensive or too difficult to justify. Second, the developers do not want to open up that possibility to other clients across the state or country because of the cost that would be involved. There are few or no economies of scale if each court gets to customize its installation.

The other element of a single provider that is difficult for some individual courts – and perhaps applicable to all courts for some changes – is that any changes are normally controlled by the commercial vendor or a "users committee" at the state level through which all requests for changes and updates must be funneled. This process, at best, is slow and time intensive. Courts that identify needs early must wait for a critical mass to identify the same need before the request is seriously considered and then for an analysis by staff and a final decision by the vendor or oversight committee. The entire process normally takes longer than it would utilizing local IT staff or vendors. Sometimes, the upgrade or change works well for some courts, but not for others. The review and approval process also inhibits courts desiring to try something new and pilot efforts statewide that require a change in the software.

There is one element of computerized case management information systems that is often overlooked by private vendors and many state-level planners: the limited and often poor infrastructure for network capacity, computers, and system applications in rural communities. Courts, the Bar, litigants, and the general public in these communities would benefit from features found in urban and suburban courts, but dependable network bandwidth capacity to remote access is limited or unreliable in many rural areas. While satellite-based broadband and continued technological advances may help rural courts overcome these impediments, they remain real, materially affect operations and court capacity, and have not yet received the level of attention they warrant.

Evaluating the Needs, Current Systems, and Opportunities for Using Technology

Workshops on case management remind participants that one of the first steps in evaluating the need for change is to identify current perceived problems and to then study those problems. One does this by collecting and analyzing data and interviewing judges, staff, and attorneys. In this process, court leaders must remain open to other issues surfacing that were not initially identified. Only after these two steps have been completed should a court decide which aspects of case management need to change. The same is true when evaluating the prospect of a new case management information system or any newly proposed technology change with the following questions asked:

- What are we having trouble managing with the current system? If data entry mistakes are causing bad data in the system, a new system may change that, at best, at the margins.[9] Likewise, if there are issues with some judges or staff not following the practices programmed into the software, new software will not address that unless all judges and court administration can agree on one process/rule.
- What benefits are we seeking with a new system and can we achieve these without a whole new system? Consider non-technology solutions after weaknesses or errors in the processing of cases are identified. Ask whether any of the following will resolve the issues the court is facing:
    - Improved training (or retraining)
    - Documents that allow quick identification of a mistake
    - A new order for completing work or reassignment of personnel
    - An additional layer of review for the process or data entry

Beyond those issues, one must ask: Will the new system bring us closer to achieving our strategic goals of transparency, accountability, accessibility, and application of the rule of law? If not, what will help us achieve them?

- What are our requirements for a new system? A comprehensive requirements analysis is needed to answer this question. The first two questions could be addressed in this phase, too, but it is preferable to answer the first two before a court spends money on this more elaborate and time-consuming step.
- Do we have a detailed timeline with specific deliverables and a budget for each phase, plus performance standards for the software before we start development? Large projects (i.e., for large courts and statewide systems) require these steps, but when implementations fail or go significantly over budget, it often is because not enough attention was paid at the beginning to asking this question and requiring answers, and/or a lack of monitoring progress.

- Will we have or can we obtain an experienced project manager on staff who can devote full time to the project? Using existing IT staff who have no or very limited experience implementing new court software or a major upgrade or installation of new hardware invites problems. Ensuring that the project manager can devote full-time attention to the project is as important as finding someone with the desired experience.

New or upgraded court software normally affects both workflow (the allocation of work among staff) and judicial and staff's support for and acceptance of the change. A comprehensive plan for achieving the change is essential to any successful effort to add or upgrade software. It must cover introducing the need for change to judges, staff, and affected attorneys and how change will be achieved. Changes of this magnitude, and frankly any organizational change of consequence, require documentation of why the change is needed, what the change will achieve, timing of the process, staff training plans, and how to inform attorneys, self-represented litigants, and other affected stakeholders. The explanations prior to implementation should also cover what will be done to determine whether the change has achieved its desired purpose(s). As important as these elements of change management are, leadership must identify the individuals who will convey these messages, as sometimes the messenger can be as important to acceptance of a change as the message itself.

A decision to buy new software or an upgrade should follow an examination of how the software will change the existing flow of work and who should complete each step in processing respective case types. Often, if a court has a firm grasp of what the new software will do, business process changes will occur that optimize its benefits. A new or updated case management information system impacts virtually all aspects of support operations and some important aspects of scheduling and organizing courtroom time. Almost all readers have been in businesses that require customers to "take a number" so service can be provided in the order in which customers arrive. Virtually all of these are simple manual customer service systems. There now are digitized/computerized versions of these devices. These systems not only provide a count of people served, but they also facilitate queue management and track how long it takes to be served and which staff person provided the service. This allows management to track the peaks and valleys in counter demand, how long it takes each staff member to serve customers, and, possibly, the type of inquiries and how long it takes to deal with each. These data can be used by managers to assess staff allocation, consider changes in procedures and/or forms, and to identify staff training needs.[10]

When designing and implementing the first generation of case management software and, to some extent, the second generation, courts tended to computerize their existing manual procedures, sometimes referred to as "paving the cow path." Case records normally became available faster and, often, to more people without having to check the paper file, but the basic workflow does not change and paper files do not disappear. The failure to change business processes can be mostly attributed to a lack of understanding about the power of the new automated case management system or, sometimes, lack of attention to modernizing existing procedures. The assembly line processing of work remains, even though computers open countless opportunities to restructure business processes and supporting staff functions. This approach at times leads to little more than speeding up parts of the record creation and retrieval processes. The result is an expense that does not fully return the myriad benefits that could have been achieved.

Court technologies can widely expand access to justice, providing online court services "anywhere, anytime" on a 24/7 basis. Some technologies help to reduce or eliminate longstanding barriers to justice, including geography (e.g., rural areas), limited hours of service and litigant costs. Court reform advocates have reconceptualized the delivery of court services, suggesting new models for creation of customer-focused "user-friendly" courts. They propose a new paradigm in which courts offer litigants both in-person services at the courthouse and a full array of online court services (Suskin, 2019).

Online dispute resolution (ODR) is one of the most intriguing and relatively new online technology solutions, successfully deployed in the private sector and a few courts at the time of this publication (Barton & Bibas, 2017). The authors anticipate increased use of ODR for selected case types (e.g., traffic, small claims, family law), with "off ramps" for staff assistance to litigants as needed during the case resolution process. Continuing expansion and refinement of technologies will likely also occur in the following areas of e-court services and end-user feedback:

- Electronic filing of cases (e-filing)
- Electronic notifications via text and email
- Electronic access to court records
- Intelligent "guided" court forms for self-represented litigants in conjunction with e-filing
- Online payments
- Off-site cash payments
- Online instructional podcasts
- Electronic exhibits
- Remote and hybrid court hearings
- Remote customer service including "chat" modes with court staff
- Judicial performance evaluations (Institute for the Advancement of the American Legal System, 2025)
- Public satisfaction surveys (National Center for State Courts [NCSC], 2005)

Court leaders must guard against being the hare when switching to new software or other technology solutions, upgrading existing software, or adding new hardware. Hurrying to replace an existing system that has become outdated does not excuse failing to obtain an understanding of the impact of the new software and/or hardware on workflow and re-engineering accordingly. The notion that "We have to get this done by (date)" may involve substantial costs in the long run and it may not fully leverage the new software or hardware.

While acquisition of new technologies requires a significant infusion of cash, courts must also take into account the substantial time commitment required of judges and staff. A court requires two oversight bodies before proceeding with a decision to obtain new software or technology. First, it requires a court-led IT governance committee to evaluate business requirements and oversee business process re-engineering and system design.[11] Second, it needs a system implementation committee to monitor progress and respond to any application issues against the planned timeline and budget.

Membership on these committees should be selected carefully and include a trusted leadership judge and/or court administrator who has some familiarity with technology chairing the committee. Senior court managers should be included, along with line staff who are familiar with court operational needs. Both the design and implementation committees also benefit from having one or more criminal and civil attorneys as members, as the legal community's needs in interfacing with the new system should be considered. Because the number of self-represented litigants continues to grow, consideration should also be given to adding one or more system stakeholders and court end-users (customers) to the committees as well. The court's leadership and committee members must understand from the beginning that being on the committee will involve a significant time commitment.

Adopting New Technologies and Impediments to Doing So

Courts are notoriously slow adopters, whether in administrative, organizational, or technological matters. This normally slow response often has been explained as courts being inherently conservative, in that they rely on existing legal precedents – looking backward rather than forward to guide case-specific decision making – and the common-law approach of limited, incremental change. The attitudes reflected in these approaches have served courts well in their adjudicative role. However, they are not necessarily beneficial to courts in leveraging the use of technology to improve service, effectiveness, and efficiency. Further, it is important to understand that modern court technologies enhance access, transparency, and accountability, and provide assistance to self-represented litigants. Technology also offers the prospect of expanding court access and improving timely adjudication of cases.[12]

There are sound, due-process-based reasons for courts not necessarily being the first early adopters of new technology: The accuracy of court records and the need for access to records – short term and, for many cases, long term – are critical for the courts, litigants, and the public. New technologies need critical "break-in" time in the marketplace before they can assure stable operation. Adopting a new technology shortly after its introduction (the definition of being an early adopter) exposes courts to the possibility of inaccurate or lost records, significant delays in accessing or providing information, and applications that prove to be counter-productive. Each of these risks, if realized, potentially undermines the judicial system and how people view the integrity or competence of courts. Courts need not be late (or very late) adopters, but it is appropriate to wait until the private sector and some well-resourced entities in the public sector have tried, tested, and proven the accuracy, stability, and value of a new technology for general public / agency use. If one thinks of the adoption curve as a bell curve (left to right: early, mass or broad, and late adoption), courts can legitimately explore and test (and/or implement) newer technologies before mass adoption, but should be very careful about doing so at the "outlier" earliest-adopter stage (Reinkensmeyer & Doktor, 2001).

We suggest several guidelines in assessing and instituting all new technologies, wherever they are on the adoption curve:

- Prioritize technologies that will improve communication with and to litigants and jurors, the Bar, the media, and the general public; and have a high probability of enhancing efficiency and effectiveness that will improve transparency; and will improve accountability. Further, look for technologies, especially video, that will expand court access and educational outreach (including courtroom procedures), completing forms, and how to obtain information about cases and/or parties.
- Do an analysis of the true nature of the problem or issue to be addressed to be sure the proposed technology will resolve the issue or problem. Sometimes new procedures, reorganizing workflow, or improving training are quicker and less expensive than technology and are sufficient.[13]
- In most cases, do not be an early adopter among all users. Courts with strong IT support and a record of successful implementations are better candidates to be adopters within the court community.
- Design pilot programs or limited testing before there is full scale adoption and check with any courts that already are using the technology.
- Always create measurable goals for the technology and then evaluate continually.[14]
- Put a high priority on training staff and other system users before implementation (near the implementation date to ensure lessons do not fade) and monitor its content and effectiveness.

- Understand that change is a constant and that technology that worked five or ten years ago may no longer be effective.
- Ensure that there is buy-in from the funding authority for technology updates as needed and ongoing system maintenance.[15]

Other Challenges

It is misleading to attribute slow adoption of court technology solely to technology-related factors. Three factors tied to public funding are equally as critical. The first is the limited amount of dollars typically made available. Court budgets at all levels are dominated by personnel costs. Many courts' operating budgets are insufficient for a fully staffed court, which leads to tension between obtaining adequate funds for staff positions while trying to upgrade technology that might supplement or reduce the need for current staff. Front end technology costs normally are seen in government as capital investment costs (at least initially) for which competition for limited funds by multiple agencies is intense. As a general proposition, courts have not done well competing for new technology funding. Both hardware and software can become antiquated before funding is obtained to upgrade or replace them. By the time a court obtains the funds to "catch up," its "new" technology solution may already be dated or obsolete.

Second, a court needs technology maintenance and system upgrades over time. The funds needed several years later may not be provided or will not meet the then-current, increased costs. We have found that the maintenance costs of a new system are, at a minimum, equal to the initial purchase price over the system's life cycle and often amount to two to three times that figure. Consequently, the court must be clear in its technology budget submission that maintenance funding will be required and it should seek a written multi-year funding commitment. Funding authorities do not necessarily feel bound by old promises, but at least the court should develop a record of technology funding agreements.

Finally, as a general proposition, private-sector salaries normally exceed public-sector wages for comparable skill and experience levels. The gap is even greater for skilled technology workers. Government traditionally has narrowed the gap by providing better job security and good benefits, particularly medical and retirement benefits. Today, however, a number of citizens see government as too costly and government employees as overpaid. The views about "overpaying" often focus on the benefit differential that normally favors the public sector or rely on misleading information about relative salaries for comparable work, experience, and skills. Moreover, too many government units have failed to fully fund pension funds for current and future retirees, making a key component of the traditional employment bargain less secure – or, in the worst-case circumstance, unavailable – to public sector employees. This reality necessarily widens the gap between public- and private-sector total compensation.

Many technology companies now offer very appealing work environments and stock ownership that may lead to greater wealth in a shorter number of years. Salaries, too, often exceed those of the public sector. This combination has proven to be very enticing to many younger workers. The technology sector's best employees often also are drawn to opportunities to work on cutting-edge developments. No government can match these non-salary inducements. Even when courts attract well-qualified technology experts, the private sector remains a strong competitor. Younger IT personnel may start in government to obtain the training that a growing number of companies are unwilling to provide. Inevitably, these now trained and experienced personnel become more desirable to IT companies, which will then pay a bonus because such personnel are highly skilled. Courts cannot compete effectively against these monetary incentives. Thus, their ability to maintain currency with developments in technology is constrained.

Courts are not defenseless against these labor market challenges, however. Court leaders should never overlook the draw of serving public needs and, especially, the mission of assisting in the delivery of justice to the community. Often, that core commitment is a primary factor in people not leaving for the private sector, despite the pay differential. Beyond that competitive advantage, the government normally offers more job security than the private sector. The depth of budget cuts during the Great Recession and, to a lesser degree, during the COVID-19 pandemic demonstrated the limits of the job security courts can provide, but overall, courts still offer more job security than private sector companies. In many cases, job benefits also are better in courts – and government generally – than those in the private sector. Lastly, courts generally offer employees a commodity that is often more valuable than money – time. Staff specialists working in court technology units are likely to have predictable schedules, typically a traditional 40-hour workweek, Monday through Friday. By contrast, salaried employees in the private sector are often expected to work longer hours, including evenings, weekends, and sometimes holidays.

One final word regarding training and the IT staff maintaining currency: courts should do all they can within their budgets to provide their IT staff and senior managers with opportunities to attend workshops and conferences to learn about new technologies and their potential use in the courts. One of the perks of court-funded professional development for court IT staff is the opportunity to earn technical certifications in critical areas like programming, network management, and cybersecurity. Similarly, membership fees for appropriate national and local organizations for IT personnel, subscriptions to leading technology magazines, and visitations to courts which are early adopters should be included in the court budget.

When a court enhances its training and learning opportunities, an unintended consequence may be making its best staff attractive to private-sector companies – and some other government agencies – which will then recruit them away. There are courts in California and New Jersey, among other states, where this is an ongoing problem. Nonetheless, it is better to have informed and trained staff capable of identifying, installing, and maintaining new technologies, even if only for a few years, than to maintain long-term staff whose skills atrophy because they are not given the latest and most relevant training.

Collectively, these factors leave courts lagging behind the private sector – and certain better-resourced government agencies, such as law enforcement – in their capacity to sustain in-house expertise for identifying and developing the latest technologies. These fiscally oriented realities have a greater impact on the ability of courts to adopt, incorporate, and use technology effectively than the previously noted cultural and legal factors. There is one additional factor that has been overlooked in some states and remains beyond the judiciary's control when acting alone. Many small, rural courts have not been able to join the technological revolution to the same degree as urban and suburban courts. As previously mentioned, the infrastructure and funding needed to support some technologies, most notably reliable network capacity to support internet and Wi-Fi access, is at best lacking and at worst not available. Additionally, the personnel or contractors with the necessary expertise are not as available in these remote areas. The COVID-19 pandemic's impact on education and remote learning has thrown a bright spotlight on this issue. Even so, the state judiciary's administrative leaders need to explore with state and local officials how best to address the infrastructure needs of rural courts so all in the state can benefit from the technological advances achieved in urban and suburban settings.

Real-Time Cyber Security Needs

The security of digital information and case management systems has been an issue for decades, but it has become a critically recognized need in the 21st century. Storing court data in "the cloud" and sharing it adds another level of security concern. Beyond spam, which is normally a nuisance, but not debilitating, there are two aspects of outside cybersecurity that must be addressed by any court software developer: malware, and unauthorized access to case records and financial systems. Unauthorized access also may involve malware, but it is important to distinguish between the two for the purposes of this discussion.

Malware and other theft efforts pose several key risks: crashing a system, locking it, data theft, and ransomware. Each of these risks implicates access to and protection of the system generally, but can also be introduced through individual accounts using passwords obtained by a hacker(s). The implications of these threats on a court are easily identified by looking at the crashes and malware introduced into corporate and government computers by (mostly) international hackers. Courts must assume that if a hacker understands the impact of attacking a court's (or all of a state's courts') systems, at some point they will try to do it and may succeed. The cost of a successful malware attack is remarkably high. The latter should lead all courts to protect their digital data and information systems to the highest degree possible. The relatively low probability of malware disrupting court data and court proceedings is not a sufficient reason to defer action.

Ransomware might appear in a court's system, often as collateral damage to ransomware being dumped into the court's data center or servers of the executive branch and/or any other systems to which the court's system(s) is connected. Clearly, ransomware is very concerning and highly disruptive. The failure to stop ransomware also undermines public trust in the court. Addressing it may require expertise outside of that found in most individual courts. This necessarily requires court leaders to address the vulnerabilities of the system with software vendors and with any agency or entity with access to the court's information system. Should court leadership have any concerns about answers being provided, it should consult with third-party experts. However the technical advice is obtained, every court should develop a plan in advance of how it will respond to attacks on its records and the manual or alternative-digital workarounds that will be put in place until the issue is resolved. The plan should be part of a court's broader continuity of operations (COOP) plan. The court also needs to ensure that there are routine, comprehensive backups of all its software and that data are securely stored offsite.

Ensuring security against unauthorized access requires attention to the design of court technology systems, the management of administrator access codes, and training users in personal responsibility, password protocols, and safeguarding physical IT assets. Increasingly, individual attorneys and litigants are being given access to case management system data for legitimate business purposes. There are ways to enable access through a separate server that will protect the court's official records storage and internal-access server(s) that should be part of the system implementation process. In addition, security training and written instructions should be provided to non-court users. Second-level security questions – i.e., after entry of a password – and two-step user authentication also should be adopted.

Increasingly, biometric systems such as facial recognition, iris recognition, and fingerprint ID are being used to facilitate access to computers and smartphones. As other technologies emerge, other sophisticated and stronger security approaches may be developed. These security measures may require specialized hardware and robust software, however. In a court environment, particularly in systems that are providing significant access to a wide variety of people and entities, there are literally thousands of access points (possibly tens of thousands in large urban courts) that can be used to compromise a system's integrity and information. Accordingly, courts should include the design of these technologies in their software acquisition plans, contingent on affordability and the wider adoption of technologies that improve security and lower costs. Failure to address these concerns at installation and continuously thereafter exposes courts to potential issues.

Unauthorized access to court records (by any means) poses a serious threat to both court operations and the integrity of the records. Instances have occurred in which deputy clerks were bribed to alter records, both paper and digital, and some jail inmates have manipulated their own records to secure early release. In a few cases, the alteration of multiple records affected hundreds of cases. Regardless of who might attempt to modify a record, court leadership must remain vigilant. Courts should protect against these risks from the outset, beginning with robust network and software security and followed by regular, secure system backups. All systems should be periodically reviewed for new vulnerabilities. For instance, regular cybersecurity audits, such as "system scans," provide a systematic approach for identifying and promptly addressing exposure points.

Another reason to guard against targeted hacks is that litigants or investors may attempt to access a judge's computer to obtain advance information about upcoming rulings or judgments, whether in draft form or before public release. Certain cases can have significant implications for a company's future or stock value, making early access highly desirable. Both federal and state courts must remain aware of these risks and continuously safeguard against them. In short, a comprehensive cybersecurity program is essential for all courts and will become increasingly more important as technology plays a larger role in creating, managing, preserving, and providing public access to court records.

Long-Term Storage of Digital Records

Records creation, management, and retention, both short-term and long-term, have challenged court leaders, essentially from the day the first court in the United States opened its doors. Until the mid-20th century, paper was the medium on which all records were created, accessed, and stored.[16] The challenges with the paper record involved having enough shelving and cabinets (physical space) for active cases, assuring that case files could be located when needed, and then long-term storage for inactive cases. Record retention schedules and best practices for how to prepare paper files for longer-term storage helped with the latter, but the process of complying with these procedures and schedules was normally time-consuming and staff intensive. Because staffing levels in a substantial number of courts have been insufficient (or barely sufficient) for the demands and deadlines of daily work, preparing files for storage and getting them to storage often were deferred or ignored. In either case, the neglect merely compounded the issues of storage space for active cases and the staff time needed to comply with record retention requirements. Many administrators viewed long-term storage of paper records as a nuisance and costly because space often had to be leased. As a result, record retention compliance was often assigned a low priority, at best.

Digital records were quickly embraced by most court administrators, in significant part because they promised to relieve courts of the burden of both short-term and long-term physical storage. An important short-term improvement was eliminating what most courts called "lost files."[17] The consequences of unlocated files for a judge, litigants, and the daily calendar were significant.[18] Digital records were available "on demand" whenever and wherever needed, including by several people at one time, which was a major improvement for most courts. Most of the promises about digital records for active cases have been realized, which is an important reason for the relatively rapid spread of digital record creation and storage.

Digital records facilitate access to and the availability of records for active cases. These advantages need to be acknowledged; they do not negate, however, the concerns expressed in the balance of this section. Raaen (2017) observed that while courts often adopt technology to improve efficiency and expand access, these benefits can be undermined – and even negated – when the technology is poorly governed or managed. There are challenges in using and protecting open digital records. Additionally, there are more challenges with long-term (in this context ten years or more) needs to use and preserve digital records for inactive files.

The first area of concern relates to active records: creating and assuring the integrity of e-filed documents, digital records created by staff, and paper documents converted to digital records after filing. Raaen (2017) summarizes the challenges succinctly:

> Technologies such as digital signatures, digital rights management, electronic "stamps," metadata, and document audits are part of the new toolbox for court records managers. Maintaining adequate metadata is a key to integrity as it provides information on the nature of a record, how and when it has been accessed, and whether any alteration has occurred. Interaction logs are useful for data authentication by ensuring that interactions with records are recorded, including any changes to the record. It should be possible to create an audit trail for any digital record that provides a history of changes made to the record, including who, when, how, and what.

The promises associated with longer-term storage issues – particularly for files that should be or legally must be retained for longer than ten years – have not been fully realized or, in many instances, recognized in full. The irony for courts believing digital records would largely eliminate long-term storage issues is that digital records actually expand and complicate those issues. Digital records present some unique issues along with some of the same challenges that paper records present.[19] The bottom line, however, is that the combination of old and new records management issues is more complex and more costly than longer-term storage of the dreaded paper records. Even worse, courts have come late to this realization (some may have not realized it yet) and have not addressed the issues at all or have taken only partial steps to deal with them. Raaen (2017) again describes the challenge:

> While it should be obvious that electronic records are entirely dependent upon technology, organizations often fail to realize that rapid changes in technology require continuous review and modification of electronic records management strategies. The challenges of technology, particularly relating to technological obsolescence and dependency, have complicated the long-term management of, and access to, information... Often, decisions regarding electronic records management have been ad hoc or based on the promise of new technologies without due consideration to long-term impact or the impact on participation in the judicial process. Therefore, judicial leaders need to approach electronic records management with a long-term vision, commitment of resources and a regard for how decisions and strategy impact access and participation by litigants, the public and the media.

He goes on to identify the unique elements of digital records that need to be addressed for long-term retention (Raaen, 2017):

> Long-term digital preservation... requires regular monitoring, frequent intervention, and the assistance of technically trained professionals. The challenge of digital record keeping is two-fold. The physical media that hold data must be preserved and protected from damage and deterioration, and the software and hardware to access and use the records must still be available... Maintaining digital records in a manner that ensures their continued authenticity and accessibility over long periods of time requires attention to factors that are unique to the digital world:

- Media Obsolescence: The options for storage and presentation of digital data continue to evolve and change, e.g., the progression of peripheral storage devices for the personal computer, and the exponential increase in storage capacity.
- Media Failure: Electronic media are susceptible to various levels of failure, including degradation as a result of poor storage or preparation.
- Media Access: Removable media such as tapes and DVDs require specific hardware to extract information from them which may become unavailable over time as manufacturers improve their products.

- Software Obsolescence: The continuing development of application software results in the rapid obsolescence of software to access and process digital information.
- File Format Obsolescence: The increasing range of formats in which data is maintained creates another challenge. Features such as "hidden text" and "change history" make digital documents more useful, but also create storage and retrieval challenges.

In recognition of these salient points, the Joint Technology Committee (2014) delineated degrees of risk for court data centers, digital archives, and digital preservation services over time.

The lack of attention to these issues within many courts may be due to training deficiencies, lack of exposure, or possibly excessive optimism about the ability of technology companies to deal with all issues before they become serious concerns.[20] At issue here is the digital data stored for ten years or more, which should give these companies adequate time to manage any concern that potentially materializes.[21] Many court leaders have not been provided the needed information to become informed consumers, so they proceed oblivious to the challenges. In other cases, they accept the assurances that any concern is overblown.

Literature discussing the needs of and how to respond to long-term storage of digital records is available and is growing. Public- and private-sector archivists, librarians, historians, and some IT professionals have been trying to shed light on these issues since the 1970s. Government is catching up, yet the gap between private and public concerns remains. In the public sphere, the U.S. Department of Defense, the National Archives and Records Administration of the national government, some state and federal executive-branch agencies, and the federal courts have begun to address the issues. State court leaders at the national level – Conference of State Court Administrators (COSCA) and the Joint Technology Committee of the COSCA, National Association for Court Management (NACM), and NCSC – have likewise produced highly instructive reports. Change at the local court level and some state administrative offices has often lagged, however. What is lacking in some state judiciaries is a broad effort in state administrative offices and many trial courts to systematically address digital court records management issues as a high-priority initiative. Because these issues involve long-term planning and are complex, there has been an "out of sight, out of mind" tendency.

One response to the challenges posed by digital records has been to re-examine and reduce the retention periods for records in some case types. The rationale for shortening retention periods is simple: "If we don't have to keep a lot of information as long as we thought when the retention schedules were created for paper records (which largely remain in place for all records), the increasing risk of losing digital records over time will not be as important. Problem resolved." A re-examination of retention schedules is always appropriate. Decisions about retention periods should not depend on the medium in which records are stored, but rather on how long they legitimately may be needed as a case record and whether they have (or may have) historical value beyond that time.

One of the reasons that paper records were not always destroyed when a retention period expired was that courts recognized that older records still may have value in later cases or continue to have value to a litigant/defendant or to those wanting a full record of a person's past activities, such as those seeking information for security clearances or particularly sensitive jobs. Courts cannot meet all needs that might arise in an indefinite future – particularly in high-volume, low-significance cases such as traffic tickets and most small claims cases – but they should not be oblivious to these potential longer-term uses of the records either. And, of course, there are laws requiring very-long-term or indefinite retention of case records in capital murder (or any murder), high-end felony cases, land-transactions, and probate cases. In one sense, digital records facilitate long-term retention of these proceedings because they require less physical space, yet retaining them, especially in large urban courts, also carries costs to address environmental issues and the need to protect against hardware and software obsolescence. Local or state archives and regional historical societies have been tapped by courts for paper records, but in some smaller jurisdictions, these organizations have declined to retain the paper records.[22] Given the challenges of retaining digital records over time, these organizations may also decline those requests.

There is one technology development still in the research stage to expand the longevity of storage – up to a billion years at the most-optimistic extreme – and to enhance the quality of the record retained. Early tests of using highly refined lasers etching glass as the medium of storage have been very promising (Lewis, 2016). The imprinting of information is done on a very small disc of glass (the size of a coin) and is subsequently stored in a space referred to as "five-dimensional storage." Caution is required among the judiciary community at this point, however, and for several years yet. Lewis (2016) offered the following caveat:

> [W]hile the researchers are optimistic about the possibilities for five-dimensional storage, the average person won't be replacing their hard drives for glass discs any time soon. Not only is it hard to get consumers [and courts] to switch... but femtosecond lasers are expensive and delicate tools that probably won't become common outside of the lab for a while. On the other hand, developing a device to read the discs wouldn't be too hard, which might make the discs more useful for institutions like libraries and museums.

Rather than wait for glass discs, states should move promptly to consider establishing state-level judicial records archives. Alternatively, the judicial branch can contract with the executive branch at the state level for records warehouse and maintenance services. This is being done in the federal government through the National Archives and Records Administration (NARA's approach may be a good model). Preserving a significant number of electronic records is expensive and challenging, both in terms of staff expertise and out-of-pocket costs. If there is a central repository, there will be economies of scale for space, equipment, and expertise. In any individual trial court or any single appellate court, the need to review the records from a number of cases from 15, 20, or 40 years ago is small. The lost data may be random within documents or result in all or most of a few documents being lost. One might argue that whatever is lost might be reconstructed or will not be critical to the reason for the review. How can a court know that today? How will lost data – possibly thousands of digital bits at the time of review – affect the reviewer's ability to understand what happened or to review and make a fresh assessment as to whether justice was done? At a macro level, the risks are small, and some would argue they are worth taking. The people directly affected by whatever data is lost will never be convinced that nothing can be done and will not blame the technology. Nor will historians be forgiving. They will fault the court and the judicial system. These are not de minimus risks.

It is possible to read the surviving portions of the Dead Sea Scrolls because of the medium used. One can read medieval parchments because of the medium used. One can read books of philosophy, medicine, and political thought printed hundreds of years ago because of the elements used and efforts made to preserve them. Original copies of America's Declaration of Independence and Constitution can be displayed because of the medium used and the great care devoted to preservation. And, the opinions of Chief Justice John Marshall are readable for these same reasons. Clearly, there are many books and records still being printed on paper. The trajectory of technology, however, suggests some people in the not-too-distant future will argue that we can abandon paper documents and records that may have historical value – or are legally required to be retained indefinitely – because everyone is using computers and digital records are sufficient. While a facile argument, we contend that it can also be misleading.

It is not acceptable that important judicial-branch documents and records may be lost to history and to parties, historians, and citizens of the future because of the medium used. However, that does not mean that all case records must still be printed on paper. Rather, more attention must be paid to the risks involved in courts' growing reliance on digital records and how to mitigate those risks. Judicial systems and individual courts must recognize that electronic records are subject to degradation (naturally over time) when they are transferred from one storage device, medium, and system to another, and because of environmental conditions. The latter is similar to the risks associated with paper; the degradation issues are unique to digital records. In time, glass discs or other storage methods may solve the long-term loss of data. It could take decades before these alternatives are perfected, however, and before they are used enough commercially to prove their worth and to lower their costs. In the meantime, courts and/or judicial systems have to develop a "Plan B" records accession plan to preclude the loss of digital records.[23]

Other Current and Emerging Court Information Systems

There are many technology solutions other than case management packages that are used in courts: financial and budgeting, jury management, personnel records and management, court security, and, in some courts, facilities management. These are important, but for the most part – other than jury management – they are commercial packages that can be used in the private or public sectors. They do not pose the same issues of usefulness without customization (in many courts) that case management information systems pose. The following discussion referencing the various court technology solutions are also noteworthy from a court administration perspective.

Automated Telephone Answering Systems

Telephone answering systems have been used by courts for decades. They also have been and are used by most government entities and businesses. Such systems normally provide a list of options that in most cases include options for each department and/or case type.[24] Once transferred to the second level, court staff may answer or there is an opportunity to leave a message. Many businesses now use voice recognition AI to have a conversation (of sorts) with the caller, providing customer service information on frequently asked questions (FAQ). Voice recognition answering systems can be as frustrating to callers as lists of "options 1 through 9," but they may also provide options more responsive to callers' needs. To the extent administrators are not already doing so, they should be moving the court toward making their websites more informative, so fewer people need to call the court for assistance. The deployment of AI and "chat bots" hold the promise of more user-friendly, timely, and accurate phone-based customer service. Court administrators must ensure that the use of this rapidly advancing technology is designed and managed to meet end-user needs, given the pressing need to increase court access.

Many, if not most, courts do not provide information on their websites about how to directly contact the court administrator, division managers, or staff. An even greater number of courts do not provide direct access information to the judges. This is largely intentional: litigants are prohibited from contacting judges directly about cases in an ex parte manner. Nevertheless, some litigants attempt to reach judges or their staff. Because of the heavy demands on judges' time, some courts avoid adding a cluttered voicemail system for judges to also review. Other courts do provide direct telephone numbers for judges, court administrators, and senior managers without compromising workflow, which may prevent small issues from escalating into larger problems. We acknowledge that such openness can promote transparency and accountability, however inefficient the results may be. At a minimum, we recognize that there should be available options that allow the caller to speak to a live person so that they can be redirected to the appropriate person in accordance with policy guidelines.

Court Reporting

The technology of court reporting has changed materially in the last 50 years. A half century ago, most reporters were stenographic reporters using the well-known small box apparatus with 22 keys to create shorthand notes they (or a "note reader") would subsequently transcribe. A minority of reporters were "pen" writers (literally using pens and pads), monitored recording machines, or, particularly in Congress and the military, were voice writers (talking into a mask as witnesses speak; the reporter's voice goes to a recording machine).

Today, many reporters are known as "real-time" reporters. They use a rectangular box that is very similar to the device used by stenographers to take notes in shorthand, just as stenographers do, but notes are converted to digital records that are read by a computer that are then translated (in draft) into English.[25] The translation occurs virtually simultaneously with the words being taken down, so they can be transmitted in "real time" to the judge and attorneys. The judge's version allows the judge to immediately add marginal notes, should they choose to preserve thoughts or to note something that they will follow-up on at a later time. The benefit for attorneys is the capacity to print the transcript immediately after the hearing or day's event concludes. This aids preparation for the next day (or proceeding) and normally saves the court money, because fewer reporters are needed to achieve the same result for the attorneys; the advantages for judges cannot be duplicated by stenographic reporters or even by a team of stenographers taking notes in tandem during the proceeding. The real-time transcription can also be displayed on courtroom monitors to provide access for hearing impaired court participants, pursuant to Americans with Disabilities Act (ADA) requirements (U.S. Department of Justice Civil Rights Division, 2020).

By the late 1980s, limited use of voice recognition technology was gaining broader acceptance and credibility in the private sector. That acceptance and its expanded use continue. Advancements in AI in recent years have enabled the quality and accuracy of voice recognition to improve materially. Accordingly, its use has expanded across numerous functions in the private sector and, to a lesser degree, in the public sector. What do these changes and the growing acceptance of its use and usefulness say about the future of court reporting? By the mid-1980s, a few people in court administration believed that voice recognition technology would largely replace court reporters within 20 years. That timeline was clearly too optimistic, but the number of people who see voice recognition software replacing some, most, or all court reporters has grown (Gaus, 2018).

Observing real-time closed captioning on television readily illustrates the challenges inherent in producing a verbatim record of court proceedings, especially during heated motion arguments or trials. Real-time closed captioning contains misspellings and misunderstood words and names, even though the material being captioned is mostly everyday English. Television dialogue rarely includes unusually spelled names or specialized technical, scientific, or medical terminology; by contrast, such language is used almost daily in courtrooms. Software designers can build dictionaries that contain the most likely used words in these categories, but inevitably, words that are important in some cases will be omitted and will need to be filled in later. AI software can be trained to recognize new words, much like word-processing dictionaries can be "taught." As the experience with closed captioning demonstrates, however, each draft transcript will require review to correct spelling, grammatical, and naming errors, as well as other inaccuracies. This is how the process unfolds today with stenographic reporters – and, to a lesser degree, real-time reporters. One of the advantages AI software might offer is fewer corrections and the proof-reader/editor may be less expensive than a stenographer. Perhaps, the amortized cost of AI software also will be less per year than a stenographic reporter, but as of now it is too early to tell. It is also important to recognize that, while technological advances are frequently assumed to reduce personnel and operating costs, these savings have been only partially realized. In many instances, new technologies have necessitated expanded technical staff, maintenance agreements, and continuing hardware and software upgrades. The possible advantage of and advances in AI in court reporting illustrate that caution and time need to be built into efforts to use technology to replace, improve the productivity of staff, or enhance customer service. The technical and programming challenges are numerous:

- The acoustics in many courtrooms are poor, making it difficult for any machine to pick up some testimony. Only a newer courtroom designed to deal with this acoustic challenge will avoid this issue.
- The locations for witnesses and the judge in a courtroom are fixed; they can be told to speak up and/or directly into the microphone. Many attorneys move around while questioning witnesses at trials and hearings. This issue has been addressed in courtrooms with audio recordings by telling attorneys not to move from the podium with the microphone.

Wireless microphones worn by wandering attorneys have separate issues and problems that thus far are not overcome by using AI.

- Staff may be needed to monitor the sound and remind everyone when the microphones have a problem picking up voices.
- Combining audio (or video) reporting with AI means many possible words – especially legal, medical, and engineering nomenclature – can be preprogrammed and AI can learn when a new word is used. Careful review and editing will be needed post-recording notwithstanding these AI advancements.
- Many attorneys and witnesses have accents or speech difficulties that may make it difficult for a machine to understand all their spoken words. Audio recordings should have an assigned monitor who also can control matters, but many courts do not use monitors. If a court shifts to an AI-enabled voice recognition recording system, it should also adopt a rule requiring parties to identify X days in advance that there are technical terms and/or one or more witnesses whose speech might be difficult for the AI software to identify. The court can then determine whether a stenographer should be used.

Several of these challenges were cited by stenographers as audio and video recording systems were introduced as alternatives. Although many of these concerns were eventually overcome or proved to be overstated, they were not fully resolved in every context. As a result, some states that have expanded the use of audio recording still require stenographers for trials in all or most case types, as well as for certain pre-trial proceedings, such as felony hearings. Perhaps courtroom voice recognition systems will be similarly limited, at least during the early phases of development. Concerns about AI replacing stenographers may simply echo the recorder-versus-stenographer debates of the 1970s and 1980s (and, in some jurisdictions and case types, which continue today). Alternatively, they may reflect the possibility that voice recognition for court reporting presents even more unresolved challenges than what was experienced with early recording technologies.

Social Media

The use of social media by judges and courts has increased exponentially in the last 15 years. Many courts now use Facebook, Instagram, X, YouTube, among other social media platforms to supplement what is on their websites, to share information about court processes and requirements, issue press releases to the media, and to maintain contact with prospective and current jurors and litigants. Judges have used it for general information about the court, for details about specific cases, and to comment on recent developments in law or policy. The use of social media will likely expand as the technical, legal, and ethical issues are resolved and as new outlets become available. Some of the useful ways a modern court can deploy social media include the following:

- As a way to expand how a court communicates basic information about court history and current developments about its calendars, judges' biographies, and how to contact departments and/or individual staff or managers.
- To provide information and training videos about how to act in court, how to present evidence or arguments at trial and in various proceedings, an outline of the life cycle of typical cases for the various case types, how to prepare and file documents, video tours of the courthouse and typical courtrooms, maps and directions on how to get to the courthouse, and new developments to expand court access.
- To maintain contact with prospective jurors due on a specific date and/or involved in jury selection or on a trial (Piper, 2020).[26]
- To provide information of interest to Bar members through an "attorneys-only" website or other password-protected platform.
- To supplement whatever means normally are used to keep media representatives advised about specific cases; it can generate significant local interest such as a notorious case, or a family law matter involving a prominent family or individual in the community (Aikman, 2004).[27]

A key concern across all social media platforms involves the ethical obligations of judges, administrators, and court staff. Judicial canons, attorneys' standards of professional conduct, and the NACM ethical principles all have been developed and modified as social media experience has been gained and new situations arise. This is an important, evolving area that should be studied and shaped by court leaders. Each court needs to adopt its own ethical standards for managers and staff, starting with the criterion adopted by the NACM and canons of judicial ethics. Administrators should also share the code of conduct with the bench to ensure they do not inadvertently do something that might be deemed an ethical violation (American Bar Association [ABA], 2020, 2026; COSCA & NACM, 2007; NACM, 2024a).

Kiosks

Kiosks are now "old" technology – having been introduced into the courts in the 1980s – but a technology that still has some practical use. Kiosks are, essentially, standing computer workstations, normally placed in the lobby or another easily accessible space, that provide general information, maps, and information about the courthouse; locations where people can find where a specific case is being heard (hopefully with directions to that courtroom or a map); places where fines and fees can be paid without having to wait for service at a counter; and dedicated space where prospective jurors can sign-in for jury duty and complete electronic juror screening questionnaires. Kiosks can improve court customer service, reduce lines at the public counter(s), and can help people locate cases and courtrooms more easily. Kiosks can be costly, particularly as features are added, but less expensive than a staff position and in the long term they may prove to be both economical and efficient. In special circumstances such as the COVID-19 pandemic, they also facilitate social distancing within the courthouse or at a remote location through enhanced electronic access. We submit that these computer structures and an expanded array of kiosk services deserve a fresh look.

Video

The use of video cameras in and by courts has had a challenging history. For decades, as television viewership and news grew into the dominant entertainment and source of information, many in the legal system – both judges and attorneys alike – resisted. At first, as the general public and news outlets wanted to follow "notorious cases" from a crime's commission to sentencing in real time through their television screens, many courts denied or materially limited video access to in-court proceedings. Then, those restrictions eased, although the majority of states normally require the permission of the trial judge prior to videotaping or live-streaming hearings and trials. There is a new generation of judges and trial attorneys who grew up in the "age of television" and thus do not see video recordings and broadcasts of live courtroom activity as a great threat to the rule of law or due process. Consequently, today, many new courthouses often are designed with video cameras in all courtrooms so the media will have access to authorized digital or recorded video, including, in a growing number of jurisdictions, live broadcasts ("streaming"). Videos of courtroom proceedings have two other benefits: first, they materially provide civic education for students and the general public, and second, they can be a valuable long-term historical record.

For at least 40 years, civil attorneys have been videotaping depositions for possible future use. Some of those recordings make it into a pre-trial hearing and/or a trial. The equipment needed to use these videotapes (or digital records) is different from the video cameras installed in a courtroom, but this demand for the use of video evidence has been part of the greater acceptance of video as a useful and, at times, essential tool. Video cameras throughout public spaces and those used for security in buildings throughout the community help solve crimes. The resulting videos become evidence (oftentimes compelling) and the same can be said of bodycam video recordings from law enforcement agencies. This, too, has influenced the acceptance of video records in court proceedings. There also are computer-aided incident reconstructions in both criminal and civil cases. These developments have resulted in a central role for video in today's courtrooms.

As video and TV quality improvements occur, courts need to keep current with their supporting technologies. Almost without question, broadcast-quality courtroom cameras and HD monitors ensure the high quality of the pictures used during proceedings for judges, attorneys, litigants, jurors (if any), and members of the public who are present. Equally important, some cases will generate significant public interest that will be covered on local – possibly national – news outlets. Courts cannot determine months or years in advance to which courtroom(s) and which judge these cases will be assigned. Thus, they must be prepared to accommodate such cases in all courtrooms and plan to use high-quality video and broadcast capabilities to enhance transparency and public education about the work of the court. For many years, Florida has been one of the states open to commercial and other television stations televising – and/or video recording for later use – in-state court hearings and trials. Florida's televised trials not only are watched in real time, but they often become part of the numerous crime-solving reality shows on television (Reporters Committee for Freedom of the Press, 2024).

The first televised trial of which we are aware occurred in Kentucky. The state had decided to use video exclusively as the medium for recording trial court proceedings following a dispute with stenographic reporters over their compensation (Steelman & Conti, 1985). Since the court video system was already installed, when a locally notorious murder trial arose in a rural community, the court arranged with a local cable station to broadcast the trial in real time. One concern was that no one would watch, but the trial became the highest-rated daytime program in the area. Viewers were rewarded with a "Perry Mason moment" when the defendant, charged with killing a person with a knife, took the stand and bragged about his prowess, demonstrating how quickly he could open and use the knife.

Artificial Intelligence

As this book goes to publication, judicial branch leaders and legal professionals are demonstrating growing interest in the application of AI in court settings. Given the myriad governance issues associated with AI, extensive policy guidance is being developed at both the state and national levels. Many state supreme courts have established standing committees to study the use of AI, while national organizations are producing workgroup reports and white papers addressing its implications for courts and legal practice. Undoubtedly, this guidance will prove critically important as courts grapple with ethical considerations and evaluate the growing array of vendor-promoted AI products and services entering the market.

The COSCA (2024) includes definitions of AI key terms relevant to the study and practice of the technology in the courts. The publication also addresses ethical considerations applicable to the Model Code of Judicial Conduct (MCJC) for judges and the Model Rules of Professional Practice for attorneys (MRPP). Similarly, the American Association for the Advancement of Science (2022), National Association for Court Management (2024b), and the ABA (2025) provide extensive guidance on AI technology solutions in courts, an AI maturity model, cybersecurity, court staffing issues (including potential staff displacement), procurement, vendor management, transparency, data quality assurance, and bias prevention. The federal government is likewise providing guidance on open data standards in the AI context (Beland, 2024), as well as an "AI Bill of Rights for the American People" (General Services Administration, 2025; White House Office of Science and Technology Policy, 2023).

Whether AI will become a valuable tool that improves access to justice and customer service remains an open question. Evidence to date is mixed. AI has a wide range of potential applications in courts and the broader legal system. These applications can be grouped into organizational, predictive, and analytical functions. For organizational and productivity tasks, AI could support scheduling, data entry, document redaction, language translation, and real-time transcription. In predictive and analytical roles, AI could model recidivism risk, perform case discovery and analysis, and offer dynamic resource allocation. Courts might also benefit from AI in judicial decision support, such as drafting judicial orders, providing expert-system advice for alternative dispute resolution, or conducting bail risk assessments. Finally, AI could serve as a 24/7 cognitive agent, offering continuous assistance to court personnel while integrating impartial reasoning with a judge's professional knowledge and experience. Collectively, these applications suggest that AI has the potential to enhance efficiency, accuracy, and decision making in the judicial system, supporting both administrative and adjudicative processes (Billotte & Reinkensmeyer, 2017; Reinkensmeyer & Billotte, 2019). Notably, there is an important distinction between productivity-focused applications and those that involve "impartial reasoning," which could be coupled with a judge's expertise. The key question in the latter context is the extent to which judges will retain final decision-making authority in individual cases. We suspect that responses to this question are likely to receive increasing scrutiny as AI capabilities expand and public concern over the quality of justice grows.

AI has multiple components and potential court uses. Some examples of existing or possible AI tool use are as follows:

- Online legal research
- Automation of routine tasks, including extraction of data from court documents to:

    - Enter information into electronic filing or case management systems
    - Complete forms automatically
    - Take action based on extracted data, such as identifying documents as confidential or sealing them
    - Assign cases to management tracks based on case type and complexity

- Document assembly
- Online dispute resolution
- Document review, such as reviewing proposed orders in family law cases
- Producing verbatim records
- Voice recognition
- Chatbots for phone-based services

Carlson (2019), a former court administrator of two large urban courts in California, adopted a broad definition of the AI term and identifies three independent methods for building AI systems:

> AI is used here to refer to any analytic, mathematical, or statistical method used to develop a tool that assists users in navigating the judicial process, making legal decisions, or resolving legal disputes... including machine learning, deep learning, neural networks, reinforcement learning, supervised and unsupervised learning, expert-system, decision theory, data mining, data analytics, etc.
>
> Broadly speaking, there are three approaches to building computer-based decision-making tools. One approach, referred to as an expert-system, is to begin by articulating all of the rules and decision logic the tool is to use in making a recommendation. Another approach is for the analysis to "learn the rules" by observation, essentially pattern recognition, and generate a tool that produces a prediction based on the pattern of past practices "learned" from examples in the training dataset. A third approach is for the analysis to "learn" by experience, either from continuous analysis of information "fed" into the analysis or from generating numerous scenarios based on fundamental rules and identifying successful strategies for making predictions... It is unclear what rules could be used in a legal setting... but it could be possible for a tool to improve its predictions by continuously analyzing new data as it is used.

The AI tool development process is remarkable in some respects, but its processing of information in almost all instances is not "intelligence" per se. It mimics being intelligent. It also works very quickly – in many instances faster than humans can process information, particularly when analyzing large amounts of the same data and information from multiple sources. The other limitation of AI tools is that they are "artificial." By definition, AI is not human. It does not process information the way humans do. These are important caveats that administrators and leadership judges must bear in mind when considering the implementation of these technologies.

Some AI tools can continuously "learn," by which we mean continuously incorporating new information into their predictions. It is possible that AI tools that will be most useful to judges in support of their decision making will need to be continuously learning, but currently such tools are not the ones being touted for courts. Carlson's remark about the third approach suggests some pause regarding which tools would be most needed for legal and court applications to be fair, balanced, and perceived as such. This also may be the most expensive approach to developing and maintaining a useful AI tool. The history of technological advances suggests that assurances of speedy improvements, of the ability to eliminate or rapidly correct built-in biases in AI, and of significantly lower costs as more courts use the tools almost never are met on the timetable indicated by vendors. Further, if and when the promises are realized, they are usually first found in the private sector, because its resources are far greater than those of the public sector and courts will remain a small market that is not prioritized.[28]

Thus, every discussion of judicial use of AI tools that we have reviewed cautions that judges cannot use the AI tool's conclusion for any purpose other than advisory information, which is not to be followed without independent, human assessment or instituting a "human in the loop" (National Association for Court Management, 2024b). In short, AI tools may be useful aids, but users must be reasonably skeptical, starting with thorough analyses as follows:

- What problems and issues need to be addressed?
- What justice system goals will be served from an AI tool?
- Are there non-technological ways to address the issues?
- Specifically, how will the AI tool help?
- Will an AI tool help the court more than a non-technical approach or using a different technological response?
- Are those who will use the tool technologically competent to use the tool properly; if not, what training is needed, how long will training take, and at what cost?
- What data-based metrics will the court use to determine if the AI application is achieving its goals?
- What upgrades will be needed over time, how frequently, and at what projected cost?
- Are there any independent evaluations in any court(s) of the use of AI tools in the application needed in the court?
- Are there any independent evaluations in any comparable organization, particularly a public agency or department, of the use of AI in the application being considered by the court?
- Who will do an evaluation of the use of AI in the court and at what cost?

One of the primary debates about courts using AI centers around decisions about who should (or could) be released pre-trial without money bail. Some courts are already using AI-based tools for these decisions, as a growing number of states have new rules authorizing the use of AI for these purposes. AI also is used in some courts as an aid in sentencing decisions (Moore et al., 2023; Rodà, 2025).

The challenges of developing and using AI tools are evident in the debate over their role in deciding whether an accused person should be released pre-trial and under what conditions, if any, beyond appearing in court. Much of the difficulty stems from building these tools using existing practices and past decisions. Research by the Ford School of Public Policy at the University of Michigan (2023) indicates that historical practices – and the biases they contained – can carry over into AI systems, influencing outcomes. As a result, these practices can increase costs for governments and contribute to negative economic and social consequences for individuals held in custody.

The debate about bail and who should and should not be required to post money bail prior to trial has led to a broader recognition of two truths: justice is more likely when decisions are individualized by a judge, and tools developed to aid decisions, whether implemented by third parties, court staff, or a prosecutor's office, should not be the result of a rote application process. The tools used by the court must also be fully transparent. Several times in his AI analysis Carlson (2019) reinforces that both humans and AI-based tools are prone to errors, so it is important to consider what, if any, constitutes an acceptable error rate. Regardless of that threshold, users should avoid relying solely or mechanically on the tool's output. AI-based tools should serve as aids for decision support rather than as replacements for human decision making. Courts should ensure that the tool's output is only one factor among many for consideration, prompting users to account for relevant factors not captured by the system. In this way, AI can enhance human judgment and decision making, rather than being a substitute for it.

It is important to emphasize here that there is a potential to use AI in ways other than to assist judges to make decisions. It is an old lesson, but the early development of case management information systems for courts should foreshadow that close supervision of and control of AI tools development by the courts is needed for the final product to meet operational needs. As Carlson (2019) also notes, there are constitutional requirements and legal mandates on courts – even ethical standards for judges and staff that are unique in society – that do not apply in the private sector or other units of government. Courts overlook these factors at their peril, whether the technology is case management information software, social media, video appearances and translators, or AI.

Final Thoughts

Today, technology is deeply embedded in court operations and the delivery of public-facing court services. That is a good thing. It is difficult to imagine how courts could operate moving forward without current technologies – principally hardware (computers and smartphones) and software (case management information systems, workflow support, jury management software, e-filing, and social media).

Court leaders need to make decisions about which technologies they will deploy, sometimes without answers to all of the questions which must be considered. Courts with a comprehensive strategic agenda are well positioned to make such decisions, leveraging current and emerging technologies in furtherance of long-term judicial branch planning. That said, managing in uncertain circumstances is par for all judicial branch leaders – judges and court administrators alike. Of course, this does not absolve senior leaders from careful research, clearly understanding how, if at all, technology will help address a court function, and articulating how the court will know if the desired outcomes have been achieved. An evaluation protocol must then be designed and implemented, continually evaluating system performance. Periodic assessment must continue through the long term, as court leaders can become complacent and technologies become dated. With appropriate safeguards, technology will not only have a larger role in court administration over time, but it will require monitoring, evaluation, and updating. Collectively, these measures will help courts to achieve their goals, mission, and vision.

Notes

1 The real-time transcripts are referred to as "drafts" because they normally contain some typos, some missed words, and/or incorrect names or words that the reporter (or judge or lawyers) can identify when the draft is reviewed before final production.

2 These case types are of "lesser significance" only in the abstract. To the individuals involved, they are of great significance.

3 The debate regarding the use of recording devices and whether they are "comparable" to live reporters was a significant issue through the 1970s and has continued, although to a lesser degree. The use of video to take the record was made a part of the debate in the late 1970s and 1980s. The use of video appearances is not without controversy today, either, particularly when it is proposed that witnesses or parties could/should appear via video from a remote location. Video arraignments of defendants in jail are used in many, if not most, courts now, but opposition remains.

4 Because of fiscal constraints at the state level and, in some states, local politics, the first system developed often was only for the state's limited jurisdiction courts (or the general jurisdiction courts). Software for the court level not covered by the first system sometimes followed several years later, but not in every instance.

5 One exception to a self-developed software package is the one developed by and through the U.S. Administrative Office of the Courts for district courts. This package is akin to a state-level system in a larger state, of which there are several (e.g., New Jersey, New York, Utah, and Arizona).

6 The elements of reports that enable good case management are identified in several reports and available through the National Center for State Courts.

7 Today, local programmers also can attend the biannual Court Technology Conference sponsored by the NCSC and other national organizations. Further, a local court can connect with one or more courts elsewhere in the state or nearby that already have privately developed software systems.

8 In the 1960s the federal government created the Law Enforcement Assistance Administration to provide states' criminal justice systems with grant funds to improve operations and undertake criminal justice research. Courts were included in the legislation creating the LEAA as potential recipients. Even so, courts across the nation received a very small percentage of the funds. From the outset, courts argued that even though the LEAA was established to help with issues of criminal justice, courts could not divide judges and staff so neatly. The fight eventually was won, but it took many years. This is but one example of how the interdependencies in courts – particularly smaller courts – are not fully understood by the two other branches.

9 Sometimes, certain kinds of data entry mistakes (e.g., dates, activity codes, and even typos) can be caught by software. Administrators must evaluate the cost and time required to provide automatic corrections and then balance between changing programming and providing staff training.

10 This data should be used to identify best practices and training needs.

11 This advice applies primarily to large projects. The planning and implementation committees for smaller projects, such as the "take a number" system mentioned above, should be smaller and staffed for the more limited scope of the project.

12 The potential of technology, by itself, to improve case processing and timeliness is limited because so many factors beyond technology impact how cases are managed.

13 This item is based on advice originally developed regarding courts' interest in a new case management approach to address delay. A major revision of how cases are scheduled and managed should not be implemented if the problem is staff shortages and an inability to update files on time.

14 For example, a goal that the technology will "reduce time spent" or "improve customer service" is not sufficient. How much time is expected to be saved by each person and in total? How will the court know if customer service is improved?

15 This point needs to be made in the initial justification and annually thereafter.

16 Exhibits are not included in this discussion.

17 Some courts, concerned about the implications of files being "lost," referred to them as "unable to locate" files.

18 A related but separate issue were files that were not provided to the judge holding a hearing when they were needed. Normally, this failure was because staff, either the court's or that of an independent clerk of court, had not finished processing one or more new documents so they kept the incomplete file rather than send it on to a courtroom. In the extreme, we are aware of a few courts in which attorneys came to leave two copies of documents, one for official filing with the clerk of court and one with a staff person dealing directly with the assigned judge.

19 The cost of storing paper records went beyond, or should have gone beyond, the rental cost of the floor space needed and, maybe, shelving. Often discounted or recognized but downplayed or ignored is the need for climate control, water protection, and fire protection in the storage facility to protect paper over time.

20 Present day and previously documented records pose a key challenge to the argument that needed technology will become available "soon" or, at least, before there is a critical problem: What happens to them in the meantime and, when the new solution becomes available, if that software (and hardware) is not programmed to address historical data? We have not yet seen an answer to that question in any report on this issue.

21 There are risks of both degradation and inaccessibility in digital records stored for less than ten years, but these are minimal and normally associated with fire, floods, excessive heat where the storage media are kept, or other major incidents affecting courts that do a poor job of backing up files and storing the backups in one or two places that are unlikely to be affected by one of these disasters at the courthouse.

22 One of the authors consulted in a small, rural court in which the court administrator had offered case records in very old cases to the local museum. The museum turned down the offer. The administrator felt some of the records might have historical value, so continued to hold on to them.

23 The same reasoning applies to important administrative records and decisions, which may be as important for historical purposes as judicial opinions and case records.

24 Contact information on court websites may be limited similarly.

25 Anyone who has seen real-time transcriptions on their television screen understands that the translation misses some words and names. Among other reasons, a mistake can be the result of a finger displacement by the reporter, a novel word that is not captured in the computer's dictionary, or the computer not understanding the strokes of the shorthand. We also note that all tests to certify court reporters allow for a small percentage of mistakes and still pass.

26 Reminders to summoned jurors about their upcoming service date and/or of changes in a trial schedule have become popular in many courts as a needed "nudge." Some research suggests, however, that these nudges may not be as effective as some have argued.

27 A "notorious" case is one that generates state and, occasionally, national interest and thus results in considerable television, radio, and print media coverage with scores of journalists and, sometimes, cameras and "broadcast tents" set up around (or very near) the courthouse.

28 One notable exception here is the large investment in advanced technologies, including AI, on the part of the military and national level intelligence and security services. Lessons learned from some of the justice-related applications may ultimately be leveraged here for "use cases" in the judicial system.

References

Aikman, A. B. (2004). From chaotic to copasetic: Lessons in media relations for courts from People v. Scott Peterson. *Court Manager, 19*(4), 6–11.

American Association for the Advancement of Science. (2022). *Artificial intelligence and courts.*

American Bar Association. (2020). *Model Code of Judicial Conduct* (2020 ed.).

American Bar Association. (2025). *Task force on AI and the courts.*

American Bar Association. (2026). *Model rules of professional conduct.* www.americanbar.org/groups/professional_responsibility/publications/model_rules_of_professional_conduct/.

Barton, B. H., & Bibas, S. (2017). *Rebooting justice: More technology, fewer lawyers and the future of law.* Encounter Books.

Beland, F. (2024, March 21). *Building trust in AI with open standards.* OASIS Open. www.oasis-open.org/2024/03/21/building-trust-in-ai-with-open-standards/.

Billotte, R., & Reinkensmeyer, M. W. (2017). Artificial intelligence (AI) coming to a court near you. *Court Manager, 32*(2), 6–10.

Carlson, A. (2019, November 11). *Using artificial intelligence and big data to develop tools used in courts* (Version 5). CourtLeader.net. https://courtleader.net/wp-content/uploads/2020/08/carlson-using-ai-big-data-to-develop-tools-used-in-courts-v5-2019nov11-36pp-saved-8-28-20.pdf.

Conference of State Court Administrators. (2024, August). *Generative AI and the future of the courts: Responsibilities and possibilities.* National Center for State Courts.

Conference of State Court Administrators & National Association for Court Management. (2007). *Resolution in support of the NACM Model Code of Conduct.* National Center for State Courts.

Ford School of Public Policy, University of Michigan. (2023). *Pretrial risk assessment tools found to be subjective and biased.* https://fordschool.umich.edu/news/2023/pretrial-risk-assessment-tools-found-be-subjective-and-biased.

Gaus, A. (2018, August 31). High hopes for artificial intelligence don't always match reality. *TheStreet.* www.thestreet.com/technology/ai-boom-or-bust-expectations-don-t-match-reality-14699427.

General Services Administration. (2025). *Artificial intelligence guidance and resources.* www.gsa.gov/technology/government-it-initiatives/artificial-intelligence/ai-guidance-and-resources.

Greacen, J. M. (2018). *Eighteen ways courts should use technology to better serve their customers.* Institute for the Advancement of the American Legal System. https://iaals.du.edu/sites/default/files/documents/publications/eighteen_ways_courts_should_use_technology.pdf.

Institute for the Advancement of the American Legal System. (2025). *JPE 2.0; Recommendations for modernizing judicial performance evaluation.*

Jaafari, J. D., & Lewis, N. (2019, February 14). In court, where are Siri and Alexa? *The Marshall Project.* www.themarshallproject.org/2019/02/14/in-court-where-are-siri-and-alexa.

Joint Technology Committee. (2014). *Developing an electronic records preservation and disposition plan* (Version 1). National Center for State Courts.

Joint Technology Committee. (2017, November). *JTC resource bulletin: Introduction to the next generation court technology standards – Application Component Model.* Conference of State Court Administrators; National Association for Court Management; National Center for State Courts.

Lewis, D. (2016, February 18). These glass discs can store data for billions of years. *Smithsonian Magazine*. www.smithsonianmag.com/smart-news/these-glass-discs-can-store-data-billions-years-180958163/.

Moore, C., Ferguson, E., & Guerin, P. (2023, August). *Pretrial risk assessment on the ground: Algorithms, judgments, meaning, and policy*. MIT Case Studies in Social and Ethical Responsibilities of Computing. https://doi.org/10.21428/2c646de5.b016a7b3.

National Association for Court Management (NACM). (2024a). *Model code of conduct for court professionals*. https://nacmnet.org/resources/education/ethics/.

National Association for Court Management (NACM). (2024b). *Courting AI: Understanding artificial intelligence in courts guide*.

National Center for State Courts. (2005). *CourTools: Trial court measures*. www.ncsc.org/our-centers-projects/courtools.

Piper, K. (2020, February 26). Why we can't always be "nudged" into changing our behavior. *Vox (Future Perfect)*. www.vox.com/future-perfect/2020/2/26/21154466/research-education-behavior-psychology-nudging.

Raaen, N. (2017). Open and transparent judicial records in the digital age: Applying principles and performance measures. In C. E. Jimenez-Gomez & M. Gasco-Hernandez (Eds.), *Achieving open justice through citizen participation and transparency*. IGI Global.

Reinkensmeyer, M. W., & Billotte, R. (2019). Artificial intelligence (AI): Early court project implementations and emerging issues. *Court Manager, 34*(3), 20–25.

Reinkensmeyer, M. W., & Doktor, J. (2001). The promise of court technology: Reality or fiction? In *The improvement of the administration of justice*. American Bar Association.

Reporters Committee for Freedom of the Press. (2024). *Open courts compendium: Florida – Cameras and other technology in the courtroom*. www.rcfp.org/open-courts-compendium/florida/.

Rodà, A. (2025). The COMPAS case: An educational journey for explaining fairness in AI-based applications. In R. Calegari, C. Castillo, S. Papadopoulos, & R. A. Søraa (Eds.), *Proceedings of the 2nd workshop on AI bias: Measurements, mitigation, explanation strategies* (Vol. 3961, pp. 1–9). CEUR Workshop Proceedings. https://ceur-ws.org/Vol-3961/paper4.pdf.

Steelman, D. C., & Conti, S. D. (1985). *Evaluation of Kentucky's innovative approach to making a videotape record of trial court proceedings* (NCJ 108026). National Criminal Justice Reference Service, U.S. Department of Justice. www.ncjrs.gov/App/Publications/abstract.aspx?ID=108026.

Suskin, R. S. (2019). *Online courts and the future of justice.* Oxford University Press.

U.S. Department of Justice Civil Rights Division. (2020, February 28). *ADA requirements: Effective communication.* www.ada.gov/resources/effective-communication/.

White House Office of Science and Technology Policy. (2023). *Blueprint for an AI Bill of Rights: Making automated systems work for the American people.* Executive Office of the President.

10 Court Community Engagement

The perceived worth of a judicial system exists in three forms of capital – human capital, structural capital, and social capital. Human capital is comprised of the people, including judges, administrators, and staff who the court hires, trains, and promotes to lead and manage the organization. Structural capital is the infrastructure and operational processes and procedures judges, administrators, and staff utilize to conduct the court's business and administer the workflow. Social capital is the trust and confidence judges, administrators, and staff convey to internal and external stakeholders regarding the court's value to the constitutional republic. Because the relative worth of the court exists first and foremost in the minds of the people, community engagement must be a requisite part of the human, structural, and social capital of the judicial branch. Having said that, we recognize that "value" in this context is subjective, shaped by impressions the court makes in its regular dealings with the public. However true and impactful that subjectivity, it still does not negate this most salient point: to sustain and enhance the court's import in a democratic society necessitates the recruitment, hiring, and development of people who aspire to make a difference in the lives of others and are aligned with working to achieve the purposes and responsibilities of the court. These individuals will *engage* with people and in processes in a way that reflects their public service commitment. Establishing a supportive, enthusiastic, and passionate network of people is one of the most critical aspects of the organization because they will be relied upon as the "face" and "engine" of the courts to fulfill its mission and vision.

Value is difficult to define vis-à-vis the delivery of "justice" or the "end product" of the courts. Consequently, there is an inherent need to operationalize what stakeholders consider to be a court-produced value – exclusive of the theoretical underpinnings and benefits of justice and empirical evidence that perhaps demonstrate

DOI: 10.4324/9781003686804-10

those judicial branch ends. Our contention is that by regularly and consistently assessing the value of the court, the judiciary can more fully leverage the benefits of programs and initiatives that are created to engage with the community. In order to do this, however, the court must be equipped with appropriate business systems and supporting technologies, guided by the kind of leaders who recognize and follow through on distilling value from the daily work of the court. Value in this context is determined by *impact*, rather than stopping short at outcome or even less desirably, by output. Courts need to innovate for the purpose of enhancing their public service value; and court leaders can only know (or at least deduce with some degree of confidence) that advancements are being made when they *actively* engage with the community.

Some private sector organizations hire Chief Value Officers (CVO) for the purpose of protecting their respective brands, while also seeking new opportunities to enhance the marketing of their products and services. These companies recognize the enormous benefit of having the right CVO as a part of their executive team, ensuring that existing and prospective customers understand the value of the organization's products and services (Barreira, 2025). Value, however, can be ambiguous, depending on how it is defined and assessed. And the value proposition of the court – the administration and delivery of justice – is oftentimes misunderstood by its "market."

Many administrators believe that an important part of their role is to manage the value of the court. While that is true in the aggregate, the specific tasks associated with creating, evaluating, and acquiring value should be assigned to designated persons who have the expertise and can focus their time for these purposes rather than attempting to multi-task these concerns along other pressing needs. For larger courts, having an office dedicated to community engagement is advisable so that information about the nature and importance of its work can be appropriately scaled. Additionally, given the complexity and pace of change in modern society, such an office becomes doubly important to communicate with policymakers, adapt to emerging trends, and respond to exogenous needs. By continuously creating, assessing, and capturing institutional value, the court can better position itself to address disruptions in the institution's milieu. This way, court structures, processes, and leadership approaches can be enhanced. Failing to reinvent itself in response to these shifts in the landscape results in diminishing worth. For the modern court, institutional value should not be viewed as a static quality, but rather as a dynamic quality that vacillates with public perception. Because the court administrator's office is responsible for gauging and responding to impressions about the contemporary value of the court and linking it to community needs, these functions are not ancillary. To the contrary, they are mission critical to the judiciary (National Association for Court Management [NACM], 2023).

Community engagement requires collaboration among internal stakeholders, as well as criminal and civil justice partners, so that the purposes, obligations, tasks, and communication outlets of all affected organizations can be coordinated to improve community relations for the justice system as a whole. Collaborating with partners, even if their organizational missions and objectives are mutually exclusive, can enhance partnerships. Coordinated efforts allow organizations to gain a deeper understanding of each other's perspectives, roles, and capabilities. Bringing court partners together allows for more comprehensive feedback, by pinpointing the most pressing problems within that particular jurisdiction. It also helps to promote a shared vision when agency heads work collectively to resolve justice "system" problems requiring the wider network of decision-makers.

For instance, when courts collaborate with criminal justice partners, they work together to determine the efficacy of current approaches and policy on the resolution of cases and sanctioning of defendants so that the costs and benefits of alternatives are clearly understood across the spectrum of the system. An assessment conducted from these varying vantage points can sometimes identify other means of accountability for those who are charged with lower-scale, non-violent offenses, and violations such as the non-payment of fines and fees or possession-only cases involving small quantities of certain types of drugs. This type of collaborative approach better positions the court and its stakeholders to consider other viable diversion programs so that the limited pool of system resources is reserved for those offenders who pose the greatest risk to the community. This also means that a court engaged with its community is highly knowledgeable about the agencies, programs, and methodologies that provide service to a wide range of people who find themselves implicated in the justice system, including victims and witnesses. In this context, the court is a resource and a conduit to those services that specialize in counseling, supporting, and advocating for people who do not otherwise have the ability or access to navigate community-based recovery.

Historically, images of courthouses and courtrooms elicit deep, broad emotions among members of the general public. We submit that this remains true because the court continues to represent the citadel of democracy, or in practical terms, it is the physical place where due process in our republic is meted out. Notwithstanding the central role courts play in society, for many, the third branch is cloaked in mystery (silent as it is often described) and steeped in tradition. Incidentally, this brings to bear both reverence and confusion regarding the roles and functions of the court. For instance, although judicial decisions can have significant policy implications that reverberate across various systems and society as a whole, most constituents have little to no direct interaction with the judiciary. When constituents find themselves in the court (most often because of a juror summons or a traffic ticket), they generally encounter a subdued room of people awaiting the judge – a person who is announced as they approach the bench while all present are directed to stand. Clad in a black robe, the judge presides from an elevated bench, flanked by court staff and sheriff's officers. The judge holds a gavel, using it to call the proceedings to order. Adversaries stand before the court, addressing this black-robed figure as "Your Honor."[1] Although attorneys argue their respective positions in the case in English, their assertions are frequently interspersed with Latin-based nomenclature that most laypeople do not understand and are left guessing about until someone can explain it to them.

The traditional court process is formal and arcane for most members of the public. The fact that the community is generally unfamiliar with the purposes of the courts and how court functions are operationalized makes it in and of itself a pivotal issue – one that court leaders should bring to bear when developing policies and procedures. Indeed, it is a critical part of what presiding judges and court administrators must do, given the profound implications that the public's view of life, liberty, and property rights has on the tenets of democracy. The general public's limited understanding about the role of the courts compels administrators (whether they realize it or not) to serve as key representatives of the third branch, as well as the government more generally. This timeless responsibility is interwoven in the Trial Court Performance Standards (TCPS) and, importantly, demonstrates that public trust and confidence are inextricably linked (be it positive or negative) to the third branch. More specifically, the TCPS recognize the profound impact stakeholder perceptions have on whether the court can achieve and carry out its purposes and responsibilities. These standards emphasize, inter alia, that public perceptions significantly affect a court's ability to fulfill its mission. Compliance with the law relies partly on public respect, ideally derived from direct citizen experience. While justice should be both done and seen to be done, public perceptions do not always reflect actual court performance. Trial courts serve multiple constituencies whose trust is essential: the general public, community opinion leaders (e.g., media, government officials), court participants (attorneys, litigants, jurors, witnesses), and judicial personnel or lawyers with inside knowledge of court operations (National Center for State Courts [NCSC], 1997).

In his seminal address, *The Causes of Popular Dissatisfaction with the Administration of Justice*, Pound (1906) submitted that courts should be regarded as "swift and certain agents of justice." Accordingly, their purpose is to administer justice such that it represents the "end of law" and an "ideal compromise between the activities of each and the activities of all in a crowded world." The court must seek to "harmonize these activities and to adjust the relations of every man with his fellows so as to accord with the moral sense of the community." A key difficulty, however, that frustrates administrative efforts in addressing the public's dissatisfaction is that it "may be minimized, but not obviated." For the court administrator, then, Pound's thesis brings to the forefront two important points with respect to the community engagement fundamental. The first involves the administrator's obligation to cultivate and preserve the court institution's relationship with the public in which it exists to serve. Second, this duty must be undertaken notwithstanding the fact that the public's general satisfaction with courts will, arguably, never be fully realized. For the administrator, measures of "success" in this realm of public service must be carefully considered and defined. As a part of this exercise, the administrator must take into account realities and what the court *should* do, given available alternatives to "harmonize" the role of the judicial branch in a "crowded world." To the extent this can be accomplished, there exists a "public satisfaction threshold" that will almost always temper it. This "reality" must also be considered by the administrator in partnership with the presiding judge so that the institutional goals that are set are *actually* attainable. Court leaders can assuage the "threshold effects" if they are adept at "marketing" the court (nota bene: engaging the community that includes the media) about the essential role and functions that make the court distinct from other government branches in serving universal interests. Standard 4.4 of the TCPS highlights "Public Education" and requires that the court directly inform the community about its administrative operation and related court programs (NCSC, 1997):

> Most public citizens do not have direct contact with the courts. Information about the courts is filtered through sources such as the media, lawyers, litigants, jurors, political officeholders, and employees of other components of the justice system. Public opinion polls indicate that the public knows very little about the courts, and what is known is often at odds with reality. Standard 4.4 requires trial courts to inform and educate the public. Effective informational brochures and annual reports help the public understand and appreciate the administration of justice. Participation by court personnel in public affairs commissions also is effective. Moreover, courts can effectively educate and inform the public by including able public representatives on advisory committees, study groups, and boards.

Similarly, the NACM (2004) *Core Competency Curriculum Guidelines* note that court leaders are urged to "educate, inform, and teach the public about the courts, but to also be educated, informed, and taught by the community."

The idea of court administration taking on the responsibility of educating an uninformed or underinformed public is perhaps more relevant today than ever. While the traditional "three Rs"[2] of reading, writing, and arithmetic remain essential (Noah Webster Educational Foundation, 2021), it may be that history is not emphasized in some school curricula. Consider a recent survey conducted by the American Council of Trustees and Alumni (2024), which assessed the knowledge of 3,026 undergraduate students on American history and government. The results revealed significant gaps in foundational civic knowledge. For instance, only 31 percent identified James Madison as the Father of the Constitution, and less than 40 percent knew key facts about current government leaders, including the name of John Roberts as Chief Justice of the Supreme Court (37 percent). Many respondents also lacked understanding of governmental structures and powers: 60 percent could not correctly identify congressional term lengths, fewer than one-third knew that the legislative branch could declare war (32 percent), and only 32 percent understood that impeachment trials occur in the Senate. Knowledge of historical documents and amendments was also limited, with only 23 percent recognizing the Gettysburg Address quote about government by the people, and 28 percent knowing that the 13th Amendment abolished slavery. The First Amendment of the Constitution, which protects several freedoms including religion, speech, press, petition, and assembly, is central to the nation's fundamental liberties. Yet, a survey on civic literacy conducted by the American Bar Association (ABA, 2023) found that some respondents demonstrated confusion regarding their First Amendment rights. For example, nearly one in five participants incorrectly believed that freedom of speech applies only to U.S. citizens, and 38 percent thought the First Amendment provides unrestricted protection to express any opinion. Sixty percent correctly recognized that the amendment allows speech with certain limitations. Perhaps most notably, respondents were also skeptical about the general public's understanding of government functions: more than half (53 percent) reported that people are not very informed, 17 percent stated that the public is not informed at all, 20 percent indicated that the public is somewhat informed, and only 3 percent considered the public to be very informed. In light of these survey findings and other similar studies, a court administrator's obligation to educate the community and to be educated by that same public cannot be overstated.

Court Communication Fundamentals

Pound's (1906) address speaks to the challenges that have long faced the courts, and the struggle court leaders continue to have in their service to the public. A former President of the Association of American Law Schools and recipient of the Golden Medal of the ABA, Pound single handedly identified most of the administrative challenges that court management addressed in the 20th century – the very same issues that courts continue to confront through the first quarter of this new century. His assertion that dissatisfaction with the courts is not a novel problem, but rather a sentiment that has always been widely held (popular), is, in part, due to the constituency's guarded opinions of legal systems – not unlike the outlook about government in general. Much of the public's dissatisfaction stems from the court institution itself; that is, the administrative structure and jurisdiction of the court, how it organizes its work, and the obscure process by which it administers justice.

Since Pound's speech, courts increasingly have been compelled to be more things to more people. Arguably, the expanded role of courts also involves being the community's moral compass as it pertains to the broad range of public policy issues at the center of criminal, civil, family, and probation dockets. These widening responsibilities, however, have not received proportionate funding or enhanced the status of courts. When the court fails to meet public expectations due to limited resources or a perceived lack of institutional value, the disdain for the judicial branch persists, regardless of the court's limited budgetary or authoritative control over such matters.

The "separate, co-equal" relationship that the courts have with the legislative and executive branches presents unique challenges, requiring court leadership to take creative approaches in intergovernmental relations. Alexander Hamilton (1788/2003) addresses this relationship in *Federalist 78*:

> Whoever attentively considers the different departments of power must perceive, that, in a government in which they are separated from each other, the judiciary, from the nature of its functions, will always be the least dangerous to the political rights of the Constitution; because it will be least in a capacity to annoy or injure them. The Executive not only dispenses the honors, but also holds the sword of the community. The legislature not only commands the purse, but also prescribes the rules by which the duties and rights of every citizen are to be regulated. The judiciary, on the contrary, has no influence over either the sword or the purse; no direction either of the strength or of the wealth of the society; and can take no active resolution whatever. It may truly be said to have neither force nor will, but merely judgment; and must ultimately depend upon the aid of the executive arm even for the efficacy of its judgments.

There is an inherent tension, integral as it may be, in the third branch between judicial independence and its accountability and accessibility. The nation's framers purposefully designed the judiciary to be the *least* political of the three branches of government; but this is not to suggest that the court is absent from politics. Of course, politics exist in courts (as they do in every realm of work life), except that they are to prevail with a lowercase "p." Consider, for instance, that federal judges are appointed for life, and more than half of the state courts have some form of a judicial merit appointment system. These systems are designed so that judges are insulated from the volatility of public opinion and the influences of special interests and popular sentiment. But, therein lies a "catch-22" when it comes to the concept that judges are apolitical when appointed to the bench. When discussing the role of politics in judicial selection, a presiding judge remarked to one of the authors:

> There is no such thing as an apolitical judge in our system. We can more easily feign our impartiality toward politics by being appointed instead of being elected, but anyone who understands the appointment process knows better. An attorney must be immersed in politics of one party or the other to even be considered by those elected in the executive and legislative branch on who gets appointed. There's no way around it. If you're not involved politically whether it be by affiliation or campaign support, you're simply not going to be in the position to even be considered. Once they're appointed, this doesn't make them illegitimate or unqualified judges of course, but to say that politics doesn't play a part in the process, and a major one at that, is untrue.

In states with elected judgeships, a variety of measures are taken to restrict judges' campaigning efforts to isolate prospective jurists from partisan political persuasions, and at the very minimum to convey an appearance of impartiality. Other measures in elected judge systems to guard against real or perceived impropriety include expanding of position qualifying requirements, extending the terms of service, reforming campaign finance rules, judicial performance review, and instituting periodic judicial retention elections. Indeed, there is a delicate balance that must be struck because albeit judges are not supposed to be political, they cannot completely disregard the interests of the public. Notwithstanding its ongoing efforts, the third branch – irrespective of the system with which judges are appointed or elected – continues to struggle with the public's understanding of the judiciary.

Public perceptions of the judicial branch are consequential to both individual constituents, as well as the court system as a whole, because they may detract from the perceived integrity of the judge's occupational status and more importantly the pivotal role they serve in a constitutional republic. We argue that however false or inaccurate those impressions might be, it remains obligatory on the part of the court administrator to consistently engage the community. Among other objectives, these coordinated efforts should demonstrate that regardless of the system that placed judges in their positions of power, they are sworn to conduct court proceedings, follow established laws to instruct juries and sentence convicted defendants, and rule on the admission of evidence and the constitutionality of various laws and legal precedents.

When laws unexpectedly yield outcomes or fail to achieve the intended objectives of the policy, courts face the same scrutiny as the executive and legislative branches because their interpretations determine how statutory language functions in real-world settings. Unexpected rulings can expose gaps between legislative intent and legal application. Inevitably, this prompts public debate, calls for reform, and in some instances, legislative amendments. The judiciary, as a result, becomes a focal point for evaluating not only legal reasoning but also the effectiveness and fairness of the policy itself. Public attention and criticism directed at the courts tend to focus less on their function of interpreting the law within defined constitutional divisions and more on the broader perception that they are part and parcel of an inefficient and ineffective "government." Consequently, public dissatisfaction with the courts is often fueled by a lack of understanding about the specific workings and limitations of the courts. These impressions have been exacerbated with the burgeoning of social media and the 24-hour cable news outlets, which promulgate the most outlandish of stories as a means of medium survival. At best, the judiciary is portrayed as sharing in the broader failings of a corrupt and incompetent government. At worst, criticism is aimed directly at the courts, seizing on isolated anomalies as a basis for attack and a means of attracting greater viewership. However inaccurate or exaggerated these accounts may be, they do not (and should not) diminish the courts' duties to engage with the public and communicate their purposes and responsibilities. In her 2009 Earl F. Nelson lecture to the University of Missouri School of Law, the former U.S. Supreme Court Justice, Sandra Day O'Connor (2009) referred to the judiciary's power as the "power of the quill," remarking that the judiciary's "power lies in the force of reason and the willingness of others to listen to those reasons."

The free exchange of ideas that are associated with self-government, individual freedom, equality, and universal education are matters that occasionally result in public dissatisfaction. We submit, however, that the benefits derived from democratic institutions clearly offset the discontent that is sometimes manifested. The judiciary's labor should approach its organization, processes, and procedures in recognition of this reality. In short, we suggest that the public's sense of discontent is not "personal," but rather is associated with the court as an institution. Leadership judges and court administrators should comport themselves accordingly, while ensuring that the court remains accessible and attentive to those concerns. Pound's (1906) remark that the "administration of justice is not decadent, it is simply behind the times" continues to reverberate today, when operations of the courts (and the public sector in general) are compared to the efficiency by which private enterprise conducts its daily business.

An awareness and understanding of modern technologies should be leveraged by court leaders as an important basis in lobbying for the necessary resources to incorporate advanced methods of managing business processes and service delivery systems. Among other considerations, as discussed along each of the parameters of the court administration framework, this requires leadership judges and court administrators to facilitate change by establishing a vision and long-term strategy, developing and sustaining justice system relationships and partnerships, recruiting, managing, and promoting the best and brightest who comprise the court's human capital, and by fostering a productive work environment. Along a similar vein and of comparative import, "community engagement" as we have come to define it, addresses those principles and practices to ensure that the court's communication channels are open and effective. We delineate the fundamentals of the court's engagement with the community along five points of reference, including information stewardship, community outreach, internal communication, stakeholder feedback, and media relations, in addressing the public's view of the American judiciary and the role of court administrators in shaping public perceptions.

Information Stewardship

Generally, individuals do not express hope and confidence in matters that they do not understand. In some instances, that lack of understanding can transmute into distrust and even fear. When it comes to the community's misapprehension of the third branch, whose responsibility is it to help them understand the workings of the judiciary? Our contention is that the onus is vested squarely with the court's administrative leadership. This is not simply an ordinary routine task, but it is rather a core fundamental of the court administration profession. In accordance with Maslow's (1943) hierarchy of needs model, when court managers are "self-actualized," they do not see their work in the courts merely as a job, but rather as a vocation; or more precisely, as a vital contribution toward achieving justice in a rule-of-law society. In the spirit of that undertaking, effective court leaders welcome the expectation to know and use positive messaging, credibility, honesty, accessibility, openness, and understandability in the course of accomplishing this key core fundamental. The public expects administrators to be conversant in the field, and proficient in communicating the ideals and objectives of the court. Consequently, court leaders must possess the ability, willingness, and capacity to serve as steadfast advocates for their court organization. This involves reaching out to the public to ensure that the institutional objectives are accurately and consistently presented in the manner intended. Community engagement promotes understanding, a spirit of cooperation, and problem-solving that is invaluable in making the court effective and, more importantly, credible in its action.

Positive Message

Court administrators are obliged to *proactively* develop positive messages about the court institution that are grounded upon court performance standards. When the message is communicated in this context, negative feelings that court users have about their case are less likely to be projected onto the court. If for no other reason, when guided and reinforced by accountability measures, positive messaging helps to mitigate instances when the court, rather than the issues of the case, becomes the object of the public frustration. For example, a disgruntled member of the public who is unhappy with a delay or the outcome of their case might come away with a better perspective of the court when they are treated with courtesy and respect. We can be assured that if they are not afforded the dignity expected of public sector professionals, their perception of the judiciary will be negative, irrespective of what transpired in the courtroom. Leaders, therefore, who train court staff to take the time to listen and explain the purpose of court processes improve the likelihood that the court is viewed more favorably, notwithstanding the case outcome. Staff designated for these positions should be trained on the principles of procedural fairness, customer service, and emotional intelligence, using court policy guidelines to ensure consistent messaging.

Institutionalizing positive messaging includes daily one-on-one customer service interactions, as well as incorporating the court's overall performance data on case management. Using the NCSC (2005) CourTools performance metrics, case management data and findings from the Public Access and Fairness Survey can be shared with the public, stakeholder groups, and funding bodies.

This kind of messaging emphasizes the court's role in protecting individual rights and liberties that are vulnerable to political influence or constraint. And this necessarily requires that the courts educate or otherwise inform the public through a variety of communication mediums about the threat posed to a society when an independent judiciary is undermined. Table 10.1 outlines examples collected from a sample of courts that developed positive messages pertaining to the relevant performance standards.[3] Although more than one performance standard may apply to a particular program, activity, or feature of the court, operationalizing these efforts demonstrates the organization's commitment and fulfillment of those benchmarks.

Table 10.1 Positive Messaging Examples Linked to Performance Standards

Performance Standard	***Specific Ways Your Court Meets This Standard***	***Positive Message***
Accessibility: Safety, Accessibility, and Convenience	Customer service kiosk that is available on expanded hours for paying fines and conducting other court business	The Hudson District Courthouse has a business center with convenient hours to make the court accessible and convenient for the public.
Accessibility: Effective Participation	Community roundtables	The Seton Municipal Court conducts bi-annual roundtable discussions to address ongoing concerns.

(*Continued*)

Table 10.1 (Continued)

Performance Standard	***Specific Ways Your Court Meets This Standard***	***Positive Message***
Accessibility: Courtesy, Responsiveness, and Respect	Customer service training	All deputy clerks at Tuers County Court are certified customer service specialists.
Expeditious: Case Processing	Reduced backlogs	The Academy City Court reduced case processing time by 15 percent in 2025.
Judicial Process Equality, Fairness and Integrity: Juries	Jury service video	The Pleasant County Court presents the video as part of its commitment to ensure a fair and reliable judicial system by supporting well-trained and informed jurors.
Equality, Fairness and Integrity: Clarity	Decision summaries	The District Court of Potenza helps the public understand the implications of cases on its docket by summarizing major merit decisions with opinions and making these decisions conveniently accessible on its website.
Equality, Fairness and Integrity: Production and Preservation of Records	Records retention schedule	The Springlake District Court adopted an improved records retention policy to maintain the integrity of these important documents.
Independence and Accountability: Personnel Practices and Decisions	Adoption of personnel policy governing "social media" use by employees	The Monza District Court adopted and instituted new policies that prohibit the misuse of social media networks, outlets, and other platforms by court employees.
Independence and Accountability: Response to Change	Adoption of a strategic plan	The Belmar County Court announced the adoption of a five-year strategic plan that was developed with community input to improve the effectiveness and efficiency of the court.

Honesty

Communicating with honesty means that the court is sharing information in a truthful, transparent way. While this proposes to never convey information that is knowingly false, it also implies being *committed* to the truth; meaning that court leaders should not distort information so that it could potentially mislead the public and media. An explanation of a circumstance or situation that casts the court in a negative light should not misrepresent the truth, hoping that it will mitigate an adverse reaction. In instances where all of the facts are not available or not entirely known, it is appropriate to simply state, "I don't know" or alternatively, "I am not at liberty at this time to share what I know, due to the court's code of ethics." This is preferable to saying, "no comment" to avoid providing information, whether the specifics are known or not.[4]

Generally, the public and media are amenable to the court's messaging, so long as it respects their desire (and right) to know. To that end, court leaders should acknowledge stakeholders in their communications and explain why the court cannot respond to a particular question, rather than offering a perfunctory two-word reply. Instead of stating, "no comment," consider the following response from an administrator who did not know the answer to the media person's question:

> Thank you. Your question is an important one and I wish I could answer it. Unfortunately, I don't know that level of detail of the case because it gets into the facts of the case. That question would probably be better directed to counsel. If you can see me afterwards, my office would be happy to provide you with their contact information so that you can reach them directly.

Likewise, courts that communicate candidly bear responsibility for correcting factual inaccuracies, irrespective of their source or timing. The oversight may have been the result of a reporter's misstatement or the public's misunderstanding, but it is important that the court address those inaccurate interpretations, however minor the fact. This applies to something as negligible as mispronouncing a party's name or a more substantive issue such as a factual error of the court record or interview. In so doing, the court assures that its communication is consistent and accurate.

Accessibility

Accessible courts eliminate barriers for members of the public who seek or require their services. To be accessible, courts develop and maintain an organizational culture which accounts for institutional operations so that *all* telephone messages, emails, and correspondence are responded to within a reasonable period. It also means that the courts work to communicate with parties so that messaging is equally accessible to disabled persons or those who do not speak English proficiently. Therefore, judiciary liaisons should be trained to ensure communication and correspondence is culturally appropriate. Courts serve diverse communities when they actively consider the varied interests of all members, including ethnic, religious, tribal, LGBTQ+, and immigrant populations. To fulfill this responsibility, court operations must be designed to identify special needs early and ensure ready access to the full array of court services for everyone who interacts with the judicial branch.

Under Americans with Disabilities Act (ADA) Title II (U.S. Department of Justice, 2024), state and local courts are required to provide communications and services that are as effective for individuals with disabilities as they are for others, including the provision of auxiliary accessibility aids, accessible forums, and modifications to policies or procedures when necessary. In addition, guidance from the NCSC (2025) emphasizes that inclusive court management practices such as culturally competent staff training (Martin et al., 2008), language access programs, and accessible physical and digital facilities are essential to ensure procedural fairness and public trust. Courts that proactively accommodate diverse needs not only comply with federal accessibility requirements, but also strengthen community confidence in the judiciary, reduce barriers to participation, and support equitable access to justice for all litigants, witnesses, jurors, and visitors.

Phone calls from reporters (including those who are disliked by court representatives or leaders) should be promptly returned. The effort to return calls and speak with the reporter, even when the court does not have anything of material value to share, conveys a sense of respect, supports positive relations with the media, and generally serves to demonstrate the court's commitment to transparency. A designated contact and liaison for the media should also be readily available to speak on the court's behalf during regular business hours, as well as times of crisis, such as during emergency situations which initiate continuity of operations plans. Much of this communication can be effectively handled and accomplished through an ombudsman or public information officer (PIO) (Bertran, 2002). For smaller courts without the benefit of dedicated staffing, it is important to clearly designate which judges and/or administrative personnel will serve as spokespersons for the court.

Openness

The court administrator must have a thorough understanding of public information laws, rules, and procedures to maintain a balance between transparency and discretion. In some instances, managers may be precluded from sharing information, given the pertinent rules and privacy laws applicable to the case. The administrator's inability to provide the information will sometimes frustrate the party making the inquiry, which can degenerate into the individual becoming verbally abusive. During one such exchange when a staff person attempted to provide only the information they were permitted by policy to provide, the litigant became incensed, calling them a "bureaubot."[5] Although these kinds of interactions in the court are unusual, they do sometimes occur given the variety of life-altering matters that the courts oversee, and the high degree of stress that accompany these issues. The anxiety for a desirable outcome or more information about a case can vex those impacted by the process – so much so that their anger is sometimes directed at those who manage that workflow, namely judges, administrators, and court staff.

Training, particularly for front office personnel, to ensure that information is communicated openly without compromising the integrity of the process, however unsatisfying it may be to the person making the inquiry, is critical. Technology allows for some case information to be available online. Court staff should work to ensure that the appropriate documents together with relevant information are accessible through that medium. While staff are generally prohibited from discussing the specifics of the case, they can offer to explain the procedural history and "background" by explaining the overall process of the court docket. In those instances when court staff are unable to answer questions because they fall outside of their scope of knowledge, members of the media and public should be directed to a different, more appropriate source.

Understandability

Engaging with the public so that the court is understandable necessarily means that "legalese" terminology should not be used when plain language is more appropriate. To the extent that technical legal jargon is required, the terms should be restated and explained in the more dominant language of the local community. Court policies and procedures should be clearly communicated by staff trained and adept in customer service. This requires assessing the strengths and weaknesses of staff skill sets in determining "best fit." Those who have a demonstratively patient and pleasant disposition in responding to the public's questions and can explain processes and policies with the same demeanor should be considered for "gateway" positions in the court; namely, customer service desks, reception and intake areas, telephone support, ombudsman and liaison offices, and jury service units.

Credibility

We examine credibility as the final fundamental regarding information stewardship because the trustworthiness of the court in many respects depends on its success with the other five communication essentials. Thus, the court is credible to the extent that it is positive, honest, accessible, open, and understandable, and it performs its constitutional role in providing justice. Moreover, a credible court is also accurate and consistent in the approach it takes in disseminating information to internal and external stakeholders. The court administrator who leads and manages the earlier stated "three Ps" – people, process, and place – so that their communication with each of these realms is positive, honest, accessible, open, and understandable will concomitantly be credible.

Community Outreach

Nationwide surveys indicate that the public generally has more trust in the judiciary compared to the other two branches, albeit racial minorities' views of the courts are not as positive as those of their counterparts. Survey findings also show that while judicial independence is commonly valued, respondents do not believe that judges are always independent and impartial (NCSC, 2023). In general, data on the public's understanding of the courts is lacking, but interestingly, knowledge is *positively* correlated with positive perceptions of the judiciary. This suggests that the more the public knows about the court, the more positively the court is viewed.

Engaging with the community requires a *proactive* approach by the courts in order for its operation to be understandable to the public. Taking the initiative to establish and maintain relationships with community members personalizes the court and incentivizes the public to become committed participants in fostering a more responsive system of justice (Reinkensmeyer & Murray, 2012). Although courts do not traditionally hold press conferences, announcing system improvement initiatives in a formal setting can demonstrate to the public the *specific* efforts that are being carried out by the third branch in identifying and addressing systemic issues that impact the community. The alternative – not taking a more proactive approach – is to allow the fictional world of television and the mass media to depict the inner workings of the court in a way that is principally driven to draw the largest number of views. In film, and even more so on television, there is a protagonist and antagonist, and an uncomplicated, straightforward court ruling that makes the intricacies of the case not only understandable, but entertaining as well. While this oftentimes does not reflect the actual machinations of the justice system, the public by and large comes to the court with these overly simplistic depictions as their point of reference.

As we discussed, courts perpetually contend with how they are portrayed in popular culture, the backdrop of the 24-hour news cycle, and on-demand programming. As Pound (1906) noted, much of the public's perspective is based on media reports that chronicle sensationalistic incidents and events that draw enough of the market to augment advertising income. Among other profound effects, these realities perpetuate a superficial understanding of the judicial branch and reinforce the public's discontent with courts. Pound's observation holds great significance now, more so than at any other time in history. To the extent that it can be influenced, setting the public's expectations of court proceedings in alignment with the purposes and responsibilities of courts is a crucial measure requiring effective management.

A *proactive* court is one which regularly engages its community and is in communication with it *before* circumstances necessitate that engagement when the state of mind of the community may not be open and receptive. Anticipatory strategies include community events, such as panel presentations and township meet-and-greet events, which bring judges and court executives together with other justice system partners in the public forum, providing the community with an opportunity for direct engagement and interaction. Furthermore, the discussions can serve to enable local bar associations, legal service organizations, and law schools in offering community members a comprehensive view of the judicial system. In this way, collaborative events allow members of the public to become acquainted with government leaders and the respective roles they play. As the neutral branch of the justice system, the court is uniquely situated to spearhead and lead these community roundtables.

These and other kinds of community dialogue also allow the judiciary to solicit feedback about how it can be more responsive to public needs in filing cases, reporting for jury service, parking, and general experiences at the courthouse. The Supreme Court of Florida (2025), for instance, offers both in-person and virtual tours for school groups, civic organizations, and leadership programs. The 45- to 60-minute tour provides an overview of Florida's judicial branch, explains the structure of the state court system, and describes how the Supreme Court functions. Tours include visits to the public spaces in the courthouse, including the courtroom, lawyers' lounge, rotunda, and library. Depending on the size of the jurisdiction, staff responsible for the technical aspects of operations and procedures can also be included in community relations on a voluntary basis. To the extent union contracts permit, court staff involvement in community engagement initiatives can be included in annual performance appraisals as an added incentive to share knowledge and represent the court.

An engaged court does not view itself as a separate entity in the community, but rather as an active participant and intermediary to the free exchange of ideas and discussion of concerns. To be clear, engagement is a "discussion" such that while administrators must be proficient at advocating the purposes and responsibilities of the court to the constituency, the court's leadership team must at the same time be receptive to being "taught" by the public.

Internal Communication

The distinction between legal advice and legal information is critical, and judiciary employees must understand and observe it to ensure equitable treatment of all litigants (Greacen, 2022). Oftentimes, staff are guided by their own apprehensions about the level and type of information they are privy to; consequently, they fail to provide any information at all, thus restricting both accessibility and understandability. Table 10.2 illustrates fundamental differences between legal advice and information that should be incorporated into staff orientation programs, customer service trainings, and community engagement seminars. More generally, the distinctions should be an ingrained part of the court culture.

Table 10.2 Basic Differentiation of Legal Advice and Legal Information

Legal Advice	***Legal Information***
• Questions typically prefaced with "Should I?" • Presenting or representing yourself in a manner which could be reasonably ascertained as taking a side in a pending or concluded matter. • Provide information to one party that you would otherwise be unwilling or unable to provide to all other affected people. • Disclose the outcome of a confidential proceeding before the matter becomes available to the public. • Recommend or suggest that a litigant take a particular course of action.	• Questions typically prefaced with "Can I?" or "How do I?" • Provide information included in docket reports, case files, indexes, documents, and other public records. • Respond to questions regarding rules, procedures, policies, or functions of the court and judicial process. • Provide templates of documents and pleadings to assist litigants in completing those forms. • Explain the meaning of terms and the relevant documents. • Answer inquiries relating to court processes, deadlines, and events.

In instances when staff are confronted with questionable inquiries, they should be guided and trained to err on the side of caution. It is better to give no information and defer the matter to a more knowledgeable co-worker, supervisor, or manager than to provide an invalid answer that could potentially compromise the integrity and impartiality of the court. Consider the Massachusetts Advisory Committee on Ethical Opinions for Clerks of the Court (1995), which prohibits clerks from practicing law and distinguishes between legal information – such as assisting with forms and providing procedural guidance – and legal advice, which involves drafting documents, taking over a case, or acting as an advocate for a litigant.

Irrespective of court size and jurisdiction, court staff interact daily with a wide range of stakeholders including the media, government officials, litigants, community members and advocates, and representatives from non-profit and corporate entities, among others. Each stakeholder group has a diverse, yet equally significant, interest in the mission and success of the judiciary. To effectively engage these groups, some larger courts have created a department (and for smaller courts, individual positions) to liaise between the court and the communities it serves. A dedicated ombudsman's office is one such example created by various courts, albeit the names of these departments may differ. An ombudsman is principally responsible for the development and promulgation of information and communications regarding the court's programs, policies, and processes, while also serving as a liaison to these services for the diverse array of court stakeholders. The overarching purpose of the office is to provide information at the time it is sought by court users. This approach is intended to ensure that litigant misunderstandings are clarified, stages of the process are clearly delineated, and general information about the court system is shared (Bertran, 2002). The following measures represent some of the court initiatives and programs managed by ombudsman-type offices:[6]

- Childcare facilities: Courthouse space for children of court users who cannot arrange childcare during reporting time.
- Citizen advisory committee: A review board that brings together business, legal, and lay leaders to evaluate and guide policy, procedure, and mandates impacting the judicial system. It can also consider public concerns and work with representatives to find solutions or seek grant funding.
- Courthouse tours: Guided visits to inform individuals and groups about the court's history and operations.
- Dissolution/Non-dissolution programs: Workshops for separating parents to understand the issues impacting their children and associated trauma.
- Engagement strategies: The court's means to develop and institute initiatives and programs so that the public is more informed about the court's purposes and responsibilities. These strategies can use various communications to inform the public about the court's mission and justice administration, protecting individual liberties and constitutional rights, and ensuring public welfare and safety. The tactics are less important than the clear and concise communication of the court's mission. This is especially relevant in an age of misinformation. These steps also include partnerships with other government branches and agencies to address implicit bias and ensure fairness.
- Exit surveys: Questionnaires grounded in empirical methods that evaluate court users' attitudes, satisfaction, knowledge, and experiences.
- Judicial performance evaluations: Anonymous surveys of attorneys, litigants, jurors, and other court participants designed to evaluate judges' legal expertise, case management, administrative effectiveness, and professional demeanor. The results are provided to judges, chief judges, and appropriate court officials.
- Mock trial or Law Day programs: Educational outreach conducted in partnership with local bar associations to engage schools and the broader public in understanding court processes, functions, and the judicial system.
- Outreach materials: Pamphlets, information sheets, media guides, juror education literature, videos, and other marketing materials to inform the public about court processes, functions, and the judicial system.
- Public access terminals: Computer systems and kiosks in the court complex for public information access.
- Public information 800 number and announcements: Telephone and media broadcasts to disseminate general court information to the community.

- Speaker series: Forums hosted by courts to address public or specific groups about court-related topics and operations, sometimes partnering with other justice system stakeholders.
- Volunteer coordination: Programs facilitated by the courts that use citizen volunteers to improve public service. Volunteers serve in various capacities, such as information aides, alternative dispute resolution, clerical aides, daycare facility aides, and Court Appointed Special Advocates (CASA) where they represent abused and neglected children in court.

The court website, in particular, should be structured and supported so that it is easily navigated by court users and members of the public. Among other things, it should provide a summary of court work units, contact directory, docket information, links to online court forms and procedures, information on court access for people with disabilities, features of special programs, and initiatives aimed at addressing community problems.

Email is a frequently used method of communication with courts and while it is important to be responsive to email messages, a balance must be struck by the ombudsman, PIO, or whomever is assigned as the court's spokesperson to ensure this routine task activity does not consume all of their time. All emails should be composed with the understanding that whatever is written will be made public; thus, efficiency in getting a message out or responding to an inquiry should not come at the expense of it being accurately communicated. Similarly, courts that are using text messaging and AI-based chatbot technologies for communications with litigants, attorneys, and members of the public should ensure the timeliness and accuracy of such automated communications.

Once a court has established email policies, personnel should be informed of management expectations. Accountability for adhering to best practices and standards should be maintained through periodic auditing and customer service surveys (Court Tools, Measure 1). Staff who deal directly with the public should include a clause below their email signature line indicating the timeframe in which a response from the court can be expected. Autoreply should be adjusted when necessary, so that it corresponds with vacation periods, protracted leave, professional development absences, or whenever the staff person will be unavailable for an extended period. While the "out of office" reply need not provide specifics regarding the absence, it should advise the sender of the name and contact information of a person who the inquiry can be directed toward in the interim. Communication guidelines should be a part of the staff orientation program so that expectations on the importance of their interactions with stakeholders are well-defined at the outset. Given the communications objectives of the court, the unit responsible for community engagement should be readily accessible to the public; thus, it becomes "mission critical" to the court to ensure that the office is adequately staffed.

The number and type of staff is ultimately determined by caseload volume and district population, but they should generally correspond to agreed-upon measurables based on current realities and workload trends. Whatever the circumstance, providing members of the public with this level and type of user-friendly "point of entry" gives them greater clarity on procedures and acquaints them with the responsible staff managing the process. A public liaison office that is adequately resourced is a very sound investment. It generates efficiencies for the court, ensuring that information is communicated accurately at the front end of the process. Other cost savings and enhanced customer service can be derived by ensuring that map directions, directories, and court access protocols are consistently updated on the judiciary's website and social media platforms.

Stakeholder Feedback

Court stakeholders should be surveyed and provided with the means to provide feedback on problems they experienced while interacting with the courts, suggested improvements, and data on their overall satisfaction. When feedback is received, the court ombudsman office should, as appropriate, follow up with users as soon as practicable. Likewise, the court office with responsibility for community relations should periodically survey the public, using electronic, telephone, or in-person methods with anonymous questionnaires. Although preserving respondent anonymity is essential, an option to provide name and contact information should be included for individuals who wish to engage in a follow-up discussion with the court personnel responsible for conducting the content analysis. As part of this methodology, the court must establish an appropriate procedure to initiate such communications. Depending on the nature of the activity or size of the undertaking that was prompted by the feedback, the court may seek to incorporate those actions in its annual report or other documents that are distributed to stakeholders.

From an analytical and managerial perspective, the goals of conducting such a study are threefold: 1) to generalize results to the wider court stakeholder population; 2) to establish a correlation and/or causal relationship between judiciary service structures and changes observed in stakeholder perceptions; and 3) to identify areas for system improvement or further analysis. Administrators whose work intersects with these tasks should have, at minimum, some familiarity with survey research methodologies that involve ensuring reliability, validity, and representativeness of the study. Reliability is a measure of the survey's stability and implies consistency such that when the same individuals under the same conditions respond to the measure, the same approximate results are generated. Validity is based on whether a particular method measures what it *intends* to measure. A valid study is one that produces findings which correspond to the actual circumstances of the court environment and which were the subject of the research (Kachigan, 1986). A survey that is valid will also be reliable, but a reliable survey is not necessarily always valid. Court managers tasked with overseeing the data collection and analysis will also need to ensure that the sample size is large enough.

The results of the study will be used to recommend and institute policy. The relative size of the sample is important because randomness does not mitigate the effects that responses from one or more subjects can have on aggregate survey findings, if the sample size is too small. Thus, there are three considerations when collecting stakeholder feedback: designing a reliable and valid study, obtaining a sample large enough to adequately represent the population of court users, and accounting for available staff resources to conduct the research.

Media Relations

A crucial aspect of the court's engagement with the community – whether positive or negative – is establishing and maintaining a professional working relationship with the media. The court faces a significant challenge, especially in high-profile cases, in striking a balance between sharing relevant information and protecting sensitive details. The court's public relations office (ombudsman or PIO) must adhere to an ethical code that ensures the information shared is appropriate, timely, and transparent (Arizona Supreme Court, 2024). Press releases, which allow the presiding judge and administrator to review and discuss the message with the public, are particularly beneficial. Briefings can be disseminated through the judiciary's website, social media platforms, and various news outlets. These platforms play a pivotal role in publicizing important information and announcements about ongoing trials, pending court matters. They can also be used to highlight special court programs, events, and system improvement initiatives, and to introduce newly appointed or elected judges and other court leaders to the public.

Notes

1 In other countries, such as Nigeria, judges are addressed as "My Lord."

2 An idiom used in Western countries to describe what is believed should be the foundational elements of education – reading, writing, and arithmetic. The phrase is used because of the "R" phoneme (sound) at the beginning of each word.

3 Court names were replaced with pseudonyms.

4 Judges and court staff are not ethically allowed to comment on pending court cases. Best practices incorporate this as a part of training so that judges and staff are advised to clearly explain the court's position to the media and public.

5 A play on words that combines the terms bureaucrat and robot to denigrate the public employee as a programmable machine who cannot think for themselves.

6 Many of the listed functions may also be found in a Public Information Office.

References

American Bar Association. (2023). *ABA survey of civic literacy.* www.americanbar.org/groups/public_education/resources/civic-literacy/survey/.

American Council of Trustees and Alumni. (2024). *New survey reveals low level of civics literacy among college students.* www.goacta.org/2024/07/new-survey-reveals-low-level-of-civics-literacy-among-college-students/.

Arizona Supreme Court. (2024). *Arizona Code of Judicial Administration § 1–303: Code of conduct for judicial employees.* https://azcjc.azcourts.gov/Portals/5/137/rules/2024%201-303%20Code%20of%20Conduct%20for%20Judicial%20Employees%2007-2024.pdf.

Barreira, T. (2025, September 18). Evolving or endangered? Why the CMO role is being redefined. *Fast Company.* www.fastcompany.com/91406065/evolving-or-endangered-why-the-cmo-role-is-being-redefined.

Bertran, M. (2002). Judiciary ombudsman: Solving problems in the courts. *Fordham Urban Law Journal, 29,* 2099–2116.

Greacen, J. M. (2022). Legal information vs. legal advice: A 25-year retrospective. *Judicature, 106*(2), 48–61.

Hamilton, A. (2003). Federalist No. 78. In C. Rossiter (Ed.), *The Federalist papers* (pp. 465–471). Signet Classics. (Original work published 1788)

Kachigan, S. K. (1986). *Statistical analysis: An interdisciplinary introduction to univariate & multivariate methods.* Radius Press.

Martin, J. A., Reinkensmeyer, M. W., Rodriguez Mundell, B., & Guillen, J. (2008). Becoming a culturally competent court. *Court Manager, 22*(4), 5–23.

Maslow, A. H. (1943). A theory of human motivation. *Psychological Review, 50*(4), 370–396. https://doi.org/10.1037/h0054346.

Massachusetts Supreme Judicial Court, Advisory Committee on Ethical Opinions for Clerks of the Courts. (1995, November 8). *Opinion 95–96.* www.mass.gov/opinion/opinion-95-6.

National Association for Court Management (NACM). (2004). *Core competency curriculum guidelines: What court leaders need to know and be able to do.*

National Association for Court Management (NACM). (2023). *Areas of responsibility of court administrators.* https://nacmnet.org/nacm-information-for-students-and-educators/areas-of-responsibility-of-court-administrators/.

National Center for State Courts. (1997). *Trial court performance standards.*

National Center for State Courts. (2005). *CourTools: Trial court performance measures.*

National Center for State Courts. (2023). *State of the state courts survey: 2023 national survey analysis.* www.ncsc.org/resources-courts/reports.

National Center for State Courts. (2025). *Serving people with disabilities and Title II of the ADA: A toolkit for courts.* www.ncsc.org/resources-courts/serving-people-disabilities-and-title-ii-ada.

Noah Webster Educational Foundation. (2021, May 6). *Why the "3 Rs" matter.* https://nwef.org/2021/05/06/why-the-3-rs-matter/.

O'Connor, S. D. (2009). The essentials and expendables of the Missouri Plan (2009 Earl F. Nelson Lecture). *Missouri Law Review, 74,* 479–492.

Pound, R. (1906). *The causes of popular dissatisfaction with the administration of justice* [Speech]. Speech delivered at the American Bar Association. https://law.unl.edu/RoscoePound.pdf.

Reinkensmeyer, M. W., & Murray, J. (2012). Court–community connections: Strategies for effective collaboration. *Trends in State Courts,* 28–33.

Supreme Court of Florida. (2025). *Visiting the court.* https://supremecourt.flcourts.gov/Visiting-the-Court.

U.S. Department of Justice. (2024). *Americans with Disabilities Act Title II regulations: Nondiscrimination on the basis of disability in state and local government services.* www.ada.gov/law-and-regs/regulations/title-ii-2010-regulations/.

11 Court Stakeholder Collaboration

Stakeholder collaboration is now recognized as a key component of the increasingly broad organizational perspective of court administration. While courts have long sought to optimize justice in individual cases, the early decades of court management in the United States focused largely on judicial branch structure and optimization of internal court operations (American Bar Association [ABA], 1974). To that end, much of the conventional wisdom on court reform centers on court unification, case management, and efficiencies in judicial administration (Berkson & Carbon, 1978; Bureau of Justice Assistance [BJA], 1988). Viewed through today's wider lens, judicial branch leaders recognize the diverse needs of individuals and entities having points of intersection with the courts. In recent years, the field of court administration has come to more fully appreciate the value of ongoing dialogue with a multitude of court stakeholders, ranging from individual litigants to large justice agencies. Such communications create a shared frame of reference for gap analysis, long range planning, and enduring improvements in the justice system. Addressing the role of these various stakeholders, Adekunle (2017) stated:

> Justice sector coordination is the harmonization and integration of activities and responsibility to ensure that the resources of each organization involved in the administration of justice are efficiently used in pursuit of the justice delivery.

Communities with robust programs of stakeholder collaboration regularly draw on the significant gains realized through cross-sector agency coordination, data sharing, and joint budget requests. Inter-branch justice ventures such as problem-solving courts (National Institute of Justice, 2020), integrated criminal justice, and the Sequential Intercept Mental Health Model (Substance Abuse and Mental Health Services Administration, 2025) are some of the myriad examples. While many local communities are making strides in stakeholder collaboration, involvement in such endeavors is often subordinate to that of day-to-day court operations.

DOI: 10.4324/9781003686804-11

In part, court management's priorities are driven by ongoing operational demands and the imperative to address pressing "issues of the day." Further, and perhaps of greater significance, the espoused benefits of stakeholder collaboration are intangible or, at least, difficult to fully ascertain. In a world sharply focused on short-term return on investment, it is not easy to address qualitative factors like public trust in the court, the community's relationship with the probation department, and citizen perceptions regarding jury service. A subtle, less obvious, factor may also involve the overriding thought that the court – a constitutionally established "neutral forum" – must remain a step removed from the community. This way, arguably, the court will not become "too closely" intertwined with executive branch justice entities and the people it serves. As such, it is the responsibility of court leaders to protect the independence of the judicial branch in stakeholder communications and inter-branch interactions (National Association for Court Management, 2011).

In our view, judicial independence can be maintained through delineation of "ground rules" at the outset of court stakeholder collaborations, inclusion of all interested parties in discussions and, in some situations, stipulating that some stakeholder forums are advisory rather than authoritative in nature. Irrespective of such precautionary measures, court leaders may find it challenging to balance the imperative of judicial independence against community demands for a "responsive court." In light of this bifurcated obligation, what steps should courts take to catalyze and actively foster collaboration with court stakeholders? Locally, to what extent (if at all) is it beneficial to create a justice system consortium and, if so, how should this be organized and staffed? How should court user feedback, public surveys, and end user focus groups be incorporated into the court's decision-making calculus? These questions and related policy and practice issues are the subject of our discussion, drawing upon our experience with justice system coordinating task forces and steering committees, supreme court judicial councils, stakeholder surveys, and community engagement in large-scale court facility projects. This particular chapter concludes with exploration of a user-centered design, a cross-disciplinary approach directly involving court participants in re-engineering of court processes. Relatively new to the courts, this promising design methodology can be leveraged to enhance access to justice initiatives.

In the broader context, exploration of stakeholder collaboration must also consider the dynamics of local community relations and the public's role in judicial branch strategic planning. Identification and engagement of court stakeholders is necessarily a locally grounded exercise; an effort taking into account the demographics, resources, and cross-sector workings of the community. While our exploration will identify key elements of stakeholder collaboration, the court's strategy for stakeholder collaboration must be thoughtfully formulated to comport with the needs and culture of its community. To this point, for example, a review of 125 studies on mentally ill people in contact with law enforcement revealed 13 different types of interagency collaboration models (Parker et al., 2018). Ultimately, it is the responsibility of court leaders to discern the justice-related concerns of the community, and to create locally based forums for meaningful, ongoing dialogue with those specific system stakeholders. As part of this leadership responsibility, court leaders can also shape local communication forums to enhance inclusion in the justice system as advocated by the Conference of Chief Justices (CCJ) and the Conference of State Court Administrators (COSCA) (2020).

A deep dive into stakeholder theory is beyond the scope of this publication. That said, it is important to acknowledge the foundational work of philosopher and educator Edward Freeman, who provides a framework for identification of stakeholders and methods for management to engage with stakeholders in a meaningful way. In discussing the concept of stakeholders, Freeman (1984) remarked:

> Simply put, a stakeholder is any group or individual who can affect, or is affected by, achievement of a corporation's purpose. Stakeholders include employees, customers, suppliers, stockholders, banks, environmentalists, government and other groups who can help or hurt the corporation. The stakeholder concept provides a new way of thinking about strategic management – that is how a corporation can and should set and implement direction. By paying attention to strategic management, executives can begin to put their corporations back on the road to success.

This broad definition of stakeholders is a marked expansion of the longstanding focus on corporation shareholders, specifically individuals having a fiduciary interest in the establishment.[1] Freeman (1984) proposes a framework for integrating the stakeholder concept into the strategic management of the organization. Stakeholder theory calls for the development of an overarching "enterprise strategy," through a process involving: 1) stakeholder analysis; 2) values analysis; and 3) identification of societal issues. Development of strategic direction requires stakeholder input, in part to gain an accurate view of the external environment and to create organizational alignment with the outside world. Facets of the stakeholder concept are integral to corporate planning, systems theory, corporate social responsibility, and organization theory – each of which can be made applicable to the workings and management of a court system.

Identification and Engagement of Court Stakeholders

In contemplating avenues for stakeholder collaboration, it is beneficial to clearly designate the judges and management staff involved in various court outreach efforts. In the authors' experience, this is an arena requiring active involvement of both the court's executive leadership and members of the bench. Typically, individual judges will have "contacts" with many different stakeholder groups and members of the community. Courts can build upon these standing relationships within various spheres, thus developing communication pathways not necessarily manifest at the court executive level.[2]

Ultimately, from an organizational standpoint, responsibility for stakeholder collaboration is formally vested in the presiding judge and court administrator. Specifically, the National Center for State Courts (NCSC, 2006) model rule for presiding judges delineates their liaison role in working with outside agencies, stakeholders, and the media. Similarly, the National Association for Court Management (NACM) (2016) has identified community relations and cooperation with stakeholders as core functions of a court administrator, encompassing the following standards of performance:

- Good judgment, understanding, and being tactful and effective in maintaining working relationships with other courts and with local, state, and federal government officials, members of the Bar, and the public
- High level of willingness to cooperate with and have trust in justice partners and stakeholders
- The ability to conduct conferences in meetings and communicate clearly in writing and speech to employees, judges, representatives of government agencies, industry, and the public

As a fundamental building block of stakeholder inclusion, Freeman (1984) recommends that organizations conduct a stakeholder analysis, stakeholder audit, and stakeholder coalition analysis. While detailed processes exist for each of these components, the main purpose here is to identify all interested parties and to develop "strategic programs" specific to the stakeholder group. Figure 11.1 presents a high-level conceptual diagram of local court stakeholder interactions, all occurring within the broad context of the local community served by the trial court. In addressing the concept of community, Dunham and associates (2015) observed:

> Lack of specificity around stakeholder identity remains a serious obstacle to the further development of stakeholder theory and its adoption in actual practice by business managers. Nowhere is this shortcoming more evident than in stakeholder theory's treatment of the constituency known as "community."

This cautionary note is instructive, highlighting the need for a carefully considered analysis of the community served by the courts. Accordingly, it is incumbent upon court leaders to look beyond the "regular cast of characters," such as prominent business owners, political leaders, and agency heads. A broader, more inclusive perspective encompasses individuals and groups from all sectors of the community – a true cross-section of the population served by the court. Noteworthy here are the extensive domains and overlapping spheres embodying the court, individual court users, and governmental entities. Our conceptualization draws a distinction between the government funding body – for example the county board or city council – and an array of government justice agencies. The nature and extent of stakeholder interactions are fluid, in part conditioned by community demands and institutional responses. The range of stakeholder interactions is also, in part, driven by the caseload mix of the court, litigant needs, and server provider resources available to the community.

Figure 11.1 Court Stakeholder Interaction Model

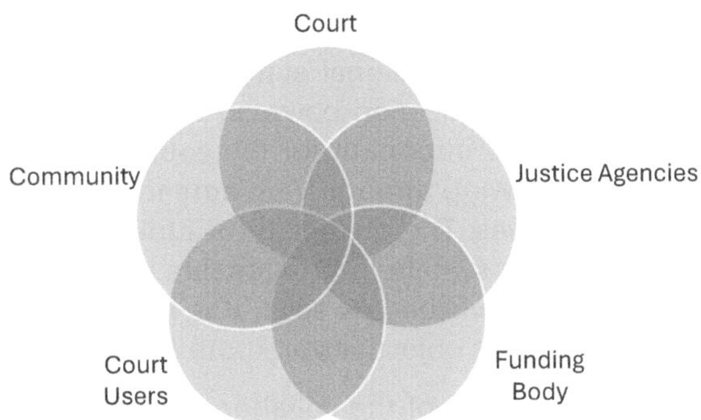

For the purposes of this discussion, the "universe" of potential stakeholder interactions with the court includes the following key components:

- Community: Members of the general public, health and social service providers, education, business and commerce, media, and political coalitions
- Courts: Judges and court staff, court administration, court programs, adult and juvenile probation, pre-trial screening and supervision, and juvenile detention
- Justice Agencies: Prosecution, defense, law enforcement, jail, corrections system including prisons and parole, and forensic services
- Court Users: Criminal defendants, parties in litigation, victims, witnesses, and juror pool
- Funding Body: City council, county board, and state legislature

Initially, with these components in mind, court leaders can inventory the array of formal and informal forums for stakeholder collaboration.[3] The more difficult analysis is to objectively assess the quality of current communication patterns, and the efficacy of permanent and standing stakeholder committees. Are the current avenues of communication really working, or, for that matter, have the stakeholder groups even met with the court leadership in recent years? Are the stakeholder groups diverse and inclusive so that membership is appropriately representative to the wide array of needs and interests? Moreover, are there missing voices, perhaps from segments of the community with special needs that seldom impact the majority, but nonetheless impact court access? With this type or similar kind of assessment, the court can take the necessary steps to dissolve inactive forums, optimize its work with productive stakeholder groups, and establish additional communication pathways to fill existing gaps. Our experience demonstrates that the planning process is best guided by a historical perspective on local court-community relations, one that brings to bear a sensitivity to the local community culture and an openness to expand the pool of stakeholder representatives. Once collaboration forums are in place, it is incumbent on the court administrator to provide responsive, professional staffing and to facilitate ongoing, bidirectional communication between the judiciary and represented groups. It is also important for the court's executive leadership to "deliver," following through with agreed-upon system changes and new initiatives. The credibility of judicial branch leadership is enhanced when system improvements are executed in a timely manner and made visible. As such, it is imperative that tasks in pursuit of the group's objectives are both measurable and attainable.

As a part of the collaboration process, it is not unusual for some stakeholder coalitions to request that the court expand program services in particular areas of interest. This can create difficulties for the court leadership, given competing demands for resources in many areas of the judicial branch. Discussing financial planning models, Freeman (1984) stated:

> I do believe that any budgeting process that is to be consistent with the strategic processes must address the overall issue of how resources are allocated to deal with various stakeholder groups.

In light of this reality, it is enormously helpful for court leaders to weigh such requests in the broad context of long-term planning and the court's overall budget strategy. The court may find in its assessment that particular requests for program expansion warrant inclusion in the court's strategic plan, while other petitions can either be deferred or addressed with an alternative approach. The overarching challenge for court leaders is to ensure that the allocation of resources remains aligned with the court's strategic vision, mission, and modern agenda.

Justice System Coordinating Councils

A review of the literature shows the wide variety of cross-sector organizational models around the country, where criminal justice entities coordinate respective spheres of work to reach mutually agreed-upon goals. Moreover, research suggests that innovations in this realm of "system" thinking and modeling will continue into the foreseeable future, given the perpetual advancement of technology and emergence of new societal issues. The courts have long played an integral role in these coordination initiatives. Some of the early state and local planning efforts involving the criminal justice system were federally funded by the Law Enforcement Assistance Administration (LEAA) and required localities to form regional planning units.[4] Criminal justice coordinating councils are now well established in many jurisdictions at the city, county, and state levels. Cushman (2002) described these bodies as follows:

> Criminal justice coordinating committee is an inclusive term applied to informal and formal committees that provide a forum where many key justice system agency officials and other officials of general government may discuss justice issues.

For those aspects of the court associated with the various components of the criminal justice system, the need for cross-sector coordination is clear. The inner workings of the justice "system" are inherently complex, given the adversarial framework, the separation of powers between the three branches of government, and the system of checks and balances. Matters are further complicated by the convergence of different levels of government, such as city-funded law enforcement, county-funded jails, and state-funded courts (Cushman, 2002). Further, some court and justice agencies are headed by elected officials, while others are led by appointed, "professional" government officials. The confidentiality of case records and separate, often incompatible agency data systems can hamper the inner workings of the justice system which ultimately impinges on the interests of the individual and the general public in the case.

Driven by necessity or sheer public demand, government leaders across various levels increasingly recognize the foregoing complexities and the need for system-wide planning and policy formulation in the justice system. Many of today's court leaders have convened or, at a minimum, actively participated in these coordinating bodies. Cushman (2002) calls for a comprehensive planning approach to "build linkages among agency stakeholders without attempting to subordinate them to a higher authority." Ideally, this "linkage" occurs at three levels – justice agency level, city/county level, and local justice system level – resulting in a coordinated plan indicative of coherent, systemic decision making.

Planning efforts, properly coordinated among these levels, have been shown to be highly effective in building linkages among interconnected (and interdependent) systems. These linkages impact a wide range of issues such as jail overcrowding, electronic pre-trial supervision, data sharing, justice facilities expansion, case management, competency evaluation, and restoration to competency. Moreover, high functioning justice system coordinating councils are well positioned to develop funding proposals that are supported and approved, typically because the program initiatives are mutually beneficial. Examples of jointly funded system-wide projects include the development of problem-solving courts (e.g., drug courts, mental health courts, and veteran courts), electronic disposition reporting, electronic warrants, and interagency data sharing. Decisions to proceed with these kind of large-scale, system-wide initiatives are often made through consensus building, as opposed to a majority vote. Given that the *active* participation of all justice system partners is generally required, creating opportunities where key agency representatives *can* participate and collaborate in the decision-making process is what makes desired outcomes most viable.

Speaking to the role of criminal justice coordinating councils, Wickman and associates (2012) noted:

> A criminal justice coordinating council is, by definition, focused primarily on policy, planning and coordination – not on operational activities. But in order to develop effective policies and plans, the council – through its members and its staff – must develop a good understanding of the core operations and operational objectives of all of the system's component parts. Optimally, the council will have a leadership role in establishing goals for the overall system, taking account of data on the crime problems and justice system management issues that face the jurisdiction.

In many jurisdictions, the membership of the criminal justice coordinating assembly is limited to executive-level representatives of the court and justice agencies. As shown in Figure 11.2 these commissions typically include delegates of the court, prosecution, defense, probation and pre-trial service, jail, and the local funding body (i.e., county or city management). Staffing for the council may be provided by the host governmental entity, be it the city or county, or shared by the court and respective justice agencies. To ensure "buy-in" from all the partnering agencies, the funding model may require the represented groups to provide budget monies for staffing and other council costs (Cushman, 2002).

Figure 11.2 Justice Coordinating Council

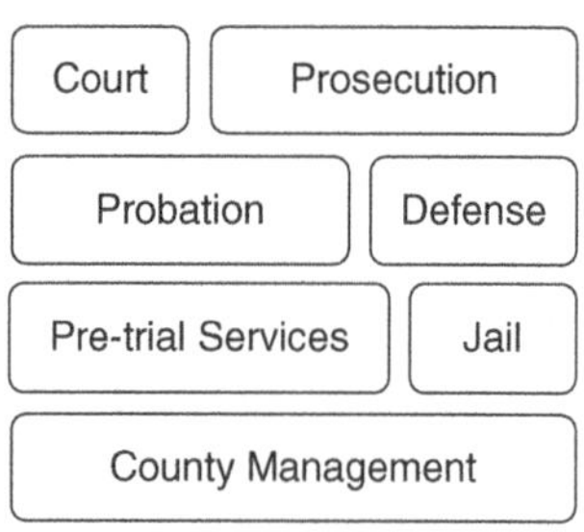

The National Institute of Corrections (NIC) (2022), among other field practitioners, recommend expanding stakeholder involvement, either in the membership of the council and/or participation in council workgroups. The NIC (2022) further suggests that a stakeholder analysis be conducted at the outset of convening these commissions so that key stakeholders are included during the early stages of activity. Among the host of other potential stakeholder groups specific to local conditions that can be included, the assembly should be representative of the following organizations and interests:

- Primary court and criminal justice stakeholders
- Executive- and operations-level committees involving "all system actors," including mental and behavioral health, social services, and re-entry services
- First-level stakeholders using the services in the areas of mental health and social services
- Other system actors such as housing, victims, community representatives, and legislators

The NIC (2022) also recommends that justice coordinating councils consider inclusion of "public citizen" members, who have a notable stake in system improvements and policy outcomes. Other than participation in these discussions, the individuals appointed to these commissions may not necessarily have any direct involvement in the courts or broader justice system (nor should it be required) (Wickman et al., 2012). Input from a broad group of stakeholders will help the council to identify and address areas of concern from the perspective of system end-users and to formulate workable, system-wide plans. As previously noted, stakeholder support for council initiatives and funding requests that are configured along these diverse efforts will be met with less resistance and dramatically enhance the likelihood of success. Figure 11.3 depicts an example of an expanded justice coordinating council membership group. Included in this broader body are representatives advocating for the interests of victims, social service agencies, mental health service providers, education, and housing.

Figure 11.3 Expanded Justice Coordination Council

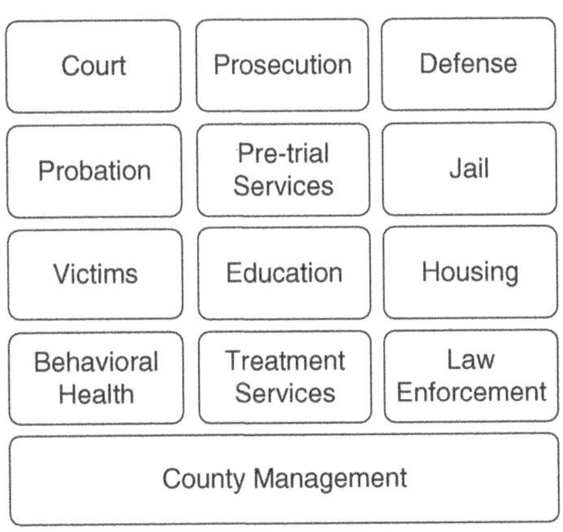

In most jurisdictions, the courts and each justice agency operate an independent, stand-alone case management system. The separate, "siloed" automation systems track duplicative and fragmented data on criminal defendants, offenses, custody status, criminal history, and court dates, among other identifiers. Unnecessary, inherently high operating costs arise from the collection, maintenance, and analysis of redundant data that is sometimes incomplete. Of greater concern, from the standpoint of public safety, data entry of the same identifiers by more than one justice agency increases the likelihood of inconsistency, which can impact decisions made during critical points of the caseflow (Scherpenzeel, 1995). This concern is raised as part of the *Data-Driven Justice* initiative, in which the National Association of Counties (NACO) advocates developing stakeholder consensus and a "shared vision" to improve outcomes for "frequent utilizers" of the justice system (NACO, 2022). Stakeholders involved in organizing and building these accords include the court, probation supervision services, criminal justice and behavioral health leaders, treatment services, mayors, city councils, county commissions, and the public.

To resolve some of the problems associated with disparate justice data systems, many criminal justice coordinating committees are created to address the need for data sharing through development of integrated criminal justice information systems. In 1997, the U.S. Justice Department's BJA created a National Task Force on Court Automation and Integration (Sullivan & Mathews, 2002–2003). The Task Force described integrated justice information systems as follows (BJA, 1999):

> Integration of justice information systems is best defined as the electronic sharing of information by two or more distinct justice entities within a system. The degree to which information systems are considered "integrated" depends on who participates, what information is shared or exchanged, and how data are shared or exchanged within the system.

Several data sharing models and supporting system architectures have evolved over the last few decades, including shared "data warehouses" and "subject in process" information systems (Cushman, 2002), as well as "intelligent" data messaging systems. The Office of Justice Programs (OJP) draws a distinction between integrated systems which allow cross-agency data "viewing" versus information management systems, which support streamlined data entry and real-time data access by authorized agencies (Sullivan & Mathews, 2002–2003).

Another important planning consideration is the distinction between horizontal data integration – held and operated among local justice entities – and vertical data integration from local agencies to state or federal criminal history government repositories, such as the FBI's National Crime Information Center (NCIC) (BJA, 1999). A 2020 inventory of integrated criminal justice "repositories" provides information on the scope of data sharing, automation architecture, funding, and supporting legislation for various state-level information systems (Ohio Criminal Sentencing Commission, 2023).

Irrespective of the information-sharing platform, the strategy generally espoused is to create a mechanism for one-time data entry and real-time data exchanges and access. Ideally, case and offender information should be collected only once (as early as possible in the process) and subsequently shared with the court and participating justice agencies, as needed and in accordance with the caseflow. One of the main goals of these integrated information systems is to enhance public safety by sharing accurate and updated information on case status, arrest warrants, custody status, and condition of release. The quality of justice is also improved when available information is consistent and reliable. Data exchanges generate greater efficiencies in data entry and reporting, thus reducing or in some circumstances eliminating the need for additional staff resources. For instance, a linear dataflow might facilitate real-time data sharing from the point of a defendant's arrest through the court's sentencing. In this scenario, law enforcement charging and case-related information is transmitted to the prosecutor's office, which is subsequently shared with the court and defense counsel. Following sentencing, case disposition data is disseminated to the corrections system (jail and prison) and provided to state and federal authorities for recordkeeping in respective criminal case history filings. A more fully developed integrated system might also include bidirectional dataflow for violations of probation, which the probation department submits to the sentencing court, prosecution, defense, and victim services. Although many of the published reports on justice system coordination center on the criminal justice system, the principles of establishing and fostering stakeholder collaboration among impacted groups are equally applicable to other areas of the legal system where interplay is critical to outcomes.

The interconnections of family courts and related dockets, mental health intervention, and consumer law represent some of the areas that would likewise benefit from collaborative partnerships. The juvenile court, in particular, and the requirement that affected parties collaborate to safeguard society, hold youth accountable, and rehabilitate minors adjudicated as delinquent, has long been recognized by judges, administrators, attorneys, service providers, and local funding bodies. Juvenile court judges are well poised to lead these efforts and convene stakeholder meetings. Not unlike the adult criminal court, strong working relationships between the court and affected parties can be forged through these collaborative efforts. Juvenile justice coordinating councils and workgroups exist in many jurisdictions, both in the areas of juvenile delinquency adjudication and juvenile dependency. To that end, the Council of State Governments and other subject matter experts in this field recommend the establishment of formal, standing bodies at the local court level to address juvenile justice issues such as recidivism rates and the use of juvenile detention. Notably, the council proposes employing "a coordinated approach across service systems to address youth's needs" (Seigle et al., 2014).

The Council of State Governments also recommends the following implementation strategies to cultivate a systems perspective among a varied set of stakeholder groups (Seigle et al., 2014):

- Establish a formal structure for collaboration, one which will foster "cross-system initiatives."
- Set shared goals, task timetables, and measures for success, as well as specific action plans.
- Establish mechanisms for cross-sector data sharing, including protocols governing data and adherence to confidentiality laws (e.g., a unified information system that automates data sharing).
- Provide cross-system training with emphasis on high-risk youth services, cross-system protocols, and interagency agreements.
- Evaluate juvenile system outcomes through "joint progress reviews" and case-level reviews, using evaluation findings to update program policies and procedures.

The BJA (2022) has examined service coordination with local courts in a multi-jurisdiction project, Models of Effective Court-Based Service Delivery for the Children and Families. Problem-solving courts programs are predicated upon close coordination with state and local service providers, such as counseling, substance abuse, and education services. The BJA (2022) observed the following dynamics from the field research of eight jurisdictions:

> Service coordination performance goals are particularly challenging for courts because they often involve issues that cannot be addressed by courts alone. To accomplish their service coordination goals, courts often must reach out to other community entities.

The BJA (2022) also identified nine "promising strategies" for systematic development of a comprehensive, sustainable approach to service coordination. Relevant to our stakeholder discussion are the key components of judicial leadership – with a judge willing to "champion" reform efforts – and establishment of an active stakeholder committee. While the stakeholder committees noted in the research are not configured in a uniform fashion, they are each structured to facilitate ongoing communication between the court and service providers. Two of the other key components noted by the BJA (2022) require the court's collaboration: 1) Centralized access to a service network for case-level service coordination; and 2) Collection and use of service delivery data for individual case tracking and for program evaluation.

Recommendations for broad stakeholder involvement and cross-sector services coordination are similarly noted in the mental health sector. It is generally advocated that the court and service providers develop a community-based response to individuals with mental health, behavioral, and co-occurring disorders (e.g., both mental illness and substance use disorders). Currently, the best practice recommendation is for local court adoption of the Sequential Intercept Model (SIM), a system designed to "ensure appropriate and holistic interventions that protect against escalation and justice system involvement" (Waters et al., 2018). Addressing the need for a systemic approach to mental health, the NCSC observed (Waters et al., 2018):

> State court leadership has recognized the importance of coordinated and comprehensive responses to mental health that focus on early diversion, redirection and treatment outside of the courts and justice system.

This is yet another forum where the leadership responsibility for stakeholder collaboration clearly rests with presiding judges and court administrators. The NCSC notes that existing justice committees may serve as a "starting point," providing a foundation for planning and governance in the mental health space (Waters et al., 2018).

The NCSC provides a vast list of stakeholders who could potentially serve on a local mental health task force. The list enumerates 36 possible participants, representing the courts, justice agencies, clinicians and competency evaluators, funding bodies, pre-trial services, emergency room personnel, public fiduciaries, employment, housing, mobile crisis units, religious leaders and several other categories (Waters et al., 2018). Accordingly, stakeholders could serve in a range of capacities such as membership on a permanent or standing committee, engagement in a SIM planning workshop, or service in a subcommittee workgroup. Another critical function in the coordinated efforts of mental health partnerships relates to the development of local justice system policies and procedures for cross-sector information sharing, as governed by the Health Insurance Portability and Accountability Act of 1996 and related state and federal privacy laws (Petrila & Fader-Towe, 2010).

Two longstanding and highly effective bodies for court stakeholder collaboration are the Council for Court Excellence,[5] serving the District of Columbia Court System, and the Center for Justice Innovation (CJI)[6] (formerly the Center for Court Innovation [CCI]) headquartered in New York City. Comprised of volunteer community members, the Council and standing committees recommend improvements to the district's courts in the areas of criminal justice, children in courts and public service. Notable achievements promoted by the Council include adoption of the one day/one trial jury trial system, improvements in the handling of child abuse and neglect cases, expanded victim rights, probate reform, and reducing civil case delay.

The Council for Court Excellence is recognized for utilizing community forum meetings, policy reports and publications, feedback from impacted residents, and coordinated efforts of various agencies to cultivate stakeholder collaboration in the justice system. The CCI (2010) proposes 13 strategies for community engagement in "problem-solving justice." One of the key strategies relates to the creation of community advisory boards, which include representatives of the justice system and the faith, business, and volunteer sectors. Other recommended strategies entail early community involvement in project planning, community forums or "open houses," task forces to address targeted issues, surveying the public, and volunteer engagement.

Stakeholder Involvement in Space Planning

Master space planning provides a unique and valuable forum for courts to engage in broad, highly impactful collaboration with stakeholders. As discussed in Chapter 12, these planning exercises define the long-term operational needs of the judicial branch, often shaping the physical infrastructure for delivery of justice services into the foreseeable future. Among other imperatives, architectural programming for new facilities addresses justice system workflows and facility contiguities, as well as opportunities to improve the provision of court services. Understandably, the long-term location, functionality, and architecture of court facilities will be of profound interest to the community; consequently, the public should be kept abreast of those planning initiatives. On a more practical note, it behooves court leaders to recognize that capital improvement projects only come to fruition through substantial investments made by the community, irrespective of the project funding model.

The large-scale capital project in the planning and construction of the "Criminal Court Tower" (the South Court Building), a 695,000 square foot facility built for the Superior Court of Arizona in Maricopa County, Phoenix, Arizona, provides a relevant example of stakeholder involvement (Reinkensmeyer & Oraftik, 2011). During the early conception of the courthouse, the court's leadership and county officials convened an extensive array of interrelated stakeholder work groups as depicted in Figure 11.4. Planning was guided by three mutually agreed upon, overarching core values: accountability, competency, and public safety. Each workgroup convened to address respective end-user needs and planning perspectives for four broad, intersecting sectors of the criminal justice system:

- Justice system: Courts, sheriff's department and law enforcement agencies, county attorney, public defense, clerk of court, court security, search warrant center, and interpreter services.
- Community: Citizens of Maricopa County, prospective jurors, people with disabilities, media, county correctional health and social services, state social services including mental health providers, housing, and economic assistance.
- Victim: Family violence prevention center, victim services unit, adult and juvenile probation, and presentence investigations unit.
- Offender: Indigent defense, probation day reporting center, probation mediation services, intensive probation, and parent coaching.

Figure 11.4 Maricopa County Criminal Court Tower Stakeholder Groups

Staffing the various workgroups and institutional planning was provided by a team appointed by Superior Court administration and county management. The planning process was fluid, evolving over a two-year period, with some stakeholders involved in early phases such as site selection, and other stakeholders participating in facility programming and schematic design. Workgroups were convened on an "as needed" basis, actively involving key stakeholders throughout the planning process. Although this collaborative approach was highly engaging and worthwhile for those involved, two practical outcomes are especially relevant to our discussion. First, individuals and organizations involved in the planning effort emerged as strong advocates for the criminal tower project, consistently voicing support for the project in the community. Community support for the project proved invaluable as questions arose regarding the "real need" for a new courthouse, the scale of the tower relative to other facilities, and the overall project cost of $450 million. Because they were fully immersed in the plan from the outset, the County Board of Supervisors (the funding body) was able to "stay the course" providing the necessary leadership and financing for the courthouse – which opened in 2012 – in addition to a series of regional courthouses.

Secondly, and of considerable long-term impact, stakeholders worked closely with the court's design team to create a facility which supported a "holistic justice" model. In this model, respective agencies are co-located at the courthouse to collectively staff early disposition courts. Stakeholders provided valuable insights regarding their respective business functions, which also provided opportunities to identify alternative workflows and re-engineer business processes. Longer-lasting system improvements and operational efficiencies also resulted from this collaborative planning process, some which factored into the county's financial analysis of operations maintenance.

Notable design features of the Criminal CourtTower include waiting areas dedicated to victims and law enforcement, bifurcated space that separates victims and their families from defendants in court proceedings, courtrooms with dual jury boxes for co-defendant cases, extensive provisions for disabled persons under the Americans with Disabilities Act (ADA), media facilities, community-based service areas for offenders, and a large-scale, user-friendly jury assembly room serving the entire downtown court complex.

Judicial Councils and Bench-Bar Committees

A critical component of modern court governance is that of judicial councils. These bodies serve as formally established standing forums for stakeholder participation in judicial branch policy formulation. Judicial councils are generally established in state and federal court systems.[7] At the state level, the judicial council may include several subordinate committees structured to address system improvements in specialized areas such as technology, probation, juvenile detention, language access, jury management, and judicial education. The chief justice may serve as the ex officio chair of the judicial council. Typically, staffing for the council and its various subcommittees is provided by the supreme court's Administrative Office of the Courts. Moreover, work assignments extend beyond recording of meeting minutes and logistical support. Senior judicial council staff work closely with the chief justice, state court administrator and committee chairs on research, agenda setting, and drafting of committee reports. Judicial council staff may also serve in a liaison role, interacting with the trial courts, justice agencies, and other state courts. Areas of focus for judicial councils vary widely from state to state and can also rapidly shift in response to unforeseen issues such as attacks on the judiciary, an economic recession, natural disasters, or public health emergency, such as COVID-19. Some of the common areas of judicial council study include:

- Access and fairness
- Beta testing statewide programs and initiatives
- Budget and resource allocation
- Court security

- Court technology
- Diversity, equity, and inclusion
- Education programs for judges and court staff
- Evidence-based practices in probation
- Facilities planning and management
- Intergovernmental relations
- Judicial selection and performance evaluation
- Jury reform
- Problem-solving courts
- Reviewing and advocating positions on legislation impacting the courts
- Statewide strategic planning for the judicial branch
- Workforce development

While some judicial councils have the authority to set and enforce policy, others hold a more limited advisory role and make recommendations to the supreme court. This is an important distinction, which should be clearly delineated in the workings of the council, enactment of judicial branch policies, and onboarding of new council members. Lack of clarity regarding the level of decision-making authority vested in the judicial council can fragment its efforts to improve operations and programs, by obscuring its objectives, goals, and mission (Durham & Becker, 2012). The Judicial Council of California, for instance, is supported by six internal committees, 25 advisory committees, and two task forces. Designated staff assist in implementing policies set forth by the council. The California Judicial Council (2025) has comprehensive policy-making authority, conveyed through its mission as follows:

> Under the leadership of the Chief Justice and in accordance with the California Constitution, the law, and the Mission of the Judiciary, the Judicial Council of California sets the direction and provides the leadership for improving the quality and advancing the consistent, independent, impartial, and accessible administration of justice.

Typically, judicial councils are composed of court officials such as judges, administrators, and clerks of court, as well as community delegates, such as citizens with an interest in the judicial system, members of the Bar, and representatives from business and not-for-profit sectors. Trial judges and court executives represent the specific interests of their respective systems, helping to bring a more local perspective into the statewide forum. The regional outlook is integral to these discussions, given the practical implications that are not immediately evident when the council seeks to institute technology systems, language access, alternative dispute resolution programs, etc. on a statewide basis. Furthermore, input from local court representatives assists in the formulation and execution of strategies by identifying issues, prioritizing court improvement initiatives, and resource allocation (Mundell & Jefferson, 2012). Finally, drawing input from the various operational levels significantly improves the council's decision-making process and the resulting policy directions.

We consider state court judicial councils to be critically important to contemporary judicial branch governance and court leadership, but not without active participation by the trial courts and community stakeholders. It is only through this committed involvement that the judicial council can serve as a trusted, transparent forum for robust information exchange and joint problem solving. This forum helps to bridge institutional fissures that almost always exist among the state supreme court / administrative office of the courts and local trial courts. In the same vein, high-performing judicial councils can also work to identify and bring into alignment key elements of interrelated strategic plans that bring to bear state and national initiatives.[8]

Collectively, the foregoing points of interaction create "golden opportunities" to strengthen state–local court partnerships and to leverage the subject matter expertise and experience of those involved in the collaboration. All of this is to say that trial court executives and state supreme court leaders will spawn more effective policy and programming when they work collaboratively than could ever be accomplished in a silo. System improvements that are meaningful also require a measure of "management by walking around," which can only be fully realized by involving the various components of the institution. As difficult as implementing change can be, it is made less burdensome when impacted entities are brought together and invested in practices that benefit the judicial branch as a whole.

Bench-bar committees provide a platform for attorneys to communicate with the court on policies, procedures, and court rules. Participating attorneys and respective clients are stakeholders in this setting, having knowledge of case management, litigation costs, and other dynamics of the legal field. These committees operate at the state and local (city and county) levels. The scope of work varies, with some groups focused on specific areas of law, such as civil procedure, rules of evidence, etc. Other ad hoc committees may work with court leadership on issues as needs manifest, such as court security, resource allocation, court technology, and justice facilities. Active bench-bar committees can be particularly helpful in court planning efforts by lending their support for additional resources and human capital (staffing and judgeships) that are sought by the court. Although recommendations by the bench-bar committee are generally only advisory in nature, given the broad administrative authority of presiding judges in policy formulation, the Bar's endorsement strengthens the court's position as it seeks to implement or change policy and procedure.

Stakeholder Perceptions: Survey Methodologies

Issue-specific survey instruments can be an effective and efficient way to gauge public sentiment on proposals for system change and judicial branch policy direction. Findings drawn from a questionnaire can also be used to develop "more user-friendly" court services and enhance litigant interactions with the judicial branch (CCI, 2019). There are assorted ways that the public sentiment can be assessed, but the court's methodology must be predicated on sound selection techniques so that conclusions drawn from the study are valid, reliable, and generalizable.

The CJI advocates "problem-solving justice" – a concept which seeks to administer justice by actively involving the people who live and work in a given neighborhood. Residents, in particular, are in a position to provide the court with the requisite perspective to identify issues relevant to that community as the court seeks to develop and institute practical solutions. Community engagement in the early stages of planning is also vital in building public support for new program initiatives, such as problem-solving courts and re-entry programs. To gauge the sentiment of the community, the CJI suggests the use of survey questionnaires (CCI, 2010):

> A survey gathers information from hundreds and potentially thousands of stakeholders, giving planners and practitioners a detailed picture of a community's priorities, expectations, and self-image. And they can be relatively painless.

Periodic surveys of the public and court users provide valuable information about the quality of judicial branch services, perceptions about the judicial branch, and in some situations, areas requiring immediate intervention. More specifically, they offer these external stakeholders the means by which to provide candid feedback about judicial branch services.

Cross-sectional surveys provide a "snapshot" of respondents' perceptions and satisfaction levels. Taken intermittently, survey findings can be used to evaluate changes in the public's sentiment (positively or negatively) regarding court services and performance, among other points of study. These data are an important touchstone for judiciary leaders in holding themselves accountable to performance benchmarks that are empirically based. One such survey is conducted regularly by the NCSC (2025). The annual study is a nationwide telephone survey designed to assess public trust and confidence in the judiciary relative to that of other government branches. Among other considerations, the assessment includes specific questions related to contemporary issues of national interest such as the court's role in behavioral health, jury system processes and reforms, and online access to court records.

At the state and local levels, court leaders are encouraged to utilize the Access and Fairness survey – Measure 1 of the NCSC (2005) CourTools. This particular measure addresses court access, as well as procedural fairness, from the perspective of court users. More specifically, it assesses the court's treatment of court users on the criteria of fairness, equality, and respect. The measure also evaluates the ease with which court users could locate and access court services that integrate factors such as safety concerns and clarity of court forms (NCSC, 2005). Administered annually or on a periodic basis, a baseline can be established by the court from which future performance can be compared. Performance can be evaluated using the cumulative index score (100-point scale), as well as areas of concern, to determine if court user experiences have improved, remained unchanged, or declined over a noted time period. The index score and trend data should be subsequently shared with court program managers and staff so that system improvements are data-driven and targeted, based on evidenced need (BJA, 1997).

For larger court systems that operate more than one courthouse, survey results can be used to juxtapose the quality of court services among the various locations comprising the complex. Court leaders might find that satisfaction levels vary considerably based on site, prompting court administration to identify and correct (to the extent possible) those factors underlying the disparity. For instance, leaders may find that a particular program or specialized service should be replicated at other court locations. Management might also find that differences in staffing or resource levels are impacting user experiences in significant ways. The same results may also be used to identify training deficits among staff that would otherwise not be known between courthouse locations.

The measure should also be used to assess deficiencies in the court's physical plant. Consider the comment made by a court user who stated, "The Google map is wrong." The court administrator's office found that the search engine's directions to a new regional courthouse building were, in fact, not entirely clear because of recent road construction. Updates were subsequently made so that the most direct route to the courthouse was known to users, who previously relied on the map and were unaware of the infrastructure changes. This type and level of "actionable" feedback is invaluable to the court because it urges the organization to take timely, concrete steps to improve access and overall stakeholder experience.

For many citizens, jury duty is one of the only points of direct interaction these members of the public will have with the court over the course of their lifetime. Although considerable progress has been made in the modernization of jury systems, the experience is generally considered tedious by many prospective jurors, who are eager to forgo the civic obligation and will request the court to defer or excuse jury duty. Feedback from this group of citizens – external stakeholders directly involved in the judicial system – is nonetheless vitally important. Surveys that include both closed- and open-ended questions provide the judiciary with insight into juror experiences throughout each phase of the selection process. Munsterman and associates (1997) recommend regular distribution, collection, and analysis of juror surveys so that trends in attitudes and satisfaction can be assessed over time. Exit questionnaires, in particular, help court leaders identify deficiencies in the system including summoning and screening processes, parking, safety and security, jury assembly and deliberation facilities, evidence presentation, courtroom experience (including sight lines, acoustics, and comfort of seating), and communications and treatment by court staff (Hannaford-Agor, 2016).

Surveys administered to the general public can be likewise helpful in determining the range and depth of needed system improvements, as well as relative support levels among the community for potential change. Documented endorsement for a new program can inform and focus the policy discussion by also accounting for the public's sentiment that could be raised as a potential political concern to block innovation efforts. For example, the NCSC (2022) conducted a national telephone survey asking citizens about the use of remote hearings and other online court services such as online dispute resolution. The findings indicated increasing public support for video court appearances, with 59 percent of respondents expressing agreement. These data points are informative to those discussions centering around the use of remote hearing technology and the extent to which these alternatives should be used in the foreseeable future, following the COVID-19 pandemic. Arizona and Minnesota, among other states, conducted similar surveys of the public, comparing in-person and remote court hearings (Arizona Supreme Court, 2022). Not unlike the NCSC study, results showed support for the continuation of the remote hearings model, findings which were also consistent with surveys administered concurrently by the Arizona judiciary and bar associations. Minnesota, in particular, organized meetings with various stakeholder focus groups. The focus group findings and recommendations favored the utilization of remote proceedings in lieu of the full-scale return to in-person hearings. These findings were shared with judicial leadership and the respective state court judicial councils, so that they could be considered in the formulation and execution of state supreme court policies governing the use and standardization of remote hearings in the post-pandemic era (Minnesota Judicial Branch, 2022).

The aggregate of stakeholder surveys must also include judicial performance evaluations. Several states have established systems that are generally administrated by a state supreme court commission to evaluate judicial performance. Surveys are one mechanism that is used to assess the performance of individual judicial officers. Typically, during a two- or three-month period, questionnaires are distributed to people who had contact with the judge being evaluated, including litigants, witnesses, jurors, and court staff. The input helps the courts ensure that all judges are provided with the opportunity to improve their work and continue their professional development, based on survey feedback. More generally, it helps gauge and maintain the quality of justice provided by the court institution. In New Jersey (2025), for instance, attorneys complete an anonymous questionnaire, which is used to evaluate judges based on more than 30 performance standards. The results are subsequently shared with the judge, the assignment (presiding) judge, the Supreme Court, the Governor, the Senate Judiciary Committee, and the Judicial Evaluation Commission and can be used as a part of the criterion for a judge's reappointment. U.S. Supreme Court Justice Sandra Day O'Connor supported the use of judicial merit selection and judicial performance review so long as it was based on the quality of the judge's work (Institute for the Advancement of the American Legal System [IAALS], 2014):

> Evaluations of judges' performance should focus on the legal analysis, clarity, and fairness of their decisions instead of the outcome of their decisions.

The ABA (2005) identified the following specific uses of judicial performance survey information:

- Self-improvement on the part of judges, thus "enhancing the quality of the judiciary as a whole"
- Effective assignment of judges and improvements in the design of judicial education programs
- Providing information to those responsible for making decisions about a judge's continued service in office, specifically for reappointment, retention or re-election of judges

The IAALS (2016) suggests that judicial performance evaluation systems utilize multiple sources of information to provide a "broad based assessment of judges' on-the-job performance." Other recommended evaluation resources include case management data, court proceeding observations (e.g., video recording audits), review of decisions/opinions, public hearings, interviews with other jurists, and self-evaluations.

Court administration personnel provide critically important, day-to-day support services for judges and their assigned staff in the local court setting. The relationship that exists between judges and personnel is considered highly valued and influential in the art and practice of court administration. As system stakeholders, judges depend on court administration for a host of enterprise-wide functions including information technology, facilities, security, and interpreter services, among other areas of subject matter expertise. The ability of the bench to fulfill its mandated functions is therefore inextricably linked to the level and quality of these administrative support networks.

In light of the integrated nature of these components within the court complex, some state court systems assess their administrative apparatus as well. The Superior Court of Arizona in Maricopa County, for instance, has promulgated an annual survey of the bench (including judges and commissioners) to assess the performance of court administration, with the aim of identifying potential areas in need of improvement. The study explores performance in the following areas (Reinkensmeyer & Hegyi, 2013):

- Central court administration
- Division administration (e.g., criminal, civil, family, probate, etc.)
- Human resources administration
- Judicial formation and education
- Jury management
- Law library
- Court reporting
- Interpreter services
- Court security
- Technology
- Facilities management

Court administration will subsequently review the survey findings and take the necessary steps to act on the input. The process is routinely repeated to gain a "Quality Cycle" perspective for continuous improvement, an integral component of the NCSC's High Performance Courts Framework (Ostrom & Hanson, 2010). Examples of respondents' comments that prompted relatively immediate system improvements included expanded hours for the juror bus service, implementation of remote video interpreter services, and enhanced communications to court personnel regarding facility projects. Of course, and perhaps most noteworthy, these kinds of efforts almost always increase the accountability of court administration (Reinkensmeyer & Hegyi, 2013).

User-Centered Design and Access to Justice

"Access to Justice" stands as one of the universal, most far-reaching strategic agenda priorities of judicial systems across the country. Although notable progress has been made in this realm, unrepresented litigants still face a number of barriers to court access. Factors that place a greater burden on certain court users include the high cost of litigation, limited courthouse operating hours, in-person accessibility, and the inherent complexities of legal procedures and processes. Bearing this in mind, many states have established commissions on access to justice to address the concerns of this unique population and to foster innovation. Programs such as self-service centers, court navigators, and online litigant service portals were developed through these and similar collaborations. Noting the importance of such initiatives, the COSCA issued a series of resolutions in 2001, urging the judicial branch's continued focus on access to justice objectives. In 2016, a joint resolution was adopted for a renewed call to action, setting forth "the aspirational goal of 100 percent access to effective assistance for essential civil legal needs" (CCJ, 2016).

Clarke and Hannaford-Agor (2020) offer an analytical tool for assessing the impact of court access measures. This instrument is designed to identify access voids or service fissures in a given court, determine the impact of proposed strategic solutions, and prioritize tasks in furtherance of key court access objectives. Flango and Clarke (2015) observed that court business processes are generally designed for the benefit of the court, judges, and attorneys. They proposed a customer-focused approach to court services, stating that "Courts should tailor their legal services appropriately and explicitly for litigants." In this context, litigants are the key stakeholders, challenged to overcome the existent barriers to access the court. Flango and Clarke (2015) suggested a paradigm shift in the court's conception of the judicial branch. In this new model, the modern court should be nimble and one which will provide early case triage, consumer choice in venues for dispute resolution, and diversion of some matters from the judicial system. Kourlis and Olin (2011) posited a litigant-friendly judicial system in earnest, characterized by processes designed to meet the specific legal needs of court participants:

> Our vision is simple: courts that are built for service to the public. Remember the "cattle call" docket that benefitted no one but the judge? In our vision, that would never happen in any courtroom in the country. Rather, every procedure would be designed for the person or party seeking justice: to facilitate just, speedy, and inexpensive access to an impartial judge and to a jury when appropriate.

Significant improvements in access to justice necessarily require a user-centered design. This approach is used extensively by businesses in consumer product construction, computer software development, and architectural layout, among industries where the good or service must optimize the customer's experience. In a user-centered process, end user requirements are considered at the outset, as well as throughout the design cycle. Users are actively involved in every facet of the iterative process, including the testing and refinement of business tasks and solutions. The design process generally includes consideration of the following factors (International Organization for Standardization, 2010):

- Context of use
- Accessibility
- Effectiveness
- Efficiency
- Ergonomics and human factors
- User satisfaction

Although user-based design is relatively new in the court administration field, there is an array of literature on these types of frameworks from which judiciary leaders can draw application (Norman, 1986, 1988). Hagan's (2018) work with self-service centers in California provides an instructive example of user-centered design in courts. The initiative included interviews with the users of those facilities, including litigants, advocates, and family members involved in the court process. Feedback from users generated a set of practical recommendations for system improvement, including wayfinding signage, user-centered design features, process-mapping tools, a more welcoming court experience, enhanced documentation, optimized workstations, and overall facility improvements. Reflecting on the importance of the user-centered approach vis-à-vis court processes, Hagan (2018) concluded:

> As we adapt human-centered design to the field of legal services, it points us to a new way to evaluate the success of services. It is about the entire service "journey" of a person going through the legal system. It is not just about improving the ability to understand how to fill in a form, or how to file it with a clerk. Rather, it is about helping the person through the series of any legal tasks. Typically, this journey includes the tasks of issue spotting, engaging with the legal system, finishing tasks, attending hearings, and coming to a resolution. We need to build for and evaluate on "sustained engagement" – whether a person can remain engaged and on track through the entire journey through a court process.

As part of the Compass Project, the IAALS provides guidance on user-centered design pertaining to the family courts (Cornett et al., 2019). The project included a series of "design sprint" workshops with self-represented litigants and stakeholders, addressing divorce and separation processes in various courts throughout the United States. Phases of the user design process included discovery, problem identification, brainstorming, building solutions, testing, refining, and debriefing. With facilitation provided by IAALS, the user-centered design sessions uncovered several problems specific to family court litigation, including burdens in accessibility, case filing costs, and complexity of court forms – the difficulties of which are heightened given the high emotional tenor of the family court docket. Consistent with the other cited instances, the user-centered approach in this example allowed the court to focus its efforts and resources so that system improvements and technological solutions were ultimately effective from the perspective of those most impacted by the changes.

Courthouse design elements are the subject of a "Procedural Justice Through Design" project at the Red Hook Justice Center in Brooklyn, New York (Pope-Sussman, 2015). Although the initiative was not a classic user-centered design exercise, stakeholders were directly involved from the early planning stages through installation of signage and program evaluation. The project design team included court users, prosecution and defense, judges and court staff, and justice agencies. Similar stakeholder-based approaches were successfully employed in the areas of courthouse architecture, training, and program development by the CJI.

The idea and promise of procedural justice require regular assessment of court user experiences. Any attempt to evaluate our system of justice without incorporating stakeholder feedback is to base program components (inputs, activities, outputs, outcomes, and impacts) at best on incomplete data, and at worst on wrong information entirely. To that end, user-centered data are not a luxury. Instead, they are an essential component of both the processes the court employs and the outcomes it seeks to achieve. For instance, user feedback is nothing short of a necessity in matters related to courtroom communications, case referrals to service providers, and post-disposition court proceedings (Embley et al., 2021). We envision a systematic revitalization of court processes and proxy services brought to fruition through a user-centered design strategy. As court leaders with decision-making authority gain more knowledge and experience in this approach of assessing and managing court operations, best practice planning models will be incorporated into the short- and long-term administration of the judiciary. The next generation of court management is situated to leverage the user-centered design, both in updating "old mainframe type systems thinking" and developing new, yet to be discovered agile service delivery structures. The quality of justice and the experience of court users (who can incidentally be the institution's best and most vehement advocates for change) will be enhanced through this interactive, customer-centered design work.

Today's court brings into view a rich mix of time-tested organizational models for stakeholder collaboration that institutional leaders can draw upon and utilize, based on the size and scope of their respective court organizations. Large, formal standing entities – such as supreme court judicial councils and criminal justice coordinating councils – stand in sharp contrast to governance in small, rural trial courts, ad hoc project workgroups, or one-time locally administered public satisfaction surveys. Indeed, courts are not characterized as organizations where "one size fits all." Rather, we find that courts which cultivate their organization, however large or small they may be, in collaboration with a "community of stakeholders" will be markedly better courts for doing so. Court leaders, namely presiding judges and court administrators, should develop and build upon innovative strategies to expand stakeholder collaboration, taking into account their organizational culture and the specific needs of the community. Ultimately, modern courts view the user-centered design approach as integral to the decisions that drive policy and practice. This is critically important because end-user perspectives bring to bear a more accurate understanding of litigant needs, mainly to broaden and assure court access. Stakeholder trust and confidence in the judiciary is enhanced through this iterative process. The complexity of access issues and the demand that the court be more things to more people means that the administration of justice simply cannot be done *without* stakeholder collaboration.

Notes

1 Freeman cites a 1963 memorandum from the Stanford Research Institute, which first noted the term "stakeholder" as distinct from that of "shareholder."

2 For example, in Arizona's View from the Bench program, legislators receive a personal invitation to spend a day "shadowing" a judge on and off the bench. Legislators are, in turn, given the opportunity to select the judge or court facility they desire to visit.

3 Freeman refers to this assessment as a "stakeholder analysis."

4 The Law Enforcement Assistance Agency (LEAA) was created by the 1968 Omnibus Crime Control and Safer Streets Act.

5 Additional information about the Council for Court Excellence is available on their website: www.courtexcellence.org.

6 Additional information about the CJI is available on their website: www.innovatingjustice.org.

7 In the federal court system, the Judicial Conference of the United States is the primary policy-making body, which also makes recommendations to Congress on judicial branch legislation. Circuit Judicial Councils oversee the administration of courts in a given regional area.

8 Synergies created through alignment of national, state, and local court strategic plans are expanded upon in the Strategic Management and Long-Term Planning chapter.

References

Adekunle, A. (2017, July). Justice sector coordination: The role of stakeholders. Paper presented at the 2017 Induction Course for Newly Appointed Judges and Kadis, National Judicial Institute, Abuja, Nigeria, July 3–12.American Bar Association. (1974). *Standards relating to court organization.*

American Bar Association. (2005). *Guidelines for the evaluation of judicial performance with commentary* (Appendix 1). www.americanbar.org/content/dam/aba/publications/judicial_division/aba_blackletterguidelines_jpe_wcom.authcheckdam.pdf.

Arizona Supreme Court. (2022). *COVID-19 continuity of court operations during a public health emergency workgroup: Recommended remote and in-person hearings in Arizona state courts in the post-pandemic world.* www.azcourts.gov/Portals/0/0/Recommended%20Remote%20and%20In-Person%20Hearings%20in%20Arizona%20State%20Courts%20in%20the%20Post-Pandemic%20World%20(2222022%20FINAL).pdf.

Berkson, L., & Carbon, S. (1978). *Court unification: History, politics, and implementation.* National Institute of Law Enforcement and Criminal Justice.

Bureau of Justice Assistance. (1988, April). *Court unification: A program brief.* U.S. Department of Justice.

Bureau of Justice Assistance. (1997, July). *Trial court performance standards with commentary.* U.S. Department of Justice.

Bureau of Justice Assistance. (1999, July). *National Task Force on Court Automation and Integration.* U.S. Department of Justice. www.govinfo.gov/content/pkg/GOVPUB-J26-PURL-LPS106671/pdf/GOVPUB-J26-PURL-LPS106671.pdf.

Bureau of Justice Assistance. (2022, November). *Strategies for court collaboration with service communities.* U.S. Department of Justice. www.ojp.gov/pdffiles1/bja/196945.pdf.

Center for Court Innovation. (2010). *Engaging stakeholders in your project* [Fact sheet]. https://csgjusticecenter.org/wp-content/uploads/2020/08/engaging_2010.pdf.

Center for Court Innovation. (2019). *Can courts be more user-friendly? How satisfaction surveys can promote trust and access to justice.* www.innovatingjustice.org/wp-content/uploads/2020/04/CCI_FactSheet_SatisfactionSurveys_04202020.pdf.

Clarke, T. M., & Hannaford-Agor, P. (2020). *Measuring the impact of access to justice programs: An assessment tool for funders and policy makers.* National Center for State Courts.

Conference of Chief Justices. (2016). *Call to action: Achieving civil justice for all.* National Center for State Courts.

Conference of Chief Justices, & Conference of State Court Administrators. (2020, July). *Resolution 1: In support of racial equality and justice for all.* https://ccj.ncsc.org/resources-courts/support-racial-equality-and-justice-all.

Cornett, L., Knowlton, N. A., Swearingen, J., & Houlberg, M. (2019). *Redesigning divorce: User-driven design for a better process.* Institute for the Advancement of the American Legal System. https://iaals.du.edu/sites/default/files/documents/publications/redesigning_divorce.pdf.

Cushman, R. C. (2002). *Guidelines for developing a criminal justice coordinating committee.* National Institute of Corrections, U.S. Department of Justice.

Dunham, L., Freeman, R. E., & Liedtka, J. (2015). *Enhancing stakeholder practice: A particularized exploration of community.* Cambridge University Press.

Durham, C. M., & Becker, D. J. (2012). *A case for court governance principles.* National Center for State Courts. www.sji.gov/wp/wp-content/uploads/Becker-Durham-A-Case-for-Court-Governance-Principles.pdf.

Embley, L., Himonas, C., & Butler, S. (2021). Usability and court dispute resolution platforms. *Trends in State Courts,* 75–80.

Flango, V. E., & Clarke, T. M. (2015). *Reimagining courts: A design for the twenty-first century.* Temple University Press.

Freeman, R. E. (1984). *Strategic management: A stakeholder approach.* Pitman.

Hagan, M. D. (2018). A human-centered design approach to access to justice: Generating new prototypes and hypotheses for intervention to make courts user-friendly. *Indiana Journal of Law and Social Equality, 6*(2), 199–239.

Hannaford-Agor, P. (2016). Jury system management in the 21st century: A perfect storm of fiscal necessity and technological opportunity. In P. M. Koelling (Ed.), *The improvement of the administration of justice* (8th ed., pp. 506–511). Carolina Academic Press.

Institute for the Advancement of the American Legal System. (2014). *The O'Connor judicial selection plan.* https://iaals.du.edu/projects/oconnor-judicial-selection-plan.

Institute for the Advancement of the American Legal System. (2016). *Transparent courthouse revisited: An updated blueprint for judicial performance evaluation.* https://iaals.du.edu/sites/default/files/documents/publications/transparent_courthouse_revisited.pdf.

International Organization for Standardization. (2010). *ISO 9241-210:2010 ergonomics of human-system interaction – Part 210: Human-centred design for interactive systems.* www.iso.org/standard/52075.html.

Judicial Council of California. (2025). *Judicial Council.* Judicial Branch of California. https://courts.ca.gov/policy-administration/judicial-council/judicial-branch-strategic-plan.

Kourlis, R. L., & Olin, D. (2011). *Rebuilding justice: Civil courts in jeopardy and why you should care.* Institute for the Advancement of the American Legal System.

Minnesota Judicial Branch. (2022). *oneCourtMN hearings initiative policy.* https://mncourts.gov/_media/migration/judicial_council_library/policies/500/525.pdf.

Mundell, B. R., & Jefferson, W. B. (2012). *Herding lions: Shared leadership of state trial courts.* National Center for State Courts. www.hks.harvard.edu/sites/default/files/centers/wiener/programs/pcj/files/ES-StateCourts-HerdingLions.pdf.

Munsterman, G. T., Hannaford-Agor, P. L., & Whitehead, G. M. (Eds.). (1997). *Jury trial innovations* (Publication R-193). National Center for State Courts.

National Association for Court Management (NACM). (2011). *The court administrator: A guide and manual.*

National Association for Court Management (NACM). (2016). *The court administrator – court administration: A guide to the profession.*

National Association of Counties. (2022). *Data-driven justice: Key stakeholders – Courts and probation.* www.naco.org/sites/default/files/documents/DDJ-Issue-Brief_Courts-and-Probation.pdf.

National Center for State Courts. (2005). *CourTools: Trial court performance measures.*

National Center for State Courts. (2006). *Key elements of an effective rule of court on the role of the presiding judge in the trial courts.*

National Center for State Courts. (2022). *State of the state courts: 2025 public opinion poll findings.*

National Center for State Courts. (2025). *State of the state courts: 2025 public opinion poll findings.* www.ncsc.org/resources-courts/state-state-courts-2025-public-opinion-poll-findings.

National Institute of Corrections. (2022). *Guidelines for developing a criminal justice coordinating council.*

National Institute of Justice. (2020). *Problem-solving courts.* https://nij.ojp.gov/topics/articles/problem-solving-courts.

New Jersey Courts. (2025). *Judicial performance program.* www.njcourts.gov/attorneys/jud-ed.

Norman, D. A. (Ed.). (1986). *User-centered system design: New perspectives on human–computer interaction.* Lawrence Erlbaum Associates.

Norman, D. A. (1988). *The psychology of everyday things.* Basic Books.

Ohio Criminal Sentencing Commission. (2023). *Examples of statewide criminal justice repositories.* www.supremecourt.ohio.gov/docs/Boards/Sentencing/committees/uniformSentEntry/RepositoryExamplesFAQ.pdf.

Ostrom, B. J., & Hanson, R. A. (2010). *Achieving high performance: A framework for courts* (Research Division working paper). National Center for State Courts.

Parker, A., Scantlebury, A., Booth, A., MacBryde, J. C., Scott, W. J., Wright, K., & McDaid, C. (2018). Interagency collaboration models for people with mental ill health in contact with the police: A systematic scoping review. *BMJ Open, 8*(3), e019312. https://doi.org/10.1136/bmjopen-2017-019312

Petrila, J., & Fader-Towe, H. (2010). *Information sharing in criminal justice–mental health collaborations: Working with HIPAA and other privacy laws.* Council of State Governments Justice Center. https://bja.ojp.gov/sites/g/files/xyckuh186/files/Publications/CSG_CJMH_Info_Sharing.pdf.

Pope-Sussman, R. (2015). *Improving courthouse signage: Procedural justice through design.* Center for Court Innovation.

Reinkensmeyer, M. W., & Hegyi, D. R. (2013). Performance assessment of court administration services. *Court Manager, 27*(4), 40–56.

Reinkensmeyer, M. W., & Oraftik, C. (2011). Today's version of yesterday's vision of tomorrow's courthouse. *Court Manager, 26*(1), 26–27.

Scherpenzeel, R. (1995). *Computerization in the management of the criminal justice system*. European Institute for Crime Prevention and Control.

Seigle, E., Walsh, N., & Weber, J. (2014). *Core principles for reducing recidivism and improving other outcomes for youth in the juvenile justice system*. Council of State Governments Justice Center. https://csgjusticecenter.org/publications/juvenile-justice-white-paper/.

Substance Abuse and Mental Health Services Administration. (2025). *Intercept 0: Community services*. U.S. Department of Health and Human Services. www.samhsa.gov/communities/criminal-juvenile-justice/sequential-intercept-model/intercept-0.

Sullivan, T. B., & Mathews, M. (2002–2003). *Metro/Davison County, Tennessee criminal justice information system: Project overview and keys to success*. National Task Force on Court Automation and Integration. www.search.org/files/pdf/TN_CaseStudy.pdf.

Waters, N., Spacek, S., & Tobias, P. (2018). *Fair justice for persons with mental illness: Improving the court's response*. National Center for State Courts.

Wickman, A., Mahoney, B., & Borakove, M. E. (2012). *Improving criminal justice system planning and operations: Challenges for local governments and criminal justice coordinating council*. Judicial Management Institute.

12 Court Strategic Management and Master Planning

This chapter situates strategic planning as the bridge between judicial leadership and court operations. Drawing on thinkers like Drucker and lessons from crises such as COVID-19, it frames planning as both a discipline and a mindset. Courts, facing relentless societal and technological change, must adopt dynamic processes that balance continuity with adaptation. Strategic planning is described not as checklists but as a values-driven framework aligning vision, resources, and operations. Long-term master planning, including courthouse design and capital projects, is presented as an extension of this strategic orientation. The chapter also emphasizes continuity of operations planning, recognizing that unanticipated crises – from natural disasters to terrorism – demand agility and resilience. When done well, planning enhances not only institutional capacity but also public trust and confidence. By integrating leadership, stakeholder input, and forward-looking strategies, courts can navigate uncertainty while strengthening their role as democratic institutions.

Strategic planning in courts inexorably addresses the elusive nature and pace of change. The Greek philosopher Heraclitus from Ephesus observed, "Everything changes and nothing remains still: and you cannot step twice into the same stream" (Bryan, 2013). Heraclitus' reflections from the 6th century are equally relevant today for the courts of this new millennia – an era characterized by change that is not only relentless, but hastened by burgeoning technology. Addressing the preparation required for change, Chief Justice Warren E. Burger advised: "More likely the pace will increase, and with it enormous stresses will be placed on all our institutions and particularly on the courts" (Burger, 1970/1990).

As the rate of societal change increases, so too does the need for dynamic planning processes. This is a universal truth across industries and sectors of which the judiciary is not an exception. Today's court leaders must, therefore, seek to draw upon a combination of best practices in project management, strategic planning, and

DOI: 10.4324/9781003686804-12

long-term master space development to continually inform their thinking and methodology in implementing select processes and wholesale programs. This chapter largely focuses on court-wide strategic and long-term master planning, examples of which are drawn from local, state, and federal courts. We explore the theoretical underpinnings of plan development and the benefits of forward-looking administration in managing a variety of capital projects, including the design and construction of new courthouses. A review of planning resources found at the national level, both from court improvement organizations such as the National Center for State Courts (NCSC), as well as other sectors, concludes the discussion.

Drucker (1973) provides an enduring "classic" definition of strategic planning in his seminal publication:

> Strategic planning is the continuous process of making present entrepreneurial (risk-taking) decisions systematically and with the greatest knowledge of their futurity; organizing systematically the efforts needed to carry out these decisions; and measuring the results of these decisions against the expectations through organized, systematic feedback.

Despite the demonstrated benefits of planning, adoption of formal programs that coordinate and organize efforts is not universally embraced by leadership judges and court administrators. Some judicial branch leaders simply do not accept the value proposition that generally accompanies strategic planning. Other leaders may not have a clear understanding of strategic planning processes or a long-term organizational development perspective. These viewpoints are further bolstered by some of the literature that expounds on the inherent limitations of strategic planning, bringing into question classic planning models. These outlooks, some which are deeply rooted in court organizations, represent a considerable challenge for the institution's leaders, who seek to institute any kind of long-term initiative requiring high-level coordination and organization.

Addressing such misconceptions, Drucker (1973) said of strategic planning, "it is not a box of tricks, a bundle of techniques. It is analytical thinking and commitment of resources to action." Likewise, formulation of a court strategic plan stretches far beyond an obligatory administrative exercise, a mere inventory of system improvement projects or detailed "to do" checklists. Rather, fully realized, a comprehensive program of strategic planning ultimately charts a clear sense of forward direction in the court and a solid framework for values-driven executive decision making.

The strategic planning element of our Fundamental Areas of Court Administration model (Figure 1.1) serves as a fulcrum, bridging the leadership of the court to essential judicial branch operations. Situated as such, planning stands out as a critically important feature of modern court governance. In *Sustainable Court Governance*,

Washington and VanDeVeer (2013) reflect on the organizational alignment achievable through strategic planning. They argued that the nature of this configuration runs deep and wide through the organization, encompassing all court business functions, communications, and education/training. When it is managed optimally, a planning program manifests the court's preferred vision, because strategic initiatives are matched to supporting resources. Consequently, the organizational capacity of the court is expanded. This "alignment process" is ultimately what enables the court to assess and improve its services and quality of justice ends. Further, and perhaps more importantly, it serves as the basis of the public's trust and confidence in the judiciary. Having said that, court leaders are challenged, given the wide spectrum of planning resources, to identify and utilize the best methodologies appropriate to their court culture (Ostrom & Hanson, 2009). These decisions are critical. Among other points, choices must consider the administrative capacity, efficacy, and sustainability of the selected planning processes. The various alternatives, in turn, give rise to a series of interrelated questions about the scope, time horizon, and array of stakeholder participants who should be involved in the plan.

Lessons Learned from the COVID-19 Public Health Emergency and Other Crises

In the early stages of the COVID-19 public health emergency, state and federal court administrative offices expedited the implementation of several wide-ranging innovations, including remote hearings (Thumma & Reinkensmeyer, 2022), digital workflow, and remote, off-site staffing. Best practices for continued provision of court services were recorded and promulgated by the Pandemic Rapid Response Team (PRRT)[1] (State Justice Institute [SJI], 2024) through a timely series of NCSC (2020) webinars and publications. Faced with the unprecedented challenges brought to bear by the protracted public health emergency, judiciaries across the system found that a high degree of organizational agility and creativity was needed in response to the crisis. Remarkably, access to vital services was not only maintained by the changes instituted during the pandemic, but it was arguably enhanced. For example, order of protection hearings in domestic violence cases and other emergency proceedings conducted via remote audio/video conference to mitigate the spread of the virus also minimized direct, personal contact between contentious litigants. Courts took similar measures to ensure court access in the wake of other crises such as the September 11 terrorist attacks (Birkland, 2004), Hurricane Sandy (United States Courts [U.S. Courts], 2012), and Hurricane Harvey (Raftery, 2017). In anticipation of such complex and far-reaching catastrophes, the American Bar Association (ABA, 2007) developed a Model Court Rule on Provision of Legal Services Following Determination of Major Disaster.[2]

Court responses to the pandemic and other crises help to inform current thinking about strategic planning, bearing in mind, as former Senate Majority Leader Mike Mansfield stated, "The crisis you have to worry about most is the one you don't see coming" (Goel, 2021). A "prepared" court leader, therefore, also recognizes that unanticipated circumstances can upend the strategic plan. Not unlike leaders of other establishments, those designated to lead the court respond to cataclysmic events by quickly assessing the situation, determining relative impacts to the institution's divisions and respective services, implementing contingency plans and solutions, and reassessing these processes as circumstances dictate. Crises such as those most recently experienced by the courts require a reprioritization of staff functions, reallocation of resources, and deferral of the projects du jour. In the aftermath, court leaders will find it necessary to recommence discussions so that the strategic plan can be reshaped in accordance with emerging realities and the "new normal."

These daunting but critically important management responses also underscore the need for courts to maintain a comprehensive and current continuity of operations plan (COOP). The court administration literature is replete with resources to help guide organizational efforts, including templates, checklists, best practices (Hall, 2021; NCSC, 2007), and "cross-sector" coordination material encompassing the judiciary, law enforcement, and public health (Bureau of Justice Assistance & Centers for Disease Control and Prevention, 2008). Contemporary COOPs also account for evolving threats to the IT infrastructure, and ensure that contingencies, including backup and recovery systems, are established and safeguarded. The Joint Technology Committee's (JTC) (2021) "Resource Bulletin," among other publications, provides court leaders with planning resources for cybersecurity and resumption of court operations.[3] The aggregate crises of the last quarter century have shown that the best strategic plans are those that are built upon a flexible framework – one which is responsive and adaptable to an evolving set of circumstances and unanticipated change impacting the short- and long-term ability of the courts to function, thus serving the public (Kleps, 1975).

Historical Context for Court Strategic Planning

While an exhaustive history of strategic planning is beyond the scope of this text, it is helpful to review the background of court planning efforts. With some notable exceptions pertinent to inter-branch criminal justice coordination, strategic management and master planning in the courts is a relatively novel concept in the field. These coordinated efforts and the strategic plan end-products that are produced by virtue of this process are now a fully developed aspect of court administration and are generally found in federal, state, and local courts.

A cursory look at history reveals countless examples of methodical planning practices, many long before the formal recognition of strategic planning as a 20th century management concept. And long before the 17th century, some semblance of large-scale "master planning" resulted in architectural marvels: Roman aqueducts, the Great Wall of China, and the Egyptian pyramids. Similarly, various forms of "action planning" aided the movement of people, goods, and services in response to an assortment of emergencies. These experiences helped to shape our understanding so that organizations (including the courts) can plan and refine their approach for the present and into the future.

Recognized as a business management thought leader, Asnoff (1965) was a pioneer in the areas of organizational problem solving and strategic planning. He advocated an iterative process, described as the "adaptive search method for strategy formulation," involving ongoing refinement of business objectives, gap analysis, and formulation of strategies. Asnoff's (1965) strategic planning framework includes the establishment of business objectives, a resources development plan, a product development plan, and an operating plan. Project evaluation and risk assessment are also emphasized in this planning model. While much of this early work focuses on the private sector and competitive advantage, the key principles are foundational to our understanding of modern strategic management. Many strategic planning concepts developed for private sector organizations were carried over to the public sector and not-for-profit organizations. Public sector planning is generally a part of budget, facility, and technology management, but it can also be found in other niche areas of non-profit entities.

Drucker (1973) recommended that all organizations institute planning processes and continuously monitor them to bolster performance. Addressing the need for an actionable planning approach, he posited:

> Formulating a theory of the business must be a forward-looking exercise. It requires creating a mission, which in turn compels the organization to systematically evaluate the emerging trends, future changes in its environments, and current or emerging social problems that may be turned into opportunities.

Kaplan and Norton (1996) advocate the Balanced Scorecard framework as a means to "communicate mission and strategy" while also providing employees with feedback on organizational performance. The scorecard draws upon four perspectives, each arguably critical to the organization's success: financial, customer or stakeholder, internal organizational processes, and innovation and learning. Using a similar method, the NCSC (2010) developed a balanced scorecard for courts, denoting four elements – effectiveness, efficiency, procedural fairness, and productivity – which collectively comprise a component of its High Performance Court Framework. This conceptualization embodies a critical dimension of organizational culture and a cycle of continuous improvement (Ostrom et al., 2005; Ostrom & Hanson, 2009). The high-performance model is predicated on four interrelated perspectives including: court customers, internal operations, innovation, and social values.

The NCSC's e-Collection library holds a significant number of court-related strategic planning documents dating back to the 1970s. Those documents include resources (guides and studies of plans) and actual court strategic plans. A seminal publication by the NCSC, *Planning in State Courts: A Survey of the State of the Art*, outlines key elements of state court planning and examines early strategic planning efforts across six states (NCSC, 1976).[4] These statewide initiatives funded by the Law Enforcement Assistance Administration (LEAA) were, in part, prompted by the justice system's "need to assist courts in establishing independent planning capabilities." The publication's foreword is instructive regarding the perceived benefits of court planning (this remains true – it is fundamental notwithstanding whatever changes have been made in the judiciary) (NCSC, 1976):

> Systematic and organized court planning represents an attempt to avoid the gap between promise and performance that sometimes characterizes public institutions. Formalizing the process somewhat may make it possible to obtain the maximum benefit from available resources in achieving responsibly set goals. Planning can help forecast future development to bring into focus participants' and users' perceptions of problems that need to be resolved.

Since the 1970s, court-related strategic plans generally fall into one or more of five categories:

1) Local court plans, made applicable to the local court system as a whole
2) Statewide, supreme court facilitated plans
3) Federal court plans
4) Plans focused on specialized areas of court administration, such as court security or court technology
5) National level system improvement initiatives, including strategic agendas and campaigns of court improvement organizations

Many courts did not embark on strategic planning until the early 1990s. The SJI assisted by providing state and local courts with federal funding. Grant monies were used for some of the early resource materials needed to develop the strategic plans.[5] The first comprehensive strategic plan for the federal courts, *Long Range Plan for Federal Courts*, was completed in 1995 (U.S. Courts, 1995). Among other key points, the plan notes the creation of the Conference of Senior Circuit Judges, the Administrative Office of the United State Courts, the Federal Judicial Center, and Circuit

Councils as foundational to the judiciary's strategic initiatives. This plan has since been updated three times – in 2010, 2020, and 2025 (U.S. Courts, 2010, 2020, 2025).

On a separate but related corollary, the federal courts also adopted a *Long Range Plan for Information Technology in the Federal Judiciary* – an effort which attempted to project technology resource needs between 2023 and 2027 (U.S. Courts, 2022). The plan addresses several features critical to its technological infrastructure, including cybersecurity, systems integration, courtroom technologies, and applications development. Many state supreme courts have developed similar plans, specific to the administration of information technology (Supreme Court of Arizona, 2013; Webster, 2008). In some states, funding bodies with oversight authority require an annual technology proposal from the courts. Plans can also be reviewed for the purposes of auditing expenditures, equipment standardization, and production efficiency. Given the fluid and complex nature of technology, incorporating these advancements into the work of the courts should be aligned with its overarching strategic plan (Webster, 2008). Accordingly, the National Association for Court Management (NACM, 2014a) *Guide to Technology for Court Managers* addresses the key considerations of IT initiatives, including return on investment, project governance, and preparation for organizational change.[6]

In the 1990s, SJI also funded national symposiums for state courts, such as *The Future of the Courts Conference*, which, among other important takeaways, raised awareness about the benefits of court strategic planning (Pankey et al., 2002). Since then, many supreme courts have created "futures commissions" and other long-range planning bodies, staffed by their respective administrative offices of the court. The planning efforts of the Hawaii judiciary, for instance, served as a model for many state initiatives and included long-range visioning, trends analysis, and scenario building – all of which accounted for the essential interacting components of driving forces, predetermined elements, and critical uncertainties (Planet, 1993). Many of the themes highlighted in the 2002 review of 27 court futures and strategic planning initiatives continue to shape practice today (Pankey et al., 2002):

- Creating "rehabilitating methods" for dispute resolution
- Enhancing public trust and confidence in the legal system
- Improving access to justice
- Improving family interventions in juvenile and family courts
- Improving judicial performance evaluation
- Modernizing and integrating court technologies

More recent state and local strategic plans expand on these earlier topics to address current and emerging justice needs. The judiciary's increasing responsibility for addressing and managing these expanding and emerging issues reflects the courts' evolving role in modern society and, more broadly, the changing role of government. In addition to the factors above, the most recent decade has brought to the fore the following concerns that are at the center of the judiciary's engagement with stakeholders:

- Community connections and stakeholder involvement
- Court performance measures, transparency, and accountability
- Matters that impact racial justice
- E-court services, including remote hearings, online dispute resolution, online payments, e-filing, e-access, etc.
- Evidence-based practices in probation and pre-trial services
- Fair justice in the criminal justice system
- Mental health
- Problem-solving courts
- Representative juries

At the national level, areas of major focus and expansive strategic initiatives are set forth by court improvement organizations like the NCSC, NACM, Institute for the Advancement of the American Legal System (IAALS), Conference of Chief Justices (CCJ), Conference of State Court Administrators (COSCA), and ABA. Plans – sometimes referred to as "campaigns" – of these national organizations highlight some of the ongoing organizational actions, while also providing planning guidance to state and local courts. For example, the NCSC (2024) "Justice for All" includes extensive planning materials on strategic planning for enhanced court access. Another example is found in the *Strategic Planning Through Sequential Intercept Model*, advocating a strategic planning framework to facilitate "cross system communication and collaboration" in the mental health arena (National Judicial Task Force, 2022).

Two recent initiatives of the NCSC are also noteworthy, providing practical guidance on trends analysis and planning in state and local courts. The Just Horizons Initiative identifies "driving forces of change," likely future scenarios and areas of vulnerability for state courts (NCSC, 2022a). Based on this wide-ranging analysis, the NCSC presents a series of action-oriented strategies in areas such as workforce development, court functions, technology, and modern court facilities. The wide-ranging action steps are stratified as applicable to strategic planning efforts at the national, state, and local court levels. Building on this work, the NCSC's "Future Ready Courts Framework" emphasizes rigorous critical analysis of future scenarios and identification of most plausible outcomes. The NCSC recommends this forecasting approach, given the current state of "profound and constant change," a trend which is accelerating in pace. Components of this planning framework are strategic foresight activities, executing and adopting activities, and strategic planning activities (NCSC, 2025a).

Strategic Planning Process

With this rich history of strategic planning, judicial branch leaders may logically conclude that every court should immediately embark on planning. However, even the most forward-thinking members of the court's management team recognize the importance of timing and support for these efforts to be successful. For the executive management team of the court, the dilemma of when (and if) to immerse itself in a strategic planning effort raises questions about the *actual* priorities of the bench and the credibility of the current management team in the long term. Realistically, reaching a state of organizational readiness for strategic planning may be difficult, if not impossible, in some jurisdictions. In undecided courts where there is a modicum of interest in planning, the court's leadership may opt to systematically build consensus in support of the initiative. This "long game" approach presents a true leadership challenge, both at the outset and throughout the court planning process. Fully leveraged consensus building requires the court's executive team to share information to influence and inform perspectives, while also facilitating honest dialogue on the value proposition of strategic planning.

Beyond internal discussions with the bench and staff, the court's executive leadership team may wish to consider the following ideas to foster and coalesce support for a planning initiative:

- A review of strategic plans developed by similarly situated courts, specifically those of the same jurisdiction level and comparable size
- Site visits to "partnership courts" which actively use their strategic plans for system improvements and resource allocation
- Identification of "hot issues" for which a strategic plan can provide direction and justification for additional resources, e.g., workforce development, case management, court access for unrepresented litigants, facility expansion, etc.
- Inclusion of "next generation" judges and court managers in the early discussions about a prospective planning initiative
- Early development of dedicated staffing capacity for the plan, including possible use of consultants, to alleviate concerns about staff workload impacts during the planning process
- Setting a reasonable and manageable scope for the court's initial plan in terms of subject matter, time horizon, and stakeholder involvement

We dedicated entire chapters to exploring the importance of stakeholder involvement in court planning, together with other meaningful community engagements. Not unlike those dynamics, the strategic planning process is deeply enhanced by broad participation of the public, system users, and justice agencies. Invariably, the court's planning process provides a unique opportunity for the court leadership to ensure diversity in the cadre of stakeholders, thus creating steering committees and focus groups that are reflective of the community served by the court. A diverse group of stakeholders will bring many valuable perspectives to the planning process, also lending credibility to the final strategic plan and the standing of the court in the community.

Martin and associates (1995) set forth a detailed process in formulating a court strategic plan, including flowchart diagrams and suggested guidelines. Used extensively in state and local courts, the authors propose the following eight-step planning process:

Step 1: Initiating and Agreeing on a Planning Process
Step 2: Identifying Organizational Mandates, Mission, Goals, and Expectations
Step 3: Establishing a Common Vision of Success
Step 4: Conducting Trends Analyses and Developing Scenarios
Step 5: Conducting an Organizational Assessment
Step 6: Developing Strategies to Manage Issues
Step 7: Operationalizing the Plan
Step 8: Monitoring Organizational Movement Toward Success

More recent guidance on facilitating this process is delineated in the strategic planning module of the NACM's (2015) *CORE*. The module presents the planning steps as a linear process – in contrast to the circular, continuous process and other variations of the classic planning model adopted by some courts. This continuous approach is illustrated in Figure 12.1. The discussion that follows draws primarily on the guide by Martin and colleagues (1995), the NACM *CORE*, and the authors' practical experience as facilitators for government and non-profit organizations.

Figure 12.1 Continuous Process of Strategic Planning – An Ongoing, Iterative Approach

Initiating a Planning Process

Our discussion of strategic planning processes starts with an assessment of organizational readiness (Pankey et al., 2002). This initial, critical step requires a realistic evaluation of the current state of affairs of the local court, the level of bench support for such an effort, and the organizational capacity of administration. Wagenknecht-Ivey and associates (2000) designed a practical and accessible survey to evaluate the organizational readiness of a court. Irrespective of the instrument used in determining whether such an initiative should be launched, the decision for planning ultimately rests with the presiding judge and court administrator.

Strategic planning literature is replete with sensible tips and suggestions for initiating the planning process. While many of the ideas sound like "common sense," the authors have learned that "getting organized" is, in fact, an imperative in court planning. Once a decision is made to proceed with planning, it is the job of the court administrator to ensure that the project is well organized, fully staffed, and ready to advance in a timely manner. Wagenknecht-Ivey and colleagues (2000) offer the following suggestions for the early launch of the strategic plan:

- Establish commitment of top leadership and name an executive leader, like the chief justice or presiding judge
- Create a strategic planning committee
- Establish regular meeting schedules and milestones for the planning process
- Designate a strategic planning coordinator
- Use experienced planning facilitators
- Consider use of a pleasant, off-site meeting facility for the group planning sessions

Most of our discussion heretofore pertains to courts embarking on a first strategic plan. Ideally, jurisdictions with a longer history of strategic planning should have instituted a fixed schedule for regular (e.g., quarterly and annually) review, assessment, and updating of their plans. Once this kind of planning regimen is established, the court may find a natural rhythm in the prioritization of new initiatives, placing some projects in a "parking lot" for consideration during the next round of planning. For example, the Supreme Court of Arizona (2019) develops five-year strategic plans which coincide with the term of the chief justice. Progress reports and plan updates are subsequently documented on an annual basis. The updates are then reviewed and refined during strategic planning retreats of the Supreme Court and the Administrative Office of the Courts.

Mission Statement and Goals

The court's mission statement should be established during the early stages of the planning process, creating a sense of direction and scale for the plan. The mission statement serves as a "necessary reference point" during the latter phases of the planning process, including the development of new plans in future years (Pankey et al., 2002). Fetter (1993) asserted, "An organization's mission is its highest level of purpose," calling for careful thought on both the mission of the court as a whole and the mission of its component parts, such as the family court. An important part of this step is an inventory of the court's mandated functions, which precisely defines the scope of the court's mission (Martin et al., 1995). A study of mandates can also be used for operations management and budget planning, particularly in the allocation of court resources (Reinkensmeyer, 2004). Together, this assessment analysis should consider applicable provisions of the constitution, statutes, and court rules.

Consider, for instance, the federal court's 2025 strategic plan, which is predicated upon a core set of values, including the Rule of Law, independence of the judicial branch, diversity and respect, accountability, and excellence in service. Centered on these principles, the federal court's mission statement underscores the neutral role of the judiciary as a separate, co-equal branch of government (U.S. Courts, 2025):

> The United States Courts are an independent, national judiciary providing fair and impartial justice within the jurisdiction conferred by the Constitution and Congress. As an equal branch of government, the federal judiciary preserves and enhances its core values as the courts meet changing national and local needs.

Vision

Creating a long-term vision for the court involves a forward-looking perspective on the uncharted future. This presents an opportunity for the planning team to formulate a *preferred* future for the court. The visioning process requires a degree of creativity, bounded by a realistic assessment of the court's potential to implement the new future within a reasonable timeframe (e.g., a three-to-five-year period). This necessarily requires that those tasked with developing the strategic plan identify trends which can potentially impact the court and should be considered in light of short- and long-term objectives. Pankey and colleagues (2002) commented on the overriding importance of vision:

> A compelling vision is often more important to implementation efforts than to strategy formation because it provides a unified sense of purpose to the often disparate units within an organization.

Schultz and associates (1993) proposed a framework for visioning workshops, which also addresses the impact of vision statements on organizational morale, productivity, and innovation. A review of state and local court vision statements reveals great variation in areas of focus, levels of detail, and scope. Kotter (1996) suggests that a credible vision should be imaginable, desirable, feasible, focused, flexible, and communicable. Communicating the court's vision to the public is particularly important. A succinct yet powerful vision statement such as the one espoused by the District of Columbia Court on the court's website, social media, signage, and court resource materials sets an appropriate and accessible tone: "Open to All, Trusted by All, Justice for All" (District of Columbia, 2017). In formulating a preferred future statement, the planning team will also want to consider ideas for "reinventing" courts and the delivery of legal services discussed in various publications that are specific to these court-related matters.[7]

Trends Analysis and Scenarios

The process of environmental scanning is vitally important in creating a context for the futures thinking involved in the other steps of the planning process. The purpose of the scanning is to identify trends and issues which will impact the court, and, more broadly, the community in the years ahead. An analysis of the macro trends[8] focuses on changes related to population growth and demographic shifts, economic indicators, and innovations in the fields of science and technology – all of which can affect the working environment of courts in a variety of ways. At the micro level, court planners might examine changes in community resources, regional service demands, and local workforce dynamics. Collecting and analyzing this wide array of information allows court leaders to consider a range of alternative future scenarios, which can be developed in tandem with responsive action planning. These considerations should also incorporate "wild card" scenarios – unlikely events which constitute a turning point in the evolution of a trend that require reliable action in managing what would otherwise be an unanticipated ongoing crisis, such as the COVID-19 public health emergency.

These analyses require extensive group discussion, along with pre-meeting staff work to gather and organize preliminary information that serves as a starting point for deliberations. Some courts will elicit stakeholder feedback using established templates and survey instruments to synthesize and assess perspectives of local, regional, and national trends and issues that could potentially impact the court and relevant agencies. Stakeholders in these exchanges are typically drawn from the organizations with which the court regularly collaborates. They may also ask subject-matter experts whose work provides in-depth knowledge of events or circumstances that, although unusual, could still leave the judiciary vulnerable. These sessions can be convened as focus groups or more formally (depending on the size of the court) as a larger scale task force. In either case, the general purpose is to help discern the needs and demands of stakeholders so that the court can reliably respond with minimal to no disruption in its operation. More broadly, this means administering justice and ensuring a well-functioning system, irrespective of those turbulent conditions that can make other organizations unstable and unpredictable.

Organizational Assessment

An assessment of the court organization is a necessary management exercise, whether it is part of strategic planning or a separate, independent application. Assessments, such as a SWOT (Strengths, Weaknesses, Opportunities, and Threats) analysis, help planners identify internal and external risks and safeguards that impact the organization (Learned & Christensen, 1965). A SWOT analysis is generally performed prior to the court's execution of an initiative, program, or institution-wide policy. The analysis is particularly helpful because it allows the court to explore and juxtapose a fuller range of alternatives together with the factors that may impact each of these choices. Moreover, the framework can be configured in concert with other stakeholder groups, in an effort to bolster respective strengths and opportunities, while also mitigating weaknesses and threats of partnerships. Other sources of data for organizational assessments include the NCSC CourTools, caseload and budget reports, organizational charts, court program evaluations, and comparison of court services to best practice standards.[9] While all of the CourTools measures should be considered in the organizational assessment, two of the measures are especially relevant to planning sessions: Measure 1: Access and Fairness (the survey of the public and court users); and Measure 9: Court Employee Satisfaction (NCSC, 2005).

Development of Strategies to Manage Issues

The work involved in devising a plan generally provides the team with a clearer understanding of the court's current reality and future challenges. This information, along with the earlier development of a court mission and vision, serves as the platform from which strategic issues will be organized and an agenda developed. Strategic issues can be grouped into broad categories such as court access, workforce development, and community relations. Higher-level classifications of strategic issues constitute the "strategic agenda." Goals and objectives should be developed for each area of the strategic agenda. Fetter (1993) emphasized the need to include a value statement – a clearly stated purpose – in each goal statement, also suggesting that most court plans should be built upon three or four major goals. These objectives should include specific milestones and other indices of progress, such as dates for deliverables and the total number of program participants. With clear goals and objectives in place, strategies can be developed for each component of the agenda, and organized into a comprehensive strategic plan document so that it can ultimately be promulgated and operationalized.

Operationalizing and Monitoring the Plan

Formal approval of the strategic plan is another important step requiring leadership on the part of the chief justice / presiding judge and court administrator. The bench and court staff should be active participants in the planning process, so that when the plan is finalized, the organization is generally supportive of the proposed initiatives. Bench endorsement of the strategic plan is required at the local court level, and statewide plans should be shared and endorsed by the supreme court's judicial council. The plan's formal ratification should be followed by promulgating it across various communication mediums so that the composite of vision, mission, objectives, strategy, approach, and tactics is made known to the various stakeholder groups that have an interest in the plan, including the public, justice system partners, funding authority, and court personnel. The development of a court strategic plan is necessarily predicated on a prioritization of stakeholder needs vis-à-vis the organizational capacity of the court. This is an area for open, candid discussion concerning the allocation of court resources. The planning framework also includes the dimension of time (e.g., a five-year planning horizon), allowing the court's workgroup or team to adopt a phased approach from inception to completion.

The subsequent steps in the planning process include assigning action items and tasks to specific staff to monitor progress. The NACM (2015) suggests that task assignments also be included in the performance evaluations of staff as a way of creating focus and incentivizing efforts toward deliverables of the strategic plan. The strategic plan should also be incorporated into the court's budget process to substantiate and justify the needs and resources including staffing, technology, facilities and security, education and training, and program-related services. Also recommended by the NACM (2015) is the designation of a strategic planning coordinator, creating a standing committee to lead the system improvement efforts set forth in the strategic plan, regular meetings held by judicial leadership to discuss the ongoing progress of the plan, and establishing a formal system of reporting. By monitoring the relative growth and evolution of the organization, court leaders can utilize these occasions to celebrate "early successes" with impacted groups, while fortifying renewed attention and momentum for the plan's goals and objectives. Those announcements can likewise be shared during steering committee meetings, as well as promulgated through press releases, websites, and social media outlets.

Strategic Alignment

Our discussion regarding alignment has largely focused on priority setting and linking business functions within a given court. At the macro level, it is also possible to connect local court strategic plans to the strategic agendas of other local, regional, and national-level organizations.The strategic agendas of national court improvement organizations will generally help define areas of broad focus, such as access to justice, mental health, and racial justice (Bell, 2022). These comprehensive themes will also garner support for national level research, grant funds, and technical assistance to the courts.

Aligning the court's strategic plan with other improvement initiatives (some of which may be a focus at the national level) helps to better position the local court in securing grants and resources that are made available by funding agencies. Alignment can also be achieved through interconnections with the state's supreme court strategic plan or a state-level futures study. One of the ways a more provincial court can help foster a sense of "collective responsibility for state-wide delivery of quality court services" is to assign a local court representative to projects and committees that are headed by the state supreme court (Mundell & Jefferson, 2012). These aggregate efforts will more fully inform court leaders about the potential issues and trends impacting their jurisdiction, as well as allowing district liaisons to draw on and share the benefits derived from innovative court program models and cross-court research findings (Labovitz & Rosansky, 1997).

Contrarian Views: Resistance and Perceived Limitations of Planning

The arguments against strategic planning are generally grounded on the practical considerations in managing the day-to-day affairs of the court and the limitations of these frameworks. In a review of planning efforts in 31 state and local courts, Kiefer (2016) found that nearly half of the courts – 14 courts in total – had no strategic plan. Interviews with judges and administrators from those courts without a plan offered the following reasons:

- Developing plans can be expensive.
- Developing a plan can be "daunting."
- Many courts are not inclined to "open up" their operation to outside "scrutiny" and business process engineering as suggested in the strategic planning literature.
- Some administrative judges do not see the value in strategic planning and may question the amount of time involved in planning versus doing "real work."

Our experience and dealings with leadership judges have not been entirely different. Some expressed similar reservations about the value and time commitment involved in strategic planning, but other judges were more open to the dividends that could be realized through such initiatives. In one exchange, a presiding judge ultimately approved moving forward with a strategic planning project, remarking:

> You administrators really like this planning stuff, don't you... flip charts and all. But it sounds like a good next step for the court. Let's go ahead with what you've laid out here. How much time do you think this will take up, say for the judges?

One of the key factors that will influence judges' perspectives on strategic planning is the expected duration of their leadership role. Kiefer's (2016) study, for instance, found that judges serving in a leadership capacity for comparably shorter periods of time (one to three years) than their counterparts are less likely to support these kinds of initiatives. Strategic plans will also have fewer sponsors during recessions or downturns in the economy because of the shift in priorities (Van Duizend & Coleman, 2009). Faced with budget cutbacks, leaders can be less inclined to champion projects or planning efforts that they perceive are a distraction and draw on the limited and decreasing set of resources they are afforded. Van Duizend and Coleman (2009), however, argue an entirely different position viewing the strategic plan as fundamental to court operations:

> Strategic planning should not be considered a luxury to be indulged in when times are good. During these difficult fiscal times, states, local governments, and trial courts around the nation are using strategic planning as a tool to identify and better manage their core mission.

Thus, planning is not ancillary, but is rather central to solutions that are being sought by the court. When methodically developed and executed, these initiatives improve justice services and reduce costs during fiscal crises by directing attention to the following critical areas:

- Constitutionally mandated court functions
- Setting and assigning priorities
- Allocation of resources
- Enhancement of revenues
- Deployment of new technologies which enhance workflow and productivity
- Justification of budget requests
- Establishing tangible measures for performance, predicated on adequate funding

Griller (2013) noted the "widespread grumbling" over strategic planning – a perspective he attributes to the considerable amount of time and resources that are invested in arguably static plans. Unanticipated events marked by turning points in the economy, healthcare emergencies, environmental disasters, or global affairs can render plans obsolete, which is used to argue against their utility. Griller (2013) added that the structured process can also create a disconnect between the urgency and importance of the plan and the pressing day-to-day demands of the court; bearing this in mind, he recommended:

> Effective present-day court leaders must be true strategic thinkers who operate from a perspective of objective insight and analytical clarity, whether or not they go through a formal strategic planning process.

Recognizing the challenges of implementing traditional paradigms across a wide array of courts, Kotter's (2012) eight-stage framework offers a viable alternative for leading major change – an approach that leverages "strategic networks" to achieve rapid system improvements. The strategic network model is comprised of the following eight interrelated "accelerators": 1) Create a Sense of Urgency; 2) Build a Guiding Coalition; 3) Form a Strategic Vision; 4) Enlist a Volunteer Army; 5) Enable Action by Removing Barriers; 6) Generate Short-Term Wins; 7) Sustain Acceleration; and 8) Institute Change.

Mintzberg (1994) asserted that the term "strategic planning" is a misnomer. He distinguishes between planning and "strategic thinking," stating:

> Strategic planning, as it has been practiced, has really been strategic programming, the articulation and elaboration of strategies, or visions, that already exist.

He proposed that formal strategic planning is inherently limited to preservation and rearrangement of present-day factors, all of which are grounded in current organizational structures. While there can be value in this kind of static model, it does not give rise to "inventing" or generating new ideas beyond the current planning framework. He further argued that conventional planning processes are also flawed by data misinterpretations and the overformalization of the planning process. Innovation, according to Mintzberg (1994), arises from the "creative act of synthesizing experiences into a novel strategy." To facilitate strategic thinking in earnest requires reimagining the conventional paradigm, which includes the following steps:

- Develop a new, expanded role for planning staff, who can serve as "catalysts" and prompt middle managers to think creatively about the future.
- Create "soft analyst" planning positions, charged to "open up" the rigid planning process, identify creative business processes and encourage others to think strategically.
- Examine and adjust the level of formalization needed in the organization's standing planning process, with an eye towards expansion of informal avenues for input.

Master Planning

At its core, a master plan is a forward-looking, long-term planning document that provides a conceptual framework to guide growth and development. It establishes connections among buildings, social spaces, and their broader environmental context, supporting coordinated and strategic decision making. One of the greatest challenges for judicial branch leaders is attaining the capital funding and approval for a new courthouse construction. This is, in part, due to the costs and complexity of facility issues, such as site selection and architectural design, in building court facilities. But, as a practical matter, over the course of their careers, most court leaders will have little to no experience in managing projects of this scale. Local politics are also often intertwined into the facilities planning process. County and city board members who are generally supportive of the court may quickly be forced to take a stand on funding priorities, the level of tolerance for debt, and competing budget demands from other justice entities. Additionally, proposals for new or expanded court facilities can get delayed or impeded over complex decisions regarding site selection, architectural design, and long-term maintenance costs.

Along with these many complications, the facility needs of local courts are often considered to be secondary to those of other entities hosted by the local funding authority. This is, in part, due to the close working relationship of the funding authority and its subordinate organizational units of government within the same branch of government. Examples include county funded and managed entities like the jail system, park district, floodplain management, and library system. Within this contextual background, the authors have also observed that government agencies governed by city or county boards are generally more likely to have current, comprehensive, long-term master space plans than their local court counterparts. In turn, the non-court entities possessing master plans are best positioned to get approval for capital improvement projects. Given these dynamics, it is in the best interest of every court – irrespective of size or location – to develop and maintain an up-to-date master space plan for acquisition of new facilities, expansion of existing buildings, and facility renovations.

Master planning encompasses many of the same elements found in court strategic planning. In fact, the court's strategic planning can serve as a foundational element of a master plan, identifying trends, and sketching out various scenarios. During a classic strategic planning process, courts can also identify general space needs and build consensus for facility projects.

Completion of a feasibility study encompasses a thorough assessment of all facility-related planning considerations and finance strategies. Among other things, the analysis will delineate alternative planning scenarios, opportunities for business process re-engineering (NACM, 2014b), and potential operational impacts. It should be noted that this level of detailed, multi-tiered evaluation is almost always a prerequisite for the funding body to approve a capital investment of substantial scope.

The NCSC's (1998) planning guide and resource explains that detailed space planning can occur over a period of years, taking into account both new and renovated facilities, but the initial study that outlines the cost/benefit of choices is an all-important consideration:

> But from an overall strategic planning standpoint, the basic roadmap for improvements should be developed before any major design activity and before the commitment of significant capital dollars.

Master planning is not exclusive to the courts or even government; rather, it is widely used in both private and public sectors such as university campuses, medical complexes, corporate headquarters, and correctional installations. Master planning is also an essential part of urban planning used by leaders of towns and cities of varying sizes and stages of development. These frameworks generally cover a period between 10 and 15 years as a way to manage sustainable growth. Akin to the courts, the master planning process helps leaders facilitate the following:

- Set priorities
- Create a phased implementation schedule
- Establish a framework for private investment
- Conceptualize urban space, including physical and spatial elements
- Engage the community and build consensus

Irrespective of the project size, the benefits of master planning are universal, allowing the court to optimize its space, unify its short- and long-term vision, create efficiencies and prioritization of work plans, enable future growth through engagement with impacted stakeholders, and to control short- and long-term costs.

There is a noted overlap in the relationship and activities between master planning and architectural programming, which incidentally may be staffed by the same team of design professionals. While it is certainly possible to staff these functions simultaneously, it requires a strong project management presence that can successfully coordinate the teams' activities (NCSC, 2025b). An architectural program is more specific regarding the utility of the court space, addressing the challenges and opportunities and ensuring that the goals are aligned with the available budget. User-needs surveys often accompany these programs so that the physical court space can be transformed in accordance with the work activity of judges, managers, and staff and the stakeholders with whom they regularly collaborate. In today's post-pandemic era where remote and hybrid court hearings are an expected norm, facilities planning must also incorporate concepts and design features of a virtual courthouse (Reinkensmeyer, 2010). All of these considerations should also be guided by space and facility standards, which delineate square footage requirements for courtrooms, chambers, jury deliberation rooms, offices, and customer service areas (NCSC, 1998; U.S. Courts, 2021).

Architectural plans must also incorporate provisions for court security, including space for entry screening, temporary holding facilities, and separate circulation patterns for inmate movement. The NCSC (2022b) also provides extensive guidance on security requirements for court facilities and is a compilation of best practices drawn from the U.S. Marshals Service, National Sheriff's Association, International Association of Chiefs of Police, Transportation Safety Administration, U.S. Department of Homeland Defense, and NACM.

Courts are part of an integrated justice system – the data and workflow of which is shared with several agency partners; as such, respective business systems must be closely coordinated. This integrated model is also not exclusive to the criminal courts, given the network interfaces that exist across the case management divisions, including family, juvenile, and municipal dockets. As previously noted, the long-term master plan should incorporate architectural design features that improve the interplay of the court's operations with the various stakeholder groups, which will function or seek service in the same space. Therefore, it is, important that a complement of individuals representing the interests of these varied groups is included in the master planning process. This is especially important today, given the courts' working relationships with state and local service providers across areas including mental health, substance abuse, housing, and education, among others. With the common goal of serving the community, some of the questions that these task forces will address include:

- What is the specific form and function of the courthouse space?
- How is the form and function of the space connected to the workflow of external agencies?
- Does the space need to be a particular design to achieve an objective set by the workflow?
- Does the space need to be flexible based on its utilization?
- What are the requirements with respect to light, security, privacy, ventilation, view, accessibility, etc.?
- Does the space need to be accessible to other areas of the courthouse or exterior location?
- What are the standard guidelines or requirements for the dimensions of the space?

Any plan that involves multiple groups of stakeholders should be mobilized (at least initially) by the presiding judge and court administrator, who are in the best position as the leaders of the court to influence active and thoughtful participation in the process. Regular engagement by these court leaders, even if only to provide a springboard and keep the plan's discussion on course, will improve the likelihood of the project's approval and overall success.

Capital funding is another important aspect of facilities planning and is a specialized part of the process that court leaders with extensive budget and planning experience may still find challenging. For those reasons, the court, as well as the funding body, will oftentimes seek outside expertise in capital financing and related areas of law. Today, the array of capital project financing options is at once both promising and daunting. Tobin's (1995) monograph on court facilities funding outlines the key decision points:

- Is financing feasible?
- Does the project require the host government to incur debt?
- What type of debt should be used?
- What revenue streams will be used for debt service?

This kind of front-end analysis regarding capital financing requires careful consideration of property ownership, legal constraints governing debt and taxation, interest rate projections, up-front costs for site selection and design, and marshaling intergovernmental relations (Byers & Swetnam, 2014).

Most large court construction projects incur long-term debt, typically in the form of general obligation or revenue bonds. A court may be asked to institute new filing fees or increase court user payments to satisfy the requirements for the revenue bond. Faced with this kind of proposition, court leaders must consider the relative impact to low-income litigants, access to court services, as well as provisions for fee waiver and deferral.[10] Time-bound tax levies (e.g., a one cent sales tax for seven years), rental income from private businesses occupying courthouse space, fees for parking, and intergovernmental agreements for judicial branch services are other types of funding that can be designated in adherence to the revenue bond (Reynolds & Hall, 2011). Public–private partnerships predicated on a contract between the host government and a private entity or private consortium that will issue certificates of anticipation or bonds offers the court another type of finance option. These arrangements have become more prevalent since the 1990s and provide for lease purchases, as well as "design-build-finance" partnerships with a private developer or non-profit entity (Eaton & Locher, 2009; Murray, 2013; Reynolds & Hall, 2011). Of course, the host government can always opt to fund the facilities project by drawing on a combination of capital finance sources, which can complicate the process further.

Planning Resources

Our discussion thus far has addressed readily available resources and recommendations for effective court planning. The current resources include planning guides, space and security standards, best practices in planning models, and sample strategic plans from every level of court. An online glossary of strategic planning terms is available through the NCSC (2025b) resources. Pankey et al.'s (2002) work, too, offers an extensive bibliography on court futures and strategic planning. Apart from these fundamentals, however, courts that seek to implement strategic and master planning must also consider staffing capacity, technical assistance by external consultants, and technological infrastructure for planning and project management initiatives. The NCSC (1976) lamented that planning for courts was – during that era – largely conducted by "non-court" entities, specifically by state and federal legislatures and executive branch agencies. The report concluded:

> Few courts or court systems have planned in a disciplined fashion to identify and attain long-term goals, in part because of the obstacles court planners have faced. Often, leadership has not believed planning to be valuable... planning support staff and information systems are often inadequate. External agencies usually control a high proportion of court finances, and the courts themselves have disjointed administrative authority.

This model was inherently at odds with the best interest of the courts, and the power imbalance this arrangement created (at the expense of the court), would prompt the judicial branch to establish its own specialized staff positions supported by other resources to enable planning efforts.

Considerable progress has been made since 1976, at least in the capacity of the courts to develop and formulate their own long-term plans. For instance, although still relatively uncommon, some state court administrative offices and large metropolitan courts now have planning units staffed with high-level personnel, dedicated for these purposes. Other courts have assigned planning functions to their research and development units or to special project staff. Courts without permanent planning staff have contracted external consultants or arranged for technical assistance from other organizations or units of government to help navigate the process. In short, while the resources that the courts can commit to these initiatives are not evenly distributed, most jurisdictions should be poised for some form of strategic or master planning that is driven principally by the court.

Educational opportunities and certification programs for project management are now widely available for those in the court administration field. These opportunities include an intensive project management program offered by the Institute for Court Management[11] in addition to project management courses that culminate in a certification from the Project Management Institute.[12] The NACM is another source of rich educational content in the area of leadership and planning. The association promotes professional development through national conferences and educational programs, a quarterly publication, *Court Manager*, member networking opportunities, mentorships, and partnership with other court improvement organizations. Central to these professional development efforts is a set of core competencies for court managers. Strategic Planning is a component of the NACM *CORE* Vision element, which also encompasses leadership and court governance. The *CORE* curriculum for strategic planning focuses on "local justice-planning networks," consensus building, and a spirit of innovation and is designed so that it can be delivered in a range of formats and for varying types and sizes of groups (NACM, 2015).

Newly developed and evolving technologies provide court managers with a greater level of ease with which to develop, implement, and monitor strategic plans (Miller, 2024). In general, computer applications support shared viewing and group updates to the plan. The applications are an important resource for project directors in managing staff assignments, tasks, action items, objectives, and goals. Some applications also support cross-linking strategic plans of distinct units or multiple departments of an organization so that respective goals and objectives are brought together under a unified mission and vision.

The latest software packages for strategic management include interactive electronic dashboards so that users can share and receive feedback from their business partners, donors, community members, or client base. In similar fashion, the courts can use these systems in cooperation with intergovernmental agencies (e.g., reports to the legislature and funding bodies), while also keeping the public apprised and soliciting input about the court's development plans. For larger scale projects such as instituting a new case management system, expanding e-court services, or renovating a building, we recommend using specialized applications to manage these initiatives. Modern applications also include integrated functions such as Gantt charting, work structure deconstruction, event sequencing and the "critical path," timesheets, and budget, among other management controls (Delos Santos, 2022). Finally, cloud-based solutions offer court leaders the ability to securely store and share information, allowing project team members to more easily collaborate.

Courts with established planning programs are ideally positioned to meet the challenges of the future. Having a unifying vision and guided by an organizational mission, the judiciary can elevate the quality of justice and enhance public trust and confidence in the courts through the development, implementation, and regular monitoring of its strategic long-term plan. Today's court leaders must leverage the strengths of their institution and advance opportunities available to modern organizations, thus helping the court to overcome new and emerging challenges that could otherwise have a deleterious effect on the administration of justice.

Notes

1 The PRRT was comprised of a group of chief justices and state court administrators, with staff support from the NCSC.

2 ABA Resolution 194 encourages states to adopt this rule.

3 The JTC is comprised of representatives from the COSCA, NACM, and NCSC.

4 This publication also includes an extensive literature review on strategic planning, both in the private and public sectors, pages 41–55.

5 Established by federal law in 1984, the SJI awards grants to "improve the quality of justice in state courts."

6 See also Joint Technology Committee. (2017). *Introduction to the next-generation court technology standards application component model.* NCSC.

7 See Barton, B. H., & Bibas, S. (2017). *Rebooting justice: More technology, fewer lawyers, and the future of law.* Encounter Books; Flango, V. E., & Clarke, T. M. (2015). *Reimagining courts: A design for the twenty-first century.* Temple University Press; Susskind, R. E. (2019). *Online courts and the future of justice.* Oxford University Press; and Greacen, J. M. (2019). Eighteen ways courts should use technology to better serve their customers. *Family Court Review, 57*(4), 515–538.

8 Information on macro-level trends can be found in futures publications such as the NCSC online library of *Trends in State Courts* and court futures surveys. Peter Kiefer also notes the availability of analyses such as PESTEL (Political, Economic,

Sociocultural, Technological, Environmental, and Legal milieu), which provides a macro-level environmental scanning tool.

9 For example, U.S. Substance Abuse and Mental Health Services Administration. (2018). *Adult drug court best practice standards*, Vol. 1.

10 The COSCA holds that courts should receive adequate funding from general fund sources, should not be dependent on court fees, and should not assess local fees.

11 A full list of courses, programs, and education offered by the NCSC is available online: www.ncsc.org/education-events.

12 Certification as a Project Manager Professional is offered by the Project Management Institute. Program information is available online: www.pmi.org/certifications/project-management-pmp.

References

American Bar Association. (2007). *Model rule on provision of legal services following determination of major disaster.* www.americanbar.org/groups/probono_public_service/policy/disasters/.

Asnoff, H. I. (1965). *Corporate strategy: An analytical approach to business policy for growth and expansion.* McGraw-Hill Book Company.

Bell, E. (2022). Helping courts address diversity, equity, and inclusion. *Judicature, 106*(2). https://judicature.duke.edu/articles/helping-courts-address-diversity-equity-and-inclusion/.

Birkland, T. A. (2004). *Emergency planning and the judiciary: Lessons from September 11.* Center for Court Innovation.

Bryan, V. (2013, July 17). *Heraclitus (535–475 B.C.E.).* Classical Wisdom. https://classicalwisdom.com/page/148/?woocommerce_netcore_subscribe=true#:~:text=Heraclitus%20(535%2D%20475%20BCE),of%20reality%20encompassed%20all%20things.

Bureau of Justice Assistance & Centers for Disease Control and Prevention. (2008). *A framework for cross-sector coordination for emergency response.*

Burger, W. E. (1990). Agenda for change. In *Delivery of justice: Proposals for changes to improve the administration of justice* (pp. xix–361). College of William and Mary Press & West Publishing. (Original work published 1970)

Byers, D. K., & Swetnam, N. (2014, February). *Guide to funding options for court facilities.* Administrative Office of the Courts, Arizona.

Delos Santos, J. M. (2022, March 24). *Best project planning software & tools.* https://project-management.com/project-planning- software/.

District of Columbia. (2017). *Strategic plan of the District of Columbia courts.* www.dccourts.gov/sites/default/files/matters-docs/2018-2022_StrategicPlan.pdf.

Drucker, P. F. (1973). *Management: Tasks, responsibilities, practices.* Harper & Row.

Eaton, S., & Locher, W. D. (2009, January). Give PP's a chance. *Los Angeles Lawyer.*

The Economic Times. (2009, July 24). Know your masters: Igor Ansoff. https://economictimes.indiatimes.com/know-your-masters-igor-ansoff/articleshow/4814072.cms.

Fetter, T. J. (1993). Planning for court management. In S. W. Hays & C. B. Graham, Jr. (Eds.), *Handbook of court administration and management* (pp. 483–496). Marcel Dekker.

Goel, A. (2021, June 23). The pandemic dramatically changed corporate leadership's traits. *Forbes.* www.forbes.com/sites/forbesbusinessdevelopmentcouncil/2021/06/23/the-pandemic-dramatically-changed-corporate-leaderships-traits

Griller, G. M. (2013). The need for nimble courts: How to develop flexible strategic networks, not rigid strategic plans. *Trends in State Courts*, 36–43.

Hall, N. (2021). *Courts continuity of operations (COOP) planning guide and template.* National Center for State Courts.

Joint Technology Committee. (2021, September 15). *JTC resource bulletin: Cybersecurity basics for courts* (Version 3). www.tmcec.com/wp-content/uploads/2025/05/JTC-Cybersecurity-Basics-for-Courts-2021.pdf.

Kaplan, R. S., & Norton, D. P. (1996). *Balanced scorecard: Translating strategy into action.* Harvard Business School Press.

Kiefer, P. C. (2016). *The role of strategic planning and management in the courts.* Institute for Court Management, National Center for State Courts.

Kleps, R. N. (1975). Contingency planning for state court systems. *Judicature, 59*(2), 62–65.

Kotter, J. P. (1996). *Leading change: An action plan from the world's foremost expert on business leadership.* Harvard Business School Press.

Kotter, J. P. (2012). Accelerate. *Harvard Business Review, 90*(11), 46–58.

Labovitz, G., & Rosansky, V. (1997). *The power of alignment: How great companies stay centered and accomplish extraordinary things.* John Wiley & Sons.

Learned, E. P., & Christensen, C. R. (1965). *Business policy: Text and cases.* Richard D. Irwin.

Martin, J. A., Wagenknecht-Ivey, B. J., Weller, S., & Price, D. A. (1995). *Strategic planning in the courts: Implementation guide.* State Justice Institute.

Miller, S. (2024, January 25). *Strategic planning tools for 2024.* Software Advice. www.softwareadvice.com/resources/strategic-planning-tools/.

Mintzberg, H. (1994). The fall and rise of strategic planning. *Harvard Business Review, 72*(1), 107–114.

Mundell, B. R., & Jefferson, W. B. (2012). *Herding lions: Shared leadership of state trial courts.* National Center for State Courts. www.hks.harvard.edu/sites/default/files/centers/wiener/programs/pcj/files/ES-StateCourts-HerdingLions.pdf.

Murray, J. (2013, December 8). Private partner could be key to building criminal justice facility without raising taxes. *Indianapolis Star.*

National Association for Court Management (NACM). (2014a). *Guide to technology planning for court managers.*

National Association for Court Management (NACM). (2014b). *Steps to reengineering: Fundamental rethinking for high-performing courts.*

National Association for Court Management (NACM). (2015). *The core.* https://nacmnet.org/nacm-core/.

National Center for State Courts (NCSC). (1976). *Planning state courts: A survey of the state of the art.*

National Center for State Courts (NCSC). (1998). *The courthouse: A planning and design guide for court facilities* (2nd ed.).

National Center for State Courts (NCSC). (2005). *CourTools: Trial court measures.* www.ncsc.org/our-centers-projects/courtools.

National Center for State Courts (NCSC). (2007). *Continuity of court operations: Steps for COOP planning.* https://ncsc.contentdm.oclc.org/digital/collection/facilities/id/75/.

National Center for State Courts (NCSC). (2010). *High performance court framework: A road map for improving court management.* www.ncsc.org/_media/Files/PDF/Services%20and%20Experts/Areas%20of%20expertise/High-Performance-Courts/High-Performance-Court-Framework.ashx.

National Center for State Courts (NCSC). (2020). *COVID-19 translated resources directory: A pandemic resource from NCSC.* https://ncsc.contentdm.oclc.org/digital/collection/ctadmin/id/2348.

National Center for State Courts (NCSC). (2022a). *Just horizons: Charting the future of the courts.* https://ncsc.contentdm.oclc.org/digital/collection/ctadmin/id/2575/.

National Center for State Courts (NCSC). (2022b). *Steps to best practices for court building security.*

National Center for State Courts (NCSC). (2024). *Justice for all guidance materials*. https://nationalcenterforstatecourts.app.box.com/s/9bg0hwcg9d2ugntxm4jodobhnwd5jex1.

National Center for State Courts (NCSC). (2025a). *A guide to building future ready courts*. www.ncsc.org/sites/default/files/media/document/Future_Ready_Courts_Guide.pdf.

National Center for State Courts (NCSC). (2025b). *Considerations for facility planning & design*. www.ncsc.org/resources-courts/considerations-facility-planning-design.

National Judicial Task Force. (2022). *Strategic planning through sequential intercept model*. National Center for State Courts. https://ncsc.contentdm.oclc.org/digital/collection/ctadmin/id/2491/.

Ostrom, B. J., & Hanson, R. A. (2009). Understanding and diagnosing court culture. *Court Review, 45*(4), 104–109.

Ostrom, B. J., Hanson, R. A., Ostrom, C. W., & Kleiman, M. (2005). Court cultures and their consequences. *Court Manager, 20*(1), 14–23.Pankey, K. G., Skove, A. E., & Sheldon, J. R. (2002). *Charting a course to strategic thought and action*. National Center for State Courts.

Planet, M. D. (1993). Future directions in the practice of court management. In S. W. Hays & C. B. Graham, Jr. (Eds.), *Handbook of court administration and management* (pp. 497–507). Marcel Dekker.

Raftery, W. (2017). How state courts are preparing for continuity in disaster. *Judicature, 101*(4), 3–5.

Reinkensmeyer, M. W. (2004). Court budget strategies: Stewardship, accountability, and partnership in Maricopa County. *Judges' Journal, 43*(3), 38–42.

Reinkensmeyer, M. W. (2010). The virtual courthouse: A clear trend... except for the human factor. In *Retrospective of courthouse design, 2001–2010*. National Center for State Courts.

Reynolds, C., & Hall, J. (2011). *2011–2012 policy paper: Courts are not revenue centers*. Conference of State Court Administrators. https://cosca.ncsc.org/sites/default/files/media/document/courtsarenotrevenuecenters-final.pdf

Schultz, W. L., Bezold, C., & Monahan, B. P. (1993). *Reinventing courts for the 21st century: Designing a vision process – A guidebook to visioning and futures thinking within the court system*. National Center for State Courts.

State Justice Institute. (2024). *Rapid response team: Pandemic roadmap to guide state courts forward*. www.sji.gov/rapid-response-team-pandemic-roadmap-to-guide-state-courts-forward/.

Supreme Court of Arizona. (2013). *Fiscal years 2014–2016: Arizona judicial branch information technology strategic plan*. www.

azcourts.gov/Portals/0/87/Documents/AJBITPlan14/AJBITSP_Final.pdf.

Supreme Court of Arizona. (2019). *2019–2024 Justice for the future: Planning for excellence.* www.azcourts.gov/Portals/0/0/Communications/JusticeForTheFuture.pdf?ver=2019-06-28-165330-887.

Thumma, S. A., & Reinkensmeyer, M. W. (2022, October 7). *Remote hearings in a post pandemic world: Adaptation and adoption of presumptive standards in Arizona.* ABA Judicial Division Record. www.americanbar.org/groups/judicial/resources/jd-record/2022/remote-hearings-post-pandemic-world

Tobin, R. W. (1995). *A court manager's guide to court facility financing.* National Center for State Courts.

United States Courts. (1995). *Long range plan for federal courts.* www.uscourts.gov/sites/default/files/federalcourtslong-rangeplan_0.pdf.

United States Courts. (2010). *Strategic plan for the federal judiciary.* www.uscourts.gov/sites/default/files/strategicplan2010.pdf.

United States Courts. (2012). *After Hurricane Sandy, courts in New York struggle to restore operations.* www.uscourts.gov/data-news/judiciary-news/2012/11/02/after-hurricane-sandy-courts-new-york-struggle-restore-operations.

United States Courts. (2020). *Strategic plan for the federal judiciary.* www.uscourts.gov/sites/default/files/federaljudiciary_strategicplan2020.pdf.

United States Courts. (2021). *U.S. courts design guide.* www.uscourts.gov/sites/default/files/u.s._courts_designguide_2021.pdf.

United States Courts. (2022). *Long range plan for information technology in the federal judiciary.* www.uscourts.gov/sites/default/files/long_range_plan_for_information_technology_in_the_federal_judiciary_-_fy_2022_0.pdf.

United States Courts. (2025). *Strategic plan for the federal judiciary.* www.uscourts.gov/sites/default/files/document/strategic_plan_for_the_federal_judiciary_-_september_2025.pdf.

Van Duizend, R., & Coleman, K. M. (2009). Why not now? Strategic planning in challenging financial times. *Trends in State Courts*, 75–82.

Wagenknecht-Ivey, B. J., Martin, J. A., & Lynch, B. (2000). *Strategic planning mentoring guidelines: Practical tips for court leaders.* Center for Public Policy Studies and State Justice Institute.

Washington, E. T., & VanDeVeer, L. R. (2013). *Sustainable court governance: The critical role of strategic management.* National Center for State Courts.

Webster, L. P. (2008). Court IT strategic planning. *Trends in State Courts*, 29–32.

13 Conclusions

The Evolving Practice of Court Administration

Constitutional Foundation of Court Administration

The book has examined the historical development, essential functions, and emerging challenges of modern judicial administration. As discussed throughout this text, courts exist to resolve disputes, protect individual rights, constrain arbitrary governmental power, and uphold the Rule of Law. These overarching purposes are enduring and foundational to judicial administration. Yet, court operations must necessarily evolve in response to changing societal expectations, technological advancements, and economic realities. Court administration plays an integral role within the judicial branch, addressing such changing dynamics through strategic management. Justice can best be achieved when court administrative systems are reliable, transparent, and competently managed.

This text has sought to illuminate court administration as a coherent, evolving professional discipline. Modern court administration draws from public administration theory, organizational development, strategic planning, performance measurement, budgeting principles, and various leadership models. While court administration is – in many respects – a profession still in its infancy, tremendous progress has been realized in recent years. In the research for this publication, the authors have been impressed by the growing body of court management resources and the strong sense of building momentum in further development of the study and practice of the profession.

Our research explored a number of longstanding, inherent tensions in judicial administration: independence versus accountability, efficiency versus fairness, innovation versus tradition, discretion versus uniformity, and centralization versus decentralization. Another critically important element of court organizational culture

DOI: 10.4324/9781003686804-13

is the tension arising from the divergent perspectives of professional and managerial cultures. The unique organizational culture of a court deeply influences how change is received, impacting system improvement efforts. These points of tension add a high degree of complexity to court administration. Among other skills and virtues, court administrators must navigate these tensions with sound judgment, patience, and diligence. Our focus here is the adoption of practical measures to understand and strategically address such organizational dynamics, all for the betterment of the judicial system.

Fundamental Areas of Court Administration Framework

The Fundamental Areas of Court Administration framework (Figure 1.1) introduced in this book provides the structural architecture for understanding the organizational complexity of modern courts. Anchored in the constitutional purposes and responsibilities of courts, and shaped by court leadership and culture, the framework integrates strategy, caseflow management, operations, human capital, finance, technology, stakeholder collaboration, and community engagement. Alignment of the court business functions is one of the most pressing functions of court administration, demanding constant attention and coordination on the part of the executive court administrator and the management team. The need for such alignment and ongoing coordination will only expand in the future, given the growth of problem-solving courts and court partnerships with justice agencies, service providers, and the community at large.

The pace of change will continue to accelerate in the years ahead, given our global economy, advancements in artificial intelligence (AI), the emergence of quantum computing, and other disruptive developments (Joint Technology Committee, 2017). Given recent trends, we can anticipate dramatic changes in court operations, some leveraging user-centered design (Hagan, 2018) and others ushering in a whole new service paradigm. Court modernization advocates propose a conceptual shift from physical courthouses to online court services (Suskin, 2019), early case triage, and "consumer choice" in methods of case resolution (Flango & Clarke, 2015). Other changes which come to mind include the potentially expansive use of AI, pre-filing court services, outsourcing of selected court services, expansion of virtual and hybrid hearings, and remote work arrangements for court staff. Amidst such transformational changes, components of the framework may necessarily shift or be entirely reformulated.

As we reflect back on our work "in the field" over many years, we are also struck by the myriad types of court structures and governance models across the United States and abroad. State and local courts across the country reveal a remarkably diverse array of unique administrative structures and operating systems. Large metropolitan courts manage high-volume dockets, supported by specialized staff and robust technology platforms. Rural and small-jurisdiction courts often operate with a limited number of generalist staff, tight budgets, and close community connections. Local courts also have a wide variety of funding models, judicial selection methods, varying caseload compositions, and distinct "local legal cultures."

Astute court administrators will fully assess both the formal and informal organizational dynamics of their courts. This is a necessary first step in strategic planning and system improvement initiatives. The framework advanced in this text is intended to be adaptable for courts of any size, taking into account their unique organizational cultures and resource levels. It does not prescribe uniform solutions. Rather, the framework offers a wide-angle lens to view and assess the degree of alignment in court staffing, caseflow management, and customer service. This kind of system assessment is an ongoing responsibility of court leadership teams – a function requiring a highly focused methodical approach. Consideration of these challenging leadership functions leads us to conclude that court management is a profession in which one can spend a lifetime learning and growing. As a foundational work by one of the co-authors suggests, effective court leadership and administration are grounded in the thoughtful integration of both "art and practice" (Aikman, 2007).

Court Governance and Executive Leadership

An effective governance structure is foundational to the vitality of modern courts. Most trial courts now operate within a shared leadership model, often described as a presiding judge–court administrator partnership or "productive pairs" (McQueen, 2015). This executive pairing reflects an important foundational premise: courts require both independent judicial officers and enterprise-wide, executive-level administrative expertise. For leadership judges and court administrators to collaborate effectively, decision rights and administrative authority must be clearly delineated.

Courts benefit from the establishment of clearly defined structures, both at the state and local levels. It is noteworthy that the formal administrative authority for courts is typically reposed in the positions of chief justice or presiding judge, per state constitutions, statutes, and court rules. That said, chief justices and presiding judges can delegate specific areas of authority to state court administrators and trial court administrators, respectively. Mature court governance systems formally document and clearly communicate such delegations of authority. Court governance also requires a transparent forum for policy formulation, clearly delineated internal and external communication channels, and regular court leadership meetings.

Enterprise-wide administrative functions – staffing, caseflow management, and customer service – must function consistently across all departments of the court. A well-defined court governance structure provides a climate for sound, evidence-based executive decision making. It also fosters trust amongst judges, administrators, and staff. In courts which have attained a high level of trust, judges and staff are likely to consider new ideas with an open mind. Engagement of the full bench can be achieved through establishment of local judicial councils, specialized workgroups, bench-bar committees, and regular departmental meetings, e.g., the juvenile court bench. This inclusive approach widens and enriches the court's planning perspective. Inclusion of judges and court staff also expands the base of support for system enhancements, while also helping the court to identify and engage prospective future leaders (Mundell & Jefferson, 2012).

Strategic Management and Organizational Alignment

Throughout this text, we emphasized the pressing need for strategic planning in the local court setting. Court strategic planning holds many widely recognized benefits, including alignment of operations with the mission of the court, allocation of resources, and opportunities for stakeholder involvement (Washington & VanDeVeer, 2013). A fully developed strategic planning process translates the constitutional purposes of the court into measurable goals, prioritized initiatives, resource allocations, and performance expectations. Budget decisions should reflect strategic priorities and technology investments should support long-term objectives. Court workforce planning should anticipate demographic and workload shifts. Facilities planning should reflect community access needs. A comprehensive strategic plan will create linkage between these domains and court operations, grounded in an agreed schedule of project deliverables (Martin et al., 1995).

These demonstrated benefits notwithstanding, many courts have not yet created a strategic plan and have no immediate plans to do so. Some courts rarely revisit or revise their existing strategic plans, many of which are substantially outdated. Likewise, many local courts lack a master space plan, which serves as a foundational document for funding and the acquisition of new or expanded courthouse facilities. This is an unfortunate and highly concerning situation, particularly in this era of increasingly rapid external changes and mounting pressures on judicial branch operations. The responsibility for strategic planning and master space planning rests squarely with court leadership. It is incumbent on presiding judges and court administrators to spearhead strategic planning and to leverage plans for court system improvements, resource allocation, and acquisition of needed court facilities. The court leadership team must tactfully convince the bench on the need for strategic planning as a value proposition, both for the court and the community which it serves. This explanation and related discussions can occur in bench meetings, judicial councils, court department meetings, memos, newsletters, and site visits to other similarly situated courts which have embraced strategic planning.

Reference to state- and national-level strategic plans can also be helpful in "selling" the concept of active court strategic planning and master space planning. The National Center for State Courts (NCSC) provides extensive information on strategic planning, including a methodology for trends analysis (NCSC, 2022, 2025). For courts which have dated or seldom referenced strategic plans, it is important to note that planning is not a one-time exercise. Rather, it is cyclical ongoing process. The planning regimen prompts courts to reassess priorities in light of evolving environmental conditions – legislative funding changes, technological advancements, demographic shifts, and public expectations. Strategic planning requires strong leadership and fortitude, as the planning process will identify both strengths and vulnerabilities of the court as an institution. It also demands clarity regarding what specific initiatives the court will not pursue. This outcome alone is enormously helpful in allocating scarce court resources, including judges, staff, equipment, and office space.

Caseflow Management and Operational Ecosystems

Caseflow management is, in many respects, considered to be "the heart" of court operations. Courts function as interconnected systems in which finance, human resources, facilities, security, jury administration, language access, technology, and specialized dockets must operate coherently. Records management is another critically important court administration function, encompassing both "hard copy" and digital records. In many jurisdictions, court operations also include probation services (adult and/or juvenile), pre-trial services, and 24-hour operation of juvenile detention facilities. Program integration is essential to prevent fragmentation, resource strain, and gaps in service delivery. The integrated court operations functions converge in caseflow management, all in furtherance of this key purpose of courts.

Effective caseflow management requires clear and realistic time standards, active calendaring practices, judicial monitoring, and reliable data systems. Differentiated case management models recognize that not all cases require identical procedural pathways. Early case assessment ("triage"), enforcement of procedural rules, and consistent case monitoring reduce unnecessary continuances and backlog accumulation (Kauffman & Knowlton, 2018). While progress has been made in some facets of case management, the authors envision a major expansion in the use of electronic dashboards, predictive data analytics, and automated noticing systems in the years ahead. While the supporting technologies for these case management tools are here "for the taking," the deployment of such technologies has been sporadic at best. Working with the bench, court administrators can facilitate widespread use of advanced case management technologies and data analytics to strengthen caseflow management.

Optimization of court services requires a high degree of coordination on the part of the court administration team and unit-level supervisory staff. In this context, it is helpful to view the court as an integrated system rather than a collection of separate operational units. Regular cross-department meetings and joint planning sessions promote coordination of business processes, information sharing, and stability in court operations. Staff onboarding programs and ongoing staff training are imperative in the court operations arena. Cross-training of court operations staff is also highly recommended, given the requirement to maintain essential court services during disasters and other exigent circumstances. These are just a few of the many communication and coordination functions of court administration. Opportunities for innovation and enhanced staff engagement abound in modern caseflow management.

Investing in Human Capital (Judges and Court Staff)

Courts are staff-intensive, fundamentally people-driven institutions. As a practical matter, personnel costs constitute the largest part of state and local court budgets. Court buildings, technology systems, and policies are also important and must be skillfully administered. That said, court performance ultimately depends upon the competence, integrity, and day-to-day hard work of judges and court staff. Therefore, human capital management is integral to the long-term organizational vitality of the judicial branch. Given this dynamic, court recruitment strategies must reflect workforce realities and evolving skill requirements. Courts increasingly compete with private-sector employers for the "best and brightest" technologically and analytically skilled professionals. Court staff recruitment and retention are most successful when predicated on meaningful "purpose driven" work, professional development opportunities, and a vibrant organizational culture.

For judges and court staff, professional development opportunities play a pivotal role in sustaining excellence. Investments in continuing education, ethics training, and cross-jurisdictional information exchange strengthen the institutional capacity of the courts. Staff professional development opportunities are offered through the Institute for Court Management, NCSC, and professional associations at the state and national levels. Relatedly, the National Association for Court Management's (NACM, 2015) *CORE* is also available for staff professional development. The *CORE* provides training resources for key areas of requisite knowledge, skills, and abilities (KSAs) in court administration.

The authors also strongly recommend mentorships for early- and mid-career court management staff. Mentoring programs help to identify and cultivate emerging leaders. Mentorships can be arranged within the court, with partnership courts, or through memberships in state and national court associations, such as the NACM, National Association for Presiding Judges and Court Executives, and International Association for Court Administration. Succession planning can and should include identification of potential leadership candidates, both internal and external of the local court.

Courts' human resources strategy must also account for generational change, evolving labor markets at the state and national levels, and shifting demographics. Workforce expectations regarding flexibility, communication style, and career progression are rapidly evolving. Included here are staff expectations regarding opportunities for remote work, alternative work hours, and employer (court) funding of continuing education (e.g., certification programs, college education, professional associations). Accordingly, courts must evaluate and adapt human resources management approaches, while also preserving the core judicial branch functions. This broad perspective is recommended, given the competing demands of in-person on-site court services and staff desires for remote work arrangements. The court administrator must consider these competing demands and various court staffing models, all in conjunction with the court's strategic plan.

Technology, Data Governance, and Artificial Intelligence

As we discussed throughout this book, technology permeates nearly every function of judicial administration. Electronic filing platforms, virtual hearing technologies, and electronic recording systems have transformed trial court operations. These innovations have expanded court access and efficiency, but they have also reshaped public expectations regarding court services. Court technology management is now more complex than ever, given the rapid development of AI and many open questions about its application in the legal setting (NCSC, 2024). At this early juncture, AI applications appear to hold great promise in the areas of workflow, productivity, and customer service. More specifically, the areas of greatest potential for the use of AI in the courts include assistance to self-represented litigants, scheduling and resource optimization, language translation, transcript production, document review, data entry and redaction, court website content, and public education (NACM, 2024). We believe that productivity tools such as these (and perhaps others not yet conceived) can yield operational efficiencies and improved customer service.

AI also introduces a vast array of court governance and ethical considerations, particularly in the realms of legal reasoning and judicial decision-making support (Conference of State Court Administrators, 2024). To what extent, if at all, will courts deploy automated decision-support systems and in which areas? Given the bias found in some datasets, can courts trust the use of AI for pre-trial risk assessment in criminal cases? These questions and other similar "use cases" must take into account "individual justice in individual cases," the requirement for transparent and explainable AI-generated decisions, and due process considerations. What is vital and must remain central in the analysis is the court's neutral role and customer service needs. To that end, courts will be compelled now and into the future to establish timely policies governing the appropriate use of AI, oversight of AI-enabled systems, and auditing of such systems (NCSC, 2024).

Cybersecurity is another major pressure point for trial courts due to the shift to fully digital court records. Data breaches, ransomware attacks, and system disruptions threaten both operational continuity and public trust in the court. As a result, cybersecurity risk management has become a sustained priority for court administration. In the current cybersecurity zeitgeist, comprehensive strategies are essential, encompassing redundancy planning, incident response protocols, staff training, and regular system audits, including vulnerability testing. Given these trends, modern courts require robust systems of technology governance and close oversight of online services. Court leaders will need to carefully evaluate their selection of vendors vis-à-vis security standards, scalability, and long-term sustainability. As courts transition to cloud-based computing services, contract management will also emerge (to the extent this is not already the case for larger systems) as a critical function of court administration. In short, data integrity and privacy must be preserved across all court platforms. The next generation of court administrators will likely spend an increasing portion of their time in technology planning and management. To prepare for these future demands, we recommend that courts establish standing technology oversight committees, both at the state and local court levels. Courts should also seek to create specialized committees to address AI applications and related policy development.

Court Culture and Capacity for Change

Court organizational culture directly influences the feasibility and sustainability of system improvements. Culture influences both internal and external court communications, tolerance for risk, and the role of court leaders. Local legal culture also directly influences the pace of case resolution and openness to court performance measurement. Some courts operate within highly collaborative environments, largely characterized by trust and a shared vision. Other courts may experience in-fighting, communication breakdowns, and informal power dynamics that complicate reform.

The capacity of courts to develop and implement strategic plans is largely contingent upon their cultural maturity. Courts that cultivate transparency, trust, and data-informed decision making are well poised to respond to external pressures. Court leaders can help to shape the court culture through consistent messaging, ongoing dialogue with the bench and staff, and skillful facilitation of change management. The court culture is deeply influenced by the views of the bench and court staff, who can either "make or break" court reform efforts. As discussed in Chapter 3, a court culture assessment can be a helpful first step in addressing the current and preferred organizational culture of a court (Ostrom & Hanson, 2009).

To effectuate change, court leaders must engage the bench, court staff, and stakeholders "early and often." In this engagement, leaders can convene meetings and provide other opportunities for stakeholder input through survey instruments and structured interviews. Court administrators play a pivotal role in these exchanges, helping to frame the meeting discussions. It is also the role of court administration to document meeting decisions and to timely follow-up on agreed upon "next steps." The credibility of the court's leadership team is augmented through this kind of iterative, inclusive collaboration process.

Leadership Continuity by Leveraging Executive Transitions

Our examination of court administration fundamentals would not be complete without discussion regarding changes in court leadership, specifically in the roles of presiding judge, court administrator, and executive department heads such as the chief probation officer or chief deputy court administrator. Court leadership transitions involve both vulnerability and opportunity within judicial branch institutions. Presiding judge rotations, elections, appointments, and retirements can introduce great instability if transitions are not deliberately managed. In contrast to many executive, legislative, and private-sector contexts, courts contend with complex relational dynamics arising from the continued presence of outgoing presiding judges within the organization (Reinkensmeyer & Billotte, 2025). Conversely, most private sector leaders leave the corporation upon the board's appointment of a new chief executive officer.

Without structured transition planning, strategic initiatives may stall, institutional knowledge may dissipate, and staff uncertainty may increase. Misalignment between new leadership priorities and existing strategic plans can generate "pendulum swings" that undermine long-term reform and diminished organizational stability. In the most challenging circumstances, disruption during court leadership change can erode momentum, impair staff morale, and compromise institutional coherence. In light of these dynamics, leadership transition planning should be understood as a court governance responsibility and a component of institutional risk management. Court administrators and executive teams play a central role in fostering continuity by aligning new leadership priorities with the court's strategic plan, clarifying governance roles, communicating transparently with stakeholders, and anticipating cultural or political stress points. Structured onboarding, succession awareness, transition memoranda, and strategic briefings provide institutional guardrails that transcend individual tenures. Effective practices also include early identification and engagement of emerging leaders, clarification of decision-making roles, and alignment of new priorities with established strategic objectives.

Court leadership transitions also present opportunities. We have found that new leaders can bring fresh perspective to new and existent problems, coupled with reinvigorated effort and focus. Some of this is indicative of the external experience they bring to the court setting. When transitions are intentionally leveraged, they can reinforce institutional congruence and deepen commitment to shared goals. In our experience, successful leadership changes depend not only upon structural preparation, but also upon authentic relationship-building, communication, and strategic continuity. Courts that institutionalize thoughtful onboarding and succession planning are well positioned to preserve stability while advancing reform. When approached intentionally, court leadership transitions can reinforce stability and revitalize a shared sense of purpose. Moreover, courts that formalize leadership continuity planning demonstrate institutional maturity – preserving stability while advancing principled reform across successive generations of leadership (Reinkensmeyer & Billotte, 2025).

Stewardship Role of Court Administrators

Presiding judges, court administrators, and senior managers serve as stewards of public resources. Modern court administration recognizes the importance of stewardship and ethical standards, both for judges and for executive and supervisory court managers. Court leaders are what Cooper (2012) describes as "professional guardians of the public good." Their stewardship role involves enterprise-wide oversight and ongoing management control of all judicial branch resources, coupled with protection of the court as a public institution. The resource management role of court administrators is set forth in NACM's (2018) Model Code of Conduct for Court Professionals, Canon 2.8:

> A court professional uses the resources, property, and funds under his or her official control judiciously and solely in accordance with prescribed procedures.

In a similar vein, the American Society for Public Administration's (2026) Code of Ethics affirms the following related principle: 1) Advance the Public Interest. Promote the interests of the public and put service to the public above service to oneself.

Peering into the future, we anticipate an expanded and increasingly complex stewardship role for court administrators. This scenario is based, in part, on the rising scale of trial court operations and commensurate budget expansion, mainly driven by population growth. The broadening role of courts is also a factor here, given the resource-intensive nature of problem-solving courts and court-annexed functions such as alternative dispute resolution, collections, parent education programs, and other litigant services. Stewardship of court resources in this context involves countless points of interaction with government and not-for-profit funding bodies, community partner organizations, and the community at large.

The stewardship role of court administrators will also be further "stress tested" in the spheres of intergovernmental relations and service provider partnerships. Moore's (2021) concept of public administrators "creating public value" is relevant here, underscoring the need for "democratic legitimization" and public accountability. In economic downturns, court administrators must work closely with funding bodies, while also maintaining core judicial branch functions and an independent judicial branch (Van Dyke, 2004). Given the foregoing considerations, the need to provide ongoing court-specific ethics training for court managers is readily apparent.

Continuing Collaboration and Call to Action

We strongly support continued investment in court-focused research and the ongoing work of court improvement organizations. Judges, administrators, and court improvement organizations have contributed to cross-court research and the development of performance standards. National-level organizations have promoted evidence-based practices, both for the courts and probation services. Professional organizations and court-improvement bodies also contribute to judicial administration through leadership convenings, educational programs, and joint system reform resolutions.

Trial courts are often the first to encounter new types of legal matters and evolving litigants' demands for service. Often, they identify and address emerging court service needs before these are widely recognized at the national level (Mundell & Jefferson, 2012). Local courts that serve as demonstration sites for pilot projects can contribute to the development of scalable practices. Court administrators can play a key role in implementing pilot initiatives and supporting program evaluations. They can likewise facilitate data collection and help translate research findings into operational improvements. In the years ahead, court administrators should pursue expanded opportunities to host pilot projects and disseminate study findings. Local courts and communities will benefit from such ventures, while also serving as a model for replication in other jurisdictions.

Relatedly, at the local level, presiding judges and court administrators are well situated to convene meetings and ongoing discussion with system stakeholders. These collaborations provide opportunity for information exchange, joint problem solving, and resource coordination. Each of us has participated in numerous high-level inter-branch meetings that could only be successfully convened by a court's presiding judge. Some gatherings included a mix of state and federal officials, while others included the governor's office and state law enforcement officials. The professionalization of court administration in recent decades has expanded the role of court administrators in inter-branch and interagency coordination. This facilitative function is likely to grow in the years ahead through continued professional development and the cultivation of emerging leaders.

Concluding Reflections

The work of court administrators requires foresight, attention to detail, and a strong commitment to the mission of the judicial branch. It also calls for close collaboration with the bench, attentive listening, and continual learning. This book invites court management professionals to view themselves as stewards of the justice system – responsible for present court operations, as well as the long-term credibility of the courts. Their efforts should remain grounded in the overarching "principles for justice administration" articulated by the NCSC (2012) and in the need for ongoing system improvement. The recommendations we offer are intended to expand court access and strengthen public trust in the branch of government responsible for administering justice.

Public confidence in courts is deeply influenced by the "everyday experiences" of court participants, along with media coverage of the judicial branch. Court administrators are in the unique position, with an awesome degree of responsibility, to directly shape the experiences of everyone who comes into contact with the judiciary. The strategies described throughout this book are aimed at aligning court operations and customer service with the constitutionally prescribed purposes and responsibilities of the courts. Courts that achieve strategic alignment and operational excellence will be best positioned to respond effectively to disruptive internal and external changes, including inevitable crisis situations.

Our work in the courts has been both challenging and highly rewarding over the years. We are each deeply grateful for the privilege of serving in the judicial branch. It is our hope that some of the "lessons learned" shared in this book will be helpful to others in the field, as well as next generation court leaders. Drawing on our professional experiences and a broad perspective of the field, it is clear that court administration has indeed "come a long way" in recent decades. Nonetheless, further development and refinement lie ahead, requiring a dedicated cadre of court administrators. The ongoing professionalization of court administration continues, guided by this forward-looking mindset.

References

Aikman, A. B. (2007). *The art and practice of court administration.* Taylor & Francis Group.

American Society for Public Administration. (2026). *Code of ethics.* www.aspanet.org/ASPA/ASPA/Code-of-Ethics/Code-of-Ethics.aspx.

Conference of State Court Administrators. (2024, August). *Generative AI and the future of the courts: Responsibilities and possibilities.* National Center for State Courts.

Cooper, T. L. (2012). *The responsible administrator: An approach to ethics for the administrative role* (6th ed.). Jossey-Bass.

Flango, V. E., & Clarke, T. M. (2015). *Reimagining courts: A design for the twenty-first century.* Temple University Press.

Hagan, M. D. (2018). A human-centered design approach to access to justice: Generating new prototypes and hypotheses for intervention to make courts user-friendly. *Indiana Journal of Law and Social Equality, 6*(2), 199–239.

Joint Technology Committee. (2017). *Courts disrupted.* JTC Resource Bulletin. National Center for State Courts.

Kauffman, B. K. T., & Knowlton, N. A. (2018). *Redefining case management.* Institute for the Advancement of the American Legal System. https://iaals.du.edu/sites/default/files/documents/publications/redefining_case_management.pdf.

Martin, J. A., Wagenknecht-Ivey, B. J., Weller, S., & Price, D. A. (1995). *Strategic planning in the courts: Implementation guide.* State Justice Institute.

McQueen, M. C. (2015). Two sides of the gavel, or court leaders as productive pairs. *Trends in State Courts,* 1–4.

Moore, M. H. (2021). Creating public value: The core idea of strategic management in government. *International Journal of Professional Business Review, 6*(1), 1–2.

Mundell, B. R., & Jefferson, W. B. (2012). *Herding lions: Shared leadership of state trial courts.* National Center for State Courts. www.hks.harvard.edu/sites/default/files/centers/wiener/programs/pcj/files/ES-StateCourts-HerdingLions.pdf.

National Association for Court Management (NACM). (2015). *The core.* https://nacmnet.org/nacm-core/.

National Association for Court Management (NACM). (2018). *NACM model code of conduct for court professionals* (with commentary). https://nacmnet.org/wp-content/uploads/Model-Code-of-Conduct-for-Professionals-with-commentary.pdf.

National Association for Court Management (NACM). (2024). *Courting AI: Understanding artificial intelligence in courts.*

National Center for State Courts. (2012). *Principles for judicial administration.* https://courts.ca.gov/sites/default/files/courts/default/2024-12/tcfwg-20130115-ncsc.pdf.

National Center for State Courts. (2022). *Just horizons: Charting the future of the courts.* https://ncsc.contentdm.oclc.org/digital/collection/ctadmin/id/2575/.

National Center for State Courts. (2024). *Artificial intelligence: Guidance for the use of AI and generative AI in courts.* www.ncsc.org/sites/default/files/media/document/AI-Courts-NCSC-AI-guidelines-for-courts.pdf.

National Center for State Courts. (2025). *A guide to building future ready courts.* www.ncsc.org/sites/default/files/media/document/Future_Ready_Courts_Guide.pdf.

Ostrom, B. J., & Hanson, R. A. (2009). Understanding and diagnosing court culture. *Court Review, 45*(4), 104–109.

Reinkensmeyer, M. W., & Billotte, R. (2025). Court leadership transitions: Leveraging organizational change. *Court Manager, 39*(1). https://thecourtmanager.org/articles/court-leadership-transitions-leveraging-organizational-change

Suskin, R. S. (2019). *Online courts and the future of justice.* Oxford University Press.

Van Dyke, R. (2004). Cutting costs through collaboration and competition. *Judges' Journal, 43*(3), 41–44.

Washington, E. T., & VanDeVeer, L. R. (2013). *Sustainable court governance: The critical role of strategic management.* National Center for State Courts.

Index

Pages followed by "n" refer to notes and pages in **bold** refer to figures.

U

V

W

For Product Safety Concerns and Information please contact our
EU representative GPSR@taylorandfrancis.com Taylor & Francis
Verlag GmbH, Kaufingerstraße 24, 80331 München, Germany